The Worship of Augustus Caesar

THE WORSHIP OF

AUGUSTUS CÆSAR

DERIVED FROM A STUDY OF COINS, MONUMENTS, CALENDARS, ÆRAS AND
ASTRONOMICAL AND ASTROLOGICAL CYCLES, THE
WHOLE ESTABLISHING

A NEW CHRONOLOGY AND SURVEY

OF HISTORY AND RELIGION

BY

ALEXANDER DEL MAR

NEW YORK
PUBLISHED BY THE CAMBRIDGE ENCYCLOPEDIA CO.
62 READE STREET
1900

THE WORSHIP OF AUGUSTUS CAESAR.

CHAPTERS.

PROLOGUE.

———

THE ABYSS OF MISERY AND DEPRAVITY FROM WHICH
CHRISTIANITY REDEEMED THE ROMAN EMPIRE
CAN NEVER BE FULLY UNDERSTOOD WITHOUT A
KNOWLEDGE OF THE IMPIOUS WORHSIP OF EM-
PERORS TO WHICH EUROPE ONCE BOWED ITS
CREDULOUS AND TERRIFIED HEAD

* * * * * * * *

WHEN THIS OMITTED CHAPTER IS RESTORED TO THE
HISTORY OF ROME, CHRISTIANITY WILL SPRING
INTO A NEW AND MORE VIGOROUS LIFE, FOR
THEN ONLY WILL IT BE PERCEIVED HOW DEEP
AND INERADICABLY ITS ROOTS ARE PLANTED,
HOW LOFTY ARE ITS BRANCHES AND HOW DEATH-
LESS ARE ITS AIMS

PREFACE.

THE collection of data contained in this work was originally intended as a guide to the author's studies of "Monetary Systems" It was therefore undertaken with the sole object of establishing with precision the dates of ancient history.

It soon appeared that many of the dates were astrological. They were grafted upon the Ecliptical Cycle and the imaginary incarnations of the Sun Such is the case with both the Indian, Chaldean, Egyptian, Greek and Hebrew dates of remote antiquity Even the epochs used by the astronomers, which were in India equal to B C 3102, in Babylon B C 747 and in Greece B C. 884, form no exception to this rule. They are all astrological.

This discovery entirely changed the author's plans. Hitherto the work had been designed merely as an accessory to other studies· it now assumed an interest and importance of its own The employment of the Ecliptical Cycle for computing the lapse of time furnished a key to the history and progress of ancient astronomy, which it was hoped might unlock at least one door to the remote past It proved to be capable of unlocking many Meanwhile the author's attention was drawn to researches of a more practical nature He brought the statistical method to bear upon a comparison of dates from ancient sources, of which he now made a more extensive collection The result was the disclosure that the Roman chronology had been altered, first, to the extent of 78 years (sunk) by Augustus, and afterwards to the extent of 15 years (restored) by the Latin Sacred College. It was also perceived that Augustus had changed the Olympiads from five-year to four-year intervals, and had thus altered many Greek and other dates to the extent of 108 years

He next found that the number of civil months in the year, and therefore also the number of days in the months and weeks, were altered The year had been anciently divided into ten months, each of 36 days, and the months into weeks of nine days Such was the case, not only in Rome, but also in the other states of the ancient world In Rome, the alteration was made by the Decemvirs; in the

other states it had been made previously   Everywhere it had marked
a revolution in government and religion

It was at this point that the author resolved to devote himself to
the serious task of tracing the alterations of the calendar and collecting such materials as might enable others to reconstruct the shat-
tered edifice of ancient history   What he saw about him was nothing
but ruins, but beneath those ruins there were evidently building materials, many of which have since been brought to light

The subject that next engaged his attention was the Jovian cycle
and worship, which could not be confidently traced backward in the
Occident further than the 11th or 12th century before our æra, nor
in the Orient further backward than the 15th century   It followed
that the duodecimal and sexagessimal cycles and institutes which
had been drawn from the orbital period of this planet, were not nearly
so old as had been pretended   A like examination of the progress
of discovery concerning the moon's node and the precession of the
equinoxes yielded analogous results   both were known very anciently,
but not nearly so anciently as had been assumed

Strengthened by these astronomical aids to research, the entire
series of chronological data were now recast, condensing them as
much as seemed consistent with exhibiting their significance and mu-
tual relations, and afterwards arranging the principal ones in clusters,
with the view to discover their origin and bearing

The result was the conviction that the basis of all ancient dates is
to be found in the religions of the Orient, and that these religions lie
at the foundation of all the religions of the Occident   In a word, that
religion was never a special creation, but on the contrary, has been
the product of EVOLUTION, an evolution which, beginning in India,
still goes on and will go on forever.

The worship of Augustus has been admitted by so many eminent critics that there can be no longer any doubt about the fact   Its religious
significance lies in the inferences that are to be drawn from it   With
these, the author has no present concern   His object has been not
to make theological deductions, but to recognize an Historical Truth,
whose admission must, in his belief, precede all attempts to compile
a satisfactory account of the Roman Empire, or of the Middle Ages

It will be shown upon ample evidences that after the submission of
the Oriental provinces and consolidation of the empire, Augustus
Cæsar set himself up for that Son of God whose advent, according
to Indian chronology, synchronised with the reappearance of the
Oriental Messiah, the date being A U 691 (B. C 63) the alleged

year of Augustus' birth; that this claim and assumption appears in the literature of his age, was engraved upon his monuments and stamped upon his coins, that it was universally admitted and accepted throughout the Roman empire as valid and legitimate, both according to Indian and Roman chronology, astrology, prophecy and tradition; that his actual worship as such Son of God—Divus Filius—was enjoined and enforced by the laws of the empire, accepted by the priesthood and practised by the people; and that both de jure and de facto it constituted the fundamental article of the Roman imperial and ecclesiastical Constitution.

Unless these evidences and conclusions are overthrown it will follow that an entirely new view of the empire, its history, its laws and its institutes, including the important one of feudalism, will demand the consideration of historians and students   Hitherto the worship of Augustus has been kept in the background of Roman antiquities It must now either be explained away, or accorded a more prominent position in the history and constitution of that great empire from whose womb has issued all the states of the modern world.

BIBLIOGRAPHY.

The following list of books is to be read in connection with the lists published in the author's previous works   The numbers at the end of each title are the press marks of the British Museum library

ABBAY (Richard)   Restoration of the Ancient System of Tank Irrigation in Ceylon.
Printed in the London " Nature " of Oct 11, 1877
ABU MASHAR (*See* ALBUMAZAR)
ACHERY (Luke D')   Spicilegium, sivo collectio veterum aliquot scriptorum qui in Galliae biblothesis delituerant.   Paris, 1723, 3 tom fol.   10 e 1-3,
ADAM OF BREMEN   Historia Ecclesiastica ejusdem auctaris libellus de situ Daniæ, 1706, fol.   158 h 14
ADAMS (Alexander), *Rev*.   Roman Antiquities, 18th ed , Edinburgh, 1854, 8vo

(This popular work was originally published in 1791, and has passed through numerous editions, both in England and America   It omits or conceals much more than it discloses concerning the religious belief and ceremonies of the Romans, and must therefore be consulted with discretion)

ALBIRUNI (Mohammad Ibn Ahmad)   Chronology of Ancient Nations   Trans by C
E Sachau   London, 1879 8vo   752 l 24
— — Institutes and Customs of India in the eleventh century   Trans by C E
Sachau   London, 1888, 2 vols   2318 h 4
ALBUMAZAR (Jafar Ibn Muhammad, commonly known as Albumazar, Albumasar, or
Albumashar)   Flores Astrologie   Trans from the Arabic by J B Sessa, Venice, 1485, 4to   718 f 2 (2.)
ALISON (Archibald), *Rev*   " Essays," political, historical and miscellaneous. London, 1850, 3 vols, 8vo
ALLEN (John) *Master of Dulwich College*   Inquiry into the Growth of the Royal
Prerogative in England   London, 1849, 8vo   2238 e 1

(A short performance, whose reputation exceeds its merit   It holds that "homage" is a custom derived from the ancient Germans, that modern sovereigns add to their titles, "by the grace of God," because the Saxon hlaford was sacred to the churl and that the king, instead of the Augustus, is the Fountain of Honour   The author has advanced no evidences to support these assertions)

ALLMER (A)   Les Gestes du Dieu Auguste d' apres l' inscription du Temple d' Ancyre   Vienne, 1889, 8vo.   7705. ee (17)
ALVIELLA (*See* GOBLET)
AMERICA   Recopilacion de Leyes de los Reynos de las Indias   Madrid, 3d edicion, 1774, 4 tomos, fol
ANTHROPOLOGY   Journal of the Anthropological Society of Bombay   Vol II, pp
164-224 Fawcett on "Festivals to Village Goddesss " London, 1886, 8vo Ac 6242
ARATUS (of Soli)   The Phænomena and Diosemeia, trans. by J Lamb. London, 1848, 8vo   There is another trans by J H Voss   1348. c 9.
ARISTOTLE   Works   Trans by T Taylor, London, 1812, 9 vols , 4to.   2052. h.
ARRIAN (Flavius)   The Anabasis of Alexander, literally trans. by E J. Chinnock,
London, 1884, 8vo   9026 ff 18.
—— — Voyage round the Euxine sea   Tr W Falconer, Oxford, 1805, 4to   200 e 18
———— Voyage of Nearchus and Periplus of the Erythræan sea. Gr with Eng Trans
by W Vincent, Oxford, 1809, 4to.   570 g 16
ASHLEY (W J)   Essay on Feudalism. London, 1887, 8vo.
ATWOOD (William)   *Barrister at Law and Chief Justice of New York.*   Fundamental Constitution of the English Government   London, 1690, fol.
AURELIUS VICTOR (S   ) De origine gentis Romanæ, 1826   Originem d' aple
Romaine, a French translation of the same work, by V A Dubois   11,3   K 9.

AYLIFFE (J) *Rev* A new Pandect of Roman Civil Law. Vol I (The only volume published) 1734, fol   500 g 14.

BAILLY (Jean Sylvain) Histoire de l'Astronomie ancienne depuis son origine jusqu'a l'establissement de l'Ecole d'Alexandrie, 2nd ed , Paris, 1781, 4to.   8562 e 14.
—— Traite de l'Astronomie Indienne et Orientale Paris, 1787, 4to,   59. h 5
—— Ancient History of Asia, a series of letters to Voltaire London, 1814, 8vo   1137 b 21, 22.
BALUZE (Etienne) Histoire des capitularies des Rois François de la premiere et seconde race Paris, 1779, 8vo   708 a 12
BANQUERI (Josef Antonio) Libro de Agricultura, traducion de Abu Lakariya Madrid, 1802, 2 vols, fol   441 I 2 3
BAUER (Bruno) Christus und der Cæsaren, Berlin, 1879, 8vo.   4534 cc (7)
BEAL (Samuel) *Rev* Buddhist Travels in the West London, 1890, 2 vols, 8vo
BEAUSOBRE (Isaac de) Histoire Critique de Manichée et du Manichéisme Amsterstam, 1734-9, 2 vols, 4to   678 e 11-12
BECK (Ludwig) Die Geschichte der Eisens Brunswick, 1884, 8vo   7104 d
BEDE. Ecclesiastical History of England and Anglo-Saxon Chronicle. Trans. by J A Giles, London, 1847, 8vo
BELL Historical Studies of Feudalism, 1852
BELLON (Peter) Travels Trans by J Ray, 1693, 8vo   978. g (1)
BELOT (E) De la revolution economique à Rome au milieu du IIIe siecle, A C Paris, 1885, 8vo   8226 eee (24)
BENJAMIN OF TUDELA Itinerary, Heb with Eng Trans by A Asher London, 1840-1, 12mo   1938 c 11
BENTLEY (John). Hist. Rev. of the Hindu Astronomy. London, 1825, 8vo 531 1 (2)
BERNARD (Jacques) Recueil de Traitez de Paix de Treve, etc., de A. D 536, jusqua A D 1700 Amsterdam, 1700, fol.   589, 1, 8
BEUDOIN Etude sur les origines du regime feodal Grenoble 1889, 8vo 6005 f 4,(1)
BEZOLD (Carl) Oriental Diplomacy London, 1893, 8vo   7704 aaa 3,2
BHAGAVAT-GITA, known also as Christna's Gospel, the Divine Song, Christna's Revelation, etc Trans. from Sanscrit into English, by Sir Charles Wilkins London, 1785, 4to.   14060. f 1
BIRCH (Samuel), (formerly of the British Museum) Records of the Past, being English translations of the Assyrian and Egyptian monuments London, 8vo, Old Series, in 12 vols , 1873-81, New Series, in 4 vols , 1880-92   2258 a 3

<small>This work is published anonymously The late Dr Birch's name is attached to it in the catalogue of the Museum Library but does not appear in the title page of the work On the other hand, the name which does appear there is that of the editor, not the author It is printed under the sanction of the Society of Biblical Archaeology</small>

BLACK (W H) The Calendar of Palestine reconciled with the Law of Moses, against the theory of Michaelis London 1865, 8vo.   4372. g 18 (9)
BLANCHET (J Adrien) Nouveau manuel de numismatique du Moyen Age et moderne With Atlas 1890, 2 tom, 8vo   12208 b
BLAVATSKY (Helena Petrôvna) Isis Unveiled New York, 1877, 2 vols, 8vo 2212 c
BOECKH (Augustus) Corpus Inscriptionum Græcorum, Berlin, 1828, 4 vols, fol   Catalogue Desk K
BOISSIER (Gaston) La religion Romaine d' Auguste aux Antonines Paris, 1874, 8vo   2212 g
BONWICK (James). Egyptian Belief and Modern Thought London, 1878, 8vo, 2212 b
BOUCHÉ LECLERC (A) Les Pontiffes de l'ancienne Rome, etude historique sur les institutions religieuses de Rome Paris, 1874, 8vo , pp 435   4506 d (1)
BOULAINVILLIERS (Count Henri de) Histoire de l'ancien gouvernement de France, Amsterdam, 1727, 12mo   897 a 14
—— History of the ancient Parliaments of France. Translated from the French by C Forman, London, 1754, 2 vol , 8vo   5424 c
—— The Life of Mahomet Trans into Eng London, 1752, 12mo.
—— Etat de la France London, 1727, 2 vols, 8vo   1857 a
BOWER (Archibald) History of the Popes Dublin, 1749-68, 3 vols, 8vo. 4855 bb
—— Another ed Phila , 1844-5, 3 vols, 8vo   4855 e
BOWKER and ILES (R. R and Geo) Reader's Guide in Economic, Social and Political Science New York, 1891, 8vo   11,900 bb 54

BRADY (John) Clavis Calendaria, or a compendious analysis of the Calendar. London, 1815, 2 vols, 8vo

BRAMSEN (W) Japanese Chronological Tables. Tokio, 1880, 8vo 11,099 b 1

BRANTOME (Pierre de Bourdeilles). *Seigneur de Brantome* Memoirs Leyde, 1722, 12mo 630 a (25)

———Another ed Paris, 1876, 12mo 8415 df. (2)

BRERREWOOD (Edward), *Rev* De Ponderibus et pretiis vetorum nummorum, etc (Edited by R B) 1614, 4to 602 e 19 (2)

BRITANNICA Monumenta Historica. (Passages in classical authors relating to Britain)

BROWN (Alex) *F R H S* The Genesis of the United States . . movement in England 1605-16, which resulted in the plantation of North America, etc. London, 1890, 2 vols, 8vo. 9602 i (1)

BRUCE (J Collingwood,) *Rev* The Roman Wall, a description of the Mural Barrier of the North of England London, 1867, 4to (Chiefly a description of Severus', properly Hadrian's Wall and the antiquities found in the vicinity) 2258 f

BRUCE (Philip Alex) Economic History of Virginia in the 17th Century London, 1896, 2 vols, 8vo 9605 c. (22)

BRUGSCH (Heinrich), History of Egypt. Trans. by Philip Smith. London, 1881, 2 vols, 8vo 2069 a

BRUNNEMANNUS (*See* Justinian.)

BRYANT (Jacob) Ancient Mythology 3d ed London, 1807, 6 vols, 8vo 86 f 11-16

This work is an elaborate effort to reconcile all the mythos, in which effort it fails, not, however, without incidentally furnishing a large fund of valuable information

BRYCE (James) The Holy Roman Empire 4th ed London, 1873, 8vo

BRYDONE (Patrick) Sicily and Malta. London, 1776, 2 vols, 8vo 10,151. d 21

BUCHANAN (George), *The historian See* Macfarlan

BUCKMAN and NEWMARCH Illustrations of the Remains of Roman Art in Cirencester, by Prof Buckman and C. H. Newmarch. London, 1850

DURIGNY. (*See* Levesque)

BURKE (Luke) "The Principles of Mythonomy", (Laws of Mythology, Systems of Zodiacs, etc) "Hebrew Chronology", "Egyptian Chronology", "Discovery of America, by the Northmen", etc , a number of articles on these and kindred topics published in the London Ethnological for 1848, 1854, and 1865-6, these being the only years of its publication. 8vo. PP 3862 a. and 295.

CALLIMACHUS. Hymns, Epigrams, etc Trans by Revd. J. Banks. Bound with Hesiod. London, 1856, 8vo. 2500 f

CANDOLLE (Alphonse de) Histoire des Sciences et des savants depuis deux siecles, suivre d'autres etudes en particulier sur la sélection dans l'espèce humaine Geneve, Bâle, Lyon, 1873, 8vo 8707 ee (15)

CAPELLA (Martianus Mineus Felix) De Nuptiis Philologiæ et Mercurii. (On the accord of Bacchus and the Logos). Ed Kopp, Frankfort, 7836, 4to 718 i (25)

CAREW (George), *Sir* Pacutu Hibernia, or History of the late wars of Ireland under Sir George Carew and compiled by his direction. 1663, fol 186 d (8)

———History of Ireland. 601 m 6

———Letters to Sir Thomas Roe Ac. 8113-71

CAREW (George), *Earl of Totness* Report of the Master of the Rolls upon the Carte and Carew Papers 1864, 8vo. 2075 c

———Calendar of the Carew MSS 1867, 8vo. 2075 c

CARLILE (Richard), The Deist, containing theological Essays by Baron de Holbach, Voltaire, and others London, 1819-20, 2 vols, 8vo 4015 f

CARRANZA (Alonso) El adjustamento y proporcion de las monedas de oro, plata y cobre, y la reducion distros metales, etc Madrid, 1629, fol. 504. g (6)

CATON (W) Abridg of the Chronol of Eusebius London, 1661, 12mo. 4530 aa.

CHARION (Edouard) Voyageurs, anciens et modernes Paris, 1854, 4 vols, in 2, 8vo 2060

CHRISTNA (Isvara), The Trans. by H T Colebrooke, Oxford, 1837, 4to 752 l l

CHRISTNA (*See* Christna's Gospel, or the Bhagavat-Gita)

CHURCHILL (Chas Henry) Mount Lebanon. London, 1853, 3 vols, 8vo 10,075. d.

———The Druzes and the Marionites London, 1862, 8 vo 10,075 d.

CLARKE (Edward), *Rev* Letters concerning the Spanish Nation (including Coins). London, 1763, 4to 179 d, 18

CLARKE (G) " Pompeii " London, 1831, 2 vols, 12mo   1157 a 21-2

CODEX ARGENTEUS Quator D N Jesu Christi evangeliorum, versiones per antiquæ duæ Gothica scilicet et Anglo-Saxonica Quaruam illam ex celeberrimo Codice Argenteo nunc primum depromsit, Franciscus Junius F F hanc autem ex codicibus MSS collatis emendatiùs recudi curavit, Thomas Mareschallus, Angius, etc Dordrechti, 1665, 4to   218 g

COLEBROOKE (Henry T) Miscellaneous Essays, containing " Religious Ceremonies of the Hindus " London, 1873, 3 vols, 8vo   14085 e 6-8

COLUMELLA (L J M) Husbandry, in XII Books French trans by Nisard, Eng trans by M. C Curtius London, 1745, 4to.   34 d. 1

CONSTITUTION and Present State of Great Britain (See GREAT BRITAIN)

COOTE, The Romans in Britain, London, 1878, 8vo   2394 e.
(A work of merit, the materials being chiefly drawn from the Roman laws relative to land and the archæological remains of Britain)

CORSINO (Edoardo) Fasti Attici, in quidus Archontum Atheniensium series, Philosophorum, oriorumque Illustrium Virorum ætas, etc 4tom Florentiæ, 1744-56, 4to   673 h (4)

COULANGES (Numa Denis Fustel de), The Ancient City, a study on the religion, laws, and institutions of Greece and Rome Trans by W Small Boston, 1874, 8vo   2259 b (e.)

—— --The Origin in Property by Land Trans by M Ashley London, 1891, 8vo.   08276 e (9)

————Histoire des institutions politiques de l'ancienne France Paris, 1891-2, 6 vols 8vo   2390 d

COUTZEN (Adamus) Politicorum libri decem in quibus de perfectæ reipubl forma, virtutibus et Vitiis, etc Moguntiæ, 1621, fol   C 24 d

———— The plot of Coutzen the Moguntine Jesuit to cheat a church of the religion established therein and to serve in Popery by Art, etc London, 1641, 4to 702 d 8 (2)

CREECH (Thomas) The Five Books of Marcus Manilius, containing a system of the Ancient Astronomy and Astrology, together with the Philosophy of the Stoics Done into English verse, with Notes London, 1697, 8vo (See Manlius and Shirburn for other editions of the Five Books called the Astronomicon) 11385 b b

CREUZER (George Frederich). Religions d' antiquité refondu, etc , par G D Guigniaut, L F. A Maury, and É Vinet Paris, 1825-51, 4 vols 8vo 2212 b

CYPRIAN, Bishop of Carthage, A D 248-58 Unity of the Church, a Sermon Trans by Revd J Fell, Bishop of Oxford London, 1681, 4to   3805, a

DAREMBERG ET SAGLIO Dictionnaire des Antiquites Grecques et Romaines Paris, 1873, 2 vols, 4to In progress In 1897 it was completed to " E ' Cat ,Desk I

DE SACY (See SILVESTRE)

DEUBER (F. H A) Geschichte der Schiffahrt in atlantischen Ozean, zum Beweis das. . der Compass . vor F G entdeckt worden sey Bamberg, 8vo 1424. c.

DIDRON (Adolphe N) Christian Iconography, or the History of Christian Art in the Middle Ages Trans by E J Millington London, 1849, 2 vols, 8vo 2502 b.

DIFFRICHSON (L) Stavkirker, or an illustrated treatise on the church architecture of Norway Christiania, 1892, 8vo

DIODORUS SICULUS History Trans by G Booth London, 1600, fol 2068 g

DION CASSIUS Rerum Romanarum, libri octoginta, ab Immanuel Bekkero Greek text Lipsiæ, 1849, 2 vols, 8vo   2052 e

——— Histoire Romaine Paris, 1845-70, 10 tom , 8vo 1307 1 (12-19)

——— An oration to Octavius Cæsar Augustus, against monarchy, taken out of the XIIth book of Dion London, 1657, 4to   E 972 (3)

——— The History of D C abridged by Xiphilinus Done from the Greek by Mr Manning London, 1704, 2 vols, 8vo 293 f (28, 29)

DIONYSIUS of Halicarnassus Antiquities of Rome Trans by Spelman London, 1758, 4 vols 4to   196 b (1-4)

DITTENBERGER (William) Corpus Inscriptionum Atticarum Berlin, 1878,fol 2068 g

DRUMMOND (W) Zodiacs of Esné and Denderah London, 1821, 8vo 1140 d 7.

DU BOS (Jean Baptiste) Histoire Critique de 'establissement de la monarchie François Amsterdam, 1734, 3 vols, 4to   182 b 8-10

DU CHOUL (Guillaume) Religion de los Antiguos Romanos Traducion en Castellano, por Baltasar Perez Leon, 1579, 4to

DUMONT D'URVILLE   (*See* D'URVILLE)

DUNCKER (Max) History of Antiquity Trans from the German by Evelyn Abbott,
  M D LL D   London 1879, 6 vols, 8vo

DUPIN (Andre M J J) *Father* Manuel du droit public ecclésiastique français Paris,
  1844, 12mo   5424 aaa 5

DUPUIS (Ch Fr) Origine de tout les Cultes   Paris, 1794, 3 vols, 4to   Plates
——— Another ed 7 v , 8vo. Plates Paris, 1795   483. a 1-7 & 484 c 22
——— An abridgment of the same Paris, 1822, 12mo   4503 a 33
——— On the connection of Christianity with Solar worship London, 1793, 8vo An
  abbreviated edition of the above work, 1877, 8vo   8632 ccc. 4 (4)

DUREAU DE LA MALLE (A J C A) Economie Politique des Romains Paris, 1840
  2 vols, 8vo   7702, bb (7.)

D'URVILLE (Dumont d')   On the Venus de Milo, contained in an official periodical
  entitled ' Recueil des Lois relatives a la Marine et aux colonies, etc , edited by
  M Bajot Paris, 1821, 8vo , part II   P P 1365

DURUY (Victor) Histoire des Romains. Nouvelle ed Paris, 1879, 7 vols, 8vo 9039 e
——— An English translation by Miss Clarke   London, 1883, 6 vols, 8vo   2382 g

DUTT (Romesh Chunder) *Barrister of the Middle Temple* A History of Civilization in Ancient India, based on Sanscrit literature London, 1890

DUVERGIER (G B Paul) La Banque Internationale Paris, 1865, 8vo 8227 h 35 (7)

DUVERGIES (Jean Baptiste) Revue Étrangère (ét Francaise) de legislation, etc 1834,
  etc , tom 7   P P 1275.
——— De l' effet retroactif des lois   Paris, 1845, 8vo   5405 d.

DYER (L) Studies of the gods in Greece London, 1891, 8vo   4506. bb. 25

EGGLESTON   English Antiquities London, 1647. (*See* Del Mar's " Money and Civilization," p 31n for reference to this work)

FITON   Origins of English History, by C J Elton London, 1882, 8vo

EUNAPIUS Vitæ Philosophorum ac Sophistarum Græca, et Latine 1849, 8vo 2051 h
——— Lives of Ancient Philosophers. 1702, 8vo   275 g. (8)

FABER (Geo S) Origin of Pagan Idolatry London, 1816, 3 vols, 4to 4504 g 12
  Though its argument, that all religions sprang from the worship of the earth and moon, may not be
convincing, its descriptions of ancient rites and symbols are useful

FAWCETT (Fr) (*See* ANTHROPOLOGY)

FERGUSON (Rob't) River names of Europe. 1863, 8vo   12901, c 24
——— The Northmen in Cumberland London, 1856

FIRMICUS (Julius Maternus) *Alleged æra, fourth century* De Frore Profanarum
  Religionum Printed in the Bibliotheca Patrone at the end of Cyprian Paris,
  1666 The Astronomicorum was printed in 1499, folio, and is bound in the
  same volume, (Astron veterus) with the Astronomicon of Marcus Manilius 715-k.1.

FISHER and SOFTBEER (E W F and A S) Greichische und Romanische Seitta-
  feln Altona, 1840, 4to   584. h (25)

FISKE (John) *Assistant Librarian Harvard University* The Discovery of America,
  with some account of Ancient America and the Spanish Conquest Boston, 1892
  2 vols, 8vo   9551 bb (13)

FOSBROKE (Thos Dudley) British Monachism 3d ed London, 1843, 8vo 2003 e.

FREEMAN (Edward) A History of the Saracens London, 1876, 8vo
——— English Constitution London, 1873, 8vo

FREHERI (*See* GRÆVIUS, tom xi)

FREINSHEIM (Johann) Alex. Mag daobus tomis repræsentatus   complectitur, alter
  (J F) com Q Curtii, libros superstites exhibet 1640, etc 8vo   584 a (9.)

FRÉRET (Nicolas) Defense de la Chronologie Paris, 1758, 4to   216. a 4

FROISSART (John) Chronicles (*See* 1337 for the title Lieutenant of the Emperor)

FRONTINUS (*See* NISARD)

FROUDE (James Anthony) Nemesis of Faith A second edition London, 1849, 12mo ,
  is the only one now in British Museum Library   2206 a
——— Cæsar, a Sketch London, 1879, 8vo   10,606. f. (3)
——— Short Studies on Great Subjects London, 1878, 4 vols , 8vo   2342 a

FULLER (Thomas) *Rev* History of the Holy War Cambridge, 1639 fol (Mentions
  a bank established in Tyre during the Crusades)   + ~ 2

FUSTEL (*See* COUTANCES)

GAILÆUS SERVATIUS   Dissertationes de Sibyllis   Amst , 1688, 4to   704 d. 22.
GARDTHAUSEN (V.) Augustus und seine Zeit   Leipzig, 1891, 8vo   9041 f.
GARKAULT (François) *Sieur des Gorges* Les recherches des monnoyes, poix, et
    maniere de nombrer des premieres et plus renommées nations du monde   .
    Reductes et rapportées aux monnoyes, poix, et maniere de nombres des François,
    etc   Paris, 1576, 8vo   522 b (4)
——— Recueil des principaux advis donnez ès assemblées   en l'abbaye Sainct Ger-
    main des prez, etc . .   Paradoxe sur le faict des monnoyes   Paris, 1578, 8vo.
——— Des mines d'argent trouvées en France   Paris, 1834, 8vo , (included in M.
    L. Cimber's "Archives Curieuses.")   805. b (3.)
GAUBIL (Antoine). Chronologie Chinoise   Paris, 1776, 4to   146 b 20
——— L'Astronomie Chinoise, Paris, 1729, 4to   50 d 10
GEIKIE (JOHN C) *Rev* Life and words of Christ   London, 1877, 2 vols, 8vo 4807 ece 6
GERMANY, Empire of Entwurf einer Grundbach Ordnung und Entwurf eines Gesetzes
    betreffend die Zwangsvoll streckung, etc   Berlin, 1889, 8vo   5604 g. 14.
GERMANY, Empire of Laws relating to Bills of Exchange   1879, 8vo   5606 b 11.
GINISLY (Paul)   "De Paris à cap Nord " Paris, 1892, 4to
GNECCHI (Ercole) Saggio di bibliografia numismatica delle zecchi italiane 1889, 8vo.
GNEIST (Heinrich R von). Hist. of the Eng Parliament Tr. by A H Keane London,
    1889, 8vo,   2394 f
——— Hist Eng Constitution Tr by P A Ashworth London, 1891, 8vo 2394 f (1)
GOBLET (Eugene) La Migration des Symboles Paris, 1891, 8vo   4503 cc (19)
GODEFROY (Jacques) De Mutationes et Augmento monetæ aureæ Helmstadii, 1732
——— Legum XII   1671, 8vo   877 i 4
GOODWIN (F) The XII Tables, (of the Roman Law,) London, 1886, 8vo. 5205 aa 17.
GOULD (Baring) *Rev* Origin and Development of Religious Belief N Y , 8vo , 1863
GRÆVIUS (Johannis Georgius) Theosaurus Antiquitatem Romanarum, Lug Batavo-
    rum, 1694-9, 12 tom fol   Tome viii contains several Roman calendars, tome xi
    contains the numismatic treatises of Freheri and Gronovius   2068 e
GRAZIANI (A) Storia della teoria del Valore en Italia. Milano, 1889, 8vo 08229 f (21)
GREAT BRITAIN   Statutes at Large (which see)
GREEK INSCRIPTIONS, Ancient, in the British Museum   Oxford, 2 vols, fol 1874-93.
    Edited by *Rev* E L Hicks, C T Newton, and Gustav Hirschfeld   2068. 9.
    (Including the inscriptions from Ephesus obtained by J T Wood in 1863-74)
GRESWELL (Edw) Fasti Temporis Catholici Oxford, 1852, 4 vols, 8vo 581 e (22-26)
——— Origines Kalendariæ Italicæ   Oxford, 1854, 4 vols, 8vo   8561 d (31)
——— Origines Kalendariæ Hellenicæ   Oxford, 1862, 6 vols, 8vo   8560 ee (10)
GREUBER (Erwin) The Roman Law of Damage to Property (Lex Aquilam, Digest,
    IX, 2) Oxford, 1886, 8vo   5205 bb 20
GROSS (J. B) *Rev* The Heathen Religion Cambridge, Mass , 1856, 8vo 4504 b.

HALE (Matthew) *Sir* The Inrolling and Registering of all conveyances of Land.
    1694, 4to   E 1973 (4)
HALIBURTON (Robert G) New Materials for the History of Man   Halifax, N S ,
    1863, 8vo   4503 bb (5)
HALLAM (Henry) Literature of Europe in the 15th, 16th, and 17th centuries Lon-
    don, 1839, 3 vols, 8vo
——— Europe during the Middle Ages London, 1869, 8vo
HAMILTON (Sir William). *Ambassador to Naples.* Discoveries at Pompeii, with Plates,
    London, 1717, 4to   662 h. 18.
HAMPSON (R T) Dates, Charters and Customs, (including Calendars of the Middle
    Ages) London, 1841, 8vo   2085 b.
——— Origines Patriciæ, or a Deduction of European titles of nobility from their
    original sources   London, 1846, 8vo   1327 g.
HANNAY (Robert). History of the Representation of England, and of the jurisdic-
    tion of the House of Commons   London, 1831, 8vo   809 g 15
HARDUINI (Joannis) *Jesuite* Antirrheticus de Nummis Antiquis Colonarium et Mu-
    nicipiorum. Parisiis, 1689, 4to   602. h 8.
——— An apology for Homer, wherein the true nature and design of the Iliad is ex-
    plained and a new system of his theo-mythology proposed Tr from the French
    London, 1717, 8vo,   11,315. c 5.
——— Chronologia Veteris Testamenti, and same in French. Paris. 1677, 4to

HARLEZ (C. de) Le Calendrier Avestique. Paris, 1882, 8vo.   4503 f 30 (2)
HARNACK (Adolf) History of Dogma. Tr by Neil Buchanan 1894, 8vo   3605 k
HARRIS (S F) Elements of Roman Law summarized, 1889, 8vo   2228 d
HELMOLDUS Chronica Slavorum Lat and Fr 1793, 4to.   158. 1. 18
HELVETIUS (Claude A) Treatise on Man London, 1810, 2 vols, 8vo
HENRY (Robert) *Rev* History of Britain London, 2nd ed 1795 8vo , 12 vols in 7
HERBERT (Henry H M) *Earl of Caernarvon* Revolutions of the Druids (or Druses)
    of Lebanon London, 1860, 8vo.   10,076 c
HERBERT (The Hon Algernon). "Nimrod," a Discourse on certain passages of His-
    tory and Fable London, 1828-30, 4 vols, 8vo   800. e 20-3.
———— Britannia after the Romans London, 1836, 4to   806 g 3
HESIOD The Theogony, also Works and Days Trans by *Rev* J Banks (Bound
    with Callimacnus and Theognis) London, 1856, 8vo   2500 f
HIGGINS (Godfrey). Horæ Sabaticæ London, 1826, 8vo , pamph   480 b 27
    An argument that the Jewish Sabbath was unknown to the Patriarchs, was not instituted until the
    time of Moses and is nowhere enjoined to be observed in the New Testament
HIGGINS (Godfrey). The Celtic Druids London, 1829, 4to.   2072 d RR
    A work of much learning, besides containing many valuable materials from Faber, Bryant, Vallancey,
    and other antiquarians, concerning ancient alphabets, mythology and Druidical remains
———— Anacalypsis, an enquiry into the origin of Languages, Nations and Religion
    London, 1836, 2 vols, 4to   2072.
HOARE (R C) Ancient Wiltshire London, 1838, 8vo
HOLINSHED (Raphael) Chronicles of England, Scotland, and Ireland, from the ed of
    1577 London, 1807, 6 vols, 4to   194 c 3-8
HOLWELL (William) Mythological Dictionary London, 1793, 8vo   696. g 3.
HOMER, The Iliad I-VIII, Tr by C W Bateman IX-XXIV, Tr by R Mongan
    London, 1848, 12mo The Odyssey Tr by R Mongan. London, 1848, 12mo
HOOPPELL (R E). Vinovium, the Roman City of Binchester. London, 1879, 8vo
HORACE Works Tr by Samuel Lee London, 1873 8vo   2282 a
HORSLEY (John) Britannia Romana, or the Roman Antiquities of Britain London
    1732, fol A valuable antiquarian work, comprehensive and concise   806 l 1
HOWELL (R) *Rev* History of the World (For Dignities of Rome, *See* II, 24-77)
HUEFFER (Francis) Life of the Greeks and Romans Tr from the German by
    F H etc London, 1875, 8vo   2031 a
———— Another Tr by Ernst Guhl and W Koner (Not in the British Museum)
HUMBERT (G) Les finances chez les Romains Paris, 1886, 2 tom, 8vo 8228 h (28)
HUMBOLDT (F H A Von) *Baron* Researches concerning the Institutions and Monu-
    ments of the Ancient Inhabitants of America with description and plates of scenes
    in the Cordilleras The "Vues des Cordilleras," Trans by Helen M Williams.
    London, 1814, 2 vols, 8vo   1050. k 13
———— Fluctuations of Gold (Berlin, 1838) New York, 1900, 8vo Cambridge
    Encyclopedia Publishing Company
HYDE (Th) *Rev* Historia Religionis Veterum Persarum Oxonii, 1700, 4to. 703. d 4.

IBN BATUTA Travels into Asia Tr by Rev Sam'l Lee. London, 1829, 4to. 752 l 1.
INDIAN ANTIQUARY (The) Bombay, 1872, 4to (In Progress)   14096 e
INGRAM (J) *Rev* The Saxon Chronicle, with Eng Tr London, 1823, 4to 2070
ISHTAR AND IZDUBAR The Epic of Babylon, etc 1884, 8vo   11652 k (12)
ISVARA CHRISTNA (*See* CHRISHNA)

JAMIESON (John, of Edinburgh) *Rev* Hermes Scythicus, or the radical affinities of
    the Greek and Latin Languages to the Gothic, illustrated from the Mœso-Gothic,
    Anglo-Saxon and Frankish, and a Dissertation on the historical proofs of the
    Scythian origin of the Greeks Edinburgh, 1814, 8vo   71 a 20
JASTROW (Ignaz). Handbuch zu Litteraturberichten im Auschluss an die Jahresbe-
    richte der Geschichtswissenschaft   11899 f 17
JOHN I , *Bishop of Antioch* Epistolæ Greek and Latin In J P Migne's Patro-
    logiæ Series Græcæ, 1857, tom 77, 4to   2011, d
JORNANDES De Gothorum Origine Lat and Fr , the latter by F Fournier de Monjan,
    included in the "Collection des Auteurs Latins " Paris, 1850, 8vo *See* NISARD.
JOURNAL OF HELLENIC STUDIES Academies, London, vol. III   2056 c.
JUAN DE PERSIA Relaciones Berlin, 1854, 8vo, broch   9455 d

JULIANUS (Flavius Claudius) *Emperor* Select works of the Emperor Julian Tr by
     J Duncan. London, 1784, 2 vols, 8vo   89 1 22-23
———— Two Orations of the Emperor Julian, one to the Sovereign Sun, the other to
     the Mother of the Gods Tr. by T Taylor London, 1793, 8vo   11391. g 1
———— Arguments against Christianity Tr from the fragments preserved by Cyril,
     Bishop of Alexandria by T Taylor Privately printed, only 25 copies, most of
     which were destroyed London, 1809, 8vo   3670 b
JUSTINIAN Codex (Text) XII libros, ed J Brunnemanus 1679 fol. 5207 h 5.
———— Institutes (Text) Latin and English Cambridge, 1876, 8vo
———— Digest (Text) Latin, with Spanish Tr by B. A Rodriquez de Fonseca
     Madrid, 1872-5, 3 vols, 4to   5207 h 3
———— Digest Introduction to the study of the, with a full commentary on the title
     De Usufructo, by Henry John Roby Cambridge, 1884, 8vo   2228 cc 6
———— Digest (Commentary) Private Law among the Romans By John G
     Phillimore, Q C London, 1863, 8vo   2238 c.
JUSTINUS Historiæ Philippicæ, cum versione Anglica. London, 2d ed 1735 8vo
     Nothing whatever is known of the soi disant Justin, who abbreviated in this, the work of Trogus
Pompeius The latter flourished in the Augustan age "Justin" was probably a monk of the seventh
(not the fourth) century
JUVENAL Satires Latin and English texts London, 1745, 8vo
KEARY (C F) "Norway and the Norwegians " London, 1892, 8vo
KEIGHTLEY (Thomas) Ovid's Fasti, with Notes London, 1848, 12mo
———— Mythology of Ancient Greece and Italy London, 1859, 8vo
     Keightley s works are more remarkable for what they ignore, than what they communicate, on the
subject of ancient mythology
KEMBLE (Johannis M) Codex Diplomaticus Ævi Saxonici Opera London 1839,
     6 vols, 8vo Containing Latin texts relating to Britain from A D 604 to 1066
———— The Saxons in England Ed W De G Birch London, 1876, 2 vols, 8vo 2071 d.
KENYON (F G) Aristotle on the Athenian Constitution London, 1891, 8vo
     In ch XLIII there are eight lines of astronomy interpolated which will not be found in the origi-
nal See Classical Review, December, 1891
KINGSLEY (C) *Rev* The Roman and the Teuton London, 1864, 8vo
KIP (William) *Bishop of California* Christmas Holidays in Rome Boston, 1869 8v.
LAING (Samuel). *The Younger* Human Origins, London, 1892, 8vo   7704 c 2.
LAJARD (Jean B F) Le Grand Bas-relief Mythriaque Paris, 1828, 4to   7820 g.
———— Mysteries de Mithra Text Paris, 1847, 4to (Les planches en folio) 557 g
———— Mysteries de Mithra Ouvrage posthume Paris, 1867, 4to   560 d
LA LOUBIÈRE (Simon de) *Le Sieur* The Kingdom of Siam, done out of French, by
     A P London, 1693, 2 tom , fol.   693 h
LANCIANI (Rodolfo), *LL D Harv* Ancient Rome in the Light of Recent Dis-
     coveries London, 1888, 8vo , illustrated
LA PLACE (P.S de) System of the World Tr by J Pond. London, 1809 2 vols, 12mo.
LAPPENBERG (J. M) History of England under Anglo-Saxon Kings London, 1845.
LE BLANT (Edmond) L'Epigraphie chretienne en Gaule et dans l'Afrique romaine,
     Paris, 1890, 8vo   07708 f 24
LECOINTRE-DUPONT (Gabriel) Lettres sur l'histoire monetaire de la Normandie et
     du Perche Paris, 1846, 8vo
LE GENTIL DE LA GALAISIÈRE (Guillaume) Voyage dans le Mers de l'Indie à l'occa-
     sion du passage de Venus en 1761 et 1769 1779-81, 2 tom , 4to.   982 h 9
LEON (Joachim Velasquez de) Management of the Royal Mines in Mexico and pe-
     tition for the abolition of the royal dues 1774, fol   9771 h. 2 (18)
LETRONNE (Jean Antoine) Observations zodiacales Paris, 1824, 8vo 1140 d g (4)
LEVESQUE (Jean L) *De Burigny* Hist. des revolutions de l' Empire de Constanti-
     nople—jusqu'a l'an 1453 Paris, 1750, 3 t 12mo   1053 a (9)
———— Hist. de la Philosophie Payenne La Haye, 1724, 12mo   525 a 19
LEWIS (Sir George Cornewall) Astronomy of the Ancients London, 1862, 8vo 2244 h 4
LILLIE (Arthur). Buddha and Early Buddhism. London, 1881, 8vo 4505 ee 11
LIUIPRANDUS Historia ejusque Legatio ad Nicephorum Phocane In Corpus
     Scriptorum Historiacæ Byzantinæ, 1828, 8vo
LOBECK (Christian A) Aglaopharmus sive de theologiæ mysticæ Græcorum causis . .
     idemque l'ostarum Orphicorum dispersus reliquias collegit, 2 tom Regiomontii
     Prussorum, 1824, 8vo   4505 aaa
———— Disputationis de mysterium Eleusinorum 1824, 4to   8357 ccc 3 (4)

LOFSCHER (Valentin Ernst) Literator Celta Lipsiæ, 1726, 8vo   1332 a 5.
LOPFS FERNANDES (Manuel Barnardo)   Memoria dos medalhas e condecoraçones
    portuguezas e das estrangeiras com relacaõ a Portugal (With plates) Lisbon,
    1861, 4to   7755 cc (15)
———Memoria das moedas correntes em Portugal desde o tempo dos Romanos, até
    o anno de 1856. Lisbon, 1856, 4to   7757 f (16)
LORD (Henry) Rev Religion of the Banians, Parsees, etc. 1752, fol. 215 e (6,)
LOWNDES (William) Essay for the Amendment of Silver Coins London, 1695, 8vo.
LYSONS (Samuel) Reliquiæ Brit Romanæ London, 1801, 2 vols, fol   562 g
MABILLON (Jean) Abbé. Vetera Analecta Paris, 4 vols, 8vo , 1675-85
MACFARIAN (Robert) Dissertation on the pretended identity of the Getæ and Scyth-
    ians London, 1799, 8vo   600 f 1
MAGNUS (Nicholas) Essay on Insurances. London, 1755, 2 vols, 4to   50 d 14
MAINE (Sir Henry) Roman Law
MALLET (Paul Henry). Northern Antiquities Trans. by Bishop Percy. London, 1826,
    3 vols, 8vo Another ed , London, 1847, 1 vol., 8vo   2500 a.
MANDRELL (Henry) Rev. Travels in Palestine, 1697 London, 1847, 8vo 2500. b.
MANILIUS (Marcus) Sometimes written Manlius Astronomicon, ex editione Bentle-
    iana, cum notis et interpre atione in usum Delphini, variis lectionibus, notis
    variorum, (Scaligeri, notas, etc) London, 1828, 2 vols, 8vo   2055 c
MARIANA (Juan de), Jesuit History of Spain Trans. by Capt J Stevens I ondon,
    1699, fol 2 pts   181 g (1)
    This work contains proofs that the Julian æra was used in Spain until about the time of the Dis-
    covery of America
MARTIN DU TYRAC, Comte de Marcellus Souvenirs de l'Orient Paris, 1839, 2 t.,8v
MASCOU (John Jacob). History of the Ancient Germans and Norsemen Trans by
    Thomas Lediard London, 1738, 2 vols, 4to   173 g 1-2
    An able and useful work, marred by national partiality According to the writer, Germany com-
    prehended Schleswig-Holstein, Scandinavia, and parts of Gaul, Dacia, Scythia, etc It was a relief to
    find that it did not also include China and America !
MASCOVIUS (Gottfridus) De Sectis Sabianorum et Proculianorum in Jure Civili, etc
    Altdorfii Noricorum, 1724, 8vo pamph , 83 pages   700 h
MASPERO (Gaston) Egyptian Archæology Tr by Miss Amelia B Edwards London,
    1887, 8vo.   2259 b 8
——— Life in Ancient Egypt. London, 1892, 8vo   7702 a 39.
MASSEY (Gerald) A Book of the Beginnings London, 1881, 2 vols, 4to. 7703 g 22.
———The Natural Genesis London, 1883, 2 vols, 4to   7703 922.
MAURICE (Thomas) Indian Antiquities London, 1806, 7 vols (in 3), 8 vo 1434 g
——— Brahminical Fraud Detected London, 1812 8vo   1114, 1 5
MELON (Jean) Essay on Commerce Tr by D Bindon London, 1738, 8v 8247 bbb.
MELVILLE (Henry) Veritas Revelation of Mysteries by means of the Median and
    Persian laws (An astrological treatise) London, 1874, 4to   1891 p 13.
MEURSIUS (Joannes), The Elder Denarius Pythagoricus sive de Numerorum usque ad
    dinarium qualitate ac nominibus secundum Pythag Lug Bat 1631, 4to 602, c 14.
——— Historiæ Danicæ Amsterdami,1638, fol.   155 b 13
MICHAELIS (J D) Hebrew and Julian months compared London,1773,8vo 0561 a 24.
——— Dissertation on the same, by W Carpenter, of Islington. London, 1825, 12mo
MIGNÉ (J P) Epistolarum, libri X, 1844, 4to   3621 a 10
MILLINGEN (James V) Ancient unedited Monuments London, 1822-6, 4to 557 c
MIR KHWAND, or " MIRKHOND " (Muhammad Ibn Khavand Shah) History of the
    Early Kings of Persia Trans by D Shea London, 1832, 8vo   752 g 19
MOMMSEN (Theodor) Zum Romischen Kalendar, 1860, 8vo   8560 c
MONASTIER (Antoine) Revd History of the Vaudois Church London, 1848, 8vo
MONTALEMBERT (Charles de), Comte The Monks of the West English tr London
    1861, 7 vols, 8vo. This work is dedicated to the Pope of Rome
MONTESQUIEU (Charles de Secondat, Baron de) Works complete Dublin, 1777, 4
    vols, 4to Another ed , London, 1878 2 vols, 8vo
MUNRO (Charles H) Digest XIX, 2, a translation of that portion of Justinian's Di-
    gest which relates to Locati-Conducti, with commentary Cambridge, 1891, 8vo
——— De Furtis (Digest XLVII, 2.) Cambridge, 1893, 8 vols 5206 aa 13
MURATORI (Ludovico Antonio) Index to the Leonine, Gelasian and Gregorian sac-
    rament aries according to M's Liturgia Romana Vetus by H A Wilson,18 2, 10

NASH (D W) The Pharaoh of the Exodus London, 1863, 8vo   9061. e 15
NEPOS (Cornelius) Lives of Illustrious Men Eng Tr Oxford, 1684, 12mo
NEWTON (Isaac), *Sir* Prophecies of Daniel London, 1733, 4to.   3185 h
NICOLAS (Nicholas Harris), *Sir* The Historic Peerage of England First ed , 1825,
    revised and continued by W Courthope London, 1857, 8vo.   2119. b.
―――― Chronology of History (Lardner's Cabinet Library) London, 8vo   2103 c.
NIEBUHR (Barthold Georg) History of Rome Tr by Hare London, 1847-51,3v.8v.
―――― Lectures on the Hist Rome,ed by L Schmitz, 3rd ed Lon ,1870,8vo 2382 c.
NISARD Collection des Auteurs Latins, avec la traduction en Français, publiée sous
    la direction de M Nisard Paris, 1848, 30 tomes, 8vo
OHLENSCHLAGER (Adam Gottlob) Die Götter Nordens Leip , 1829,8vo 11,557.bb.17.
OPPERT (Gustav) Aborigines of Bharata-Varsa (India) Lon , 1893,8vo 10,007.cc.15.
OSBORN (Robt D) Islam under the Arabs London, 1876, 8vo
―――― Islam under the Khalifs of Bagdad London, 1878, 8vo
OVERBEEK VAN (Bonaventure) Les Restes de l'ancienne Rome Paris, 1700, fol.
―――― Stampe degli avanzi dell'Antica Roma rinovata Londra, 1739, fol.   561 f.
OWEN (T M.) Hist of England to the Norman Conquest London,1882,8vo 9503,c 10.
PAGNINI DELLA VENTURA (Giovanni F) Della Moneta de Fiorentin (In Lanetti's
    Nova racialta delle monete, etc) 1755, etc, fol   603 1 9.
PALGRAVE (Sir Francis) Rise and Progress of the English Commonwealth London,
    1832, 2 vols, 4to   597 h 13.
―――― History of the Anglo-Saxons London, 1887, 8vo
PARRY (Ch H) The Parliaments and Councils of England London 1839,8vo 809 g 1.
PAUILY (A F von) Realencyclopädie Stuttgart, 1893, 8vo   2282 f 2.
PENN (John) *Of Stokepark, near Windsor* Observations in Illustration of Virgil's
    Fourth Eclogue London, 1810, 8vo   1000 1 20
PERROT AND CHIPIEZ A History of Art in Ancient Egypt, from the French of
    Georges Perrot and Charles Chipiez London, 1883, 2 vols, 4to
PERSIUS (Aulus Persius Flaccus) Satires (Written about A. D 60) Tr by Sir
    Wm Drummond London, 1797, 8vo   237 f 33.
PETAU (*Father* Denis) History of the World London, 1659, fol   1309 k 4
―――― De Veteri anno Rom Kalendarium vetus Rom 1694, etc., tom 8, fol 2068 e
PETER (Carl) Zeittafeln der Romischer Geschichte Hale, 1841, 4to   1307 1
PFEFFEL VON KRIEGELSTEIN (Christian Frederich) Abrège Chronologique de l'his-
    toire et du droit public d'Allemagne Paris, 1766, 2 vols, 8vo
PHLEGON (*of Tralles*) De mirabilibus et longævis libellus Eiusdem de Olymp
    Fragmentum Greek and Latin 1568, 8vo   704. b. (21)
PIKE (L Owen) The English and their Origin London, 1866
PINKERTON (John) *Geographer, Medalist, and Antiquarian of Edinburgh* History
    of Scotland to Malcolm III , (A D 1056,) with a Dissertation on the Origin and
    Progress of the Scythians New ed Edinburgh, 1814, 2 vols, 8vo 10,370 d 3
―――― Dissertation on the Goths London, 1887, (reprint,) 8vo   1194 g 1
PITTAKYS (K S) L' Ancienne Athène, ou la description des Antiquities d'Athène
    et de ces environs Athens, 1835, 8vo.   1299 c 8vo
PLATO The Dialogues (*including the Laws*) Tr B Jowett Oxford,1875, 5 vols, 8vo
PLINY (*The Elder*) Natural History London, 1848, 6 vols, 8vo [Some portions
    of a much better English translation were published by the Wernerian Club of
    Oxford now defunct]   2500 g
PLINY (*The Younger*) Panegyric upon Trajan London, 1730, 8vo   5 1633-5
―――― Epistles London, 1786, 2 vols, 8vo Melmoth's Translation
PLUTARCH Lives Tr by J Langthorne London, 1825, 2 vols, 8vo.
―――― Isis and Osiris Tr by Rev Samuel Squire, Bishop of St David's Greek and
    English Cambridge 1744, 8vo.   704 8. 10
POCOCKE (Edward) India in Greece, containing the sources of the Hellenic race, the
    Buddhistic propaganda in Greece, etc London, 1852, 8vo   4505 c
POCOCKE (Richard) *Bishop of Ossory and of Meath* Description of the East. Pinker-
    ton's Voyages London, 1808, 4to   2057 d
POLLUX (Julius) Textrinum Antiquorum, with an appendix on the Onomasticon, by
    J Yates London, 1843 8vo   1400 g. 3
POLYBIUS The histories of Trans. by E S Shuckburgh Lon ,1889,8vo 9041 b (38)
POOLE (R S) Chronology of Ancient Egypt London, 1851, 8vo   9061 e (11.)

POIHIER (Robert J) Pandectæ Justimianæ. Paris, 1748, fol.   5205 h (1.)
—— Another ed Paris, 1818, 5 vols, 4to   17 b 13-17.
—— The Law of Contracts Eng Trans. London, 1806, 2 vols, 8vo   496 e 16.
—— Another ed Philadelphia, 1853, 8vo   5423. dd 3.
—— Contract of Sale. Boston, 1839, 8vo   496 d 20.
POTOSÍ Un Memorial, etc A memorial on the affairs of Potosí addressed to the King
    of Spain, by J de Ibarra Gueztaraen Madrid, 1618, fol.   1324. k. 5. (16.)
—— Los Azogueros dueños de minas, etc A memorial of mine proprietors to the
    King Madrid, 1620, fol   1324 k. 5. (85.)
—— Gremio de los Azogueros. Madrid, Nov 12, 1636, fol   725 k. 18 (32.)
PRIDEAUX (Humphrey), *Dean of Norwich* Marmora Oxoniensia ex Arundellianis ..
    Conflata . Recensuit Oxonii, 1676, fol   604 h 3
PRIESTLEY (Joseph), *Rev* History of Early Opinions concerning Jesus Christ Bir-
    mingham, 1786, 4 vols, 8vo
    The philosophical and theological works of Priestley of which latter this is the principal one, are
    both numerous and verbose They wholly fail to explain the history of Christianity
PROBUS (Marcus Valerius) Leipsig, 1826, 8vo   2053. g.
PROCOPIUS, *of Cæsarea* Wars of Justinian Lon ,1653,f Tr Sir H Halcroft 9073 h 5.
—— Secret Hist. of the Court of Justinian Tr into Eng , 1674,Lon ,8vo 1053 a 2.
—— Histoire secrete de Justinien. M Isambert, Paris, 1856,8vo Gr and Fr 9135 d
PRUDENTIUS (Aurelius Clemens) Selections from Prudentius, trans into English by
    F St J Thackeray London, 1890, 8vo   3435 gg 1.
    These selections are from the religious hymns and poems adapted by Prudentius from the ancient
    liturgy, or ascribed to him by later composers
PTOLEMY (Claudius) Tetrabiblos Tr by J Wilson London, 1820, 12mo 718 c 39
—— Hypotheses et Epoques des Planetes,by the Abbé Halma Paris,1820,4to 49 e 5.
—— Table Chronologique des Reynes, by the Abbé Halma Paris, 1819, 4to 49 e 4
QUATREMÈRE (Étienne Marc). Memoires geographiques et historiques sur l'Egypte,
    etc Paris,1811, 8vo (Describes the Egyptian Gold Mines of Antiquity) 1298 c 11
QUATREMÈRE DE QUINCY (Antoine Chrysostome) Sur le statue antique de Venus
    Paris, 1821, 4to   561 *d 29
QUINCEY (Thomas de) Works of Edinburgh, 1889-90, 14 vols, 8vo   12,274. c
RAMBAUD (Alfred) History of Russia London, 1882-6, 3 vols, 8vo.   2392 d.
RANKE (Carl F) De Lexici Hesychiani Lipsiæ, 1831, 8vo   12,923. b 14
RECLUS (Élisée) The Earth New York, 1871, 8vo
RECUPERO (Giuseppe) Storia naturale e generale dell'Etna Opera postuma Catania,
    1815, 2 tom , 4to   1254 k 19 20.
REEVES (John) History of the English Law from the Saxons to Philip and Mary
    London, 1787-1829, 5 vols, 8vo.   508 b 17-22.
REITEMEIER (J F.) Geschichte des Berghauses Gottingen, 1785, 8vo   725 a 24
RHALLES (Georgios Alexandros) and POILES (Michael) Canons of the Greek Church
    Athens, 1852-59, 6 vols, 8vo   05107 ce 1 (2)
RICKARD (R) The Era Calendar Birmingham, 1884, 12mo   1881 a 4 (67)
RIVERO AND TSCHUDI Peruvian Antiquities Tr by F L Hawks N.Y.1853,8vo 9772 d
ROBERTSON (W A. S) Roman Canterbury London, 1883, 8vo
RODIER (Gabriel). Les races humaines, chronologie, etc Paris, 1862, 8vo 9006 gg 18.
ROUGEMONT (Frederic de). L'histoire de l'astronomie. Paris, 1865, 12mo   4378 b
—— La Peuple Primitive. Geneve, 1855-7, 3 toms , 12mo   10,006 d e
RUDBECK (Olaf) Linguæ veteris Scytho-Scandicæ sive Gothicæ Upsalæ, 1691, fol
—— Atlands Swedish and Latin texts Stockholm, 1863, fol (Originally printed
    in Upsal, 1702 The fourth vol , which was only completed to p. 210, is here re-
    printed in facsimile)   9435 1
RUGGIERO (Ettore) Dizionario Epigrafico de Antichita Romane Roma (Loreto
    Pasqualacci) 1886-93, 8vo In 1898 it was completed to the letter C.   769
RUSSELL (Dr William) History of Europe London, 1810, 6 vols, 8vo
RYGH (O) Norse Oldsager Christiania, 1835, 3 vols, 4to
SACRO BOSCO (Joannes de) La Sphere pour prouver que l'astrologie est très utile et
    nécessaire au genre humain. Paris, 1584, 12mo   533 b 5 (2)
SAINT-CHAMANS (August de) *Viscount* Traité d'Economie publique suivé d'un
    aperçu sur les finances de la France 3 tom Paris, 1852, 8vo   8206 d (29)
SATOW (Ernest) The Jesuit Mission Press in Japan,1591-1610 1888 4to 11, v h 33
SAVARY (C L) Letters on Egypt Tr from the French London, 1787, 2v 4vo 4047 f 7

SAVIGNY (Fred Karl von) Geschichte des Romischen Rechts. Heidelberg, 1815-31, 6 vols, 8vo

SCARTH (H M) *Rev* Roman Britain London, 1883, 8vo An able and interesting work drawn from antiquarian sources 4419 1 39

SCARI FI (Gasparo) L'Altimonfo From the 1582 folio edition, included in the Scrittori Italiani Classici. 1803, 8vo 1140 e

SCHRAM (Robert). Eclipses of the Sun in India 1896, 8vo 8561 h (44)

SCOTT (Wm. A) *Ph. D.* Repudiation of State Debts 1893, 8vo 08,225. ee.

SCOTUS (Johannes Erigena) Ein Beitrag zur geschichte de Philosophie und Theologie im Mittelalter 1861, 8vo (Including Usury, etc) 8466 bbb (27)

SELDEN (John) Titles of Honour London 1631, fol 2119 f.

―――― Liber de Nummis London, 1678, 8vo

―――― Table Talk (Reprint) London, 1869, 8vo

SENECA (Lucius Anæus) De Beneficiis (lib V is cited in the "Mixt Moneys " case).

―――― Claudii Cæsaris Apocolokintosis A work in which the author ridicules the deification of the Emperor Claudius

SEWELL (Robert) First report on the Kristna district of the Madras Presidency. Madras, 1878, fol 7702 k (13)

―――― Southern India Chronological Tables, 1894 8vo. 8562. ff (34)

SHARIF (Jafar) Customs of the Musselmans of India Madras, 1863, 4to 10,056 f

SHARPE (Samuel) *Orientalist* History of Egypt London, 1849, 2 vols, 8vo 2502 d

SHIRBURN (Sir Edward). The Astronomicon of M Manilius London 1675, 8vo

SILVESTRE DE SACEY (Antoine Isaac), *Baron,* Essai sur les Mystères d'Eleusis, etc. 1816, 8vo. 1363 f (39)

―――― Exposé de la Religion des Druzes et la vie du Khalife Hakem, etc Paris, 1838, 8vo , 2 vols 696 k (20-21)

SMITH (Ch R) Antiq. of Richborough, Reculver and Lymne Lon ,1850,4to 10,350 d

―――― Antiquities of Trèves, Mayence, Wiesbaden, Niederbieber, Bonn and Cologne London, 1851, 8vo 7707. c 26

―――― Illustrations of Roman London London, 1859, 4to 2259 f

SOLTBEER (Adolphe) Litteraturnachoveis über Geld und Munzwesen insbesondere uber der wahrungsstreit, 1871-91, etc Berlin, 1892, 8vo 08,227 e 35

SONNERAT (Pierre) Voyage aux Indes Paris, 1806, 2nd ed , 8vo. 566 d 6

―――― Voyage to the East Indies and China Tr by F Magnus Calcutta, 1788-9, 3 vols, 8vo 010,057 ee 22.

SOUCIET (Father E) *Jesuit* Observations mathematiques, astronomiques, geographiques, chronologiques, et physiques, tirées les anciens Chinoises. Paris,1729, 4to. 50 d 10.

SPEED (John) History of Great Britain. London, 1650, fol.

SQUIRE (Samuel), *Bish of St David's* Greek Chronol Cam , 1741, 8vo 580 e 26.

STANLEY (Thomas), *the Elder* Hist of Philosophy. Lon , 1743, 4to , 4th ed , 523 k 5

STATE PAPERS Calendar of, Domestic Series, (annual,) London, 1866, 8vo

STATUTES AT LARGE (of Great Britain) Edited by Danby Pickering, Reader of the Law Lecture to Gray's Inn Cambridge, 1762, 8vo

STOW (John) *Antiquarian* Survey of London Carrisbrooke Library, reprint London, 1889, 8vo 012,207 1.

STUBBS (William), *Rev , late Regius Prof of Mod Hist ,* Oxon. Chronica Magistri, Rogeri de Hovedene London, 1858, 8vo 2073 g.

―――― Constitutional History of England Oxford, 1880, 3 vols, 8vo 2320 b 5

―――― Seventeen Lectures on Medieval and Mod Hist Oxford, 1886, 8vo 9073 e 13

―――― The Early Plantagenets, 2nd ed , 12mo London, 1877

SUIDAS Cæsarum Vitæ 1563, fol 815 m. 3.

SULLIVAN (J) La Féodalité Jersey, 1885, 8vo A brochure on the feudal system and especially as to existing survivals in the island of Jersey

SUMNER (Wm G) The Financier and the Finances of the American Revolution New York, 1891, 8vo 08,227. h. (15)

SYMMACHUS Epistolacum Symmachi V C præfecti Urbi, libri duo 10 905 c 37

TAYLOR (Robert), *Rev* The Diegesis, being a Discovery of the Origin, Evidences and Early History of Christianity London, 1841, 8vo

―――― Syntagma London, 1884, (Reprint,) 8vo

TAYLOR (Thomas). *The Platonist* Eleusinian Mysteries. 1790, 8vo. 704. e. 12.
———— Aristotle's Treatise of Animals 1809, 4to 520. e 5.
———— Fragments of a Treatise on Religion by the Emperor Julian, (A D 361-3.) preserved by Cyril, Bishop of Alexandria, to which are added some other fragments of Julian's, relative to the Christians Tr into Eng London, 1809, small 8vo pp 98 (Very rare, only 25 copies having been privately printed, nearly all of which were destroyed) The same reprinted in London, 1873. 3670 b
———— Iamblicus on the Mysteries of the Egyptians 1821, 8vo 8460 d
———— Mystical Hymns of Orpheus. 1824, 8vo 11,335. c 33
———— Pausanias. Itinerary of Greece Tr into Eng London,1824,3 vols,8vo 1299 c 10.
———— Translations of the Fragments of Ocellus Lucanus (B C 500), on the Nature of the Universe, Taurus, (the Platonist,) on the Eternity of the World, Julius Firmicus Maternus, on the Thema Mundi or Geniture of the World (from the third book of the Mathesis), and Proclus, (A.D 412-85), on the Perpetuity of Time. London, 1831, small 8vo, pp 96. 8461 bbb 15.
TEIXEIRA DE ARAGAO (A C) Descripcao historica das moedas Romanas existentes no gabinete numismatico de Sua Magestade El Rei . . . Dom Luiz I. Lisboa, 1870, 8vo, pp. 640. 7756 bbb (7)
———— Descripcao geral e historica das moedas cunhadas em nome dos reis, regentes, e governadores de Portugal. Lisboa, 1874, 8vo 7757. dd.(7.)
TERRIEN (de Lacouperie) *Mem Soc. of Bib. Archæol* Early History of Chinese Civilization London, 1880, 8vo. 9057. a.
———— Paper Money of China. London, 1882, 8vo. 7756. bbb 16.
THEODOSIUS Codex Theodosianus. ed. G Haenal. 1841, 4to. 705 h (17-18).
THEOGNIS *the Megarean* Fragments. Tr. by Rev J Banks Bound with Hesiod. London, 1856, 8vo 2500 f.
THIERRY (Aug) The Norman Conquest of Britain London, 1856, 8vo
THOMPSON (Henry), *Rev* History of Roman Literature London 1852, 8vo
  On page 120 appears a representation of the Obelisk of Augustus
THUCYDIDES. Tr by Rev. William Smith, about 1740 Reprint, London, 1892, 8vo.
TORFÆUS (Thormodus). "Arcades," or Ancient History of Orkney Tr by Rev. A. Pope. Wick, 1866, 12mo 9509 e 3.
TOULLIER (Charles B M) Le droit civil expliqué Paris, 1845, 8vo. 5403 ee.
TOWNSEND (George H) Manual of Dates London, 1877, 8vo.
TROPLONG (Raymond T) Le droit civil. Paris, 1845-55, 8vols, 8vo. 5403. e.
TURNER (Sharon). Tal-iesin, the Bard London, 1803, 8vo. 1064 l. 1.
———— History of the Anglo Saxons London, 8vo
TWISS (*Sir* Travers) Money and Currency Oxford, 1843, 8vo 1390 f 50 (3)
———— View of the Progress of Political Economy in Europe since the 16th Century. London, 1847, 8vo. 1390. d. (12.)

ULUGH BEG, *afterwards christened Juan de Persia, q v.*
UPHAM (Edward). History of Buddhism. London, 1829 fol 1232. k.

VAIRASSE (Denis) A voyage to Sevarambia Tr from the Fr ed of 1675 Included in "Travels into several remote nations of the world " Vol. III, p. 12 London, 1727, 8vo 12,612. d 22
VALLANCEY (Charles). Ancient History of Ireland Dublin, 1786, 8vo 982 d 8
———— Primitive Inhabitants of Britain and Ireland Dublin, 1807, 8vo. 5795 (1.)
VALERIANI (Gætano) La Vita di Gesu Cristo, (reprint) 1869, 8vo 4807 aa
VEDAS, THE The Threefold Science of the Iyotish udhyayu of the Veda. Rev. J. Stevenson Bombay, 1833, 4to 14,007 c I
———— The Main Results of Modern Vaidaik Researches, by Ram-chandra Ghosha Calcutta, 1870, 8vo , pp 57 4505. c 10
———— Hymns of the Rigveda R T H Griffith Benares, 1889, 8vo 14,007 cc 17
———— Sacred Books of the East. Max Müller Oxford, 1879 8vo 2003 b
VERSTEGAN (Richard). A restitution of Decayed Intelligence in Antiquities, concerning the most noble and renowned English nation (Eds , Antwerp, 1605, London, 1628, 1634; 1655, and 1673) London, 1673, 8vo 7707 b 29
VINING (Edward P) An inglorious Columbus or evidence that Hwui Shan and a party of Buddhist monks from Afghanistan discovered America in the fifth century. New York, 1885, 8vo. 0551 i, 5.

VOLNEY (C F Chassebœuf de), *Count* Œuvres completes Paris, 1838, 8 tom , 8vo
   (These works include Meditations on the Ruins of Empire, Travels in Egypt and
   Syria, Climate and Aboriginal Inhabitants of the United States of America, New
   Researches into Ancient History, and Treatise on the Alphabets and Languages
   of Europe and Asia)   12,235 k 2
VOLTAIRE (Arouet de)   Essai sur l'histoire générale Paris, 1756, 7 vols in 4, 8vo
———— History of Europe. London, 1754, 3 vols, 8vo.   582. d 2-5 (1)
———— Another ed , 1758, 3 vols, 8vo.   582 b. 3-5.

WEEDEN (William R) Economic and Social History of New England, 1620-1789.
   New York, 1890, 2 vols, 8vo   9602 de g
WHISTON (William A) Vindication of the Sibylline Oracles; to which are added the
   genuine Oracles themselves, in Greek and English. London, 1715, 8vo 873. 1 23
WIARDA (Tileman Dothias) Geschichte und Auslegung des Salschen Gesetzes. Latin
   and German texts Bremen and Zurich, 1809, 8vo.   5606 c
WILLIAMS (Sir Monier) Buddhism in its connection with Brahminism and Hinduism
   2nd ed London, 1890, 8vo.   2212 c 1.
————Hinduism Published by the Society for the Promotion of Christian knowl-
   edge London, 1877, 8vo   2212 a.
WIMMER (Ludv. F.A) Die Runenschrift Ed by Dr. F Holthausen Berlin, 1887,
   8vo.   7708 ee 41
WORSAÆ (J. J A) The Danes and Norwegians in England. Tr. from the Danish
   London, 1852, 8vo
———— Ancient Norway Tr from the Danish
WRIGHT (Thomas) The Celt, the Roman and the Saxon. London, 1885, 8vo. (An
   able work drawn chiefly from antiquarian sources)   2258. b.

YANGUAS Dictionario de Antiquedaaes , art " Moneda "
YARRANTON (Andrew) England's Improvement by Sea and Land; to Outdo the
   Dutch without Fighting, to Pay Debts without Moneys, to set at Work all the
   Poor of England with the growth of our own Lands, to prevent unnecessary Suits
   in Law, with the benefit of a voluntary Register (registration of land titles), directions where vast quantities of Timber are to be had for the building of Ships,
   with the advantage of making the great Rivers of England navigable, rules to
   prevent Fires in London and other great Cities, with directions how the several
   companies of handicraftsmen in London may always have cheap Bread and Drink.
   London, 1577, 2 vols, 4to. (An ingenious and extremely rare work.)

ZASIUS (Joannes U) Epitome in usus feudarum Lugduni, 1544, 8vo   5306 a. 2.
ZOROASTER Boum-Dehesch, cosmogonie des Parsés, trad, par M Auguetil du Perron Paris, 1771, 2 tom , 4to.   696 1. 6 8.

THE WORSHIP OF AUGUSTUS CÆSAR;

A NEW CHRONOLOGY AND SURVEY

OF HISTORY AND RELIGION.

CHAPTER I.

THE CYCLE OF THE ECLIPSES.

OF all the nations of antiquity, the East Indians are the only ones whose chronology, albeit like the others fundamentally astrological, possesses any such astronomical harmony or such symphony of dates as, even with the greatest prudence, can be made to yield useful and reliable results. The different æras which are still used in various parts of India for the computation of time, afford valuable side-lights on this difficult but strangely interest ng research The employment of the statistical method, in bringing together a vast number of dates, both from India and the numerous other countries into which the Brahminical and Buddhic religions and their derivatives have penetrated, adds great strength to the deductions derived from other sources. Finally, the employment by the Indians of two principal and several other sets of Divine Years, all founded on the Cycle of the Eclipses, brings the whole body of research to such satisfactory conclusions, that it would seem to require an overwhelming mass of evidence to upset them

It is hardly too much to say that a knowledge of the Cycle of the Eclipses and of its astrological derivatives ranks with the most important historical information within the whole range of human attainment, for upon it have been erected all the Divine Years, upon these all the mythologies, and upon the mythologies, all the history of the ancient world It is the guide to all religious myths, dogmas and doctrines; the clue to religious evolution; the key to chronology; and the finger-post to ancient history It is older than theMahabharata epic, it is younger than the present decade, for it was made the basis of a proclamation by the Emperor of China so late as January 28th, 1898; it is the father of the gods, of the zodiac, of the calendar, and of all the festivals of all the churches both Oriental and Occidental.   Philosophers have sold the knowledge of it to the temples, and the temples have employed it to amaze, terrify and rule mankind.   Conquerors in all ages have wielded it as a weapon, more potent than armies, or fleets, with which to subjugate states or destroy opposing races   Yet, to-day, notwithstanding its extreme simplicity, its vast antiquity and its sinister career, it is but imperfectly known even to the learned and an absolutely sealed book to the masses.

The conquests of Darius, Alexander, and Seleucus in India, of Titus in Greece, Scipio in Spain, Pompey in Syria, Cæsar in Gaul, Mahomet in Arabia, Cortes in Mexico, Pizzaro in Peru, and many others were all made in the name of Messiahs drawn solely from this Mystic Cycle, and whom astrology had taught the conquered nations to believe would visit the earth at these periods [1]   Indeed it has served as a *ruse du temple* and a *ruse de guerre* for upwards of thirty centuries   India has lately been disturbed by seditions, which can be traced directly to this source   China is alarmed at the coincidence of a New Year's Day and a solar eclipse, while the brother of the German Emperor, who must have learnt from the German missionaries in China that a recent year marked the dawn of a new Brahma-Buddhic manvantara has exposed himself to the suspicion of using this information in order to strengthen his position at Kiao Chao

It is a more or less commonly accepted belief, that astronomy is the offspring of astrology.   The writer's reading and observation has led him to the opposite conclusion, namely that astrology is a development of astronomy, in other words, that nearly the entire mass of fancies, verbalisms, and conceits, known as astrology, owes its origin and its strength to previous discoveries in astronomy   Astronomy no sooner discovered a fact, than astrology at once turned it to practical account   The date of one is, therefore, an almost infallible guide to that of the other   The Rev Edward Greswell (Oxon), who has left us twenty volumes of misapplied learning on the subject of the Calendar, laboured hard to prove that the eclipse credited to Thales of Miletus, B C , 585, was not fore-told from observation, but by means of the Cycle of Eclipses which he supposed Thales to have discovered, forgetting that the cycle itself could only have been the product of previous astronomical observation, extending over long periods of time, and also, forgetting that in another part of his work he pointedly affirmed that this

---

[1] The Aztecs, Peruvians, Chibchas, and other American nations were looking for the reappearance of a Messiah when the Spaniards landed in America

cycle was known to the Egyptians so early as the tenth century B C

The use of the Cycle of Eclipses can not only be traced in Miletus to the period of Thales, it belongs to an older period in Egypt and Chaldea, and to a still older period in India. Man has practised the arts of imposture from so remote an epoch, he has been so ingenious in perverting the truth, that no safe reliance can be placed upon anything that he has directly affirmed or written with reference to antiquity. History is not to be gleaned from the memorials which have been preserved, but rather from those which have been lost, neglected, or forgotten Man, when viewed generally, is a constitutional romancer, one who is altogether too cunning to be convicted out of his own mouth The progress of astronomical knowledge, which he can neither forge nor pervert, affords much more reliable testimony concerning the progress of astrology, and therefore, of religion and history, than anything which he has written on these subjects. Prominent in this range of knowledge was the Cycle of the Eclipses and the sinister use to which he put it

Upon this basis the Brahmins erected the most stupendous system of superstition of which it is possible to conceive. Upon this system of superstition, they superimposed an ecclesiastical organization and canon, contrived to last for several thousand years, compared with which the most venerable organization of the Western world is but a thing of yesterday This system had probably lasted one divine year, before the failure of Parasurama unexpectedly exposed its weakness, and opened it to attack. Yet, such was the strength of their ecclesiastical organization that it required another divine year before this attack succeeded, not, indeed, in overthrowing, but in modifying the system of the Brahmins This modification began with the calendar, the precise point of the Parasuramic fracture. The man who detected and exposed this fracture, was he who is known as Buddha, Tat,[2] or Gotama, and the least obvious, yet, practically the most important, of the reforms that he instituted, was to alter, or at least to suggest the means of altering, the division of the zodiac, and of the year, from ten to twelve equal parts.

It is probable that the change from a ten to a twelve months' year had its origin in the failure of Parasurama, the tenth incarnation of Brahma, or Vishnu, who was to have wound up the affairs of the

[2] The Brahmins afterwards appropriated this name "OM, TAI, SAI, these are considered as the three designations of Brahma" Ies Chrishna to Arjuna Bhagavad Gita, XVII, 23

world, and to have brought mankind to judgment in the year 1206, 1143 or else 1128 B C   But at that distant period a political or religious revolution, without adequate astrological support, was practicably impossible, while astrology, without a positive astronomical ground-work, was out of the question   That the Parasuramic failure was indeed followed by a long period of disturbance and civil wars, ending with the Buddhic reform of the calendar, can only be attributed to the discovery, or disclosure, of some great astronomical fact which furnished the basis of such reform; and this is most likely to have been the discovery of the planetary nature of Jupiter, and the determination of the Jovian cycle of twelve years   The Indians and Chinese indeed carry their Jovian cycles back to much more remote periods   But it is easy to prove that these are comparatively modern inventions based upon Buddhic divine years, and that the actual æra of the Jovian cycles is not much, if at all, earlier than the eleventh century, B C   This was the phenomenon needed, and this was the phenomenon employed not merely to explain away the failure of Parasurama, but to obtain a further lease of power for the Brahminical church.   Nevertheless, the movement thus begun was disputed for centuries by the contending sects which arose out of the Parasuramic failure, and it was not until the second Buddhic period or the seventh century in India and China, the sixth century in Miletus, Chaldea, Egypt and Greece, and the fifth century, B C , in Rome and the West, that the change from a ten to a twelve months' year was effected.   It is not necessary in this place to dwell upon the causes of this remarkable change, we are here only concerned with the fact and the evidences of the change, and with the marks which still remain of it in our laws and customs.

For example, four holidays are still observed in the British Isles, and in Gaul and in Germany, of whose origin nobody has yet offered a satisfactory account.   These are Martinmas, November 11th; Candlemas, February 2nd, Whitsuntide, May 15th; and Lammas, August 1st.   Such are the dates of the Cross Quarter days as fixed in Scotland, where they always fall on the same days of the solar year.   In England, Whitsuntide "term" is May 15th, whilst Whitsuntide itself is moveable, because it occurs so and so many days after Easter, which, being a lunar festival, becomes, in a solar calendar, a moveable day.   But in Scotland, where the year for all purposes is solar and "Julian" (i e , consisting of $365\frac{1}{4}$ days) the Cross Quarter days are fixed   Leases are usually dated from two of them, or from an approximate day bearing a fixed and permanent relation to them, the removal terms in leases being May 28th and November 28th In England, hunting and fishing leases are usually dated from Martinmas Similar customs prevail on the Continent.[3]

On the other hand, the usual English quarter-days for leases, taxes ("rates"), interest-payments, the liquidation of tradesmen's accounts, and many other periodical events and settlements are Lady Day, March 25th, St. John's Day June 25th, Michaelmas September 29th, and Christmas December 25th, answering to the equinoxes and solstices

Why is it that these last-named English quarter-days are not enough for the whole kingdom, and that four other quarter-days are found to be in common use, not merely in Scotland, but also (as to hunting leases) in England, while as popular holidays, or festival days, they are observed as universally in one country as the other? It is true that Candlemas and Lammas are no longer popular festivals, but this cannot be said of Whitsuntide nor of Martinmas, both of which are widely observed Moreover, why is it that these submerged Cross-Quarter days are still venerated in France and Germany?

Why is it, also, that except as to Michaelmas, which, however, is only four days out, the usual quarter-days are just three months apart, whilst in the case of the Cross-Quarter days it is two months and a half from Martinmas to Candlemas, three months and a half from Candlemas to Whitsuntide, two months and a half from Whitsuntide to Lammas, and three months and a half from Lammas to Martinmas?

The solution of these problems belongs to the changed division of the year, from ten months of thirty-six days to twelve months of thirty days (with five epagomenæ), and it incidentally brings to light some of the most interesting and significant facts in the whole range of ancient history and religion

---

[3] "In England for many municipal and parochial purposes the year is reckoned from Lady Day or (else from) Michaelmas Day The tenure of lands is generally computed by the same periods In Scotland the period in contracts of landlord and tenant is often dated from Lammas or Candlemas " Sir Geo Cornewall-Lewis, "Anc Astron," 29 Many interesting survivals of Whit-sun (Baal-time) and of Martinmas, such as Weeping for Thammuz, or Osiris, called the "Festival of the Dead," will be found in Haliburton's work

CHAPTER II.

THE ANCIENT YEAR OF TEN MONTHS

TO begin with, the Roman calendar, our own calendar, has been seriously altered By this is meant not merely that it was altered ten days by Pope Gregory in 1582, or eleven days by the British act passed in 1752, but that, to say nothing of other alterations, it was altered long before either of these dates, by changing the ancient year of ten months, aggregating 365 days, to a year of twelve months, aggregating 365 days The date of this alteration in the principal states of the world was approximately as follows ·

Country	B C	Remarks
India	662	Digambara aera of Buddha
China	657	Rev E Greswell, Fasti Catholici, I, 509
Miletus	592	Thales, or else Anaximander
Persia	590	Zoroaster.
Babylon	582	Nebu-chadn-Izzar
Athens	582	Solon changed 10 x 36=360, to 12 x 29½=354.
Egypt	547	Calendar falsely attributed to "Ramses III."
Syria	524	Cambyses, of Persia, "King of Asia "
Rome	451	Calendar of the Decemviri

To be told that the months anciently had 36 days each, or even an average of 36 days, will probably surprise the majority of our readers, yet there is scarcely an institute of antiquity so well attested

"According to the Babylonian Table the zodiac contained ten gods called the 'Ten Zodiac Gods ' [1] The commentators, more intent upon identifying Xisthrus with Noah, have entirely overlooked the significance of the Ten zodions of Babylon, whose numbers prove not only a division of the zodiac and the celestial sphere into ten parts, they also imply a division of the year into ten months and indicate the epoch of the Table This must be assigned to a period after the very ancient division of the year into eight and before its comparatively later division into twelve, civil months.

[1] Doane's " Bible Myths," p 102, citing Dunlop's " Son of the Man," p 153, n.

The prytanes or Senate of Athens consisted of 500 persons, 50 from each of the ten tribes, into which the whole population of Attica was divided. Each of these bodies of 50 representatives, served the public a tenth part of the year. None of them could serve less than 35 days nor more than 38, the last only in an intercalary year   It follows that the months contained on the average between 35 and 38 days   The Choiseul Marble, on which the course and succession of the prytanes for the whole year is recorded, proves that in fact the months had 35 or else 36 days each   Numerous other inscriptions prove that the current day of the month and the current day of the prytanea were the same [2]

"In the time of Homer, as in that of Romulus, the year was not divided into twelve, but into ten months"—*annum fuisse non duodecim mensium, sed decem*   Aulus Gellius, III., 16.

It may be added that Homer's "Odyssey," XI , 313, attributes to Poseidon, who is speaking to Tyro, an expression which implies a year of ten months.   Greswell, "Kal Hellenicæ," VI , 394

The day sacred to Hermes and to Maia, the fourth day of the tenth month, when Hermes, Mercury (or Ies) was born, as mentioned in Pisistratus' version of Homer's Hymns, is also regarded as an implication of the same fact   The day sacred to Hermes and Maia was Martinmas.

The prytanes also prove by their number and function the ancient division of the Greek year into ten months   Cf Potter's Antiq Greece, I, 507

"When the Founder of the City (that is to say, Romulus, who in the Augustan age was also alluded to as Quirinus) divided the periods of time, he appointed that there should be twice five months in the year   .   The first month was Mars .   .   .   But Numa added two to the ancient months   .   The market day (that is to say, Mercury's day, merk-day, mess-day, mass-day, the middle-day, etc) always returns after the ninth revolution."   Ovid, Fasti, I, 29. 38, 43, 54.

"Numa's first undertaking was to divide the year into twelve months according to the course of the moon " Livy, I, 19

' Junius Gracchianus, B C 124, Fulvius, B C 189, Varro, Suetonius and other writers all agree that the Roman year was divided into ten months   According to Fulvius it was Numa, while according to Junius it was Tarquin (Superbus) who altered it to twelve months."   Censorinus, de Die Natale, XX, (written A. D 238)

[2] Rev. Edw Greswell, K. H., I, 84-88

"Romulus divided the year of the Romans into ten months   The first (month) was March." Macrobius, Sat I, 12

Augustine of Hippo also mentions ancient "years" (evidently meaning months) of 36 days, "the tenth part of the lunar year " "City of God," XV, 12

Geminus, in his "Uranologia" testifies that the Roman year was originally divided into ten months.

Eutropius, I, 3, says "Numa Pompilius divided the year into ten months " Except that Romulus and not Numa was the supposed author of the ten months' year, this testimony is corroborative

Says Diodorus, lib I· "Even at this day, now that there are twelve months in the year, many (persons) live a hundred years "

"The fifth month in the Sibylls is July, because anciently the first was March and there were but ten, until Numa " Procopius, Bell. Gothica, I, 19.

"Nor did the ancients have as many calends (a metonym for months) as there now are, their year was shorter (in months) by a couple of months " Ovid, Fasti, III, 98

The Pythagoreans regarded the number Ten as perfect

"The number Ten was then in great esteem   .   For that reason Romulus respected the conventional number in forming the year (of ten months) " Fasti, III, 132

Livy says of the year of Rome 291, or B C. 463, that "The elections were then held and Lucius Æbutius and Publius Servilius being chosen consuls, they began their office on the calends of August, which was at that time considered the beginning of the civil year " As March was by all accounts originally the first month, a change from March to August in a twelve months' year would have been a change from the first to the sixth month, a difference of only five months   Such a change being more than a quarter of a year and less than half a year would have entailed great inconvenience and confusion   But in a ten months' year no such mischief would have resulted, because in such a year the change from March to August would have amounted to exactly half a year   There can consequently be but little doubt that at the time this change was made in the New Year Day, the year was divided into ten months [3]

While all the authorities agree that the division of the year was

[3] It will not do to argue that the ten months' year was not a full year of 365 or at least 360 days with 5 epagomenæ, for it is in such years that Livy, Cicero, Dion and Plutarch computed the reign of Romulus at 37, while other ancient writers computed it at 38 years, an interval that forms a definite part of the accepted chronology

changed from 10 to 12 parts (duodekameria) there is some diversity as to the year when the change was made   Many of the authorities piously assign it to Romulus, or Numa, while M Fulvius Nobilior, who was Consul B. C 189, is reported to have said that the change from 10 to 12 months was made by Manius Acilius Glabrio, B C 191, only two years previously   (Macrob Sat I, 13, § 20)   How- ever, Fulvius was confuted by Varro, who cited a brass tablet of Pinarius and Furius, B C 472, "which was dated by a reference to intercalation," says Sir Geo Cornewall-Lewis, evidently meaning an intercalation designed, like those of the Hindus and Chinese, to harmonize the 10 and 12 months' year   This "intercalation" will be explained further on   The most authoritative statement on the year of the change from 10 to 12 months was made by Cassius He- mina and M Sempronius Tuditanus, the last of whom was Pontifex- Maximus of Rome B. C 185-76 They said that the change from 10 to 12 months was made by the Decemvirs (B C 452-450), and this was probably the fact   The apparent disagreement between the date of Varro's tablet and the acra of the Decemvirs may be due to the alteration of the Roman chronology explained in another place. [5]

Such are the literary evidences with regard to the change from a ten months' to a twelve months' year.   It is perhaps unnecessary to state that the two new months in the Roman calendar were January and February, which are now intercalated between the previously last or tenth month, December, and the previously first month, Primus, afterwards called March; unnecessary, because the names of these months alone would prove the whole case   But there are other proofs.   The ancient ordinal names of the last four months still remain in use to prove not only that the year was anciently divided into ten months, but they also attest the place of intercala- tion   December is a word which relates to ten, yet December is now the twelfth month; November which relates to nine, is now the elev- enth month; October which relates to eight, is now the tenth month; September which relates to seven, is now the ninth month.

Still other evidences of the ten months' year are derived from com- parative philology; yet these will be adduced last of all, because al- though the most popular, they are the least reliable   The calend of March was called Messo, from Mesotheus, a surname of Bacchus,

[4] Mrs Gatty dates the change from a twelve to a ten months' year in B. C 293. According to Pothier, Cicero (de Legg, ii,) fixes it in the consulate of Dec. Brutus, which by our computation would be B C. 200   The statement of the Roman Chief- pontiff is far more authoritative.

Janus, or Mercury, the god of the open door. In like manner the calend of August (five months later) was called Messa, a surname of Ceres, the goddess of harvests From these names sprang the metonyms *messis* for harvest times, *messis*, a crop and many other words of like import Again, as the calend of March, the ecclesiastical New Year day, was called *par excellence* the Messo, or High Mass-day, so the calend of August, or the ecclesiastical Mid-year, was called the Lesser Mass, or, according to the Rev Sam'l Johnson, the Latter Mass, corrupted, as he asserts by the English, to Lammas So distinctively was this name of *messa* attached to the middle day of the year, that afterwards it was also given to the middle of anything, for example *mesa*, the middle part, Pliny XIX, 9, *mesaula*, the middle salon or hall of a house, Vitruvius VI, 10, *mese*, the fourth or middle string of the seven-stringed lyre, Vitruvius, V, 4: mess-day, Mercury-day, merk-day, market-day, or the fourth, or middle day, of the septuary week, which day is still the market day in all rural places within the limits of the ancient Roman empire, Bru-mess, or midwinter, another name for Brumalia, or the festival of Bacchus, *mezzanine*, a middle flooring, *mezzo*, the middle or half of one, and so on The mediæval monks, in order to dispose of this tell-tale word, said that *mess*, or *mass* came from *missio*, to dismiss, but this was simply their *ipse dixit*. They offered no proofs to support such a derivation, and they made no attempt to explain the numerous applications of the word mess or mass, which had nothing to do with dismiss or dismissal Mess is a word of very high antiquity. It was used in India, Tibet, China, Egypt, Greece, Persia and Rome In all these countries it meant the Messiah, the mediator, the intercessor, the one who stood in the middle, between God and man Not to go any further backward in time than the Greek period, it was given to Bacchus, who was called Meso-theus, or the Mediator, to Poseidon or Neptune, who was called Mesopontus from *meso*, the middle and *pontus*, the Sea (Racine), to Mithra, because she stood in the middle between the opposing forces of Ormuzd (Oromesus) and Ahriman (Racine), and at one period even to Jupiter, called Messapea, because he was then regarded as the Mediator between Saturn, the Supreme, and his handiwork, the human race

Similar evidences are to be found in the names of the Hebrew, Syrian, Babylonian, Greek, Egyptian, Chaldean and Indian months They all exhibit in their names an original Ten and an added Two, to make up the present Twelve. Take the Syrian months for example. they are Eloul, Tisri I, Tisri II, Canoun I, Canoun II,

Sabat, Adar, Nissan, Iyar, Hisiram, Thammuz and Ab It is evident that Tisri II and Canoun II are after-thoughts, or months intercalated after Tisri and Canoun, in order to make up a present Twelve out of an ancient Ten

Until this accumulation of evidences is overthrown, it must be conceded that the year was anciently divided into ten months. This places us in a position to add the corroborative, though less positive, testimony of the Cross-Quarter days

When the year consisted of ten equal parts or months it could only be otherwise equally divided into five periods of two months each, or two periods of five months each, for ten cannot be equally divided by any other numbers than one, two, five, or ten itself As the quarter days did not fall on the same day of the month, rents were probably paid—and the existing Scottish practice is a proof that in fact they were so paid—every half year, that is to say, at the end of every five months, or 180 days [5] In a period of industrial activity —and it will scarcely be denied that in commercial countries, even in very ancient times, such periods occurred—a half yearly period for rentals and other settlements must have become inconvenient Though the origin and the motive of the change was of a far more important and significant character than mere convenience, yet convenience may not have been without influence in rendering the change acceptable When the change did take place, the half yearly removal and rent and settlement days had to be—and they were in fact—exchanged in favour of quarterly periods We have now to describe the process It will bring to light some strange matters

Let us take Rome for example The date is B C 452 The year consists of ten months, each of 36 days with five intercalaries. It begins March 1st In order not to disturb the customary half yearly rent and settlement day, occurring August 1st, which was also at that period the consular day, or beginning of the civil year (Livy III, 6), the plan of changing to a twelve months year is to divide the first half of the current year into five months each of 36 days and the second half into six months each of 30 days, and in the following year to render the change complete by dividing the year into 12 months each of 30 days This is the "intercalation" previously mentioned. Rents, etc., are henceforth to be paid quarterly When

---

[5] In the Bhagavad Gita, a work which Dr Lorimer assigns to about the year 400 B C , but which may be nearly as ancient as the period of the second Buddha, the year is divided into two seasons of six months each, that of "the Sun's northern circuit" and that of his 'Southern circuit' I. C VIII, 24-25.

does the first quarter become due? The middle day, the ides of May, which in the 36 day month falls on the 18th The long subsequent decree of Pope Gregory changed the 18th to the 28th This accounts for the Whitsun term, still employed in Scotland When does the second quarter become due? Three months (now of 30 days each) from August 1st, namely, on November 1st. Add Gregory's ten days to this and we have November 11th This is Martinmas. The mid-year day, August 1st, is Lammas Six months (each of 30 days) from Lammas is February 1st This is Candlemas eve

It is true that while the Gregorian change disturbed the ancient dates in November, it did not disturb the ancient dates in May; but in respect of the Whitsun term the ten days change had to be made in order to keep these two rent days at the customary distance, 166 days, apart In other words, when Martinmas was advanced from November 1st to the 11th it became necessary, without altering any of the other festival dates in May, to advance Whitsun from May 18th to the 28th; and this accordingly was done [6]

We have thus accounted for the Cross-Quarter days, but we have not yet disposed of this anomalous year The year B. C 452 con-sisted of ten months each of 36 days (with five epagomenæ), the year B C. 450 consisted of 12 months each of 30 days (with five epago-menæ), both of them commencing March 1st; but this particular year B. C 451, the Year of Change, although it consisted like its predecessor and successor of 360 days (with five epagomenæ) yet it included only 11 months. In order not to disturb Sextilis 1st, or Lammas day, when the consuls entered upon their office and the half year's rents were due in the ten months' year, the first half of the year had to have five months of 36 days, while the second half had six months of 30 days, total, 360 days, (with five epagomenæ), but only eleven months. The year of the change began on March 1st; it ended with the last day of January; consequently in that year there were only eleven months in the calendar The crowded-out month first made its appearance in the calendar of B. C 450; and as this month was largely devoted to purification and preparation for the New Year, it was called February, after the god of purifica-tion, whose name was Februus

The long subsequent year, when Julius Cæsar rectified the Roman calendar, consisted of 445 days and it was called the Year of Confusion

[6] The American Encyc Brit , art "May," remins us that on the Ides of May was celebrated the feast of Mercury The Ides of May in the ten months' year was Whit-suntide, the 18th. It is quite likely that one festival arose out of the other.

This affords warrant to suspect that the remoter year, when the months were begun to be changed from ten of 36 to 12 of 30 days each, was called "The Year of Change." Ovid, Virgil, Pliny, Servius, Hyginus and other ancient authorities allude to a once-existent zodiac of 11 signs and therefore to a year of 11 months; a number and mode of division, which, if employed permanently, would have led to extreme confusion and inconvenience. For this reason these allusions can only be reasonably applied to the unique Year of Change, the only year, which, according to our view, ever really consisted of eleven months or was represented by 11 zodions.[7]

There is indeed a Greek legend that "Musaeus," who is assigned to a very remote age (B. C. 1406) invented the zodion of the Archer, which might be taken to imply that before his time the Greek zodiac had but 11 signs and the year only 11 months. On the other hand, the legend may merely mean that the Hindu sign of a human-archer, Dhanaus, or Danaus, was altered by "Musaeus" to the Greek sign of the centaur-archer. The former is to be seen on the gold coins of Darius; the latter is in the zodiac of to-day. Seriously, however, a Musaeus of the 15th century B C belongs not to history but to mythology. The date B C 1406 is astrological. Musaeus is the Greek form of Moess, one of the names of the god Dionysos, Bacchus, or Buddha. It was adopted by several Dionysian writers, the latest of whom flourished in the fourth or fifth century of our æra and composed a work entitled "The Loves of Hero and Leander," some lines of which were borrowed from Nonnus, the Dionysian, another follower of the same cult. As for the legend in Servius that in the Alexandrian zodiac the Scorpion occupied the space of two-twelfths of the zodiac, until one-twelfth was given to its Claws in order to form what is now known as the Balance—we may consign it to the realms of poetry.[8]

[7] The American Encyc Brit , art "Zodiac," gets rid of the difficulty by reciting that "the earlier Greek writers—Eudoxus, Eratosthenes, Hipparchus—knew of only 11 zodiacal symbols, but made one do double duty, extending the Scorpion across the seventh and eighth divisions." This scheme, which creates the Balance from the Scorpion's claws, admits twelve divisions but only eleven signs, an incongruity that the succeeding sentence tries but fails to explain. "The Balance obviously indicating the equality of day and night, is *first mentioned as the sign of the autumnal equinox* by Geminus and Varro and obtained through Sosigenes of Alexandria official recognition in the Julian calendar." The point is not who first mentioned the Balance as the sign of the autumnal equinox, but when was the zodiac first divided into twelve parts and into how many parts was it previously divided, not during some exceptional year, but permanently.

[8] Cf Drummond on the Zodiac, p 76

Pliny (N. H , II, 6) credits the invention of zodiacal signs in the Western world to Cleostratus of Tenedos, who first invented, adopted, or added, those of Aries the Lamb and Sagittarius the Archer. *" Signa deinde in eo Cleostratus, et prima Arietis ac Sagitarii "* Pliny makes Cleostratus later than Anaximander, whose æra he fixes in Olym 58 (B C. 548)   In the Periplus of the Pseudo " Scylax of Caryanda," Cleostratus is alluded to as a contemporary of the real Scylax   This makes him later than the Indian expedition of Darius Hystaspes, the maritime portion of which was conducted by the real Scylax, about B C 508   If these dates could be depended upon, the period when the Athenians adopted, what will appear to be the Buddhic subdivision of the zodiac into twelve parts and changed their year from ten to twelve months, was, according to our present calendar, about B C 508.   The subsequent alterations of 108, including 78 years in the calendar, which were effected by Augustus Cæsar, a subject yet to be treated herein, has thrown many ancient dates out of joint   Could they be re-established, it would probably be found that the adoption of the 12 months' year in Greece took place somewhat earlier than B C 508; most likely between that year and the date of the calendar reform of Solon; in other words, about B. C 550.

However, it will be observed that in addition to several explicit accounts of the change from a ten to a twelve months' year, we have several accounts of changes in the zodiac   One says that " Musæus" invented the sign of the Archer, another, that two zodions were made out of one, namely, the Balance and Scorpion out of the Scorpion); while still another asserts that Cleostratus first gave to the zodiac the Lamb and the Archer   The Rev. Dr Greswell, without even suspecting that the zodiac previously had but ten signs, believes that the most recent zodions are the Waterman and the Fishes, [9] but his evidence on this point has to be weighed against that of Pliny

If these conclusions concerning a ten months' year fail to agree with the appearance of a 12 months' year in the Hebrew Scriptures or with the opinions of those expositors who claim for the Hebrew Scriptures a greater antiquity than the time of Solon, it is because such a claim lacks the support of evidence   There is nothing whatever but conjecture in favour of the greater antiquity of the existing version of the Old Testament   There is no extant manuscript of the Bible older than the Christian æra, nor indeed is there one so old,

[9] Cf Fasti Catholici, III, 397-8, 410.

whilst the Bible itself does not pretend to be older than the period when Hilkiah the priest found the Book of the Law and carried it to Shaphan, the scribe. This was about B. C. 454 [10]

So far as they relate to the order and succession of the zodions and months the foregoing explanations rest to a certain extent upon the assumption that the Censors permitted the Augustan writers to tell the whole truth with regard to this matter and that therefore such order has not been disturbed, but a passage in John of Nikios throws some doubt upon this point. That chronicler states that Augustus caused the months of August and February to change places in the calendar [11] This may only mean that originally when the two additional months and signs were added by the Romans, one each was placed at the end of the fifth and tenth month, namely February after Quintilis and January after Decembris; and that afterwards Augustus placed them where they are now. (See chapter VII, year B C 452) In several other states of antiquity the added months were placed one each after the original fifth and tenth month; but the practice was not uniform, for in some of them the added months were both inserted (at least so they appear now) after the original tenth month, whilst in other states the added months were inserted (at least so they appear now) in other parts of the calendar.[12] It is not necessary for present purposes to go any farther into this part of the subject The reader who desires ampler information will find it in the author's monograph on "Ancient Calendars" [13]

The Calendar has been a potent instrument in the hands of imposture. The Egyptians realized this so keenly that they seized a propitious interval in their long life of slavery to make their kings swear never to alter the calendar.[14]

The classical Greeks carved their planispheres and calendars upon

[10] I Kings, xii

[11] On this point consult Ovid, Fasti, II, 47, and John of Nikios.

[12] Clinton, Fasti Hellenicæ III, xii, censures Archbishop Usher for venturing to make precise calculations as to the position of the months in the calendar prior to and after its correction by Julius Cæsar, "a precision for which we have no authority." Sir Geo Cornewall-Lewis, in his "Historical Survey of the Astronomy of the Ancients," p. 237, has something to the same effect

[13] It may, however, be stated in this place that Plutarch, Cicero, Varro, Ovid and Macrobius agree in asserting that "anciently" February was the last month. As there was no February more ancient than the twelve months' Consular year which began with Lammas, it would appear that February was originally placed between Quintilis and Sextilis, or July and August.

[14] Nigidius Figulus, as quoted in the Scholiast on the Aratus of Germanicus Cæsar, Dupuis, II, 122, Greswell, II, 389, Wilkinson, II, 255.

monuments of marble, but one has only to examine the ingenious alterations in the pieces of this description now in the Museum of the Louvre, to be convinced how vain was their precaution [15] The Romans of the Republic insisted upon a nail being driven each year into the facade of the ærarium   The Koran forbids intercalation [16]

All to no purpose   The calendars have been altered repeatedly, not only as to days and months, but even as to years   The most remarkable of these alterations were effected by Augustus Cæsar.

[15] See Chapter XI, herein
[16] Sura IX, 37 cited by Albiruni.

CHAPTER III

THE LUDI SÆCULARES, AND OLYMPIADS

THE great festival of the Ludi Sæculares which marked the sexagessimal subdivision of the Divine Year, was probably inherited by the Romans from the Etruscans It is said to have been fully explained in the "Life and Customs of the Romans" by M Terentius Varro, a work written, as we learn from passages in Pliny, Nonius and Cicero, in A. U 704, or 705, but now lost [1] According to Censorinus, Varro stated that the Etruscans had celebrated seven of these festivals at the following intervals of time 105, 105, 105, 105, 123, 119 and 119 years, total 781 years This information Varro said he got from the Annals of Etruria, written in the eighth cycle; octavum tum demum agi (Censorinus xviii), that is to say, the eighth cycle was then begun If A U 704 means 50 years before our æra [2] and Varro wrote directly after the beginning of the eighth cycle, it follows from the foregoing data that the Etruscan æra, from which the Cyclical Games took their periods, began before B C 831 On the other hand, if, as we shall presently furnish reasons to believe, the Varronian date, A U 704, means 35 years before our æra (a difference from the previous hypothesis of 15 years) then the Etruscan æra began on or before B. C 816, thus, 35 plus 781=816 According to Dodwell, the Etruscan æra began with Procas, king of Alba, B C 816, the very same year to which the present calculation conducts us [3] According to Sir Isaac Newton the Roman æra was 120 years wrong What we shall endeavor to prove is that it was formerly 78 years and is still 63 years wrong

It was a common custom in ancient times for conquerors to adopt the æra of the conquered and call it by a new name Thus the Babylonians, when they overthrew Nineveh, adopted the æra of

---

[1] Nat Hist XIV, 17, Nonius, voc Cœcum et Obstrigillare, Cic ad Att VIII, 2

[2] To use the word "æra" or its corrupted form "era" with reference to any period before Augustus, is, strictly speaking, an anachronism, however, the word has now a broader meaning than it had originally.

[3] Dodwell's Chronology "De Veteribus Græcorum Romanorumque Cyclis"

Tiglath-pil-Esar II, B C 748 and called it that of Nebo-Nazaru, the date being that which is recorded by Ptolemy and the orthography being that of Censorinus. The Persians, when they conquered Hither India, or Beluchistan, adopted the æra of the Cingalese Buddha and called it that of Cyrus. While the Moslems, who conquered the Persians, adopted the æra of Iesdigerd and called it that of Mahomet's Flight. When, probably during the fourth century *before* our æra, the Romans found it necessary to adopt an æra from which to date their mythology or history, they had before them only the æras of Nebo-Nazaru and Procas; for, as will presently be shown, the Greek Olympiads were not used in Roman works until Timæus wrote his history about B C 300. As between an unfamiliar and comparatively recent and a familiar and more ancient æra, it can scarcely be doubted that the Romans previous to this date preferred Procas to Nebo-Nazaru, and that in fact they adopted the Etruscan æra for their own and gave it the name of Romulus. In such case the received æra of the Nativity, which begins with the 754th year of Romulus, is out of harmony with the calendar of the Roman Commonwealth, to the extent of 63 years. It is not meant by this that we of to-day are in fact 63 years more distant from Romulus or the pretended Foundation of Rome than is shown by the calendar; but that we are in fact 63 years more distant from the period which was assigned by the Romans of the Commonwealth to that astrological personage and misdated event, and therefore that our calendar is out of harmony with Commonwealth dates to that extent. It is also out of harmony with Oriental dates to the same extent. To the Romans of the Commonwealth there was nothing before Romulus. He was the Son of God and Founder of the City. To the writers of the Augustan age (who had the annals of Etruria before them) there was Procas before Romulus and there were two generations of time between Procas and Romulus. Livy, who was a preceptor in the household of Augustus and whose History of Rome was read by that prince before it was published to the world, tells a pretty story of Numitor and his daughter Rhea Sylvia, who was a vestal virgin a century before vestal virgins were created in Rome, and who in that anachronical and immaculate capacity begat Romulus and Remus and floated them in an ark among the bulrushes, but nobody believes this story now, and the two generations between Procas and Romulus may be summarily dismissed to the realms of the imagination

With regard to the length of the Etruscan cycles it will be observed that the first four were of equal length, namely, 105 years.

Then occurs a great change from 105 to 123 and next to 119 years
The change was doubtless due to the discovery by the Etruscan
astrologers that they had previously miscalculated the annualised
cycle of the eclipses and that instead of being 105 x 6=630 years, it
was as they next supposed 666 years, and that to the first four cycles
of 105 years there should be added two more each of 123 years to
complete the term. But before the sixth Ludi Sæculares came
around it seems to have been discovered that not 666 but 662 years
was the true period of the node; hence to the first four cycles of 105
years and the fifth cycle of 123 years they added 119 for the sixth
cycle; and this interval remained unchanged until Etruscan astrology was superceded by Roman In the meantime the Greek astrologers had learnt from the Orient the true period of the ecliptical cycle, which is neither 630, nor 666, nor 662, but 658⅔ years This
cycle, upon being divided by six, gave approximately 110 years for
the Ludi Sæculares, and, as appears from the following lines of
Horace, written A. U 738, such was the interval adopted by the
Romans:

> Certus undenos decies per annos
> Orbis ut cantus referat que ludos
> Ter die clara, totiesque grata
> Nocte frequentes

The seventh Etruscan cycle (of 119 years) when added to the others, makes an average of 111 years, or only one year more than the
"ten times eleven years" immortalized in the Sæcular Hymn.

A glance at our chapter VII on Æras will convince the reader that
most, if not all, of the æras of ancient nations were based on the
Eastern incarnations Thus the Assyrians adopted the æra of Ies
Chrishna and assigned it to Tiglath-pil-Esar; the Chaldeans adopted
the same æra and ascribed it to Nebo-Nazaru In each case a few
years were added The Hindu date of the re-incarnation (birth) of
Ies Chrishna was, B C 736 (Table B) The Assyrians and Chaldeans added 12 years to this and made their æra B C 748. To this
the Etruscans added 68 years to make the æra of Procas, which to
the Romans of the Commonwealth, was the æra of Romulus. Proofs
of these alterations will be furnished as we proceed

In erecting a new æra, the first and most necessary step is the
acceptance of the established one for the basis of the proposed one
Universal custom, the arrangement and due order of historical data,
the accepted chronology of events and numerous other circumstances
stand in the way of change Hence Julius Cæsar, alt   the odd

period of his assumption of divinity must have impressed upon him the desirability of altering the established æra of Rome by many years, is not known to have pursued any such attempt, unless indeed he tampered with the Greek olympiads, of which we cannot be certain. However, as time advances, opportunities occur to render such changes practicable and these opportunities have usually been seized upon to establish a new æra and efface or conceal the true origin and identity of the æra which it was desirable to displace

Such an opportunity presented itself to Augustus After the battle of Actium and the closure of the temple of Janus, the world was at the feet of this prince and it was in his power to make whatever changes he pleased His assumption of sovereignty took place at a period when no known incarnation of the deity, whether Chaldean, Greek or Roman, was precisely due, although one had just passed Therefore to make himself out to be that Son of God, that incarnation of the deity, which the poets and astrologers of his court pretended was presaged in the Sibylline books and which character he afterwards assumed and proclaimed upon his coins and marbles, it became necessary for him to fit his Apotheosis to the Ludi Sæculares, or rather the Ludi Sæculares to his Apotheosis, for there was nothing equally available in astrology to hang it on This, by itself would not have been difficult, for the Ludi as we have seen, had not previously been celebrated with very scrupulous regularity, and the confusion and demoralization of the times lent every facility to his object But it so happened that Rome was now placed in direct maritime communication with India and that the period of the Indian re-incarnation (that of Quichena or Salivahana) had arrived [4] The immense body of religious mythology generated in the Orient had long since scattered its seeds throughout Bactria, Western Asia, Greece, Egypt and Etruria, regions which were now comprised within the Roman Empire and whose religious prepossessions it was to the last degree important for Augustus to utilise [5] The problem for the Roman astrologers was therefore to fit the Apotheosis of Romulus Quirinus and seven Ludi Sæculares to the proposed Apotheosis of Augustus Quirinus. In other words, it was necessary to

[4] " Embassies from the Kings of India have been many times sent to me, which has never before occurred under any Roman ruler." The Testament of Augustus, Son of God, engraved upon the Temple of Ancyra, art XXXI

[5] I have seen in the possession of General Sir Montague McMurdo some sculptured heads of Ies Chrishna or Salivahana, of the Græco-Bactrian aera, which unite the placid calm of the Indian conception of Buddha with the intellectual features of the Greek school, the combination producing an effect both noble and fascinating.

prove, so far as the calendar could be made to prove it, that the recent Indian re-incarnation was a false one and that of Augustus the true one, the sequel to that of Romulus Quirinus, the incarnation foretold by the Cumæan Sibyl and long expected by the Western world To achieve this result it was necessary for the Augustan astrologers to destroy 76 or 78 years of recorded time; in other words, to sink that number of years from the Roman calendar [6]

Let us now examine the various accounts that have been permitted to reach us of the year of Romulus, or the year when Rome is said to have been founded by Romulus. These accounts may with convenience be divided into two classes I, Those written during or after the age of Augustus; and II, Those written before the age of Augustus. As it is the Augustan chronology which is on trial, we begin by dismissing Class I without discussion It comprises Dionysius of Halicarnassus, M Terentius Varro, as reported by Plutarch, Pomponius Atticus, Cornelius Nepos, as reported by Lactantius, Messala Corvinus and Eutropius, all of whom give the foundation of Rome in Olym VI, 3, equal to B C 753; Censorinus, who gives Olym VI, 4 or B C 752, Porcius Cato, Solinus and Eusebius, who give Olym. VII, 1, or B. C 751; and Diodorus Siculus, as reported by George the Syncellus, who gives Olym VII, 2, or B C 750 There is also a mutilated passage in C Valerius Paterculus which gives Olym VI, 2, or B C 754 and the statement of Orosius, which places the æra of Romulus, some time during Olym VI If, as we shall endeavor to prove, Augustus altered the calendar, it is useless to look for the truth in any of the direct or explicit statements made on this subject during or after his reign It may occur in some round-about way; for the most subservient writers have sometimes taken the pains to preserve an important truth in a disguised form, it may be deducible from other circumstances; but it is not to be looked for on the surface; for to place it there meant death, or else exile and oblivion.

Class II comprises Timæus, the Sicilian, who lived during the fourth and third centuries before Augustus and who is alleged to have stated that the æra of Rome began 38 years before the first Olympiad (that is, the Olympiad employed by Dion. Hal.), Quintus Ennius, who died B C 169 and who tells us that Rome was founded since "*Septigenti sunt paulo plus vel minus anni,*" Polybius, who lived during the second century before Augustus and who fixed the

[6] Just one Calippic cycle.

æra of Rome at Olym. VI, 3; Quinctus Fabius Pictor, who flourished over two centuries before Augustus and who gave the æra at Olym. VIII, 1; L. Cincius Alimentus, of the same period, who fixed the æra of Rome at Olym. XII, 4; and Cicero, who in his Republica fixed the æra of Rome in the same year as Timæus. All these writers, except Ennius and Cicero, are reported by Dion. of Halcarnassus (Ant. Rom. I, 74), their own works having perished.[7] But let us listen to Dion's exact words: "Timæus, the Sicilian (by what computation I know not), places it (the last re-inhabiting or building of the City, or by what name soever we ought to call it) at the same time with the building of Carthage, that is, in the 38th year before the first Olympiad; Lucius Cincius, a Roman senator, about the fourth year of the twelfth Olympiad; and Quinctus Fabius, in the first year of the eighth Olympiad."[8] Polybius is mentioned by Dion. in another place. When converted into the Christian æra, that with which we are most familiar, these æras of Romulus stand as follows; Timæus and Cicero, B. C. 814; Ennius, about B. C. 876; Polybius, B. C. 750; Fabius Pictor, B. C. 747; and L. Cincius Alimentus, B. C. 728. Among these various dates that of Timæus has the following recommendations in its favour:

First. He was the earliest writer of all; and it was during his æra that the calendar was first published in Rome (B. C. 304).

Second. He was the son of K. Aromachus of Tauromenium and was universally regarded as an historian of credit, a fact which is vouched for by the frequent references to his works in Dionysius, Cicero, Livy and other writers. The former especially lays great stress on his varied learning and his exactness in chronology.[9]

Third. Timæus was a Sicilian Greek and had no interest in misstating the date which the Sicilians or Romans of his time believed be true.

Fourth. He wrote before the Incarnation myth was revived, which Julius Cæsar formulated and Augustus personified and upheld, in Rome; and which had to be maintained at the expense of chronology by making it fit the Ludi Sæculares, or else some other epoch of astrology.

Fifth. In choosing an æra for the Incarnation, or else the Apotheosis, of Romulus, it is inconceivable that the Romans of the Commonwealth should have chosen one more recent than that of Nebo-Nazaru,

[7] The fragments of Polybius mention no date.
[8] This work of Dionysius was written 30 years after the Apotheosis of Augustus.
[9] Dion. Hal. Book V.

or that of Procas   In the fixing of mythological or religious æras the remotest one is usually of the most recent manufacture; otherwise the myth to which it is attached runs the risk of losing every advantage that is to be gained by the assumption of superior antiquity Indeed this may be termed the very basic law of mythological chronology; and examples of its operation may be found in the histories of all the ancient states [10]

Sixth.   Evidences that the Augustan chronology was currupted appear in every direction.   The works of the earliest Roman historians have all disappeared   Of Quinctus Fabius Pictor, Lucius Cincius Alimentus, Marcus Portius Cato, Lucius Calpurnius Piso, Lucius Callius Antipater, Cnæus Gellius, Caius Licinius Macer, Lucius Ælius Tubero, Quintus Valerius Antias, or Lucius Sissena, not a vestige remains, beyond the brief references to these authors which appear in the works of the Augustan writers.   Under the pretence of piety Augustus ordered the collection and destruction of numerous ancient and contemporary works   Of these, two thousand perished in a single *auto da fé* (Suet Aug. 30)   Of the few that were spared, all have been mutilated   Quintus Ennius is known to us by little more than his name.   Polybius is hacked to pieces; the historical works of Cicero have all perished, Cornelius Nepos is in fragments and without dates; of 142 books in Livy's History of Rome, but 45 remain, and many of these are mutilated or corrupted, of Ovid's Fasti, out of 12 books, but six remain; Manilius has been largely tampered with; many others have been divested of dates: and Varro, the most voluminous of the Augustan writers, is known to us only by two detached and imperfect pieces.   In all these works the chronology, when any chronology appears, is suspicious and bears the look of having been altered.   Names, generations and dates fail to agree The lives of men are thrown into one age, while their works furnish evidence that they lived in another, and the archæological remains bear similar testimony. [11]

Seventh   During the Commonwealth it was not the custom to

[10] " Athens, Thebes, and other states employ fables to add dignity to their history." Lucian, Dialogue on Falsehood, ed Irwin, p 128

[11] An instance of this sort appears in Plutarch's Camillus, where he says that Heraclides Pontus lived shortly after the capture of Rome by the Gauls   Heraclides was a disciple of Plato and afterwards of Aristotle   Plato was 41 years of age when Rome was taken, and he died in his 80th year   Aristotle was not born until a year after Rome was taken, and he died aged 63 in Olym , CXIV, 3, (B.C 321). At the period assigned to Heraclides, Aristotle could hardly have been old enough to teach.

reckon from Romulus, but by the consulates (Pliny Nat Hist. III, ix, 13) Timæus, who was not a Roman, is the earliest writer known to us who together with the Olympiads used the æra of Romulus. Piso the historian, if indeed he used the æera of Romulus at all, was probably the earliest Roman who did so Therefore the Olympian equivalents of Commonwealth dates which are furnished by some of the Augustan writers are of suspicious validity.

Eighth. The early records of Rome were all destroyed when the City was burnt by the Gauls, and there appears to have remained no Roman official documents upon which the Augustan writers could have constructed a valid and continuous chronology; so that they must have either accepted or altered that of the republican writers, or else drawn one from their own imaginations

Ninth The Ludi Sæculares, mentioned by the historian L. Calpurnius Piso Frugi, as having been celebrated in his own time, were dated by him, A U. 596 This is evidently a date by the Timæan calendar, that of the republic, in which the year of Romulus was fixed 38 years before the first four-year Olympiad; for A U. 596 (Timæan) agrees with A U 518 (Augustan) in which year, according to the Augustan Quindecemviral records, the fifth Ludi Sæculares were actually celebrated, and these were undoubtedly the Ludi mentioned by Piso Frugi

According to the post-Augustan Fasti Consulares, one Piso (the name was legion) was consul in B C 133 This would be A U 620-1 (Christian) or else A U 605 (Augustan) or else A U 681 (Timæan) If Piso was consul that year, he could not, upon our hypothesis, have been the historian Piso, or, if meant to be the historian, then the Fasti have dated him, as they have dated many of the events and notabilities of the Commonwealth 78 (since altered to 63 years) out of his time, but this was only a trifling alteration to the calendar-makers whom we are discussing, and if they misdated Piso they probably did so without the slightest hesitation or compunction The names of the consuls given by Censorinus are of course from the same source as the 15 year alteration which appears in most of his dates But the post-Augustan astrologers did not do their work skillfully. They should have wholly destroyed the book, or effaced all the dates. Unable to perceive the significance of Piso's date in Censorinus, the recensors left it unaltered That date and the remark from Piso that a New Cycle began in his time prove that Piso's date of A U. 596 is by the Timæan calendar.

COMPARISON OF THREE CALENDARS:

Timæan.	Augustan	Post-Augustan

From A U. 814 (deduct 76)=738 (add 15)=753, for the altered year of Rome B. C.

From A. U 816 (deduct 78)=738 (add 15)=753, for same.

From A. U 596 (deduct 78)=518 (add 15)=533, for the Ludi Sæculares of Piso

Tenth   The Ludi Sæculares furnishes conclusive evidence on the subject. This Cycle and Festival, which according to Horace (and, in accordance also with the astrology of the Alexandrian and Augustan periods), recurred every 110 years (and which, therefore, should have been celebrated in the years 110, 220, 330, 440, 550, 660, 770, 880, of Rome), was in fact not celebrated in those years, if we reckon by the chronology of the Augustan writers. The Augustan chronology therefore is false   And so the sovereign-pontiff Claudius declared, who celebrated this festival in the 800th year of Rome, according to the Augustan chronology, or the 876th according to that of Timæus [12] Even the year last named was not the precise year for the Ludi, which should have been celebrated in the 880th year of Romulus, according to Timæus   But the date given is within either two or four years of the proper time, an apppoximation sufficiently near to indicate its supposed or attempted correctness. On the other hand, the Ludi celebrated by Augustus and Agrippa were altogether out of time with the Horatian and astrological intervals. The conclusion is therefore unavoidable, that the year of Romulus, as accepted during the Commonwealth, was altered by the astrologers of Augustus This alteration amounted to either 76 or 78 years

Eleventh. The alteration made no practical difference to the Romans. Until after the conquest of Etruria, Rome was a City, not an Empire, and long æras, if ever used at all, were borrowed from the Chaldeans, or the Greeks, as the Nebo-Nazarene Æra, or

[12] Says Suetonius in Claudius, 21 "Claudius, assuming that Augustus had anticipated the Ludi Sæculares, which he had celebrated out of their true season, caused them to be re-celebrated,   When (according to custom), the herald proclaimed that Ludi would take place 'which no living person had ever seen or would ever see again ' he was laughed at (by the Augustans), because there were several persons then living who had seen the previous Ludi Sæculares and some even, who, having taken part in those, now took part in these " Says Pliny (N H VII, 49) "Stephanio   danced in two Ludi Sæculares, those celebrated by the god Augustus ('divi Augusti') and those by Claudius Cæsar in his fourth consulship, considering that the interval which elapsed between them was 63 years," instead of 110 Says Tacitus (Ann. XI 11) "During the same consulship .   . the Ludi Sæculares were celebrated, an interval of 64 years since they were last solemnized in the reign of Augustus. *The chronology observed by Augustus differ.d from the system of Claudius,* but this is not the place for a discussion on that subject "

the Fall of Troy, or the Olympiads, rather than from the comparatively recent adoption or invention of the incarnation of Romulus.

Twelfth   The Timæan date of 38 years before Ol. I, 1 (equal to
B C 814) also appears in Cicero's "Re Publica," I, 38, 39, 58, and
II, 70; as that of the foundation of Rome. This is an especially
valuable corroboration of Timæus, because a great part of this work
of Cicero was recovered in recent years from a palimpsest and therefore it had probably not been subjected to that general alteration of
dates by the Latin Sacred College which befell the other works of
classical antiquity.

Thirteenth   The Timæan date, as corrected, namely, to B. C 816,
is also that of Porcius Cato, the Censor, who declared that the
Foundation of Rome was 432 years after the Capture of Troy, an
event that, according to several authorities current in Cato's time,
synchronised with the First Panionic Cycle, B. C 1248. Thus
1248—432=816   It is true that Dionysius of Halicarnassus, who
reports the Roman æra of Cato, has put, or has been made to put, a
different construction on it, by using the date for the Capture of Troy
which is attributed to Erastothenes; but there is no evidence that
Cato wrote anything which would authorise Dionysius to limit his
æra of Rome by using such a measure of Troja Capta.   Moreover,
we only know Erastothenes through Clement Alexandrinus   We are
therefore warranted in rejecting the Troja Capta imputed to Dionysius and in retaining the years of Troy and Rome left us by the older
historians   These dates are B C 1248 for the former and B C 816
for the latter [13]

Fourteenth.   Upon referring to chap IX herein it will be observed
that Tacitus stated that the same interval of time existed between
the Foundation of Rome and its burning by the Gauls, as between
the latter event and the burning in the reign of Nero. The burning
under Nero occurred in July, A D 64; the burning by the Gauls in
B C 384, an interval of 447 years and a fraction   Add 447 years
to B. C 384 and the Foundation would appear to have been in B. C.
831   Deduct the 15 years since added to the calendar by the Latin
Sacred College and the result is B C 816, the year of Piso
Cicero, etc

Fifteenth   The Timæan chronology tallies with the Etruscan æra
as well as the Etruscan cycles   The æra of Procas was B. C. 816,
that of Romulus according to Timæus was B C 814, and according

[13] Cicero on c't , Dio Hal   , II, 2; Herodotus, Eterna

to Cicero, Tacitus, and probably also Cato, B C. 816 The corroboration here is both striking and circumstantial.

These circumstances and considerations alone warrant us in rejecting the Augustan chronology and accepting that of Timæus; but there is more behind When the dates of the Ludi Sæculares are arranged in tabular form, the motive of the alteration will be more clearly perceived, it was evidently done in order to bring the Ludi Sæculares to the Apotheosis of Augustus, which it was intended to celebrate in the consulate of C. Furnius and C. Silanus Deduct from the Augustan corruption of 76 years the 15 years correction of the Christian chronologers and we have the Roman æra of Timæus and an explanation of the difference which now exists between the Oriental and Western æras [14] As dates are often as difficult to succinctly explain as to understand, let us recapitulate, even though at the risk of being deemed tiresome.

The re-incarnation of Ies Chrishna or Salivahana occurred, according to the Indian chronology, in B C 736 To this the Chaldeans added backward 12 years, making it B C 748, and called it the æra Nebo-Nazaru To this again the Romans of the Commonwealth added backward 66 years, making it B C 814, and called it the æra of Quirinus or Romulus. (Timæus) Thus 78 years were added backward, to the æra of the incarnation. From the ancient (the republican) æra of Romulus, Augustus subtracted 76 years and thus made the Augustan æra of Romulus B C 738 (Cincius says Olym XII, 4, a difference of ten years). Reckoning the Ludi Sæculares at intervals of 110 years from the dates at which they were alleged to have been formerly celebrated they were next due, according to the Augustan calendar, in A. U 738, which year Augustus determined to distinguish by his own Apotheosis, only, it is to be observed, that six Ludi make 660 years, whilst the astrological interval between one incarnation and another was 658 years, a difference of two years To this æra of A U 738, later astrologers, after having adopted the Augustan æra for that of Jesus Christ, and so used it for several

---

[14] It is curious to observe how repeatedly this corruption of the Oriental calendar obtrudes itself into a comparison of æras From Ies Chrishna B C 736, to Romulus B C 814 (Timæus), is 78 years, from the re-incarnation of Ies Chrishna B C 78, to the beginning of the present æra is 78 years, from the Christian æra to Vicramaditya is 78 years, from the Apotheosis of Romulus to the first Ludi Sæculares, according to the Augustan chronology, is 78 years, while between the Ludi of Augustus and those of Claudius, plus the 15 years since added to the calendar, is 78 years Many more similar instances of the kind could be ?

centuries, added 15 years, and thus made the present æra. By this addition of 15 years to the Roman reckoning they made the year of Romulus B. C 753 and the Apotheosis of Augustus B C 15, whereas in fact the æra of Augustus (his Apotheosis) and the æra of Jesus Christ were identically the same down to the time of that later astrologer, whoever he was, that made or completed the restoration of 15 years to the calendar.[15]

TABULAR SUMMARY OF ALTERATIONS TO THE CALENDAR.	B. C.
Hindu æra of the birth of Ies Chrisna, or Quichena . . .	736
The Chaldeans added . .	12
Making the Nebo-Nazarene æra . .	748
The Romans of the Commonwealth added two generations	66
Making the æra of Quirinus, or Romulus, according to Timæus .	814
Or, if according to Piso, for which see further on, add . . .	2
Making the æra of Quirinus or Romulus according to Piso . .	816

According to what was evidently the scheme of the Augustan astrologers, the Ludi Sæculares celebrated the Birth, not the Apotheosis of Romulus, which was removed to, or is pretended to have occurred in, his 33rd year. Hence the first Ludi fell 110 years after his Birth, or 78 years after his Apotheosis and the remainder of the Ludi at intervals of 110 years, in A U. 188, 298, 408, 518, 628, and 738, the year selected by Augustus for his own Apotheosis, By deducting 76 instead of 78 years the Ludi Sæculares and the Augustan Apotheosis would come together, hence from Timæus deduct 76 or from Piso . 78

Augustan æra of Romulus, or Quirinus . , .	738
Deduct for one Ludi of 78 years and six Ludi each of 110 years, total .	738
Apotheosis of Augustus, the second Quirinus completion of the Seventh Ludi	o
The Latin Sacred College added to the calendar, years . . .	15
Thus throwing the Apotheosis of Augustus back (to where it now stands) .	15
Add to B C 15 the years of the Augustan æra of Romulus, makes	B C. 753

The reason why Augustus fixed his Apotheosis and Æra in A U 738 was to fulfil the prophecy of the Cumean Sibyl The rebellion of Marc Antony had deferred the Peace which the Sibyl foretold would mark the Advent of the Son of God and which Virgil somewhat prematurely sang in his Fourth Eclogue The battle of Actium had yet to be fought; and until this was over and the temple of

---

[15] Ten years of this appear in the difference between the present Anno Mundi of Greece and Rome This alteration has been ascribed by the Benedictine authors of "L'Art de Verifier les Dates," to the period of Diocletian, but the authority is suspicious It is not stated when or by whom the remaining five years of alteration were made The whole extent of the post-Augustan alteration—15 years—makes just one Indiction

Janus permanently closed, the prophecy awaited fulfillment This
famous battle was decided in A. U 723 or 724 After this, and only
after this, was the temple of Janus permanently closed, and the Peace,
thus signalised, marked by the Apotheosis and Æra of Augustus
Cæsar

Following this date it appears to have been the common practice
of the Roman Church, whether pagan or christian, to employ the æra
of Augustus, or Anno Domini the year of our Lord; the pagans
meaning our Lord Augustus Cæsar and the christians our Lord Jesus
Christ; but both referring to the same year, namely A. U. 738 (now
known as A U 753). The object of the 15 years afterwards added
was evidently to destroy the identity of these two æras The occasion of the alteration was an astrological event In other words, the
reason why an interval of just 15 years (no more nor less) was created between the æras of Augustus and Jesus was evidently the discovery of that astrological conjunction recorded by Antimachus (who
flourished B C. 403) as having occurred in Olym VI, 3, which is
equal to the 23rd year after the beginning of the four-year Olympiads (Plut in Rom) This was 15 years before the æra of Romulus, as fixed by the chronology of Augustus The discovery may
have been made directly after Plutarch published his book, that is
to say, in the reign of Hadrian, who, by the way, was a great admirer
of Antimachus and whose example doubtless led to a wide reading of
that ancient author. But, as stated above, it does not appear to have
been definitively utilised until the Middle Ages To win the Romans
from the degrading worship to which they had been forced by the impious decrees of the Cæsars, the christian authorities were constrained
to employ such devices as were suited to the opinions and prejudices
of the times. Among these was that well established law of astrology, that incarnations would or must occur only at the period of a
conjunction of the Sun and Moon. Hence the Latin papacy proclaimed that Jesus was born at Midnight, on the winter solstice and
was conceived on the preceding vernal equinox, when "the Sun and
Moon conjoined over Jerusalem " To connect the incarnation of
Jesus with that of Romulus was an obviously indispensable condition
to the firm establishment of the christian religion in Rome. This
was done by fixing the year of Romulus in Olym VI, 3, in which,
according to Antimachus, such a conjunction had actually occurred
Olym VI, 3 was the year B C 753, according to the present chronology. Consequently this year was indicated by the christian chronologers as that of Romulus; and thus the æra of Augustus was

forced backward 15 years and made to appear 15 years B. C.; whereas it was not and it is not the fact

The Augustan æra (that of the Apotheosis) is preserved by the poet Ansonius in two places   In Epigramatica IV, 11, 148, he says:

Annis undecies centum conjunge quaternas=	1104
Undecies unamque super treiterida necte 11 plus 3—	14
Hæc erit æternæ series ab origine Romæ	1118

And in Epigramatica, III, 149, he says. *Mille annos centumque et bis fluxisse novenos*, (*i e , 1118.*)   The year 1118 is given as that of the current year since the Foundation of Rome in the year A D 380, when Ansonius was consul, under Gratian   Subtract 380 from 1118 and the quotient is A. U 738, which is the true æra of Augustus in the Augustan chronology.   Had the christian æra, as now settled, namely A U. 753, been known to Ansonius, he would have had to date his consulate in A U 1133, thus: 753 plus 380=1133

We are now prepared to arrange the Roman Ludi Sæculares in tabular form with the view to exhibit their relation to the 15 year change in the calendar which was made some time during the Middle Ages

THE LUDI SÆCULARES

Actual year A U of celebration Censorinus *	Proper Year A U *	Reputed Consulate or reign, from the Quindecemviral records	Years from Augustus	Equivalent in Christian æra
78	78	————	660	B C. 675
188	188	————	550	565
245 or 298	298	M. Valerius and S P Virginius	440	455
305 or 408	408	M V Corvinus and C Petilius	330	345
518	518	P. C. Lentullus and C L Varus	220	235
605, 608 or 628	628	M. E Lepidus and L A Orestes	110	125
737	738	Augustus Cos C Furnius & C. Silanus [16]	0	15
841	848	Domitian Suetonius Dom 4.	110	A D 95
957	958	Septimius Severus.	220	205

* These years of Rome, " A U ," are according to the received chronology

The last figure of the first column shows the year when, according to the Quindecemviral records quoted by Censorinus, the Ludi Sæculares (all excepting the first two) were actually kept; the observance of the the first two cycles not being recorded   Hence Censorinus calls the third one, the first ; but this can only mean the first one actually kept, for it was unquestionably, at the lowest calculation, the third Cycle   In addition to the Cycles shown in the table, Censor-

[16] This consulate fell in A U 738, by the Augustan calendar. In most modern date-books it is dated A U 727 or B C 27, the discrepancy is explained by the ten years' difference mentioned in a previous note, plus one year, due to the modern custom of subtracting " B C " dates from A. U. 754 instead of A. U. 753, as formerly

inus, in another place, informs us that Piso recorded a New Cycle in
A. U. 596. As shown above, this was evidently the year of Romulus by the Timæan calendar and means the Cycle observed in the
year A. U. 518; the difference between 596 and 518 being exactly
78 years. Another Cycle was celebrated by the emperor Claudius
in A. U. 876 (Timæan) or A. U. 800 by the Augustan calendar. This
was evidently meant for the Eighth 110-year Cycle from the Nativity of Romulus, which cycle would occur in A. U. 880 (Timæan); a
subject treated in another place. It must be remembered that the
interval of the Ludi Sæculares was as nearly as practicable, but not
exactly, one-sixth of the astrological cycle of 658⅔ years. Hence
between one Great Cycle and another, two years had to be dropped
to make the Small Cycles (the Ludi) agree with the Great Cycles.
As the period of 876 years embraces the whole of one and part of
another Great Cycle, the approximation of four years (as between
876 and 880) is sufficient to indicate the identity of the two intervals. Corroboration is derived from a curious phrase in Censorinus,
which, probably because it was not understood, was left unaltered
by the corruptors of his manuscript. He notices an alteration of the
calendar that was made in the second consulate of the emperor Antoninus Pius and C. Bruttius Præsens, which was "just 100 years"
previous to his own time and 876 years forward from Nebo-Nazaru;
from which it would appear that Antoninus Pius celebrated, in some
way or another, precisely that same number of years from Nebo-
Nazaru that Claudius did from Romulus, namely 876. Censorinus
adds that "we are to-day really in the hundredth year of this Annus
Magnus," which can only mean 100 years from the Eighth Age of
the Great Year of Nebo-Nazaru, celebrated by Antoninus Pius.

According to Basil Kennett (Rom. Antiq., p. 301) there is ancient
authority for the belief that the Third Cycle was celebrated in A. U.
330, which was the proper Timæan year for it; but we have not yet
been able to discover the original passage from which Kennett drew
this information.

Sylla's abortive aspiration to become the Sacred Personage whose
cycle was indicated by the Ludi Sæculares, which, says Plutarch,
were predicted and expected in his time, affords a further corroboration of the Timæan calendar. According to the present chronology
Sylla was born in A. U. 616 and the Sixth Ludi had been celebrated
either a few years before, or after, he was born, i. e., either in 605,
608 or 628; hence, as their interval was more than a century, it is
inconceivable that he should have expected them to be celebrated

again in his own time   But if we admit that the Timæan calendar
was still used by the Romans, the difficulty is at once removed   By
the Timæan calendar the Sixth Ludi were due in A U 660 and if,
as it is most likely, the date of Sylla's birth was borrowed from that
calendar, before it was changed, then he would be 44 years of age
when the Festival recurred; a conclusion that agrees with the other
details of his biography   Carr (Rom Antiq p. 65) also states that
a Cycle of the Ludi was celebrated by Caracalla in A U 952; but
unless our calendar is wrong this would relate to his father Septimius Severus, for Caracalla did not obtain the throne until A U
964   Still other Cycles were celebrated by the emperors Phillip and
Honorius in A U 1000 and 1157 respectively.   These last it will
not be necessary to discuss [17]

The second column shows the years when the Ludi Sæculares
should have been kept and a New Cycle begun   According to this,
Augustus celebrated the Cycle one year before the correct time,
even by his own chronology; but such was the case only in appearance. The year of Romulus began in April, that of Augustus (based
upon the Julian year) began with March or January   If the New
Cycle was celebrated, as is likely, on Pariliana, it was in the year 737
Old Style, or 738 New Style

The third column shows the consulate, or else the reign, during
which the Cycles are said to have been celebrated   These consulates
are from the Quindecemviral records   As whoever altered the
Augustan to the present dates was compelled to alter the names of
the consuls, it is all but certain that the consulates given in the table
are spurious, and probably of less value than the alternates mentioned by Censorinus, which may possibly be genuine

The fourth column shows the number of years counting from
Augustus backward or forward   A person living in the reign of
Augustus would by this computation be obliged to believe that the
Cycles had been duly celebrated in the past at the correct astrological
interval of "eleven times ten years"; and therefore that Augustus
must be the veritable re-incarnation of Quirinus, between whose
Apotheosis and his own there were precisely Six Cycles or (barring
two years) exactly one astrological Great Year of 658 years [18]

[17] On January 1, A D 1300, the Ludi Sæculares were revived by Pope Boniface
VIII, with the object of attracting pilgrims to Rome   They were at first appointed
for every 100 years, then for 50, 33 and 25 years   After 19 such festivals were observed, the Reformation put an end to them   Gibbon, VI, 558

[18] For another explanation of the two years of discrepancy see Chap VII, years
B C 814 and 707

Augustus' Cycle was the seventh; beginning the (ecclesiastical) year in March, he was born in the seventh month; his zodiacal sign was the seventh, or Capricorn, which he stamped on his coins, etc.   This astrological twaddle and more of the same sort the reader will find in the garrulous Suetonius

The fifth column shows the result produced by the 15-year alteration of the calendar effected by the post-Augustan astrologers and pontiffs.   This alteration indicates that the christian æra, which it is pretended was discovered, invented, or deduced, by Dionysius Exiguus, is nothing more nor less than the Augustan æra, which the christian astrologers found in common use and were therefore fain to accept and adopt   In short, the present æra of the Incarnation is really the Augustan æra, altered by 15 years, just as the Augustan "A U 738" is the æra of Quirinus altered by 78 years, while that of Quirinus is the Nebo-Nazarene æra altered by 12 years   It is evident that the æra of Augustus was invented for him by Manilius, or some other astrologer of his own court   As to the period and authors of the post-Augustan calendar we have sufficiently indicated them in other portions of this work.

The reader will bear in mind that it is not the existence, nor the story, nor the heavenly mission, nor the divine attributes of Jesus that are herein questioned; it is simply asserted that the æra which we now use is in fact the æra of Augustus, altered by post-Augustan astrologers, under direction or with consent of the Latin Sacred College, to the extent of 15 years, and that, leaving out of present view the intermediate alteration made by Augustus, the year of Rome now used is 63 years out of harmony with the year of Rome, as reckoned at the time of Timæus, Piso, Ennius, Sylla, Cicero and Tacitus [19]

Under all the ancient hierarchical governments the æra was invariably reckoned from the Nativity, Apotheosis, or Ascension of an Incarnated god, or Deified Ruler, witness the æras of Ies Chrishna, Buddha, Nebo-Nazaru, Romulus, Alexander the Great, the Seleucidæ, the Ptolemies, Julius Cæsar, etc   Under the ancient republics the

[19] If it be admitted that Julius (or else Augustus) altered the Olympiads from five to four-year intervals and their epoch from Iphitus B C 884 to Corœbus B C 776, then in such case the date of L Cincius Alimentus, namely Olym. XII, 4, receives a new significance.   In the four-year Olympiads this is equal to B. C. 729, which is an inadmissable date, while in the five-year Olympiads it is equal to B. C 826, which is within ten years of the æra of Piocas, and of the Foundation of Rome according to the various authorities quoted   The ten years of discrepancy is accounted for in a previous note

æra was reckoned from the incumbencies of public officials, as the archons of Athens, or the consuls of Rome   Sometimes, though much more rarely than is represented by chronologists, the æra was reckoned from the foundation of cities   But under the hierarchies the æra was invariably reckoned from an Incarnation   In fact the practice continues to the present day, both in India, Thibet, China and Abyssinia.   The fulsome and impious acclamations of Manilius, Virgil, Ovid, Horace and other poets of the Augustan court leave leave us no room to doubt that this practice was followed by Augustus, and that to bring the Ludi Sæculares to the year of his own Apotheosis he sank 78 years from the calendar of the Commonwealth and destroyed or altered all the literary works that were supposed to clash with his pretension of superhuman origin and the theory it involved of synchronism with the sacred period of the Divine Year, the Incarnations and the Ludi Sæculares

Still further corroboration of these views is derived from those passages of Censorinus, which, not being attached to any precise date. were probably, for that reason, left unaltered   For example, his quotation from Piso is taken from the latter's Annals of the Seventh Cycle (Annali Septimo)   This agrees with the Timæan chronology, but not with the Augustan, according to which Piso lived in the sixth cycle, the seventh only commencing with Augustus. Again Censorinus says that " the eighth (Etruscan) cycle " had begun "in Varro's time "   This agrees with the chronology of Timæus   In an another place (XVII) Censorinus says that " the day of the death (of Romulus) marked the end of the first cycle "   Therefore the Second Cycle began with the 33rd year of Romulus, reckoning from his Apotheosis, or the 37th of his reign, which was precisely the theory advanced by the Augustan astrologers and afterwards supported by the testimony of Dionysius of Halicarnassus and Plutarch [20]

[20] Plutarch in "Numa" places the death and ascension to heaven of Romulus in "the 37th year from the building of Rome and his reign "   In " Romulus " he says that " Romulus is said to have been 54 years of age and in the 38th of his reign when he was taken from the world "   Dionysius says that Romulus died in the 37th year of his reign, which he begins with the first year of the decennial archonship of Charops of Athens, which he places in Olym VII, 1   (In the five-year Olympiads this would be B C 817 or 816)   In the chronology of Rome, Dionysius makes Numa succeed immediately after Romulus and says nothing of an interregnum, neither does Plutarch, whilst Livy mentions it specifically, and though he says in one place that it lasted for one year, he stretches it in his chronology to two years, killing Romulus in A U 37 and enthroning Numa in A U 39.   To render matters still worse Dion-
is m.   hrs   ten kings

So much for the Ludi Sæculares; now for the Olympiads There
are reasons for believing that either Julius Cæsar or Augustus, or
both of them together, altered the olympiads from five to four years
and their epoch from Iphitus to Corœbus.   These reasons will now
be briefly set forth.

First   The Olympiads were always called by the Greeks pentaeteris and by the Romans quinqennales, both of which terms mean
periods of five years; not of four years   Some examples of this
practice occur in the passages cited below   In ancient times, when
the year consisted of ten months each of 36 days, the pentaeteris
were celebrated every fifty months   The five-year period was called
pentaeteris for the same reason that a five-sided figure is called penta-
gon, and the five first books of the Bible the pentateuch. The reason
is that penta is the Greek word for five.

Second   Writers previous to the Augustan age and some even
during the Augustan age, especially the poets, whose verses could
not be so readily altered as prose writings, explicitly stated that the
olympiads were periods of five years, the same as the Roman lustra
Where Ovid, who was at the time, (as he tells us in another passage),
just fifty years of age, writes that his lifetime is equal to ten olympiads, he makes a similar statement by indirection   Among the
writers alluded to are Pindar, *Olymp* , III, 33, X, 67, Nemea
XI, 30, Ovid, Pontics, IV, 6, Tristia, IV, 8, IV, 10; Metam XIV,
324, Martial, IV, 45, 3, Suetonius, Nero, 53; Josephus, Wars, I,
xxi, 12.

Third   The olympiads were solemn festivals, kept with a political
object, the sports and exercises being merely of a secondary or in-
cidental character   The duration of the festival was five days and
its object was to appropriate—and by such appropriation to mark—

of Rome, which he gives separately at 37, 43, 32, 24, 38, 44 and 25 years and adds
up together as 244, whereas they only make 243. Finally, Plutarch in 'Numa" says
that the Olympiads (and therefore, we may infer, the archonships with them) were
corrupted by Hippias, the Elean   Amidst this discordance, blundering and corruption of texts, about an astrological myth, the astrological Cycles (658, 110, and 33
years respectively), remain our safest guides to ancient dates. According to Michelet
(Hist Rom Rep , 44) Servius, a commentator on Virgil, who is attributed to the
end of the fourth century, wrote as follows "The Emperor Augustus related in his
Memoirs that at the apparition of the comet observed at the funeral of Cæsar, the
aruspex Vulcatius said in the Comitia that it announced the end of the ninth and commencement of the tenth Cycle." If Augustus wrote this in his Memoirs (of which
not a line remains) then he admitted that the Etruscan calendar was over two Divine
years older than the Roman, a circumstance which indeed is deducible from the chronology of Ennius and which nobody at that period disputed

the five superfluous days, or epagomenæ, which constituted the difference between the ancient solar year of 360 days and the later solar
year of 365 days In short, it was a Monument of the Equable solar
year, and as such, it became a bulwark of Popular Liberty, against
the insidious and always menacing device of a lunar year. The
olympiad opened with sports, it closed with sacrifices; and its honours and rewards were the highest objects of Greek ambition When
Julius Cæsar established by law a solar year of 365¼ days, the need
for a quinquennial ceremonial lost its force. Confident that his institute of the Julian year would not be overthrown, the quinquennial
festival was apparently abandoned, as having outlived its usefulness
Why continue to rejoice over the 365-day year of king Iphitus, when
Cæsar, who was a King of kings, had safely anchored, in the laws of
the empire, a better and more perfect year of 365¼ days? In his
turn and in his usual devious and prudent way, Augustus also shelved
the quinquennial olympiads, by depriving them of their religious
character, ceremonial and support Known in his reign as the
"Cæsarian," they were afterwards called the "Augustan" games,
and, carrying out the plan of Cæsar he substituted in their place
the quadrennial games to which he gave the familiar name of Olympiads, coupling them with the ancient ceremonial, religious sacrifices
and secular rewards Henceforth the olympiads celebrated not a
dead Charter of Liberty, but a living one, not a period of five
epagomenæ, to be huddled into a short month (Cronia) every five
years, but a living Charter of Liberty, a leap-year day, to be celebrated ever fourth year forever

Fourth After a critical examination of the Greek and other ancient authorities, Sir George Cornewall-Lewis (op cit 117) declared
of the quadrennial cycle, or four-year Olympiads, that there is "no
historical trace of its actual use in any Greek calendar" The reason
of this is quite simple the Greeks never used a quadrennial cycle
Censorinus indeed says that they used a quadrennial intercalation,
but that it recurred every fifth year! Stobæus, "Ecl Phys.," I, 8,
mentions four "great years" of four, eight, 19 and 60 years respectively, but in the corresponding pasages of Plutarch, "Plac" II, 32[21]
there is no four-year cycle and the 60-year one is given as 59 years
Pliny, II, 48, attributes a four-year intercalary cycle to Eudoxus, but
no evidence of it can be found in any of the calendars extant and
even if it could be found it would not mean the Olympiads, because
they were not used for the purpose of intercalating the calendar, but

[21] Also Gell..........Plutarch XV 54

as the steps of a chronological æra for marking the flight of time.

Fifth   It remains to consider the effect upon chronology which followed this alteration of the Olympian intervals   If we accept the computation of Erastosthenes, as reported by Clement Alexandrinus, the Olympiads of King Iphitus began with B C 884; if of Callimachus, they began B C 828   Between these dates and the epoch conferred upon the Olympiads named after Coroebus, B. C 776, the interval was either 108, or else 52 years, or, if we reckon from Iphitus *inuente* to Coroebus *exuente*, it was just 56 years.   If Cæsar had already sunk 108 years from the Greek calendar, Augustus had only to sink 30 years less from the Roman calendar, to be enabled to utilize all the historical events which the chronologers had assigned to the years between B C 776 and 884   According to Cicero[22] the date of Callimachus is not, while that of Eratosthenes, is, correct   Hence, the quinquennial Olympiads began B C 884 and the alteration made by Cæsar amounted to 108 years [23]

Sixth   The reason for ascribing the alteration of the Olympiads to Julius rather than Augustus is derived from the statement in Cicero's Republica II, 10, where the æras of Lycurgus, and Iphitus are fixed at 108 years before the first (quadiennial) Olympiad.   This is precisely the beginning of the first (quinquennial) Olympiad and also the beginning of the tables of Eratosthenes, namely B C 884.   As Cicero was murdered by order of Augustus and Marc Antony, before the reign of the former began and therefore before he had lawful power to alter the Olympiads, it may be reasonably concluded that they were altered by Julius.[24]   However, there are reasons for believing that the alteration was not completed by Julius but by Augustus

This alteration of the Olympiads did not affect the fasti of Rome, all of which were later than the æra of King Iphitus, nor did it affect the historical, but only the mythical or fabulous fasti of Greece; because the former were also later than Iphitus   In the fabulous fasti

----

[22] Repub., II, 10

[23] See Ch. VII, B. C. 884 and 828

[24] If it be assumed that the quinquennial olympiads began with the date assigned to them by Eratosthenes, then the two series of olympiads would meet in B C 344, which would terminate the 108th and begin the 109th 5-year olympiad from B. C 884   It would also terminate the 108th and begin the 109th 4-year olympiad from B C 776.   If the quinquennial olympiads began at the date given by Callimachus, then the two series would meet in B C. 568, which would terminate the 52nd olympiad in both.   The former, the date of Eratosthenes, is regarded as the correct one   The meeting of the olympiads was therefore in B. C 344.

there was but a single date which affected the historical fasti   This
was the date of Troja Capta   As this varied in the classical authors
from a period that synchronises with B. C 1334, down to one that tallies with B C. 1049, there was abundance of room between these ex-
tremes in which to fit any event that was deemed worthy of preserva-
tion in the historical fasti

It should be added that most of the æras of Troja Capta that still
survive are worked backward from the Olympiads, so that when these
were shifted, Troja Capta was shifted with them   For example, several of the Greek chronologers counted from the first Olympiad backward to the return   the Heraclidæ 328 years, and to the Capture
of Troy 80 years more   Many of the other dates of Troja Capta
come from suspicious sources, as that imputed to Eratosthenes by
Clement Alexandrinus, who is assigned to the third century of our
æra, but who (or his work) may be later.   The original of the
canon of Eratosthenes is "lost," the MSS of Milan and Venice dis-
agree, while both contain Hebrew dates [25]   These circumstances indicate that it was composed or else altered (probably altered) during
the medieval ages.   Other æras of Troja Capta, as that of the Parian
marble, are anonymous; they lack authority; or, as in this case, they
have been tampered with and altered [26]   It is a suspicious circumstance that the canons of Eratosthenes and Callimachus vary by 56
years until they reach the date B C. 776, when they at once harmonize   It is also suspicious that not a single chronological æra is left
in Herodotus or Thucydides   As for the canon of Censorinus, it has
evidently been thoroughly "revised" and altered by the Latin Sacred
College   In short, we have no reliable, no original date of Troja
Capta; and if we had one, unless it was recorded in terms of the
Brahminical or Hindu Divine Year, or of some other astronomical
conjunction, there would remain no event by which it could be fixed
in time

[25] Clinton.   [26] Rev. J. Robinson.

CHAPTER IV

ASTROLOGY OF THE DIVINE YEAR.

WE now come to the most significant and important of the various influences that have governed the calendar, the key to the æras, and the corner stone to astrology This is the Divine Year, or Cycle of the Eclipses, consisting of 223 lunar revolutions or 6585⅔ days (approx) or 18 years and 10 or 11 days (approx) During this period there will usually be 41 eclipses of the sun and 29 of the moon Familiarity with the cycle will enable anyone to foretell an eclipse with almost unerring certainty; so that in ages when ignorance and superstition were rife, the few possessors of this information were armed with almost supernal power over the human mind Although there can be little doubt that Thales was familiar with the Cycle of the Eclipses and therefore with the periods of lunar as well as solar eclipses, yet a century after his time, the Greek priests caused Anaxagoras to be thrown into prison for daring to reveal these periods One of the consequences of this ecclesiastical monopoly of science was the defeat of the Athenian army before Syracuse, an event which both Thucydides and Plutarch impute to an unexpected eclipse of the moon

Said Plutarch· "The first person who wrote a clear and bold solution of the enlightening and obscuration of the moon was Anaxagoras, who now (time of the defeat before Syracuse) had not long been dead, nor was his account in everybody's hands, but concealed, imparted only to a few, and that with caution and assurances of secresy " Five centuries later than these events Pliny wrote in his Natural History, XXV, v.: "It is long since the means were discovered of calculating beforehand not merely the day or night, but even the very hour at which an eclipse of the sun or moon is to take place, yet the majority of the lower orders still remain firmly convinced that these phenomena are brought about by enchantments " But we are not left to rely upon these ancient authors for examples of the popular ignorance of eclipses. It is but a brief period since the Chinese were greatly disturbed by the inauspicious occurrence of

a solar eclipse on their New Year's day, while very recently the
Second Adventists of England were awaiting the Reappearance of
Jesus Christ, which according to their perverted use of the Cycle of
Eclipses, was to take place within a brief space of time, commencing
at Easter in the year 1898 It is hardly too much to say that the
moralist still uses this cycle to awe the sinner, the general to terrify
the enemy, the hierophant to govern nations

When the Cycle of the Eclipses was first determined is unknown;
when it was first imparted to the public has not been ascertained
with certainty. It was known to Thales of Miletus in the 6th century B C It was known in India long before the second Buddhic
period, possibly before the first one. because the Brahminical theogony and the myth of the Ten Avatars was based upon it [1]
Though known to the Greeks before the reign of Darius, it was
probably not openly connected in the Occident with the Indian myth
of the Incarnation before the conquest of India by that monarch;
for Darius himself was one of the earliest actual "incarnations" of
the Occident and yet one whose story of godship is not entirely
free from suspicion of having been constructed in after years by the
grateful priests of Egypt, whose temples he had spared In the Orient,
the Cycle of the Eclipses constituted what might be termed the nundinal year of Maha-vira or Brahma-Buddha, of which the astrologers
counted 36 to each Divine Year or cycle of the Incarnation, or 360
(equal to ten incarnations) in the lifetime of the earth.   Thus:

Cycle of Eclipses, 223 lunations, or . . . 6585⅔ days
Divine Year, consisting of as many months as there were days. in the
  Cycle of Eclipses, hence . . . . 6585⅔ months
Great Year. [As at that period there were ten civil months to the
  common year the Divine Year would therefore consist of 658 common
  years and a fraction. By some writers this was called a "Great Year"
  (Plutarch, in Sylla) At its recurrence the incarnated Sun (Ies, Iss,
  Issus, etc), was to be born anew]   . . . 658 years
Lifetime of the World, consisting of as many years as there were
  months in the Divine Year, hence . . . 6585⅔ years
Day of Judgment At the end of this period the human race would
  be brought to judgment and our planet destroyed by fire

The astrological elements of these Divine Years can be observed
in memorials which are separated by 30 centuries of superstition.
There were 36 deities and ten columns, say Perrot and Chipiez in
their illustrations of "Egyptian Art" I, 389.   There are 36 stages
in the great Eclipse Cycle, said the second Adventist president of

[1] Story of the Cool , "Gadma "

the British Chronological (but very illogical) society, in January, 1898   To concede what this system claims, is to grant to a clique of jugglers and impostors the ecclesiastical Empire of the earth for a period of 6585 years, because to expose its falsity by means of an object lesson would require the whole of this immense period of time.

The astronomical appearance is that once in 6585⅔ days an entire cycle of the eclipses takes place, until the initial eclipse recurs and the mechanism of the universe has undergone a complete revolution This appearance would have been the same in a ten months' year as in a twelve months' year; so that the change in the mode of dividing the year is no argument against the antiquity of the knowledge of the Cycle   Upon the period of this cycle the busy minds of hiero-phants erected a theory at once pleasing and terrifying to the superstitious multitude.   If in 6585⅔ days (as appeared to be the case) the movement of the universe was practically renewed, then as a matter of course in 6585⅔ months it would be morally redeemed and in 6585⅔ years it would be both practically and morally de-. stroyed   Such is the astrology of this cycle and such the logic of the Ten Incarnations of Iesnu or Vishnu, to each one of whom was appropriated a zodiacal sign, a month of the year and a divine year of 658 solar years   What the Hindus called a Kalpa, was to the Persians a Nauroz and the Greeks a Great or Divine Year   The Romans both of the Republican and Augustan ages divided it into six parts, each one of which was called a Sæcular period and con-sisted of 110 years.   The Romans of the Dionysian age (between the Augustan and Christian) had a cycle of 532 years composed of 6580 months; a basis which is very nearly like the Cycle of the Eclipses menstrualized   According to Albiruni, a Moslem writer of the tenth century, (ed 1879, p. 63) the Jews of that century used this same Cycle as a Paschal period.   Perhaps they had it at an earlier date.   The earliest valid mention of it as a christian paschal cycle, is by Argyrus, who wrote in 1372, but I am inclined to believe that it was used in the Roman Church by Gregory VII., A. D. 1073-80

Although both of them have the same astronomical basis in the astronomical Cycle of the Eclipses, the Divine Year is practically astrological, while the Paschal Cycle is practically astronomical; and as it is with astrology and not astronomy that we are dealing, we will at present confine our attention to the Divine Year of the ancients

The sign·ficance of this cycle, though obliterated and lost sight of in the Occident, since the eleventh century, yet still retains all of its ancient vitality in the Orient It is the foundation of religious faith not merely with the Brahmins, but also with the Brahma-Buddhists and the Moslems Aristotle cautiously said that at the end of every such a cycle a metaphysical revolution occurred, which statement was then true of all the world and is still true of the Orient; for have, or had, we not Mirza Ghulam Ahmad of Quadian in the Punjab, as well as the late lamented Mahdi of the Soudan and the M'lenga of the Mashonaland, to say nothing of the prophets Dimbleby in London, Antonio in Brazil and Schlatter in New York and Mexico? In an obscure allusion to the same significant cycle Sir William Jones said with increased caution, "I propose the question, but I affirm nothing " As for belief in the annualized cycle or Lifetime of the Earth we still have the Millenarians, the Millerites, the Second Adventists and others to remind us that one of the grossest of astrological superstitions has not yet lost its hold upon upon the minds of civilized peoples. Ever since the Cycle of the Eclipses was discovered mankind has dreamed of a Renaissance which was to redress the balance of antiquity in a halcyon age That age has never come and it is safe to say that it never will come until the human race has the moral courage to repudiate this cyclical phastasm and seek its welfare by the aid of its own powers and opportunities.

² Said Ies Chrishna "Whenever there is decline of righteousness and uprising of unrighteousness, then I project myself into creation For the protection of the righteous and the destruction of the evil-doer and for the proper establishment of the law of righteousness, I appear from age to age   At the end of a Kalpa, all things return into my nature and then at the beginning of a Kalpa I again project them " Bhagavad Gita, IV, 7, 8, IX, 7

CHAPTER V

THE JOVIAN CYCLE AND WORSHIP

THE Jovian Cycle, an interval of 12 years and five days, marks the orbital period of the planet Jove, or Jupiter Anciently, it appears to have been regarded as a period of exactly 12 years. Upon this period astrology built a sexagesimal cycle, consisting of five periods of Jupiter, or 60 years, and this was used and is still used for the computation of time. Reminiscences of both of these cycles, the astronomical and the astrological, appear in the number of our zodions, months, apostles, paladins, jurymen, etc , in our subdivisions of the sphere; in the hours and minutes by which we mark the time; and in many other institutions and customs We have now to enquire when the Jovian Cycle of 12 years was first discovered, or employed

The modern Hindus employ 60 and 90-year cycles which go back to B C. 3185, 3174, and 3114, all of which epochs are evidently derived from, or connected with, the Calijoga (æra) of B C. 3102 As that æra is anachronical (Laplace, Brennand,) therefore, they are all anachronical The Chinese employ 60-year cycles beginning, according to various authorities, in B C 2717, 2687, 2627, 2397, 2357, 2337, and 2217 Those of 2357 and 2337 (this probably means all of them) are connected with the divine Yao, or Jove; but sexagesimal cycles of these remote dates are all anachronical [1] There was no known astronomical fact, no sexagesimal, no duodecimal period, to build them upon They must all be regarded as spurious until some important astronomical fact connected with them is proved

---

[1] In the Bhagavad Gita X, 21-39, Chrishna declares among other things that he is himself Vrihaspati, or Jupiter, the supreme god. The English translator, Mohini M. Chatterji, claims that the work which contains this declaration is 5,000 years old But such a claim is preposterous In VIII, 24-25, Chrishna incidentally alludes to the year of 12 months, an almost certain proof that at least this part of the scripture is later than the second Buddha However it is possible that the part in which Vrihaspati is mentioned may be as ancient as the era assigned herein, or less Chrishna. Dr. Lorimer's date for the whole work is about B C. 400

to have been known at periods when such cycles commenced; for astrology never built upon sand   Its whole strength was due to the circumstance that its basis was sound   It need scarcely be added that that was all that was sound about it, its minor premises and conclusions being merely rubbish   The Brahmins built their astrology upon a system of five planets, to wit, the Sun, Mercury, Venus, Earth and Mars; and this system continued in vogue for many centuries after the various dates above mentioned.   The Egyptian 60-year cycles, mentioned by Martin[2] and conjecturally assigned to about B. C 1650, are anachronical.   The Greek five-year pentaeteris of B C 1406, which were credited by some to Zeus-pater and by others to Jasius, are barely possible   As for the Persian sexagesimal cycle, beginning in B C 5054 and known as the Turki Cycle, it is hardly worth discussing   There is not a scrap of evidence to support its claim to antiquity, and in all probability it is not so old as the Dionysian or else the Christian mundane æras of the Dark Ages, from one or the other of which it appears to be derived.

The utmost antiquity that can reasonably be assigned to the discovery of the period of Jupiter, or to the Jovian Cycles, is that of the occultation of Purvaphalgunibava (Jupiter) in B C 1426, the Sun-æras of India, B C 1312, or B C 1306, the corrected Yao æra of China B C 1311, or else the Sun or Pan æras of Greece, B C 1260, 1248, 1219, or 1206, because, according to Diodorus, Pan was meant for Jupiter.   As for the æra of the Assyrian Sun-God Shamash, this has not been ascertained   Neither has the age of the magnifying lens found by Layard in the ruins of "Nimroud," an instrument whose employment it has been claimed could not long have preceded the discovery of the period of Jupiter   The scriptologists who have been pleased to identify the City of "Nimroud" or Belus, with the astrological personage called "Nimrod," ascribe this relic to the 22nd century B C.   Unfortunately for this theory, Herodotus has left us a chronology of "Semiramis," the mythical daughter-in-law of Belus, which will not admit of Belus or his city being assigned to a higher date than the ninth or tenth century B C Dyaus-pitar, from whom some of the writers hold that the Greeks derived their Zeus-pater, will be found in the Vedas; but it is difficult to determine when these scriptures were altered, or interpolated

The th   Jupiter (Rohineya,

[2] Theon Smyrnaeus, Liber de Astronomia, ed Martin, Paris, 1849; 8vo

Maghabha, Ashhadhabhava, and Purvaphalgunibhava) the four daughters of Soma (the Moon) and claim that their occultations were observed during a period of 16 months in B C. 1424-6, at which time Saturn (Chyasuta) was not known to them as a planet This is possible, but not probable. Brennand is of the opinion that Jupiter was known to the Hindu astronomer Parasara, who flourished about B. C. 1181, but he does not appear to be willing to assign a higher date to this knowledge. Moreover, neither the observance of an occultation nor the knowledge that Jupiter was a planet bespeaks a knowledge of its period, which alone is what we are seeking Finally, as Brennand justly remarks, the association of the planet with the name of the Buddhist "sage" Vrihaspati implies some connection between the planet and the Buddhist religion, which he evidently assumes is of a much later period than Parasara But here he is mistaken, for the first Buddha is earlier than, or at all events as early as, the Hindu astronomer However, if the connection between Jupiter and Buddhism was the discovery or employment of Jupiter's period, then all these apparent discrepancies may be reconciled by supposing that Jupiter was perhaps known to be a planet B C 1426, but that his period of 12 years was not determined until the æra of Parasara, B C 1181, and that it was then, or even at some more recent date, utilized by the Buddhists, who gave to the planet the revered title of Vrihaspati Jupiter and his orbital period and the sexagesimal cycle are all mentioned in the Surya Siddhanta; but this proves nothing, because we do not know when that work was composed [3]

We have thus far followed the dates on this subject downward to B C 1181, let us follow the remaining dates upward. Jupiter is said to be indicated as a planet upon the Chinese chart of the heavens which is ascribed to the year 600 B C and upon which 1460 stars are accurately depicted This chart is said to be in the National Library at Paris [4] But this does not prove that the period of Jupiter was known In the sexagesimal cycle of Jove, as it is employed in India, China and Japan, each year of the 60 has a proper

[3] The Surya Siddhanta recognizes the planetary character of both Saturn and Jupiter and gives their orbital periods it employs the sexagesimal cycle, and it reckons twelve months to the sidereal year It is probably a work of the second Buddhic period An English translation of the work by Rev E Burgess appears in the Journal of the Am Orient Soc. 1860

[4] Haydn, Dic Dates, art. "Planet" 7¹ num¹(r(f st¹r₌ ¹¹   ¹ˑ ⁺ is suspicious, it exactly corresponds with the ¹⁻¹   ¹¹ years in ᵗhe ₛᵤₜᵗ₌ ᵗᵥ((ₛ

name· According to Freret (XIII, 303-4) there is reason to believe that the Chinese names were bestowed by the astronomer Sze-ma-ts'ien, who flourished in the reign of Woote B. C. 86   This astronomer drew up a table of sexagesimal cycles, to the years of which he affixed names which ran backward to B C 841.   There does not appear to be any reason why he should have stopped at that particular year unless it was the year when the orbit of Jove itself was determined, or at least the knowledge of it was brought into China   At the same time it is to be remarked that even according to Chinese accounts the sexagesimal cycle was invented in order to reconcile the old series of ten with the new series of 12 years and therefore that there is some reason to suspect that the sexagesimal Cycle is far less ancient than the Cycle of 12 years.

Herodotus, Mel 5, says that Targitaus the first King of the Scythians lived "just a thousand years" before Darius Hystaspes invaded their country.   This fixes the æra of Targitaus in B C 1495   Now Targitaus was reputed by his countrymen to have been a son of the god Jupiter, a belief which, could we be sure of the period when it was entertained, would carry the worship of Jupiter back to the 15th and near the 16th century B C   But it would be venturesome to attach any date to the worship of Jupiter from this passage   All that can be said is that Herodotus, a writer of the fifth century B. C , evidently regarded the worship of Jupiter as very ancient

If the poems assigned to Orpheus, who is described as one of the Argonauts, and whose æra was therefore the 12th century B C., could be regarded as belonging to this remote period, they would carry the Jovian cult and cycle back to his imputed æra, but the known facts will hardly warrant such a conclusion   The doubts which some two thousand years ago were cast upon the genuineness of the Orphic lays have never been removed '

Among the more positive evidences which we possess of the Jovian worship are those which appear in the works of Homer and Hesiod; indeed, so far as concerns the occident, these poets may have framed the Jovian theogeny   "Whence each of the gods sprang, whether they existed always and of what form they were, was unknown, so to speak, until yesterday.   For I am of opinion that Hesiod and Homer lived *not more than* four hundred years before my time and these fr   ι ι ι   ι ι ιιι Greeks ιιd gave ιaιιιs to the gods

[5] Diod

and assigned to them honors and arts and declared their several functions "[6] The birthplace of Homer is undetermined: but it is generally agreed that he was an Asiatic Greek   His æra is uncertain   Frederick Augustus Wolf, in his celebrated " Prologemena ad Homerum " 1795, says that " the voice of antiquity is unanimous in declaring that Pisistratus first committed the poems of Homer to writing and reduced them to the order in which we now read them "   Charles Lachmann, 1837-41, showed that the Homeric poems consisted of no less than 16 different lays brought together by Pisistratus, who enlarged and interpolated them B C 561   Xenophanes, who flourished B C 540-500, the earliest writer who mentions Homer, complains of the false notions which the poet taught, an expression which rather conveys the implication that in his time, and at least in Greece, such notions were new, or at all events were not old enough to have obtained popular assent, much less that official sanction and endorsement, which, probably at a later period, required them to be read aloud at the Panathenaic festival.   Herodotus, our principal witness, says that Homer lived " not more than " 400 years before his time, which was about B C 450.   This expression assigns Homer to any date *not more than* 400 years before the time of Herodotus, while the expression "yesterday " leaves it to be inferred that such date was not very distant   We are informed by Cicero, Pausanias and Diogenes Laertius'[7] that the works of Homer were revised and edited by Pisistratus, the deified King of Athens, who reigned something less than 200 years before Herodotus wrote   So far as we know, this period, say about B. C 600, marked the earliest publication of the Homeric poems and the Jovian theogony in Attica   Indeed the oldest inscriptions which survive of the Greek language do not ascend beyond the middle of the seventh century   These are the marbles of Thera, Melos and Crete about B. C. 620, and the Ionian slab of Psammeticus in Upper Egypt, which is of nearly the same age

Another straw which points the same way is the fact that the Romans associated their earliest legends—those which relate to the Foundation of the City—not with Jove, but with the god whom the Greeks regarded as his predecessor, Saturn.[8]   It was Saturn and not

---

[6] Euterpe, 53   [7] Cicero, Orat , III, 34; Pausanias, VII, Diogenes Laertius, I, 57.

[8] According to Brennand, 54, Jupiter was known to the Indians before Saturn, while in the Greek states, at all events in the Greek colonies of Asia Minor, Saturn was known as a planet and worshipped before Jupiter   If it could be assumed that both of these opinions were correct, this would narrow the field of our researches.

Jove who visited Janus in those great galleys whose rostra became the emblems of the Eternal City Had Jove been worshipped, or even known to the Romans when these legends were invented, it seems more likely that he would have been the Supreme of the Janus legend, rather than Saturn The legend therefore indicates that at the period of the Foundation, say B C. 816, the Romans, or the Albans, worshipped Saturn and not Jove, as the Supreme God

The period beyond which, according to these views, there is no warrant for carrying the antiquity of the Homeric theogony, namely about B C 600, marks the conquest or colonization of the Crimea by Greeks, and the establishment of Greek trading-posts and emporia close to those of the Iezyges, who with them conducted the overland trade from the Volga to the frontiers of India

There is a passage in Herodotus which by implication carries the Jovian worship back to the ninth or tenth century before our æra, not indeed in Attica, but in Sparta. "Lycurgus, a man much esteemed by the Spartans, having arrived at Delphi to consult the oracle, no sooner entered the temple than the Pythian spoke as follows 'Thou art come, Lycurgus, to our famous temple, beloved by Jove and all (the gods) that inhabit Olympian mansions. I doubt whether I should pronounce thee god or man; but rather god, I think, Lycurgus '"[9] Tradition assigns Lycurgus to the æra of Troja Capta, Herodotus implies that he lived in the tenth century B C , Thucydides and Cicero, our best authorities, fix him in the ninth (B. C 884), Aristotle alludes to his legislation as ancient, but fixes no date; Thirlwall and Grote regard him as a real personage of the ninth century Assuming the story in Herodotus to be authentic it carries the worship of Jove in Sparta back to the tenth century before our æra

The pentaeteris were originally not Greek, but Oriental festivals They are mentioned in the Vedas (Brennand, 159; Colebrooke I, 106) and were brought into Greece by the Veneti, who were worshippers of Ies Chrishna, or as Grecianized, Ischenus The festivals were called Ischenia The period of their importation was probably near the close of the 13th century before our æra They celebrated the equable year among the Iesyges, the Veneti, the Phœnecians, Pelasgii, and other kindred peoples; but not among the Greeks, who so far as we are aware, had no knowledge of the equable year until after

[9] Clio 6c

their colozmation or conquest of the Crimea in the seventh century, B C [10] Indeed, they themselves explicitly ascribed the discovery of the equable year to Thales, a Phœnecian Greek of Miletus Until the Greeks employed the equable year, they certainly did not celebrate it with the pentaeteris The previous celebrations must have been those of the Eleans and Pisans before their cities were taken by the Greeks In short, there seems to have elapsed a period of several centuries between the introduction of Jovian worship and the observance of the pentaeteric festival by the Greeks.

Pococke, 258-262, believed that the worship of Carnos (or Cronos) was the earliest form of religion which was brought into Greece from the Orient and that this was followed by the "establishment of the Jania sect, by the Jania pontiff of Thessaly," whose title was "Jeyus or Zeus" and his residence Oo'Lampos, or Olympus. According to this author, the worshippers both of the Greek Zeuspater and the Roman Jupiter took the name of their god and his fane from the Jania religion of India If this opinion were supported by satisfactory evidences, in place of those adduced by this somewhat venturesome author, both the discovery, the name and the worship of Jupiter in Greece might be carried backward with confidence to the æra of Ies Chrishna, or the first Buddha; but we are not as yet prepared to follow Mr Pococke thus far.

From these various considerations the determination of the Jovian cycle is narrowed down to some period near the æras of Ies Chrishna in India, [11] Ieschenus in Pisa, and Lycurgus in Sparta

To sum up The remotest admissible æra of the discovery of the planetary character and cycle of Jupiter in the Orient is the 15th century, whilst among the Greeks (this does not include the Eleans or Pisans) no plausible evidences of it have been found earlier than the tenth century [12] A reasonable date for its discovery in India is a mean between these two dates, say the 12th century B C With-

[10] Our Thors-day and the Roman Dies-Jovis answers to the Vrishpat-var of the Hindus, as written in the code of Manou. Dyaus-pater, Vrishpati, Brihaspati, Zeuspater and Jupiter are all variations of the same name and mean the same thing See Chap VIII for Vrishpat.

[11] A 30 year cycle (exactly one-half of the Jovian sexagenary) belongs to the religion of Ies Chrishna. See "Story of the Gods," IV, 4

[12] While the author sees no reason at present to alter this conclusion, he nevertheless believes that some weight should be accorded to the fact that the Romans associated one of their earliest legends, that of Janus, or "Father Jasius" (Virgil), with Saturn and not with Jove. This would imply that the Jovian worship was unknown to them or their ancestors at the period assigned to Janus or Jasius.

out venturing to suggest that the discovery of Jupiter's planetary character or period had any direct connection with the overthrow of the original Brahminical system, it will scarcely be denied that the assistance which it was capable of affording to a rival astrology would not be without its influence in strengthening that more popular worship which sprang up after the close of the Mahabharata wars and which afterwards in India took its name from Ies Chrishna, or the first Buddha and in the West from that of Ischenou, Hermes, Bacchus, or Dionysius.

CHAPTER VI.

VARIOUS YEARS OF THE INCARNATION.

THE following table shows the years of the incarnation of the Deity according to the Brahminical religion, all of the years being cast into the conventional or familiar Christian æra. The dates are those of the last year of the avatars as numbered.

TABLE A BRAHMINICAL DIVINE YEARS.

Ordinal Number of avatar *	Indian or Pre-Augustan Chronology	Roman or Augustan Chronology	Modern, or Christian Chronology	Ordinal Number of avatar	Indian or Pre-Augustan Chronology	Roman or Augustan Chronology.	Modern, or Christian Chronology.
	B C	B C	B C.		B C	B. C.	B. C
I	7128	7050	7065	IX	1864	1786	1801
II	6470	6392	6417	X	1206	1128	1143
III	5812	5734	5749	—	548	470	485
IV	5154	5076	5091		A.D	A D	A D
V	4496	4418	4433	—	109	187	172
VI	3838	3760	3775	—	767	845	830
VII	3180	3102	3117	—	1425	1503	1488
VIII	2522	2444	2459				

* The ten avatars of Iesnu, or Vishnu, or the names of the ten different forms under which he appeared or was to appear to mankind, were as follows I, Iesnu or Vishnu, the Matsya, II, Courma, or Kurm, III, Varaguin, or Varaba, IV, Nara-Sima, or Nara-sing, V, Vamen, or Vamuna VI, Rama Krakuchouda, VII, Bala-patren, or Karaka-muni, VIII, Parasurama, or Kasyapa, IX, Chrishna, or Saca-muni, X, Kalpi, or Maittreya The interval between them was always the same, namely, one ecliptical cycle, but the names and periods pertaining to each one do not appear to have remained unchanged

This table is constructed upon the following hypotheses 1, That the Calijoga (B C. 3102) is the conventional date of a Brahminical incarnation, a date which has been long accepted throughout the Orient, 2, That the Brahminical incarnations were 658 years apart, 3, That the Augustan dates are 78 years later than the Indian, and 4, That the Christian dates are 15 years earlier than the Augustan.

The following table shows the years of the incarnations of the Deity according to the Brahma-Buddhic or Hindu religion all of the dates being cast into the conventional or familiar Christian æra

TABLE B   BRAHMA-BUDDHIC DIVINE YEARS OR INCARNATION CYCLES

Indian, or Pre-Augustan Years		Roman, or Augustan Years.		Post-Justinian or Christian Years	
Buddha's birth	Buddha's death	Buddha's birth	Buddha's death	Buddha's birth	Buddha's death
B C.	B C	B C	B C	B C.	B C
6658	6578	6580	6500	6595	6515
6000	5920	5922	5842	5937	5857
5342	5262	5264	5184	5279	5199
4684	4604	4606	4526	4621	4541
4026	3946	3448	3868	3963	3883
3368	3288	3290	3210	3305	3225
2710	2630	2632	2552	2647	2567
2052	1972	1974	1894	1989	1909
1394	1314	1316	1236	1331	3251
736	656	658	578	673	593
B.C.	A.D.	A.D.	A.D.	B C	A D
78	1	0	79	15	64
A D	A D	A D	A D.	A D	A D
579	659	658	737	642	722
1237	1317	1316	1395	1300	1380
1895	1975	1974	2053	1958	2038

This table is constructed upon the following hypotheses 1, That previous to the Augustan age the Indian date of the nirvana of Buddha was equivalent to the Christian B C, 656; 2, That the alteration of the Calendar by Augustus removed this date to B C 578, and 3, That the Calendar was subsequently, probably about the 11th century, altered by the Latin Sacred College to the extent of 15 years, thus casting the nirvana of Buddha into B C 593; 4, That his nirvana occurred in his 80th year, 5, That the various nirvanas of Buddha are 658 years apart.   A difference of one year is sometimes to be observed in ancient dates which is due to the common practice of omitting A. D. 0. in calculating their Christian equivalents, and sometimes to a change in the new-year day

It will be observed that between the dates in Tables A and B there is a difference of 108 years   For example, in Table A the Augustan year of the tenth avatar of Iesnu is B C 1128, while in Table B the nirvana of Buddha is fixed by the Augustan chronology in B C 1236; the difference being 108 years.   In other words, the Brahma-Buddhic incarnation dates are 108 years earlier than the Brahminical   This discrepancy is continued throughout all the divine years   Its effect is to bring one of the divine years—that of the re-birth of Ies Chrishna, Quichena, Buddha, Dionysius or Salivahana (for they were all one) to the Christian B. C 15, or the Augustan A D o, the year of the Apotheosis of Augustus, and third closure (during his reign) of the temple of Janus.   If we turn back to chapter III, it will be observed that the difference between the epoch of the quin-

quennial olympiads B. C. 884 and that of the quadrennial olympiads
B. C. 776 is precisely the same—108 years. This coincidence when
strengthened with other evidences enables us to detect the author
and the motive for sinking 108 years from the Brahminical chronology,
or in other words, for adding 108 years to the Buddhic. The author
was evidently Augustus and the motive was to prove by the calendar
that he himself was that self same Ies Chrishna, Quichena, or Quirinus,
whose re-incarnation had been predicted and who was expected to
appear to mankind both in the Orient and the West. It is quite
possible that the olympiads were altered from quinquennial to quadrennial intervals by Julius Cæsar—indeed the æra of Iphitus given by
Cicero rather indicates this—but as stated in chapter III the alteration appears to have been completed by Augustus.

TABLE C.

Occidental Divine Years employed in Chaldea (Babylon), Assyria,
Persia, Arabia, Egypt, Greece, Gotland, Etruria and Rome—658
years apart.

B. C.

2064. Bel-Esus; Chres; Cres; Deluge of Ogyges; Anno Mundi
      Eusebiano (?)

1406. Nin-Ies; Jasius; Eric-theus; Eleusinian Mysteries; Ousurt-
      Esen; Marina.

748. Tiglath Pil-Esar; Nebo-Nazaru; Osiris; Adonis; Pheidon;
      Messenia's "Third Age"; Tat; Janus Quirinus, or Romu-
      lus; Numa Pompilius.

90. Woden, or Wotan; Minius Ieus; Etrurian doomsday; Kab ben
      Luayy; Sylla; Quintus Sertorius.

A. D.

567. Ies Chrishna (re-appearance); Meshdak; Mahomet (birth).

1225. Divine years now became obsolete in the West; though they
      continued to be observed in the Orient. At Rome the
      second coming of Jesus Christ was expected down to the
      year 1260, q. v., after which date this expectation, so far
      as the ecclesiastical authorities are concerned, seems to
      have been abandoned.

It will be observed that between the Indian incarnation dates of
Buddha's nativity in Table B and the Occidental incarnation dates
in Table C there is a discrepancy of twelve years. The origin and
period of this dislocation have not been satisfactorily settled, but
it seems likely to have been established before the Augustan æra.

TABLE D.

Buddhic, Bacchic, or Dionysian Divine Years, in cycles of 552 years reckoned backward and forward from Salivahana

Indian B. C	Christian B. C.	Augustan. B. C.	Indian. B. C.	Christian B. C.	Augustan B. C.
7254	7239	7176	2286	2271	2208
6702	6687	6624	1734	1719	1656
6150	6135	6072	*1182	*1167	*1104
5598	5583	5520	630	615	552
5046	5031	4968	+78	63	+0
4494	4479	4416	A D.	A D.	A. D
3942	3927	3864	473	488	551
3390	3375	3312	1025	1040	1103
2838	2823	2760	1577	1592	1655

* Reputed æra of the Indian Bacchus who conquered the West   This is evidently the same god or hero that was worshipped by the Jains   See next chapter, year B C 1219

† Variant æras of Salivahana, the re-incarnation of Ies Chrishna

TABLE DD.

Buddhic, Bacchic, or Dionysian Divine Years, in cycles of 532 years, reckoned backward and forward from Salivahana

Indian B C	Christian B C.	Augustan B C	Indian B C	Christian B C	Augustan. B C
6994	6979	6916	2206	2191	2128
6462	6447	6384	1674	1659	1596
5930	5915	5852	*1142	*1127	*1064
5398	5383	5320	610	595	532
4866	4851	4788	+78	63	+0
4334	4319	4256	A D	A D	A D
3802	3787	3724	453	468	531
3270	3255	3192	985	1000	1063
2738	2723	2660	1517	1532	1585

* Reputed æra of the Indian Bacchus who conquered the West   † Salivahana

TABLE DDD would be similar to Table DD, only instead of counting backward and forward from A D o the cycles would count from B C 8, which was the year of the apotheosis of Augustus in Egypt. A table of this character was evidently used in constructing the paschal periods of Hippolytus, a writer attributed to the third century. also by Dionysius Exiguus, who is assigned to the sixth century See Chapter VIII, under "532 years," where this series of Dionysian divine years is again mentioned

TABLE E

Brahma-Buddhic *lokkals*, 2700 years apart, according to various authorities

Varaha-Mihira. B C.	Gen. Cunningham B C	Sewell and Duff Rickmers B C
6077	6777	5777
3377	4077	3077
677	1377	377

If we consider the hundreds of æras which have been or are still being used to mark the flight of time, they will be observed to arrange themselves into groups or constellations, of which the principal ones relate to either Ies, or Brahma, or Buddha For example, it will scarcely be doubted that of the numerous æras shown in the next Table, F, ranging from B C. 771 to B C 527, the majority, indeed perhaps all, of them relate one way or another to the second Buddha; and that they cluster around the last quarter of the 7th century B C as a common centre. It may fairly be deduced from Arrian and Diodorus that at this period the Indian states enjoyed one of their few intervals of freedom These authors, following Megasthenes, accord to the ancient Indians three periods of political liberty, one each of 200 (?), 300 and 120 years; but they do not mention the dates at which such periods of liberty prevailed We may reasonably assume that the two last periods followed respectively the establishment and restoration of the Buddhic religion; but there is no guide to the occurrence of the first Some other aspects of this subject are dealt with further on in the text. Baron Bunsen's treatment of the matter is based on the assumption that Syrian mythology and historical fact are one and the same thing; an extravagance by no means confined to that eminent author.

Ascending from the 7th century B C and guided, through what otherwise were absolute darkness, by the light of the Divine Year, we are enabled to perceive that in like manner the various æras which centre in the 13th century B C relate to the first Buddha See Table G.

On the other hand, there are numerous æras pertaining to gods, hiercharchs and tyrants, which evidently do not belong to Buddhic clusters, but to some other chronological constellations For example, in the 11th century, Table J, we find a cluster of so-called Indian "Buddhas" who taught not the principles of political liberty, but those of a penal code The divinities of this cluster are evidently related to one another, but not to the Buddhic gods They are Brahminical They commemorate no period or impersonation of liberty They mark the triumph of hierarchical tyranny and its concomitants feudalism, caste, slavery, mysticism, priestcraft and superstition. We shall consider this and its cognate clusters of æras in their proper place and endeavor to point out their relation to the Brahamical messianic theory and the influence of the latter upon the creation of new myths Meanwhile let us deal with the Buddhic constellations The following dates are found upon coins or epigraphic monuments, or in literary works, or else are deduced therefrom as set forth in Chapter VII.

TABLE F

Æras of the Second Buddha, B. C. 771-527.

	B C.		B C		B C
Messenic æra (by the		Thammuz,	673	Buddha, birth,	598
5 yr Olympiads)	771	Numa, death,	672	Solon,	592
Tat, or Tatius,	769	Lao-tsze, China,	667	Panionic Cycle,	592
Romulus, Quirinus,		Buddha, nirvana,	662	Zoroaster, birth,	590
or Quichena,	753	Jimmu, regnal year,	660	Mad-ies, Khazaria,	584
Tiglath, Pil Esar,	748	Iesnara, Scythia,	658	Thammuz,	582
Messenic æra (see 685)	—	Buddha, Crimea,	658	Servius Tullius,	578
Nebo-Nazaru,	747	Buddha, nativity,	658	Jain Mahavira,	569
Phoroneus,	747	Chinese æra,	657	Gotama, nirvana,	567
Adonis,	747	Buddha, nirvana,	656	Buddha, birth,	557
Chinese æra,	742	Chrestonian æra,	656	Buddha, nirvana,	554
Numa Pompilius,	738	Nana-Sabesia,	645	Buddha, Burma, nir	552
Salivahana (Ies Chrish-		Mithra,	645	Armenian æra,	552
na)	736	Ianus Quirinus,	644	Confucius,	551
Ies Chrishna, birth,	724	Ies Chrishna, ascension,	644	Perseus,	548
Buddha, birth,	721	Thammuz, nirvana,	641	Æsculapius,	548
Sargon II (Iesargon?)	717	Solon, birth,	639	Jain Mahavira,	545
Jimmu, birth,	712	Buddha, Pegu,	638	Buddha, Siam, nir	544
Cyaxares (see 632)	710	Buddha, China,	638	Buddha, Ceylon, nir.	543
Zoroaster,	710	Fetzana æra of Buddha,	633	Buddha, Ava,	543
Giemschid,	703	Cyaxares,	632	Buddha, Burma, nir.	533
Ectzana, Burma,	701	Zoroaster, death,	630	Swetambara Vira,	533
Iesyges, Tarentum,	694	Jain Mahavira,	629	Cyrus, deified,	533
Thoth, Egypt,	692	Buddha, Ceylon, b,	619	Pythagoras, advent,	533
Burma, Sacred æra,	690	Servius Tullius,	612	Pisistratus, deified,	527
Messenic æra (Third age)	685	Adrastus,	610	Mahavira, nirvana,	527
Fod, or Budda, birth,	677	Lao-tsze, China,	604		

It is regarded as quite possible that were the sources of these various æras closely examined they could nearly all be resolved into one; in other words, that the difference in years between most of them could be accounted for by the various changes which have been made in the calendar. Many of them relate to ideal personages whose mythology is built upon the oft-repeated incarnations of Iesnu, or Vishnu, while others are those of historical characters who sought to exalt their power by connecting themselves with the same wide-spread myth.

TABLE G

Æras of the First Buddha, B C 1406-1193

	B C.		B C		B C
Buddha-Brahma,	1406	Buddha,	1336	Perseus,	1291
Nin-Ies, or Ninus,	1406	Troja Capta,	1334	Bacchus, Aretes,	1290
Ousurt-Esen,	1406	Ies Chrishna,	1332	Troja Capta,	1290
Jasius, Crete,	1406	Buddha-Brahma,	1332	Pan, of Arcadia,	1260
Eleusinian æra,	1406	Maryamma,	1332	Pan, of Ionia,	1252
Greek, Buddha (Eric-		Ies Chrishna,	1332	Pan, of Ionia,	1248
theus,	1406	Pelasgian æra,	1331	Ies Chrishna,	1248
Buddha-Brahma,	1394	Thoth, or Mercury,	1322	Troja Capta,	1248
Marina, Scythia,	1394	Ies Chrishna,	1315	Theseus,	1235
Buddha-Brahma,	1391	Kwar Ismian æra,	1312	Jason, Venetia,	1225
Ies Chrishna,	1391	Yao, China,	1311	Ies Chrishna,	1219
Bel Issus,	1390	Ianus,	1306	Ischenou, Elis,	1219
Buddha-Brahma,	1366	Duiga,	1306	Thammuz, Egypt,	1200
Thoth, Ies-iris, or		Ies Chrishna,	1300	Pelasgian æra,	1200
Osiris	1350	Bacchus (More?)	1300	Parasurama,	1193
Pan (Eric-theus),	1346	Troja Capta,	1202	Inachus,	1193

The evidences of a Buddhic or Bacchic religion, during and shortly after the Mahabharata wars, both in India and the Western countries, which, at this period, were doubtlessly largely peopled by refugees from India, are so numerous and convincing, that it would be rash to regard all these æras and personages as fabulous; although such is probably the case with most of them. That the Mahabharata wars left in India a popular leader or leaders who inculcated the principles of liberty, and the right to carry arms, will scarcely be doubted, especially by persons familiar with the customs and traditions of the Sikhs, the Bheels and other very ancient races, which still survive in their native country. All these are warrior races, and some of them make a practice never to go unarmed. While accepting the peaceful tenets and social aspirations of Buddhism, they evidently believe that liberty is not to be preserved through the unaided medium of faith; but that it needs also the bulwark of courage and the defense of arms. That these principles of liberty were carried into the Occident and furnished a foundation for the free states of Scythia, Asia-Minor and Greece, has been maintained with no little ability by Buchanan, Jameison, Pococke and others. Whether the name of the Oriental hero was Chrishna, Buddha, Pan, Mercury or Janus, is of no practical consequence. The principles represented by his name and the periods when and where they were promulgated, diffused and adopted, are alone important. In this sense the first Buddha must be regarded as much an historical personage as the second or the third Buddha. He certainly existed in men's minds, and for present purposes that is enough. Diodorus Siculus says that some of the Greek writers denied the reality of Bacchus, while others contended that there were three of this name, or one who revisited the earth at intervals; that the first one was born at Nissa, in India, and having been deceived by Lycurgus king of Thrace, he marched into that country and executed the treacherous monarch by nailing him to a cross.*

Among the modern writers on Indian antiquities who have asserted or assumed the existence of a First Buddha and the practice of a Buddhic religion in India during the period above indicated are Jones, Prinseps, Marsden, Wilson, Tod, Pococke and Colebrooke. The last one especially has some strong passages on the subject.

Beside the opinions of these writers there are the well known evidences afforded by the Buddhic or Brahma-Buddhic monuments of

*Dio. Sic. ed. 1700, pp. 116-19.

India, many of which are evidently much more ancient than the Second Buddha, and the fact that the Phœnicians who appeared in the Levant long before the period of the Second Buddha carried Buddhic images upon the prows of their galleys The worship of Thammuz (Buddha) in Syria may not have been earlier than the Second Buddha, but that of Thot (Taat, or Buddha) in Egypt was certainly as ancient or nearly as ancient as the period of the First Buddha.

TABLE H

Æras of the Third Buddha, B C 90, A D 65.

	B C.		B C		B.C
Woden,	90	Deiotaurus,	53	Pontine æra,	2
Minius Ieus,	90	Æra of Antioch,	49	Diviatiacus, Gaul,	57
Doomsday, Etruria,	88	Julius Cæsar, apotheosis,	48	Salivahana,	2
Woote,	86	Æras of Tyre, Antioch,		Apollonius of Tyana,	1
Sylla,	84	Pontus, Thessaly, etc.,	48	Buddha, Table B,	0
Pontine æra,	82	Æra of Rhodes,	42		A.D
Salivahana,	78	Sextus Pompeius,	41	Buddha, Table B,	1
Ptolemy, as Dionysius,	78	Herod, deified,	40	Chinzapagua,	1
Æra of Mecca,	78	Augustus, advent,	40	Augustus, Egypt,	8
Quintus Sertorius,	78	I eucadian æra,	36	Abyssinian æra,	8
Æra of Sinope,	70	Marc Antony,	36	Augustus, ascension,	14
Æra of Antioch,	64	Æra of Pontus,	36	Æra of Comana,	35
Augustus, conception,	64	Issus, son of Mariam,	25	Cingalese æra,	40
Salivahana,	63	Buddha, Table B,	15	Moorish æra,	40
Augustus, nativity,	63	AUGUSTUS, *apotheosis*,	15	Pontine æra,	64
Pompey, apotheosis,	63	Augustus, Egypt,	8	Fod, China,	65
Samvat Vicramaditya,	57	Pontine æra,	7	Indian Vrihaspati,	65

Many of these æras relate to historical personages, who, aware of the recurrences of the oriental Divine Year, sought to impose themselves upon the world as the predicted and expected king of kings Woote was an actual emperor of China who assumed the Mongol and Scythic name of the Messiah. Minius Ieus, Sylla Sertorius, Pompey, Diviatiacus, Deiotaurus, Julius Cæsar, Sextus Pompey, Marc Antony, Augustus and Apollonius are well known to history

We now turn backward to what, for the sake of avoiding confusion, we have ventured to term Brahminical æras, though so far as concerns many of the personages or names of personages connected with them, they are in fact not Brahminical, but Brahma-Buddhic

TABLE I

Brahminical æras, ninth avatar, B C 1897-1650

	B C		B C		B.C
Isaac, or Iesac,	1897	Phœnix æra,	1847	Cycle of Yao,	1650
Inachus,	1869	Ies Chrishna,	1786		
Iesnu, ninth avatar,	1864	Mahabharata wars,	1050		

The last incarnation of Vishnu, or Ies-nu, appears to have been expected previous to the Mahabharata wars, when the destruction of the world was to take place It is not improbable that the failure of this event had something to do with the revolt from Brahminism which characterized those wars and the reconstruction—after an Interregnum—of the ancient astrological system, into the later Brahma-Buddhic form which it still bears. There are no other traces of the earlier Brahminical æras now extant, though as we shall presently see, there are numerous marks of a later series.

TABLE J.

Brahminical æras, tenth avatar, B. C. 1300-1000.

	B.C.		B.C.		B.C.
Ies Chrishna,	1300	Ischenou,	1219	Bacchus,	1144
Rites of "Bacchus,"	1300	Theseus, death,	1206	Brahma, end of 10th av.	1128
Troja Capta,	1292	Rhampsinitus,	1200	Chaldean æra,	1106
Perseus,	1291	Parasurama,	1193	Josh, or Joss,	1104
Inachus,	1290	Inachus,	1183	First Zoroaster,	1076
Lykæa,	1260	Parasurama,	1182	Ies Chrishna,	1036
Troja Capta,	1258	Ies Cnrishna,	1178	Fod, son of Mai,	1036
Ionian æra,	1252	Parasurama,	1177	Fod, Brahma-Buddha,	1027
Ionian æra,	1248	Jovian orbit det'd,	1176	First Buddha (a	
Troja Capta,	1248	Parasurama,	1176	Brahma-Buddha),	1207
Theseus,	1235	Inachus,	1171	Buddso (Brahm-Bud)	1000
Jason,	1225	Ies Chrishna,	1156	Code of Manu, circ.	1000
Ies Chrishna,	1219				

These dates are Brahminical; the names, with few exceptions, are Buddhic; the combination is Brahma-Buddhic.

TABLE K.

Brahminical æras, 11th avatar, B. C. 590-388.

	B.C.		B.C.		B.C.
Zoroaster II.,	590	Darius,	521	Druid Cycles,	470
Mad-Ies,	584	Gebel-Eisis, (Hesus)	495	Hesus,	470
Servius Tullius,	578	Hesus, Spain and Gaul,	480	Phœnician æra,	389
Cyrus,	533	Chrysis,	479	Zoroaster II.,	389
Pisistratus,	527	Roman lustra adopted,	472		

In this series appear the names of several historical personages, who, being aware that a Divine Year was about to commence, or had just passed, assumed to be that predicted Son of God, who was expected to regenerate mankind and inaugurate a reign of universal peace and happiness.

TABLE L.

Brahminical æras, 12th avatar, A. D. 121-271.

	A.D.		A.D.		A.D.
Attic-Hadrianic æra,	121	Gupta,	167	Caracalla,	211
Osiris,	136	Commodus,	188	Elagabalus,	220
Barco-cheba,	136	Manes,	195	Sassanian æra,	223
Antonius Pius	138	Ardisher (shah-in-shah),	205	Kalachuri Samvat,	250
Gupta,	166	Gupta,	206	Manes, ascension,	271

It may be asked what warrant there is for regarding certain of these æras as Brahminical, or Brahma-Buddhic, or as having anything to do with the theogonies of India. The answer is that the heroes of these æras all impiously proclaimed themselves in Rome as the

Son of God, or the Messiah, that they evidently did so on or about
the occurrence of a Brahminical divine year, that the Messiah was
only expected, whether in the East or West, upon the occurrence of
a divine year, that they were all founders of new forms of religion,
and that they were all of them, as well Pompey, Julius and Augustus
before them, familiar with the Oriental theogony and the influence
it possessed both in the East and West, to command the obedience,
not merely of the superstitious multitude, but also of vassal kings,
pro-consuls, tetrarchs, and distant officials, as well as to ensure rich
offerings and endowments to the temples in all parts of the empire

The æras of Osiris, Barco-cheba and Manes are sufficient to establish the recurrence, rehabilitation and renewed observance of the
Brahminical divine year down to near the middle of the third century
of our æra, for it should be remembered that these Messiahs were
worshipped by vast multitudes in Persia, Syria, Egypt, and also the
the Western provinces of the empire   This induction derives additional support from the recrudesence of the Brahminical divine year
and its accompanying Manifestation in the ninth century of our æra,
as shown in the following table:

TABLE LL

Brahminical æras, 13th avatar, A D 722-971

	A D.		A D		A D
Quetzalcoatl,	722	Brahma,	846	Mansur, the Almighty,	922
Aera of the Papacy,	752	Aera of Tartary,	846	Ibu-Abi-Zakarriyya,	937
Aera of Jesus Christ		Nepal æra,	870	Abd-el-Raman III ,pre-	
first used,	781	Khri-l-de-Ssrong,	880	tended son of Marv,	936
Amogavarsha,	800	Nepal æra,	880	Peruvian Manifestation,	937
Sergius,	800	Salivahana,	890	Kalachakra æra,	965
Charlemagne,	800	Obeidallah,the Messiah,	909	Seljuk, son of Alanka-	
Parasurama,	825	Al Hallaj,	914	van,the Virgin Mother	971

It will scarcely be denied that these various clusters of earthly
divinities and æras, centering as they do on or about the periods of
the Brahminical divine years shown in Table A, evince a remarkable
persistence in the messianic belief, and that this belief had much to
do with the progress of religion and the history of states

If our historical knowledge were sufficiently extensive and accurate,
it would probably appear that many of the ideal Messiahs were
based upon actual pretenders who arose previous to the date assigned
to them and from whose worship that of the ideal Messiah was a re-
action or protest   In such case the æra of the Ideal was invented
at a later period and had to be thrown backward some centuries
before the period of his invention, in order to invest him with the
attribu   an mity surround him with superstitious r   ,   y, and

thus procure for him the veneration due to antiquity. For example, in the history of Assyria, Tiglath-pil-Esar was an actual personage who pretended to be a Messiah and who demanded to be worshipped as such. The same impious demand was made by his royal successors, until a time came when their evil and tyrannical lives rendered this demand so odious and intolerable, that it was resisted even by the degraded multitude. This then was the moment for organized revolt; but revolt, without an Ideal, a perfect Messiah, to take the place of the real but imperfect one, would in such a country and under such circumstances, have necessarily proved abortive. An ideal had, therefore, to be invented; and, in fact, he was invented and called Nebo-Nazaru, Nebo being the equivalent of Bacchus, Mercury, or Liber Pater, the god of freedom; and Nazaru possibly the pretended place of his miraculous advent. To complete the imposture, he had to be thrown backward in time. As Herodotus, who wrote B. C. 445, says nothing about him, he probably was not invented until after the immortal Greek composed his history. Let us say that he was invented about B. C. 400. The æra of the pretended Nebo-Nazaru was fixed in B. C. 747, the same as that of the real Tiglath-pil-Esar; he was, therefore, thrown back in time, or antedated, about 350 years. The divine attributes and mystery with which this degree of antiquity enabled the Ideal Messiah to be surrounded, might have rendered his name the battle cry of a holy war, and summoned millions in arms to sweep away the detested tyranny that had called the new Saviour into existence.

Such was probably the case not only with Nebo-Nazaru but also with many other of the Ideal incarnations of the past; but which were the real and which the ideal Messiahs, is a matter that cannot at present be determined upon grounds that would be likely to meet with general acceptance.

CHAPTER VII

ÆRAS

IN the following collection of Æras (Table M) all the dates have
been couched in the Vulgar Æra beginning January 1st, A D 1
This date coincides with the year 4004 of the World, according to
Bishop Usher, 3760 of the modern Jewish Anno-Mundi; 3102 of the
Brahminical Calijoga, 884 of the five-year Olympiads; 816 of Rome,
according to Timæus, Cicero and others; 776 of the four-year Olympiads, 753 of Rome, according to Varro; 747 of Nebo-Nazaru, or
"Nabonassar" and 15 of Augustus   It should be observed that the
Greek Olympiads, which were originally five-year periods or pentaeteris, whose epoch was in B C. 884 were altered during the Augustan
period to four-year periods or tetrateris, whose epoch was fixed in
B C 776, thus making a difference in many deduced dates of 108
years.   It should also be observed that the æra of Rome from which
many dates are commonly deduced by the equivalent A U 753=
A D 0, or A U 754=A. D 1, has evidently been altered twice;
that the antiquity of Rome was reduced by Augustus from B. C 816
to B. C 738 whilst it was afterwards augmented by the Latin Sacred
College to B. C. 753, which has long been and is still its familiar æra.
When these changes were made, the various manuscripts within reach
of the college, whether Augustan or medieval, in which deductions
from, or comparisons with the Greek Olympiads or other foreign
æras occurred, were altered to tally with such changes of the æra
But in such a vast undertaking some of the equivalent dates were
overlooked; manuscripts then lost to view have since been recovered, and above all, immense collections of ancient coins and marbles have been brought into view in recent years; all of which evidences unite to restore the ancient dates and prove the age and extent of the alterations   In the present work, except where explicit
notice is given to the reader, these alterations of the Sacred College
have not been touched   No attempt has been made to reconstruct
the accepted chronology   Nevertheless, it is but proper to advise
the reader that the alterations of the Roman æra above alluded to

were not made without introducing a host of conflicting dates into
history, which hitherto the modern critic has sought in vain to reconcile with probability. A large proportion of these dislocations arise
out of the 15 years of alteration which was made or completed by
the Sacred College, probably during the pontificate of Gregory VII,
A. D. 1073-85. Many dislocations which arose from the Augustan
alterations of 108 and 78 years, are still to be observed in historical accounts.

The boldness with which these alterations of the Western Calendar were made raises the suspicion that similar alterations have been
made in the Eastern Calendar. "Joannes Moses, collector of the
land-tax for the province of Pegu, said that whenever the king
thought the years of the æra too many, he changed it." (Dr. Francis
Buchanan, in Asiat. Res. VI, 171.) But this statement only relates
to one province and to the last century. However, there are reasons to believe that a similar remark is applicable to earlier times.
Col. Wilford says that several "corrections" of the Indian Calendar
have been made at various times, especially one of 14 years, the
length of his reign, ascribed to Bhartrihari. (Asiat. Res. IX, 200.)
But neither he nor any other chronologist has yet impugned the in-
tegrity of the more ancient Indian dates.

In this maze of alterations and dislocated dates the Divine year
will be found a steady light which, though not absolutely reliable,
affords a guide where otherwise all were darkness, doubt and confusion.

————

B. C. 6984, Europe.—Dionysian Anno Mundi, computed by Alfonso X, King of Castile and Leon and published under his patronage
in A. D. 1488, in about which year the end of the world had been predicted. This collection of astronomical and astrological materials is
known as the Alfonsine or Alphonsine tables. According to Muller,
the Anno Mundi of the royal astrologer was B. C. 6984; while
Strauchius says it was B. C. 6484. Assuming Muller's equivalent to
to be the more correct one, the Anno Mundi of Alfonso appears to
have been constructed of 13 Dionysian divine years (each of 532
common years), dating backward from B. C. 78. This would carry
it to B. C. 6994 instead of 6984. See Table D.

B. C. 3777, N. India.—Bacchus. Says Pliny, Nat. Hist. VI,
xxxi, 5: from Liber Pater (Bacchus, or Bacchos ... ...sus),
to Alexander ... ... the Indias ... ... three

months "—"*Anni* VI, *MCCCCLI adjiciunt et menses tres* " This
æra began on the autumnal equinox, or "*menses tres*" before the anniversary of the Apotheosis of Alexander the Great, which latter
event was celebrated in Egypt on the winter solstice. The 6451
years are reckoned backward from Alexander's Conquest of the Punjab, B C 326 The figure given by Pliny, namely 6451 years from
Dionysius to Alexander, is supported by Solinus, who in ch 64 (53)
has the same figure for the same interval Arrian's figure of 6042
years from Dionysius to Sandrocottus is substantially the same
thing. It measures the interval from Buddha, B C 6384 (Table D)
to Chandra Gupta, B C 342 Pliny and Solinus adopted the method
of computation reported by Megasthenes, while Arrian preferred the
Dionysian method which had become popular in the West

B. C. 6777, N. India.—Saptarshi-Kal, or Lok-Kal, or the æra of
the Seven Rishis, or asterisms, of the Great Bear: a Brahma-Buddhic
æra of Ies Chrishna employed in Cashmere and Northern, but unknown in Southern, India Gen Alex Cunningham, "Book of Indian Æras " He employs this æra by synchronising it with Pliny's
6451¼ years, added to 326 (B C), the year of Alexander's Conquest of the Punjab His authorities for the æra of the Saptarshi-
Kal are Vridda Garga and the Puranas, who accord an interval of
2700 years between one Lok-Kal and another, or 100 years to each
of the 27 Lunar Mansions into which the Hindus divide the ecliptic
Hence, the succeeding Lok-Kal was in 4077, "when Chrishna, the
the Splendour of Vishnu, ascended to Heaven," etc Vrihat San-
hita, c xiii, 1-4 Cunningham's rendition of the Lok-Kal is not un-
disputed. According to Varaha Mihira and the later astronomers,
the Lok-Kals occurred in B C 6077, 3377, 677, etc Sewell has
still other periods (See Table E, herein) But Cunningham's
seem to be the best authenticated and he is supported by Stokvis
and other chronologists

B. C. 6717, N. India.—From Buddha (or Bacchus, or Dion-Isus)
to the ascension (reign) of Sandracottus, or Kandra Gupta (B C
315) the Indians calculated, according to Magasthenes, in Arrian's
"India," just 6402 years Hence 6402 plus 315=6717 Dunckei's
"India," 72-4. This computation has neither significance nor value
It is based on an exceptional ms of Arrian and an uncertain date of
Kandra Gupta

B. C. 6658, N. India.—Brahma-Buddhic æra, 6402 years before
the death and bodily ascension to heaven of Sandracottus, or Kandra
Gupta (B. C. 256). Magasthenes, in his version of Arrian' "India"

employed by Duncker. Bearing in mind the astrological significance of the Divine Year, it is evident from this and the foregoing
dates, all of which were deduced from the accounts brought to Europe by Megasthenes, that in the time of Alexander and Seleucus
the Hindus looked for the Dissolution of the World and the Day of
Judgment within a comparatively brief period. The lifetime they
assigned to the world was equal to ten ages, avatars, or incarnations, each of 658 years and according to this one, the lowest of the
Megasthenic computations that has come down to us, the Day of
Judgment was due in B. C. 78, the period of Quichena, Ies Chrishna
or Salivahana. Thus, 6658 less 78, equals 6580 years, which was the
period that the Brahminical astrologers assigned to the lifetime of
the world from beginning to end. The date above assigned to
Kandra Gupta, who was a contemporary of Alexander and Seleucus,
is that of his death according to Bunsen. See B. C. 330 and 315 for
æras of Kandra Gupta.

B. C. 6369, India.—Brahma-Buddhic æra. According to Col.
Wilford in Asiat. Res. V, 242, etc., and Dr. Hales I, 195, Megasthenes (they say) reported the Indian Anno Mundi at 6042¼ years
before Alexander's invasion of India in B. C. 327. Hence the Indian æra was in B. C. 6369. This computation couples the fixed year
of one account with the running year of the other.

B. C. 6369, Persia.—Eudoxus and Aristotle held that the first
Zoroaster lived 6,000 years before Plato. Pliny XXX, 2. As Plato's
æra was B. C. 427-347 this computation will bring the æra of the first
Zoroaster to about this date. Hermippus, B. C. 210, thought that Zo-
roaster flourished about 5,000 years before the Trojan war. Pliny,
XXX, 2. Niebuhr believes that he never existed at all. He is prob-
ably a Persian adaptation of one of the numerous creations of
Brahma-Buddhic astrological fancy. See B. C. 630 and 590.

B. C. 6310, Rome.—Anno Mundi calculated by Onuphrius Panvi-
nus, about A. D. 1560. Hales I, 211.

B. C. 6204, Antioch.—Anno Mundi, according to an Indian account of Megasthenes, cited by Hales. This is evidently a blunder.

B. C. 6174, Arabia.—Anno Mundi of the Arabians, cited by
Hales. See B. C. 6065.

B. C. 6158, Babylon.—Anno Mundi of the Chaldean chronicles,
cited by Bailly.

B. C. 6157, China.—Anno Mundi according to the Chinese chronicles, cited by Bailly.

B. C. 6138, Alexandria.—Anno Mundi according to Diogenes Laertius of Cilicia who died B C 222. Playfair

B. C. 6128, Egypt.—Anno Mundi of the Greeks in Egypt Bailly.

B. C. 6110, Russia.—Anno Mundi of the modern Russian Greek church Whittaker's Almanac, 1896, p 66

B. C. 6081, Greece.—Anno Mundi of Diodorus Siculus, according to Playfair Diodorus died in tempo Augusto

B. C. 6077, India.—Hindu incarnation, or year of the Lok-kal according to Varaha Mihira. See Table E

B. C. 6065, Arabia.—Æra of "the Great Isskander of the Two Horns." (Isskander Zu al-Karnayn) Epoch, Safar 10th, or March 25th, the vernal equinox This is evidently meant for Ics Chrishna, Bacchus, or Buddha The æra is curiously preserved in the "Tailor's Story" of the Arabian Nights, the scene of which is laid in Baghdad, Safar 10th, A H 653, or March 25th, A. D 1255, which is said to be the 7320th year of the æra In Sir Richard Burton's "literal translation" (1885) the "Two Horns" are omitted and in a foot-note to his "Terminal Essay" the æra is referred to, but misunderstood, and explained away. See another Arabian Anno Mundi herein under B C 6174 This is evidently the same æra, the difference being 108 (109) years: an explanation of which will be found in Chapter VI herein

B. C. 6000, India.—Pre-Augustan date of Buddha's birth See Table B.

B. C. 6000, Byzantium.—Anno Mundi according to Suidas, A D. 1090 Playfair.

B. C. 6000, Antioch.—Anno Mundi of the "primitive church ' founded on the "Septuagint." Gibbon, "Dec. and Fall," I, 562, *n*. See A D 1000

B. C. 5877, Egypt.—Anno Mundi of Manetho, B C 304. Hales, I, 241

B. C. 5872, Judea.—Anno Mundi of the Septuagint. Putnam. This æra was calculated by the Jews of Spain in the 12th or 13th century of our æra

B. C. 5812, India.—Pre-Augustan date of the third incarnation of Brahma. See Table A

B. C 5598 Byzantium —Anno Mundi of the Greek church Wooll

B. C. 5512, Byzantium.—Anno Mundi of "the Christians," as reckoned during the tenth century of our æra, according to Albiruni; ed 1879, p. 18

B. C. 5509, Byzantium.—Sept 1. Anno Mundi employed by Argyrus A. D 1372 and by Bury and Stokvis. See B C. 5508 and 5493 and A. D. 1492.

B. C. 5508, Byzantium.—Anno Mundi attributed to Julius Africanus, who is said to have flourished A D. 222, to Lactantius, who is assigned to the beginning of the fourth century and to Panadorus, the Alexandrian, fifth century, subsequently adopted by the Italian papacy under Leo VI , A. D 886-911 (Greswell F C. II, 120) It commenced 1st September. Cf The Pandits, G. C. Tarkalankar and P N Saraswati, in "Chronological Tables," p xxix (largely copied from Lieut Col John Warren's "Kala Sankalita ") The Russians continued to employ this æra until 1700 (reign of Peter the Great) and although the ecclesiastical new year day fell, according to some authors, on 21st March and according to others, on 1st April, yet the civil year began on 1st September Picot, "Tab Chron " I, 245. See B C 5500 The same year (5508) was deduced by Joseph Scaliger from the Septuagint Clinton says B C 5508 Nicephorus says B. C. 5507, or 5506 According to Bailly, the (modern) Persian chronology gives B C 5507 Bury says (for Byzantium) 5509 "Later Rom Emp " II, xxii The Rev Dr Hales gives 120 different years for the creation, varying from B C 6984 (Alfonso X, King of Spain) to B C 3616 (Rabbi Lipman, in Universal History ") and adds that this number might be swelled to 300 Dr Hales himself fixes the Creation at B. C. 5411.

B. C. 5506, Byzantium.—Anno Mundi deduced by the Latin Sacred College from the chronological work of Nicephorus Gregoras, a Greek ecclesiastic, and at one time a favorite of the emperor Cantacuzenus Nicephorus was born about A D. 1283, died about 1360. He wrote the history of his country in 38 books, extending substantially from the Fall of Constantinople in 1204 to the year 1358 The last 14 of these books remained unpublished until after the Italian Revolution of 1848, a delay which is attributable to obstacles interposed by the Papal See. Nicephorus, possessed of great learning, was especially skilled in astronomy and chronology, one proof of which is that he proposed to correct the Julian year. He thus anticipated by more than two centuries the calendar reform afterwards accomplished by Pope Gregory XIII The work of Nicephorus opens with the Nativity of Christ, which he fixes in the 42nd year of

Augustus.   Originally this synchronised with A. D. 15; but, owing to the 15 years' alteration of the Latin Church, it now agrees with A. D. o. or A. D. 1, or, according to Latin chronology, as applied to the tables of Nicephorus, with the 15th year before the reign of Tiberius.

After the recovery of Constantinople by the Byzantines in 1261 efforts were made to reconcile the Greek and Roman religions, chronologies, etc.   In these negociations Nicephorus took an active part. A portion of his contribution consisted of introducing into the chronology of the Greek Empire as many years (15) as had already been added to the chronology of the Roman Empire by the Latin Church. Three of these years he inserted between the reigns of Pertinax and Diocletian, two in the reign of Valens and four in that of Justin II. The remaining six years were distributed throughout a dozen reigns, as is shown in the following table:

Nicephorus Lib.	Page	This Liber ends with the—	Nicephorus. A. M.	Equal to A. D.	Roman Fasti A. D.	Difference
I	125	19th Tiberius	5539	33	32	1
II	219	14th Nero	5575	70	68	2
IV	341	Death of Pertinax	5701	196	193	3
VI	437	14th Diocletian	5795	290	284	6
VIII	667	Death of Constantine	5847	342	337	5
IX	809	" " Constantius II.	5872	367	361	6
X	104	" " Jovian	5875	370	364	6
XI	216	" " Valens	5891	386	378	8
XII	336	" " Theodosius	5909	404	395	9
XIII	430	" " Arcadius	5923	418	408	10
XIV	581	" " Theodosius II.	5965	460	450	10
XV	635	" " Leo	5990	485	474	11
XVI	727	" " Anastasius	6034	529	518	11
XVII	803	" " Justin II.	6098	593	578	15

B. C. 5503, Alexandria.—Anno Mundi of the Greek Church of Alexandria.   The Pandits' "Chron. Tables," p. xxiv.

B. C. 5502, Alexandria.—Anno Mundi of the Copts and the Greek Church of Alexandria.   Cf. Stokvis, "Chron." and Woolhouse "Measures and Moneys."   From this æra ten years were subtracted by the Latins.   See below, B. C. 5492.

B. C. 5500, Byzantium.—Anno Mundi, commences 1st September (29th August?), attributed to Julius Africanus.   "We know from Syncellus and a fragment (supposed to be) of Julius Africanus himself that he assumed the year of the world, 5500, to be that of the Incarnation."   Rev. E. R. Hodges' rendition of "Cory's Fragments," ed. 1876, p. 98.   George the Syncellus, (i. e., cell-companion) was a fellow-monk of the Greek patriarch of Constantinople and was born about A. D. 800.   "Africanus, in his Chronicle, reckoned 5500 years from the creation of the world to the age of Julius(?) Cæ-

sar. Nothing remains of this work but what Eusebius has pre
served." Rev. J. Lempriere, Class. Dic. By the "age of Juli
Cæsar " is probably meant the Apotheosis of Augustus Cæsar (S
below, B. C. 15) which according to several of the Byzantine chrono
gists marked the 5500th year of the world. The period of 5500 ye
is precisely 50 Ludi Sæculares. The date which is clearly astro¹
cal was probably shifted from Augustus to Christ some time d
the eighth century.

B. C. 5500, Byzantium.—Anno Mundi attributed to Hipp
who is said to have suffered under Septimius Severus, A..
See A. D. 1. It was probably shifted from Augustus to Chr
ing the eighth century.

B. C. 5493, Abyssinia.—Coptic æra commences 29th of
Old Style. The Pandits' "Chron." p. xxiv and Stokvis. '
is evidently derived from the Byzantine B. C. 5502, whilst t
that of the death of Augustus Cæsar. See A. D. 14.

B. C. 5493, Antioch.—Epoch Aug. 29. Anno Mundi employed
by Theophanes, A. D. 751-818. "It differs from the more common
Byzantine æra of the Nativity, viz., A. M. 5509, by 16 years." Bury
"Later Rom. Emp.," I, xxii and 413. Bury says it (5493) was "the
æra of Antioch (or rather of Panodorus, the Alexandrian) which was
used by Theophanes." Ibid, II, 425. The real difference is one indiction, or 15 years. Stokvis says B. C. 5494. See B. C. 5508.

B. C. 5492, Antioch.—Epoch Aug. 29. (Stokvis says Sept. 1.)
Anno Mundi of the Latin Church. The subtraction of ten years
from the Greek, to make the Roman Septuagint æra, is usually attributed to the age of Diocletian; but there is no valid proof that
the Greek Anno Mundi was employed at that period. The earliest
Greek Anno Mundi must have been fixed later than the adoption of
Constantinople as the capital of the Empire; indeed later than the
canon ascribed to Dionysius Exiguus. Cf. " Middle Ages," ch. VIII.
See also B. C. 5506.

B. C. 5469, Rome.—Anno Mundi attributed to Sulpitius Severus,
who died A. D. 420. Hales, I, 211.

B. C. 5411, Byzantium.—Anno Mundi of the Greek Church.
Hales, p. 101.

B. C. 5369, Antioch.—Anno Mundi, based on Megasthenes.
Hales.

B. C. 5344, Judea.—Anno Mundi of the Talmudists. Putnam·
Not of the Talmudists, but of the commentators on the Talmud,
about the 12th or 13th century.

B. C. 5342, India.—Birth of Buddha   Divine Year   Indian date.
ᵀable B.

B. C. 5206, Mexico.—Anno Mundi of the native astrologers, ac-
ˌrding to Boturini in Lord Kingsborough's "Mexico," VI, 176
ggins, Anacal , II, 25

'. **C. 5200, Caesaria.**—Anno Mundi of Eusebius, Gibbon, I,

ᴗ. **5199, Mexico.**—Anno Mundi of the laity of Mexico accord-
the early christian converts in that country   Boturini, op cit
'. **5054, Persia.**—Turki æra of the Creation. " From the
⌐ Timur until Julal-ud-din Mohammed Akbar, there were three
ᵜ use, the Hegira, the Turki and the Julal-ud-din   The Turki
ᵥith the Creation of the world and is computed ˌn (Jovian)
ᵙ 12 years   In Maharram A H 1138, there had elapsed 565
ᵼd the fourth year of the following cycle was in progress
ᵻr begins with the new moon of the month Jeth (Jaistha, or
          e Hindu calendar; and the months are lunar   Intercala-
tion is made at the end of each two or three years "   The Pandits'
"Chronology," p xviii, quoting from a Persian ms belonging to a
gentleman of Benares (see A. D. 1075)

B. C. 4825, India.—Erroneous æra of Parasurama, employed
in some works of reference   See B C 1176 or 1175 and the recurrence of the Parasuramic or Kollam ages at intervals of a millennium
thereafter

B. C. 4714, Europe.—January 1st, commencement of the "Julian
period," an astrological cycle invented by Joseph Scaliger, in 1583,
to avoid the uncertainty of mundane æras.   It begins with a Solar-
lunar conjunction and continues for 7980 years, an interval formed
by multiplying the approximate periods of a solar cycle of 28, a
lunar cycle of 19 and an indiction of 15 years, in other words, 15
Dionysian Divine Years of 532 years each.   Stokvis, Chambers,
Woolhouse, The Pandits, and Robert Sewell, "Indian Calendars,"
all commence this period January 1st, B C 4713

B. C. 4700, Judea.—Anno Mundi of the Samaritan Pentateuch.
Putnam.   Abendana says that the earliest use of any mundane æra
among the Jews was about A D. 1000   Lyons, "Jewish Calendar,"
p. 26

B. C. 4684, India.—Hindu re-incarnation.   Table B.

B. C. 4658, Judea.—Anno Mundi of Josephus   Putnam

B. C. 4346, China.—Anno Mundi invented by Liu-Shu, A D.
1068, in his book "Wai-ki "   Fergusson, 110

B. C. 4026, India.—Hindu re-incarnation. Pre-Augustan date of Buddha's birth. Table B.

B. C. 4007, Rome.—Anno Mundi. Hutton; the Pandits; etc.

B. C. 4004, Rome.—April 21st. First day of Creation and Anno Mundi of the English Bible. Pascal and De Sacey (authors of Port Royal); Usher; and Greswell. This is the æra commonly used in Protestant states. The difference between this and the Septaugint and Samaritan æras is attributed to the fact that the latter add greatly to the ages of the patriarchs. The epoch is the Roman Palalia.

B. C. 4000 Rome.—Anno Mundi of Bell's "Pantheon"; article "Merodach."

B. C. 3996 England.—Anno Mundi of the Second Adventists. Epoch, the autumnal equinox. "Lime-light views were given of the Zodiac in order to show that there could not have been any eclipses before (this) Creation year"! J. B. Dimbleby in Proc. Br. Chron. and Astron. Ass. London, January, 1898.

B. C. 3950, Judea.—Jewish Anno Mundi of Scaliger, apud Putnam, p. 3.

B. C. 3780, Judea.—Anno Mundi of the Jews, as reckoned during the tenth century of our æra, namely, "3448 years before Isskander (Alexander)". Albiruni, op. cit. 18. This was the earliest calculation of any Mundane æra among the Jews. Abendana, apud Lyons.

B. C. 3761, Bombay.—Anno Mundi of the Bombay Jews, that is, the "ancient æra" . . . which is "never used by chronologists, but for times before Christ." No explanation is given by the Pandits of this alleged custom. This æra began with Nissan (about the vernal equinox), whereas the years otherwise employed begin with Tishri (about the autumnal equinox). Stokvis says October 5. The ancient Jews are alleged to have employed the æra of Nebo-Nazaru. (But this began on February 26th. See B. C. 747.) The chief difference between the Oriental and Western Jewish calendars is that the former place the embolismic days of their lunar year in any of the five longest solar months, whereas the latter invariably throw them into Adar. Intercalation in Bombay is made on the 3rd, 6th, 8th, 11th, 14th, 17th, and 19th years of the Metonic cycle. This custom cannot be traced higher than the 14th century of our æra, although some chronologists have assigned it to the 11th century. The Pandits' "Chron". The æra itself can hardly be older than the 10th century of our æra.

B. C. 3760, Cordova.—Molad Tohu (Birth of the Void) or Mundane æra of the Modern Jews. Rabbi Abendana (d 1685) says that this æra was first used by the Spanish Jews during the tenth century. There are some reasons for believing it to have been fixed in the twelfth century   The Calendar is lunar, the year consisting of 354 days with an intercalary thirteenth month (Adar II,) every third year, to take in the lost days of the solar year. The New Year's day is Tishri 1st, which falls about the autumnal equinox and is celebrated as Rosh Hashanah, and also as the feast of Trumpets   It has been alleged (See B C. 3761) that the "ancient" Jews used the æra of Nebo-Nazaru, but there are no coins, or other monuments to substantiate this statement, which negatively is contradicted by the entire absence of dates in the Hebrew Scriptures written after this period   In B C 524 (Greswell) the Jews gave their present names to the months of the year, most of such names being those of Oriental gods, as Nissan, Ayar, Zif, Sivan, Thammuz, Abib and Elool for Nyssa, Ashar, Deva the Zif, Siva, Thammuz the Buddha, Aswin and El. At the same time they changed the composition of the year from ten civil months of 36 days to twelve civil months of 30 days each with intercalaries, such added months being Tishri II, and Kanoon II   The earliest Jewish æra of which any explicit monumental or literary remains exist is that of the Asmonean republic   (See B. C. 143). The next is that of Rabbi Hillel (B C. 112-A. D. 8) who is said to have fixed the Mundane æra in a Greek year corresponding with B. C. 3700. Scaliger says that though the modern rabbinical calendar professes to go back to the date of the Creation, its true date is not older than A D 344   Rev E Greswell, F C, Intro. 103 and II, 115 is of the same opinion   But see B C. 3780 for Albiruni's statement with regard to the Jewish Calendar   In the 11th century the Alexandrian Jews fixed the Mundane æra in B. C. 3752. Albiruni. (See B C 3780 and 3752) In the 11th or 12th century the Jews of Cordova fixed upon B C 3760, the æra which through the influence of the Spanish and Portuguese Jews, has since grown into common use.   In the 13th century Abulfaragi, an Armenian bishop, said that the "Eastern" Jews fixed their Mundane æra in B. C. 4220   In the Sedar Olam Sutha, or "Small Chronicle of the World", attributed to the year A D 1121, the Mundane æra is fixed in B. C 4359, which is precisely one Brahminical Divine year earlier than Hillel's date; just as the Jewish æra of Cordova is precisely one Brahminical Divine year earlier than the post-Augustan date of the Brahminical Calijoga, a fact that stamps all of these æras

as astrological and serves to mark the period of their invention
With regard to the head of the year, Dupuis (II, ii, 59, 285) says that
Thammuz, (which is the same as Thamos, Tamus, Thamies, Thor,
Thoth, Teut, Tat, Taat, Tatius, etc), at present the fourth month
of the Hebrew year, was anciently the first month, that it was sym-
bolised by the zodion of the Ram, and that the New Year began
on the winter solstice, which is the birthday of Buddha   The
scriptural New Year is Nissan 1st, which, in a solar calendar would
fall on the Vernal equinox and in a lunar one, on some day near it.
According to Rabbi Joshua this was the day of the Creation, while
Rabbi Eleazar, with equal reason, proves that the world was created
at the autumnal equinox.   Cf. Philo Judæus, Josephus; the Talmud
("Rosh Hashanah"); Albiruni; Maimonides, R Menassah ben Is-
rael's "Conciliator," I, 127, ed. Lindo; Rabbi Isaac Aberbanal's
Commentaries; Rabbi Jacques J Lyons and Abraham de Sola,
"The Jewish Calendar," Montreal, 5614-1854; and "Middle Ages
Revisited," App. P.

B. C. 3760, Masonry.—Mundane æra of the Feeemasons, which
is the same as that of the Jews   Another Masonic Anno Mundi is
B C. 5000.

B. C. 3758, Ghazaria.—Anno Mundi.   Diodorus Siculus, lib.
II, iii, says that in the island of the Hypoboreans they observe a
cycle of 19 years during which time "the stars perform their courses
and return to the same point; for which reason the Greeks call this
revolution of 19 years the Great Year " Booth, the English translator of Diodorus, supposed this "island" to be Britain, but there
is nothing except national partiality to sustain this conjecture.
Britain was well known to the Greeks as the Cassiterides and to the
Romans as Britain.   The uniform testimony of the Greek writers indicates that the Hypoborean regions were in Scythia, that the Greek
knowledge of them was earlier than their knowledge of Britain and
that such knowledge came with the Greek trade that flowed through
Ghazaria and the Caspian sea.   This trade extended westward as far
Messapia in Italy, close to Sicily, where Diodorus, who was a Sicilian Greek, probably got his information.   "Island" may mean in-
differently an island or a promontory, as in the well known case of
Jutland.   The Holy Land of the Ghazars or Khazars appears to have
been situated in the northern part of the Caspian Sea and this is
probably the place favoured with the miracle presently to be mentioned   The cycle alluded to is evidently the Metonic, of 235 lunations, about 19 years   At the end of the same chapter Diodorus

says that the 197th cycle of the Hypoboreans was celebrated by
Apollo in person, who with harps and other musical instruments
chaunted the praises of his own glory, these heavenly strains lasting
from the Vernal equinox to "the rising of the Pleiades." Diodorus
omits to say in what year Apollo thus appeared upon earth; but as he
wrote during the Augustan age and employed the Augustan chronology, there is warrant for believing that the story was intended to
synchronise with the period of the Roman incarnation, or B C 15
In such case the Anno Mundi of the Hypoboreans was 197 x 235=
46,295 lunations, equal to something over 3743 years before the
Apotheosis of Augustus; in other words, about 3758 or 3759 years
B C. This is one divine year or 658 common years before the Indian Calijoga It coincides very closely with the Anno Mundi of the
Jews, who evidently got more than one of their institutes from the
Gharzarians It is hardly necessary to add that this Anno Mundi is
of Brahminical origin This chronology of the Messianic myth was
revived in the 13th century by Genghis Khan the monarch of Zagatai (North Caspian) and the conqueror of China. See A D 187,
845, 1206 and 1227

B. C. 3752, Alexandria.—Anno Mundi of the tenth century
Jews, who counted from Adam to Alexander 3448 years and from
Alexander to Jesus, 304 years   Albiruni, p. 18.

B. C. 3714, Cashmir, or Little Tibet.—Æra mentioned in
Taylor's History of India.

B. C. 3590, Persia.—Anno Mundi used by the Persians of the
tenth century of our æra, who counted from the beginning of the
world to Zoroaster, 3000 years and to Alexander, 258 more   Albu-
rini, op cit , 17.   Assuming the æra of Alexander to be B. C. 332,
we have 3000 plus 258 plus 332=3590

B. C. 3562, Persia.—Anno Mundi of the tenth century Persians,
based upon the medieval Christian assumption that the æra of Alexander was B C 304   Albiruni. See B C. 3590.

B. C. 3368, India.—Hindu pre-Augustan date of the Divine Year
dating back from the birth of Buddha.   Table B

B. C. 3185, India.—Beginning of the Vrihaspati or Jovian 60-
year cycles according to the Surya Siddhanta   See B. C. 3174 and
1176 and A D. 1796

B. C. 3174, India.—Beginning of the Vrihaspati or Jovian 60-
year cycles of the Surya Siddhanta, the 69th cycle having ended in
A D 965-6.   The Pandits "Chron"   See A. D. 1025.

B. C. 3164, India.—Brahma Kalpa   Higgins, "Anacal " I, 182.

This may be a corruption of the Calijoga, from which it differs by 63 years.

B. C. 3128, India.—Barhaspatya Kala; or beginning of the Jovian 60-year cycles. Stokvis.

B. C. 3114, India.—Beginning of the Vrihaspati or Jovian 60-year cycles by the Telinga account. The Pandits' "Chron." See A. D. 1025 and 1807.

B. C. 3102, India. The Calijoga, sometimes written Kaliyuga; Kali, meaning time, and joga or yuga, conjunction. Oppert, however, translates Kali to mean "first." The Calijoga commemmorates the end of the seventh and beginning of the eighth incarnation of Iesnu or Vishnu, "who manifested his glory to mankind" in the name and form of Ies Chrishna; Ies meaning the Sun and Chrishna meaning black, probably referring to a solar eclipse. Hence it is that the statues of Ies Chrishna represent him with a black face, complemented with woolly hair. Father Sonnerat (Voyage aux Indes) regards the Calijoga as the beginning of the Fourth Brahminical Age which began 4883 years before his time, A. D. 1782. This relation and year both agree with the determinations of Mr. Halhed in his Preface to the Code of Manu. Father Sonnerat goes on to say that the Calijoga was marked by the erection of a great temple to Juggernaut, between whose devotees and the celebration of the Calijoga he thus establishes a connection. The great antiquity of the Calijoga is confirmed by a variety of evidences. It is alluded to in the Puranas; it is employed as the starting point of the Brahma Siddhanta and Surya Siddhanta, two of the oldest astronomical treatises of the Hindus; it is the starting point of the Chrishnabouram or astronomical tables of the Siamese Chrishna, obtained in 1687 by Father Loubère and compared with the Tables of Tirvalore during the 18th century by Father Le Gentil; it is older than the Anno Mundi of the Jews and Free-masons, both of which are based upon the Calijoga; and it is older than the æra of Liber Pater brought into Europe by Megasthenes and preserved by Pliny and Arrian, because that æra also is evidently based upon the Calijoga. The reverence in which it is still held is evinced by the fact that it was employed so recently as the last century in dating the gold mohurs of Hyder Ali, Sultan of Mysore, A. D. 1760-82 and those of his son Tippoo Saib, A. D. 1785-99. (Kelly's "Cambist.," II, 217.)

The Hindu astronomers assert and Bailly believed that the Calijoga was the date when a conjunction of the sun, moon and several of the planets was actually observed and recorded. Laplace could find no such conjunction without going back to B C 4300. He, therefore, concluded that the Hindu and Siamese astronomical tables had been modified in modern times, a conclusion in which he was corroborated by Playfair. (Trans Royal Soc Edinb. 1790) As these eminent savants were not aware of the alteration in the division of the Hindu year from ten months of 36 days to 12 months of 30 days each, their calculations will require revision On the other hand, Brennand (Hindu Astron 1896) and Rev E. Burgess (Jour. Am Or Soc. 1895) regard the year of the Calijoga as having been fixed before or during the Mahabharata wars; a conclusion which appears to be corroborated by numerous convincing evidences The same year, B C 3102, is deduced by Max Duncker (India, p 72) from the Puranas As will appear further on, when discussing the epoch of the Calijoga, this seems to have been originally fixed on or about the winter solstice, and afterwards changed to Feb. 17-18, a change which had the effect to alter the year from B. C. 3102 to B. C 3101. (Wm. Marsden, Phil. Trans. LXXX, pt. ii, 565) But it is not certain that the epoch fell originally on the winter solstice, because the epoch of the æra reported by Megasthenes fell on the autumnal equinox

An attempt was made by Rev Wm. Hales to lower the antiquity of the Calijoga to B. C. 1913, 1905, 1370 and 1078 and by Baron Bunsen to lower it to B C 1448, but the methods employed by these chronologists do not warrant the conclusions they reached The Calijoga may not be what the Hindus have pretended, namely, the æra of a quintuple conjunction observed and recorded at the time; but it certainly is an æra invented not later than the 12th and possibly the 15th century B. C , which, like the Julian æra of Scaliger, was designed to afford a basis for astronomical calculations and one which has actually served that purpose ever since (Brennand; Burgess.)

Owing to numerous changes of the Indian calendar—from solar to lunar and from lunar to sidereal reckonings, from ten to 12 months' years and from years beginning with one particular month to years beginning with others—it is impracticable to trace the epoch or New Year's Day of the Calijoga with precision According to the date preserved by Pliny the year of Liber Pater in the time of Megasthenes commenced on the autumnal equinox; but it is not certain that such was also the case with the Calijoga. The beginning of the Hebrew year on or about the same day seems to confirm the day given by Pliny, but the Hebrew New Year day appears to have been of Seleucidan origin and of not very ancient date. Albiruni fixes the epoch of the Calijoga on the first Aswin, which in the Tamil calendar fell in 1897 on September 16th. On the other hand, Stokvis, Brennand, Duff Rickmers, Sewell and other modern astronomers and chronologists fix the epoch of the Calijoga on the 17th-18th February, B. C. 3102; and there we must be content to leave it. Cf. Bailly, "Astron. Ind.;" Col. Wilford in Asiat. Res., IX; Prinsep, "Useful Tables;" Brennand, 82; Colebrooke's "Essays;" Sir Geo. Cornewall-Lewis, etc.

B. C. 3102, Arabia.—Anno Mundi of the ancient Arabians. Max Idler, "L'ere des Arabes," p. 32.

B. C. 3100, India.—Tamil Durmuki Kali. Pandits "Chron." p. xix.

B. C. 3098, India.—Varapa Kalpa. Higgins, Anacal. I, 182.

B. C. 3076, India.—Saptarshi. Robt. Sewell, "The Indian Calendar," Table III. Duff, p. 4, calls it the "Laukika, or Saptarshi" æra, traditionally used in Cashmir, adding that it reckons by cycles of a hundred years. On p. 62 it is called the Saptarshi or Lokakala cycle. Epoch, Chaitra 1st.

B. C. 2757, China.—Beginning of the 60-year cycles according to Brennand, "Hindu Astron.", p. 7.

B. C. 2717, China.—Supposed beginning of the 60-year cycles. Souciet. (See below, year 2337).

B. C. 2710, India.—Hindu re-incarnation reckoning backward from the Augustan date of Salivahana. Table B.

B. C. 2697, China.—Beginning of the 60-year cycles. The Pandits. See A. D. 1804.

B. C. 2687, China.—Reign of the mythical Ti-hoang, orHoang-ti. The 60-year cycles "invented". Du Halde. (See below, 2627.)

B. C. 2637, China.—Æra of the pretended incarnation of Fo-hi, according to Rev. C. Gutzlaff. This æra was revived and legalised by the Emperor Kienlong, A. D. 1735-95. Gibbon, II, 575, n. It commences on the winter solstice. Cf. the Pandits' "Chron". According to Stokvis the Jovian cycles of China and Japan commenced this year.

B. C. 2627, China.—Sixty-first year of Ti-hoang, or Hoang-ti. The 60-year cycles "established," according to Freret, who, however, makes the 61st year agree with B. C. 2636. See B. C. 1965.

B. C. 2540, India.—According to Higgins, Anacal. I, 251, this year the Sun entered the sign of Aries, from Taurus; the Indians, hitherto of one religion, split into Brahmins and Buddhists; and the latter were driven out of India This is as bad as the astrologers. There was no 12 sign zodiac with Taurus and Aries at this remote period. The entire scheme is fanciful. See B C 380.

B. C. 2474, China.—Æra of Yao, or Jove, who divided the year and regulated the calendar. The Hebrew name for Jove is also Yao.

B. C. 2448, Cashmir.—Epoch of the chronicles called Rajahtarangini Prof Wilson, "Asiatic Researches," vol XV; Pococke, p 131

B. C. 2397, China.—February Chinese æra, as computed by certain of the Jesuit missionaries (Prinsep).

B. C. 2357, China.—Incarnation and Investiture of the divine Yao Du Halde. This is feigned to have occurred at the winter solstice McDowell Higgins Anacal I, 330, contends that Yao, Jove, Jupiter, etc, are the same In such case the divine Yao was of a much later period, the planet Jupiter, as such, being, as yet, unknown and the ancients worshipping only planets.

B. C. 2337, China.—Nineteenth year of Yao. The 60-year cycles "commenced" Du Halde, Hist. China, I, 282 This is the Chinese æra used throughout his history. Other Jesuits reckoned from 2397. Prinseps See A D. 1024

B. C. 2256, India.—Incarnation of Buddha Col Tod Winter solstice.

B. C. 2235, Assyria.—Incarnation of Bel-Issus, or the Lord Issus (Clinton; Vernal equinox?) Hales begins this æra with B C 2254 (See below, years 2064, 1406 and 1390)

B. C. 2234, Chaldea.—First year of Chaldean astronomical records found on tablets of baked clay (Rawlinson). This date is 1903 years before Alexander visited Babylon, B C 331, and is from Callisthenes Freret, Mem Acad. Inscript XVI, 205, prefers B. C. 1532. These records were undoubtedly concocted at a later age, to support the myth of Bel-Issus See B C 2235, also, "Middle Ages Revisited," ch. I, n 15

B. C. 2218, China.—Third cycle, second year Accession of Ta-Yu, first emperor of Hia dynasty, and the so-called first "certain" Chinese date

B. C. 2163, China.—Incarnation of Yao, according to Bunsen, III, 388

B. C. 2157, Chaldea.—Epoch of Chaldean "historical" æra. Jules Oppert, cited by Gustav Oppert, p. 331

B. C. 2064, India—Brahmo-Buddhic incarnation of Ies Chrishna, evidently invented after the Mahabharata wars The proper date is B C 2052, q v.

B. C. 2064, Assyria.—Incarnation of Bel-Issus, or Bel-Esus. According to Eusebius, "Chronol." I, 12, "Castor reckoned 1280 years from the first Ninus to a second Ninus, or Nin-Ies, successor to Sardanapalus ". This would throw the æra of the second Ninus into the 8th century B. C. and the æra of the first Ninus into the 21st century B. C., making it coincide with the æra of Bel-Esus. The whole mythos is Oriental, astrological, and pre-dated. See B. C. 1406 and 1390.

B. C. 2064, Assyria.—Approximate æra assigned by Assyriologists to Sargon I, who was evidently merely a mythos of the Sun worship. He is said to have been born miraculously and in some obscure place, his father being unknown and his mother a person of royal descent, by whom he was deposited in an ark of reeds and bitumen and left to the care of the River. He was carried by the stream to the dwelling of a ferryman, who reared him as his own son until the time came for the disclosure of his true rank, when he was acknowledged by the Assyrians as "The constituted king," (such being the meaning of his name), and he took his seat upon "the throne of his ancestors." His palace was at "Agane, a suburb of Sippara." . . . "There was born to him a son named Naram-Sin." All this and more of the same sort appears in the ninth edition of the Encyc. Brit. art. "Babylon," wherein Sargon is treated as an historical character "about B. C. 2000" who possesed a library and a catalogue. His son, Naram-Sin, is overthrown in battle by Khammuragas, another "historical " character who has left us an inscription which is now in the Louvre! After the incredibly remote dates which the Assyriologists have thrust upon us, we dare not wonder at libraries or inscriptions 4000 years old, but we certainly have a right to draw the line of credulity at Naram-Sin, in whom we clearly recognize the fourth incarnation of Vishnu; the mythical spawn of a Brahminical astrological conceit, here smuggled by ignorance into the domain of history. Cesnola found a cylinder in Cyprus bearing the name of Nara-Sin, son of Sharrukin, "who knew not his father". This last is evidently Varuguin, the third incarnation of Vishnu. Andrew Laing, "Human Origins"; M. A. R. c. I, n. 1.

B. C. 2064, Argos.—Incarnation of Cres (him of the Eight Curetes, or Danoi). Legendary æra of Dan-aus or Dan-Ies in Argos. (Dhanaus was the Indian name for the zodiacal sign of the Archer). This æra is assigned, by Herodotus, to Bacchus. Euterpe, 145.

B. C. 2064, Attica.—Censorinus reckons from the Deluge of Ogyges to the first Olympiad (Olympiadem primam) "about 600 years "   The first Olympiads were celebrated at Athens B C. 1406, q v   If to this is added one divine year, which answers to "about 600 years," we have B. C 2064 for the Deluge

B C. 2052, India —Birth of Ies Chrishna, or Buddha, (pre-Augustan date) the third avatar before that of Salivahana, B C. 78. Table B.

B. C. 2016, Greece.—Anno Mundi Eusebiano, as used in his chronology. Epoch, at midsummer   Clinton, Fasti Romani, II, 217   This æra was also used by Hieronymous   It is probably couched in the Cæsarian æra and should be B   C   2064

B C. 1965, China —Conjectural original æra of the supposed incarnation of Hoang-ti, the second messiah of the ancient Chinese mythological scheme, the first being Fo-hi with eight disciples, and the third being Yao, with twelve disciples, Hoang-ti having had ten For Fohi see B C 2637 and for Yao see B C. 1311   This year, B C 1965, is that given by Hwang-fu-mi, the Chinese astrologer (B C 300, for the incarnation of Yao, which in fact, that is to say, in the mythological scale, was one divine year later than Hoang-ti (The Chinese divine year was probably 654 common years See Chap VIII). Hoang-ti was miraculously born; ere he left the breast he could speak   To the sweetness of an infant he united the penetration and judgment of a sage   He commenced to reign when he was only twelve years of age   He invented the cycle which reconciles the ancient divisions of Ten with the later divisions of Twelve; he erected temples; instituted Ninths to support the priesthood, encouraged agriculture and the culture of the silk-worm, he introduced the com-. pass, abacus, decimal system, knife-money, uniform weights and measures, etc   One of his disciples, Chao-hao, suppressed a religious insurrection; introduced church music, established the nine classes, five of whom were to govern the five guilds of artisans and the others to preside over tillage and—like the Roman emperors of a later period—regulate the manners of the people.   Another disciple, Tchuen-hio, regulated the mines (this is probably meant to include money); joined the crown to the pontificate; extirpated heretics; reformed the canon law; regulated the choice of animals for sacrifice; reorganized the priesthood; and altered the calendar, beginning the year "on the first day of the month in which the Sun should be nearest the fifteenth degree of Aquarius." Du Halde.   All this, except the Ten disciples, is clearly of a post-Jovian and post-Buddhic date.   See B. C 2687 and 2627.

B. C. 1913, India.—Erroneous æra of the Calijoga, computed by Hales. See B. C. 3102.

B. C. 1905, India.—Erroneous æra of the Calijoga, computed by Hales. See B. C. 3102.

B. C. 1897, Judea.—Miraculous conception of Sarai, who is married to Abram, her half-brother, (Gen. XX, 20). When Abram is 99 years old and Sarai is 90, they converse familiarly with God (Gen. XXVII and XXVIII), who thereupon promises Abram a child, to be born exactly a year later. (Gen. XXVII, 21). That a year in this place originally meant ten months, is deducible from the Chaldean word Sar, which, says Rev. Dr. Greswell, is the root of saros, and therefore also of Sarai, or Sarah, meaning ten. This son, the miraculous issue of the Creator and Sarai, (Gen. XXI, 1, 2) was called Isaac. Abram was afterwards ordered to sacrifice this son and he obeyed; but at the critical moment his hand was arrested by the Creator and Isaac was saved. Abram lived to the age of 175 and Sarai 127 years. Most of the details of this mythos are of Hindu origin. Abram or Bram is an impersonation of the Creator; Isaac is the Hindu sun-god Ies-aac, which is still the name of one of the Hindu months; the marriage of brother and sister was a distinguishing characteristic of the Oriental, and Egyptian, and even of the Peruvian incarnations; the full year, or ten months, of gestation, is another one; the order for the destruction of the divine child; his imminent peril; and his providential escape from impending death—these and other features of the story—are evidently oriental and astrological; and they cannot be accepted as history. It is not difficult to recognise in them a distorted account of the ninth incarnation of Brahma, which fell due B. C. 1864, just 33 years after the date assigned by the scriptural chronologers to the conception of Sarai. See Table A.

B. C. 1869, Argos.—Æra of Inachus, the reputed founder of the kingdom of Argos, in the Peloponnesus, "Betwixt the 2120th and 2150th year of the World." Bell's Pantheon. As Bell's Anno Mundi was B. C. 4000 this would fix the æra of Inachus about B. C. 1869. Inachus was one of the names of Bacchus, whose cult is asserted to have been introduced into Argos from Crete. The Inachia were Cretan festivals in honour of this divinity. The date assigned to Inachus by Bell is probably the invention of a long subsequent age.

B. C. 1864, India.—Ninth avatar of Brahma, or Vishnu. See Table A, chap. VI.

B. C. 1847, Egypt.—Phœnix Æra, or first (original) Julian cal-

endar, or calendar of 365¼ days to the year, beginning Thoth 1st,
or Nov 18th, B C 1848, afterwards altered to Tybi 7th or March
24th, B C 1847, from which date its author calls it the Epoch of
the sphere of Mazzaroth. Rev Edwd. Greswell, F C, I, 552
As Dr Greswell failed to observe the change from the year of ten to
that of twelve months, in Egypt and elsewhere, the æras he deduces,
when they are older than the eighth century B C, are only of literary interest and have no historical value

B C. 1786, India —Augustan date of the Brahminical Ies
Chrisnna, the ninth avatar of Brahma, afterwards called Iesnu or
Vishnu, this being the termination of his manvantara. This was anciently regarded as the final metamorphosis of Vishnu, when the
world would be destroyed and the human race brought to judgment,
a prediction whose failure must have greatly weakened the foundations of the Brahminical system   The Banians, though they accepted
this system, yet believed in a tenth manvantara, that of Kalpi, who
was to appear in future and whose zodion is a winged horse, three of
whose feet rest apon the earth, while the fourth paws the air   When
this foot descends upon our planet (time not fixed), the end will
come   Noel, "Dic Fable"   See B C 1332 and 1315   The system of nine (or ten) incarnations has been greatly extended by the
Brahmo-Buddhists

B. C 1650, India —Remotest probable æra of the Mahabharata
wars   Pococke, 149-51, prefers B C 1480, Wilson says B C 1430;
Wilford says B C 1370; Prinseps, "Useful Tables," 217, says B C
1367; Robertson's "India," p 329, says "before 2000 B C.;" but
this is inadmissible. See below, year 1430.

B. C. 1650, India.—At some indefinite period the 60-year cycles
of Yao (China) were adopted in Egypt.   Martin, "Hist Sinica," p.
14, Bunsen's "Egypt," III, 385, *n*   For reasons given above and in
"Middle Ages," Appendix P, n 14, it is believed that these cycles
were not actually employed in India until long after the Mahabharata
wars   Their employment in Egypt must be assigned to a very much
later date.

B C 1590, India —Epoch of the "Line of the Rishis," constellation of Ursa-Major, commencing with the first of Magha, as
fixed by observation at that time, according to Brennand, "Hindu
Astronomy," p. 82.   For further information on this subject see chap.
VIII herein.

B C 1528, Egypt.—Æra of Busiris, a king or lieutenant under
and contemporaneous with Osiris, according to Orosius, who fixes

the æra of Busiris at 775 years before the foundation of Rom.e Eusebius fixes the same æra at about 700 years before the foundation of Rome. On the other hand, Eratosthenes, cited in Strabo, declares that there never was a king or tyrant called Busiris. The name is probably a variant of Hesiris, Osiris, etc. See B. C. 1235. The æra is anachronical.

B. C. 1506, Athens.—The image of the Mother of the Gods is brought from Mount Cybele. The Parian marbles. This is a Scythian date, probably connected with Targitaus, Tages, Taygetus, etc., and adopted by the Athenians during the Solonic period. See 1495.

B. C. 1495, Scythia.—The first king of the Scythians was Targitaus, who according to Herodotus lived "just a thousand years" before Darius Hystaspes invaded their country. As the last-named event occurred in B. C. 495, this would fix the æra of Targitaus in B. C. 1495. Targitaus is evidently a name of Buddha. "As one of the Tathagates he preached to all mankind the mystery of suffering." Trübner's "Oriental Record," 1889, No. 243, p. 5. The Etruscans, whose Divine Years occurred in B. C. 1474, 816, etc., worshipped a Divine Child whose brow was adorned with the Sacred Ram's horns and whose name was Tages. F. A. David, "Antiquites Etrusques," V, pl. 57. There is a possible connection between these two divinities; also with the cult of Tay-getus, Son of Jupiter in Laconia, because Targitaus was also the Son of Jupiter, the Supreme God. Herodotus, Melpomene, 5. In Terpsichore, 3, the same author says, that the Getæ, or Scythians, were, next after the Indians, the greatest nation on earth. Diodorus Siculus makes a similar remark. Pococke proves that they colonised Greece and Etruria.

B. C. 1480, India.—Mahabharata Wars. Pococke, 149-51.

B. C. 1451, Judea.—Nativity of Moses, 1571; promulgates the Ten Commandments, 1494; ascends bodily to heaven, 1454. Haydn. See B. C. 509.

B. C. 1448, India.—Erroneous date of the Calijoga. Rev. Wm. Hales, "Chronology." See B. C. 3102.

B. C. 1432, Candia.—Iron found on Mt. Ida by Jasius and the Dactyles. The Parian marbles. But see B. C. 1406 and 1394.

B. C. 1430, India.—Mahabharata æra. Prof. Wilson, Analysis of the Puranas, As. Jour. XIII, 81. Pococke, 149. See B. C. 1650.

B. C. 1430, Eypt.—Conjectural æra of the tablets of Tel-el-Amarna, according to Dr. Sam'l Birch, in "Records of the Past,"

New Series, II, 57   This date is based upon the fancied resemblance of Nahrima, mentioned in one of the tablets and Chushanrishathaim, in Judges, III, 8, a clue whose little worth is admitted by Dr Birch himself, op. cit., III, 55.   These tablets constituted part of the official records at Thebes, whence they were removed to Tel-el-Amarna, a place midway between Minieh and Siout, on the east bank of the Nile.   They are stamped with the cuneiform letter, in the Babylonian language, which hitherto has only been imperfectly mastered and translated.   Many of the expressions in them point to a date several centuries lower than that conjectured by Dr Birch   They were discovered in A D. 1887.   See æra of the Hycsos, B. C 1106.

B. C. 1426, India.—Year when the Equinoctial point V E was in Crittica (one of the Pleiads)   Crittica now marks the third, whereas formerly it marked and gave its name to the first, nachshatra.   Colebrooke   This was a period of great activity in Hindu astronomy   It was also the period when Mercury, Venus, Mars and Jupiter were in occultation, B. C. 1424-6   Brennand.   Laplace appears to prefer fixing the period of astronomical activity in B C 1491   At all events there is a substantial agreement between Jones, Bailly, Laplace, Colebrooke, Bentley and Burgess that in the 15th century B C. the Hindus were acquainted with the equable year, the nodical cycle, the Precession of the Equinoxes and the period of Jupiter   These phenomena form the astronomical bases of the astrology of the Hindu Ies Chrishna, the Egyptian Hes-iris, the Greek Jasius and the Roman Janus

B. C. 1406, Assyria.—Incarnation of Nin-Ies, or Ninus, probably invented during the eighth to fifth century B C   See B C 2064.   Ninus was foretold by prophets; his celestial father was Ies; his putative father was Belus of the royal line of Ies, his virgin mother was Semiramis, although the Rev Alex. Hislop says her name was Rhaah, or Rhea, the Gazing Mother, his star was the Messianic; he was born at the Vernal equinox amidst flowers and the sounds of heavenly music; he was recognised as the Messiah by the seers or astrologers; his head was surrounded by a nimbus of light; he performed numerous miracles; his favorite disciple, of whom he had ten, afterwards 12, was Argon or Arjon; and after saving the world from sin he was persecuted and crucified to death at Babylon on the winter solstice, descended to hell; rose again after three days and nights, and finally ascended bodily to heaven   His principal sacrament was baptism, his epigraphic symbols were the + and † and his zodion was the Lamb.   The æra and worship of Ninus, like that of Belus, were probably instituted many centuries after the date ascribed to him on the monuments.

B. C. 1406, Crete.—Æra of Jasius, Lord of the Ten Incarnations of the Sun. These "incarnations" (his followers) were afterwards called the Ten Dactyles of Mount Ida, the inventors of iron and founders of the pentaeteris or five-year Olympiads, sometimes called Panathenæa, mentioned by Diodorus and by Plutarch in Theseus. Diodorus, V, 4, says that the Dactyles "practiced sacred rites and mysteries," and were "adored and worshipped as Gods." The years were of ten months each. Potter, Ant. Gr. I, 507. Hence the pentaeteris were celebrated every 50 months. This year, 1406, was exactly one astrological cycle (658 years) before the incarnation of Tiglath-pil-Esar II, the Nebo-Nazaru of the Chaldeans. Censorinus; Noël, Dic. de la Fable; Townsend, Dic. Dates, p. 499. The Ten Dactyles were preceded, or else followed by the Nine Curetes, priests of Cybele. Diodorus says the Dactyles were followed by the Curetes, but as both were imaginary, and only relate to matters of belief, the order of precedence is only important when it relates to the history of the belief. The five-year Olympiads were "revived" by Iphitus, B. C. 884, q. v. Pausanias, Eliacs, V. 4, 8; Potter's Ant. Gr. I, 507. The names of the Ten Dactyles partly from Pausanias and partly from Strabo were Jasius, Hercules, Peoneus, Epimedes, Idas, Carybas, Hercules (Mercury?), Salaminus, Damnaneus and Acmon. Hercules is repeated, while Mercury is omitted. Pausanias names Pyrrhicus as one of the Curetes.

B. C. 1406, Attica.—Eleusinian æra. Myth of the Thracian (Scythic) king Eric-Theos, Eric-Theus, or Eric-thonius, Son of Vulcan and Athena, mother of gods. Union of the (Twelve) states of Attica. "The Emolpides, or descendants of the High Buddha Priest, were now appointed to the administration of the holy rites." Pococke, 270. Cf. Jamieson, 40; Strabo, Geog. VII, VIII, and X. Greswell, Kal. H., IV, 11. "Eu-mol-pides" was afterwards converted into "Eumolpus, the first hierophant." The scheme is astrological and anachronical. The Eleusinian festival was originally held on the winter solstice and, after the Seleucidan æra, on the autumnal equinox. It was observed down to the year A. D. 396. Townsend; Pausanias, Eliacs, V, 4, 8; Potter's Ant. Gr. I, 507. See B. C. 1346, 1219 and 776. Townsend (Dic. Dates) says that Ericthonius introduced silver into Attica. This is a feature of the messianic myth, which ascribes all good things to the Messiah.

B. C. 1406, Attica.—Greswell. Kal. Hell. I, pref., alludes to "the Athenian solemnity" of B C. 1342 Add the 63 or 64 years dropped from the Roman calendar and we have B C. 1406, the æra of Jasius and the Eleusinia.

B. C. 1406, Egypt.—Deification of Ousurt Esen, sovereign-pontiff, XIIth dynasty. Perrot and Chipiez, p. 335 The date is gained approximately by allowing an average of 12 or 14 years to the reign of each of the kings mentioned by Bunsen in his correction of Manetho's dynasties It is fixed precisely in B C 1406, because that is the christian date of the Assyrian and Greek incarnations. (Table C.) Bunsen, by allowing 33 years to each reign, carries Ousurt-Esen back to the 24th century B C , but there is nothing to justify such a computation

B. C. 1394, Scythia.—Marina, queen of the Amazons, over-runs Cilicia, Syria, Arabia and Egypt, in which last-named country she makes a treaty with Horus, the miraculous offspring of Osiris and Isis. On her way to Asia, Marina worships the Mother of God at Samothrace, and grants freedom to Cilicia She builds many cities, including Mitylene in Lesbos Upon her return from Egypt she passed through Phrygia and settled at Marina, a place which she named, on the river Caicus, between Pergamus and Larissa Here she was attacked by the Thracians, who killed her and drove her army into Libya, where it perished Diodorus Siculus. This is a Scythian legend connected with the worship of the Matrem Deorum, which Tacitus observed was practiced by the Scythian tribes of the Baltic and of which very ancient traces will be found scattered all through Scythia, from Bactria, westward to Scandinavia and Thrace The year above attached to the legend of Marina is the Hindu date of the birth of Ies Chrishna, the first Buddha (Table B)

B. C. 1394, India.—Hindu re-incarnation, reckoning backward from Salivahana (Table C) Probable period of the discovery of iron and steel in the Orient See B C 1432 for a pretended earlier discovery in Candia

B. C. 1391, India.—Parasara's astronomical observations go back to this date Rev Ch Pritchard; who also assigns the Vedas and the Mahabharata wars to the same period Parasara's observations were probably designed to commence with the birth of Ies Chrishna, or the "First" Buddha " (See above, year 1394) The three years' variation are explained in " Middle Ages Revisited," ch VIII and App. S. See B. C. 1181 and B. C. 576.

B. C. 1390, Assyria.—Incarnation of Belus, or Bel-Issus (See above, years 2235 and 2064) A small stone cylinder in the British

Museum is ascribed to Budi-ela, "king of Assyria," and is dated by the Museum authorities "B. C. 1350." All the dates connected with the worship of Belus are anachronical. The cult of Belus is probably not older than the 12th century, B. C. This messiah was variously called Belus, Bel, Bel-Esus, Bala, and Baal. His coming was foretold in the sacred books of Chaldea. The name of his celestial father is given by the Greek writers as Jasus, or else Acrisius. His putative father was Ies; his virgin mother was Semiramis, or Astarte. His birthplace, in Baalbec, was indicated by the Messianic star which stood over it. He was born on the vernal equinox (the festival of beltane) to the accompaniment of flowers and heavenly music. He was recognized as the Expected One by the astrologers, (belephantes). Accompanied by his faithful disciple. Oannes, one of ten, he performed many miracles, which were recorded in the now lost sacred scriptures of his native county. For preaching strange doctrines he was crucified in his 33d year, on the winter solstice; descended to hell; whence he rose again and ascended bodily to heaven. His principal sacrament was baptism, both by water and fire; his epigraphic symbol, the cross, which appears on numerous Assyrian and Chaldean cylinders; and his zodions were the Bull and Ram (belier). Many remains of this cult still exist in the popular customs of the older states of Asia Minor and Europe; some perhaps in the British Isles. Among several æras ascribed to Belus, ranging from B. C. 2064 to B. C. 1390, the lowest one has been selected, as being the most plausible, though even this one is probably too ancient.

B. C. 1370, India.—End of the Mahabharata wars. Col. Wilford; Pococke, 149 n.

B. C. 1370, India.—Erroneous æra of the Calijoga. Rev. Wm. Hales. See B. C. 3102.

B. C. 1366, India.—"Earliest Buddha," according to Prinseps, "Useful Tables," p. 164. "Brahminical æra of Buddha," according to Asiatic Researches, vol. II. This is the "First Buddha" of the Hindu pantheon, and there are many indications that the date is more or less correct, though the mythos evidently belongs to Ies Chrishna. This Messiah was foretold by prophets; he was the son of the Holy Spirit and the Virgin Maia; he was born in the village or town of Rajagriha; was recognised and worshipped by the Magi and by kings; the messianic star stood over the place of his nativity; a brilliant nimbus of light surrounded the holy infants' head; his complexion was black; his hair woolly; he was prematurely wise, and as he grew up, his doctrines, embodied in the Puranas, were promulgated by ten disciples Though he came to reform mankind and save the world, he was himself persecuted by the reigning king, who caused him to be crucified at the age of 33 years To judge the dead, Buddha descended to the nether world where he remained three days and nights. Then he arose and ascended bodily to heaven His sacraments were the eucharist and baptism, his epigraphic symbols were the cross and svastica; his zodion was the Bull; and his images are represented in a sitting posture, cross-legged.

B. C. 1350, India.—"Modern computation" of the date when the vernal equinox corresponded with the first point of Cartica, the Hindu-date being 1426. Brennand's "Hindu Astronomy," London, 1896, p 54 See Chapter IX herein.

B. C. 1350, Egypt.—First æra of Ies-iris (or Osiris) and Isis Epoch, 1st Thoth, then the 22nd July, agreeing with the heliacal rising of Sothis in Heliopolis at that period (We would prefer B C 1250 to B C. 1350) The orthography of Ies-iris is so given by Hellanicus, who visited Egypt during the 5th century B C. (Plutarch, "Isis and Osiris," 34). Sothis, called by the Greeks Sirius, was the star of Heavenly Conception; sothis meaning conception Isis was both the Wife and Mother of the Sun; Ies-iris was the progeny, his name signifying Son of God The names of the twelve months of the year cannot be traced higher than this date Rev. Dr. Greswell, Fasti Cath , III, 138, 170, 193; Kal Hell , IV , 131-3 Dr. Greswell may have safely extended this last observation another astrological cycle of 658 years later The names of the twelve months do not appear to be older than the 7th century B. C., and all western monuments which mention them and profess to be of an older date must be regarded with suspicion The 12 signs (and therefore inferentially the 12 months) are ascribed to Anaximander of Miletus, B C 610-547. Sir Wm Jones declared that the Greeks and Arabians derived their zodiacs from the Indians. So did the Egyptians. The Twelve months are distinctly Buddhic and are certainly not older than the second Buddhic æra See B C 692. Some writers say that the celestial father of Osiris was Ammon, or Amen; others say Seb, or Set, others again, that his putative father was Menuis His mother's name is variously given as Isis, Neith, or Nout, and Marionymous, or the Thousand-named His natal star was Sirius; his natal day was at one period fixed at the winter solstice Plutarch in ancient times and Haliburton in modern, (F. D 30, 32) fixed the resurrection of Osiris in our November These variant dates may be due to the change from a ten to a twelve months year, or to some other alterations of the calendar. Osiris was sun-rayed; his complexion was black, and his hair was woolly. He was included in a slaughter of innocents ordered by Typhon, from which he of course escaped. His legitimacy was proved by numerous miracles; some of his doctrines appear in the Book of the Dead; the number of his disciples was 10, afterwards 12; he was crucified on the vernal equinox (probably an altered date;) he descended to hell, where he remained three days and nights to judge the dead, and he rose again and ascended bodily to heaven. His principal sacrament was baptism; his emblems were the "Latin" cross, the crux ansata and the Christian monogram, while his zodion was the Bull or Calf (Apis). His name is variously written Osiris, Hes-iris, Ies-iris and Em-esa. Ies-iris (from Hellenicus) is probably correct. Em-esa as the equivalent of Orisis is given by the Edinburgh Review, July, 1893.

B. C. 1346, Greece.—Panathenaic calendar of Ericthonius, July 21. Greswell, F. C. I, 553. "Panathenaic" is doubtful.

B. C. 1336, India.—First Buddhic æra, according to Abul-Fazl. The Pandits' "Chron." See B. C. 1366.

B. C. 1334, Troy.—Fall of Troy, oldest date; but see B. C. 1292 and 1248.

B. C. 1332, India.—Approximate æra of Maryamma, wife of Jamadagni, a village carpenter, and the virgin mother of Ies Chrishna, the ninth incarnation of Iesnu, or Vishnu. The name of this divinity is written Maryamma by Oppert and Mariatala by Noël. The latter regards her as the mother of Parasurama; the former as the sister of Ies Chrishna. Oppert explains that amma means mother; hence Maryamma means Mother Mary. She is also called Ganagamma, or Ganga-gamma, Mother of God, and has many other names. She is worshipped all over India, especially at Canaanur, in Trichinopoly, Chrishna's birthplace. Annnal festivals to her honour are celebrated with great solemnity on the seventh day of the light fortnight of the month of Sravana. This brings the beginning of the festival to the day before Ourgati Tirounal, or birth-day of Ies Chrishna, which day, the use of a lunar calendar, has shifted about three weeks back from Aswin 1st. The festival is called Sitalasaptami and lasts seven days. At these festivals Maryamma is carried about on a gorgeous car with the same pomp as are the statues of Vishnu and Iesora, the latter being the god with the Bleeding Heart. "*On célèbre sa fête avec beaucoup de solemnité, et on le mène en procession sur un char avec autant de pompe que les grands dieux*

Vishnu et Ixora " (Noel) Ordinarily the sacrifices consist of buffalo bulls, heifers, or black rams, but there have been occasions when human victims were immolated, by being persuaded to throw themselves under the car, similar to the practice of Juggernaut. Until forbidden by the British authorities, hook-swinging, as an act of piety and penitence, by her worshippers, was common; and in spite of the legal interdict, a sacrifice of this character occurred recently in Colavandan. Maiyamma is also worshipped daily in the form of a black stone called Baddukal, which is regarded as a sort of household deity among the Indian villagers, each of whom possesses one The worship of Maryamma anciently became so popular among the Sudra class that the Brahmins, who were unwilling to kneel to the same divinity as their inferiors, reduced her caste by circulating the following legend Maryamma was the principal one of the nine saktis (graces) and was originally placed by the supreme deity in command of the elements, an empire which she could retain only so long as she remained unchanged When her commerce with the grand-overs (winged spirits of the air; auræ; sylphs) was discovered, Jamadagni persuaded his son to deprive his Holy Mother of life The request was obeyed, but Parasurama's grief for his mother was so intense that his putative father permitted him to recall the goddess to life She was accordingly resurrected, to the great joy of Parasurama (or Ies Chrishna), who, however, in joining the decapitated head of his mother to a human form selected the body of a Sudra woman, so that Maiyamma was no longer holy enough for the worship of high caste Brahmins The Sudra class make up for this by placing Maryamma above the supreme deity While the Brahmins insist that she is now only a goddess to invoke heaven against diseases and especially the small-pox, the Pariahs venerate her and her infant son as the most exalted of all the divinities, " *Les Parias partagent leurs adorations entre sa mère et lui . . . qui la mettent au dessus de Dieu* " (Noel) Her symbol is a branch of the margosa, which in all cases of sickness is suspended over the bed of the sufferer The cocoanut, which is thrown and broken on the threshold of the temple, offerings of myrr and frakincense, the wood of the Nimb tree, upon which Ies Chrishna suffered; and the custom of treading on embers and walking through bonfires, are also peculiar to her worship She is the only deity to whom salted fish and other cooked dishes are offered "She removes the sin of those who address her with the holy five letters, pancasara" Like the Greek Medusa, the hair of Maryamma is made of twisted serpents, these animals being an object of sacerdotal significance to the Hindus. (So were they to the Assyrians, Egyptians, Greeks and Romans, as witness the stories of the conceptions of their various incarnations). The rites of Maryamma have undoubtedly been altered since their first inception. The length of the annual festival, which is now seven days, was probably nine days in more ancient times. The worship of Maryamma can be traced from India into Asia Minor, with the Urtuki Turcomans or Venetians, of Pontus and Bithynia, who, many centuries before our æra, raised a shrine to her at Piscenus in Mariandynia, a province which was doubtless named after this goddess. As in India, she was worshipped at Piscenus in the form of a black stone; probably an æreolite. This sacred stone having been captured and removed to Elam by a King of Assyria, was afterwards restored by Assur-bani-pal, in B. C. 645, q. v. We next find the worship of Maryamma utilized by the deified Cyrus of Persia, who bestowed her revered name upon his own mother, a device which was imitated by Alexander the Great, who conferred upon his mother the sacred name of Olympia. See B. C. 533. The Tauri, probably related to the Iesyges, established the worship of Maryamma in the Crimea and the vicinity. See B. C. 658. At a later period this venerable goddess was removed from Piscenus to Rome, where she became an object of profound adoration to the pious, especially to those of the gentler sex. See B. C. 205. The black stone of the Caaba, in Mecca, appears to be related to the same worship. The Matrem Deorum subsequently made her way into Gaul (see B. C. 470) and the Gothic countries of the Baltic (Tacitus), in all of which places she was the especial divinity of the poor and afflicted. Gustav Oppert, op. cit.; Fr. Fawcett, "Festivals to Village Goddesses" in Jour. Anthrop. Soc. of Bombay, II, 164-224; and the other authorities above cited. Mr. Fawcett's account includes the significant circumstance that the services at the annual festival to Maryamma have to be conducted by a carpenter. Mr. Oppert copied all of Fawcett's account verbatim except the sentence which mentions the carpenter.

B. C. 1332, India.—Birth of Ies Chrishna, the ninth incarnation of Iesnu, or Vishnu. Some authors say B. C. 1315. (See B. C. 1786.) The name is spelt by the Abbé Raynal as Christna. The name of the sacred river of India upon which his principal temple stands is spelt Kristna. This is also the name given to his images in the Musée Guimet. Father Sonnerat, "Voy. aux Indes." I, 30, says it is written in the various idioms of India as follows: Crisnen,

Criten, Crixnou, and Quichena, all of these words meaning *black*.
Noel gives Kistner for another variant   Crixnou is probably the
origin of the Greek Ischenou, while Quichena is that of the Roman
Quirinus, from which comes the existing Quirinal   The advent of
Chrishna was foretold in the sacred books, also by Nared, the astrologer   His celestial father is variously called Ies-saca and Brahma,
his putative father, Josa, Jesa, Nanda and Jamadagni   Some authorities say that the latter was a carpenter; others, a shepherd.   He
was of the royal line of Yadu or Yudava   Chrishna's virgin mother's name is variously given as Maiyamma, Maritala, Mai, Lakshmi,
Decki, Devaci, Adita and Vasudeva   The Messianic star indicated
the place of Chrishna's birth, which took place at Canaanur, or
Mathura (Brahmin) or Gorakpore (Buddhic), and on the winter solstice.   He was born in a cave, among cowherds   The nativity was
ushered in with flowers and music.   He was recognized by the Magi
and presented with gifts of sandal wood and perfumes   At the period
of the nativity his putative father was called away to pay the taxes
Chrishna's head shone with a divine effulgence, his complexion was
black and his hair woolly   A slaughter of the innocents was ordered
by King Kansa with the object of destroying the infant Messiah,
who, however, escaped   He was transfigured and performed many
miracles   The doctrines which he preached are contained in the
Vedas and Puranas   These caused his betrayal and death   He partook of a last supper with his ten disciples and was condemned to
death by Kansa and crucified at Kusinara, upon a Nimb tree, on the
Vernal equinox in the 33rd year of his age   To judge the dead he
descended to the nether world (bhuvana) where he sojourned three
days and nights, after which he reappeared upon earth, only to
ascend bodily to heaven (mocksha)   This event is commemorated
by the festival of Houli, for which see B C 1219   His principal
sacraments were the eucharist and baptism; his epigraphic symbols
were the cross, the bee and the mystic letters O M, or A U M;
his zodion was the Bull.   His favorite disciple was Ar-joona, or Ar-
jun; some say Jain; others, Jon   His carne-vale (masupadu) lasted
exactly 40 days   At his death the sun was eclipsed, the earth shook
with violent commotions and ghosts stalked the highways   His favorite plant, or that of his followers, was the margosa, or passion-
flower   The sole of his foot was marked with the lotus   The attribute of his images was the spotted fawn-skin mantle   The sign of
his future or last coming will be his re-appearance as Kalpa, mounted
upon a white horse

B. C. 1332, India.—Æra used by Kalhana Pandit, in his "History of Cashmir." Prinsep. This is evidently the æra of the Buddhic Ies Chrishna, whose later incarnation Ramchandra Gosha fixes in B. C. 644.

B. C. 1331, Samos.—Pelasgian æra. Approximate date of the colonisation of Cipar-Issa, afterwards called Samos, by an Oriental race from Pontus, who are known by the name of Pelasgi, and who appear to have been connected with the Iesiges of the Cimmerian Bosphorus, the Iesiges of Tarentum, the Phœnicians, the Veneti, the Leuco-Syrians, etc., in short, an Oriental maritime and trading race, who previous to the rise of the Greek power, established a series of factories or trading-posts stretching from the Palus Maeotis along the Southern shores of the Pontus and the Byzantine Bosphorus to the Ægean sea and afterwards along the coasts and upon the islands of the Mediterranean to the Western Ocean. The date is deduced from several circumstances:

1: Thucydides (Intro.) says that before the Trojan war the Pelasgians occupied the principal coasts of the Levant.

2: The foundation of Cadiz by the Phœnicians, among whom must be included the Samians, is ascribed to the year 1101, and it must have taken many years to found the series of intermediate island colonies which enabled them to push thus far westward.

3: The Samians worshipped Jasion and the Eight Cabiri, or Children of the Sun. At the head of these Disciples was Dardanos, the god or genius of the Sea. (The Prince of Mingrelia, in Colchis, who rules a remnant of this ancient race, still calls himself the Dardianos, or Ruler of the Sea. He is again mentioned below.) The relation between Jasion and Dardanos in the Samian cult seems to have been similar to that of the Ies Chrishna and Jain of the Hindus, or that of Messiah and Disciple. For these sacred characters, the Greeks, when they supplanted the Iesiges in the Crimea, substituted the Dioscurii. The period of the cult of Ies Chrishna and Jain in Rajputana and Guzerat, varies from B. C. 1332 to B. C. 1219.

4: The year 1331 marks the re-incarnation of Buddha, (Table B), a period when it is most likely that a schism would arise in the Buddho-Brahminical church and when new forms and mysteries of worship and the migration of non-conformists would take place.

A peculiar custom appears to connect the ancient trading race of Pontus, Samos and Venetia: that of marrying the sea with a ring. A remnant of the Pontine race, who were driven by the Romans from the Cimmerian Bosphorus into the mountains of Colchis, existed

so late as the 17th century of our æra and perhaps exists yet.   The
Prince of Mingrelia still called himself Lord of the Sea and annually
wedded the ocean with a ring, though he possessed neither a sea-port
nor a ship   Malte Brun, I, 304   The story of Polycrates and the
emerald ring which he cast into the sea, is evidently a Greek perversion of the custom which that commander probably found and suppressed or modified at Samos   Pliny says that the ring of Polycrates
was shown at Rome in his day, but he evidently doubted the Greek
story and regarded the ring as spurious   The later custom of the
doges of Venice is well known, and though it is said to have been
invented by one of the five Popes of the year 1197, it was in fact
extremely ancient   Samos is said to have been successfully invaded
by the Ionians under Proclis about B C 1050 and to have had factories or emporia at Perinthus, (Propontis), Nagidus and Celendaria
(Cilicia).   After this invasion, Samos became a member of the Ionic
confederacy

By the end of the 7th century B. C the Samians were so much
behind the age as to be obliged to send to Corinth for Aminocles, a
Greek ship-wright, that he might build ships for them   (Thucydides)
In B C 639 Colæus, a Samian captain with a Greek crew, was driven
westward to Tartessus, near the mouth of the Guadalquiver and
made a profit of 60 talents by trading with the natives   Herod Mel.
52; the date being computed by the Encyc Brit   Samos possessed
what Herodotus considered the largest temple in Asia Minor   This
was erected to an Asiatic goddess, the Matrem Deorum, whom the
Greeks call Demeter, or Hera, and whose image, as seen upon coins,
resembled the goddess of Ephesus   Samos was famous for its trading
fleet, the art of casting images in bronze, which was here first practised in the Western world and for its pottery or Samian ware   The
principal divinity of Samos, Jasion, invented the Mysteries, patron-
ised the culture of the vine and generally possessed the attributes of
Hermes or Dionysius   Herod. Thalia, 41, Pliny, xxxiii, 6; xxxvii, 2,
Cicero, de Fin , iv

It can scarcely be doubted that it was the race of traders and
navigators here alluded to, whether called Pelasgii, or by some
local or else characteristic name, who introduced from the Orient
into the West the Brahminical theory of divine incarnations, media-
tors, or messiahs   Leaving out of view writings, because writings
are easily forged, the earliest valid monuments of the West are not
only later than those of the East, they are later than the invention of
avatars, or incarnations; for they all bear some impress of this

mystery. The superior learning, skill and resources of the Phœnicians naturally provided a ready acceptance for their religion. But after they had accepted it and modified or coloured it with their own myths, the natives everywhere evinced an anxiety to get rid of their teachers; perhaps in order that their own versions of Chres, Jasius, Jason, and Dionysius might go unchallenged. The desire to supplant their envied visitors in the lucrative trade of the Orient and of the Western coasts might have had no small share in this resolution. However this may be, the Assyrians, the Egytians and the Greeks attacked them upon every occasion or pretext that offered; yet it was not until after some centuries of exhausting resistance that the Phœnicians were eventually overcome. In the 6th century B. C. the Greeks captured the Phœnician cities of the Ægean and of the Pontus, eastward to Colchis and the Palus Mæotis; whilst the Egyptians under Necho cut a canal through the Isthmus of Suez and diverted the oriental trade, or at least a portion of it, into the Red Sea. Even when the power of the Greek States declined and the remnants of the Phœnician communities along the coasts of Europe and Asia Minor once more raised their heads, they were assailed by a new set of conquerors, the Romans, with the same bitterness that had characterized the Greeks, Egyptians and Assyrians. They were all but extirpated at Tarentum, Lissa, Santa Maura, Corfu, Trapesus and other places along the coasts of Greece, Italy and Pontus. Almost the latest identification of this people was at Samos, B.C. 36 (?) when Marc Antony, the Roman Bacchus, made that port the refuge of his fleet.

B. C. 1322, Egypt.—Thoth 1st. Egyptian æra, evidently taken from the Nebu-Nazarian epoch of the Sothiacal period ending with the Divine Year A. D. 139. Censorinus. Cf. Theon Alexandrinus, (4th cent.) as quoted by Biot, "Recherches, sur l'astronomie Egyptienne," Paris, 1823, p. 303. The equivalent Roman day, July 22nd, is given by Greswell, F. C. III, 158. In the Alexandrian Augustan calendar Thoth 1st corresponded with August 29th, the birthday of the Indian Dennus and long afterwards the day of Augustus' Ascension. Theon gives this year as the æra of Meno-phres or Menephres, who is unknown to history. The scheme is essentially Chaldean and astrological. Cf. Hales, Chron., p. 40; Prinsep, Ind. Ant. II, 140; Records of the Past, II, 208; and Plutarch, De Is. et Os., xiii; xlii; xliii. Biot's year for this æra shows the 15-year discrepancy between the Augustan and Christian calendars.

B. C. 1315, India.—Era of Ies Chrishna, of his death, according to ancient Indian dates, of his birth, according to Augustan dates. His coming was predicted or foretold by prophets; he was born of a Virgin; at Mathura; cradled and fostered by shepherds; concealed soon after his birth for fear of being destroyed by the tyrant Kansa, who had ordered all the male children to be slaughtered, etc All this is sculptured at Elephanta "Over the head of the principal figure of the group (which portrays the Slaughter of the Innocents) are to be seen the mitre, the crosier and the cross." Higgins, Anacal I, 133, Chrishna, though he had a staunch friend who stood by him in all his trials and sufferings, yet he died a martyr on the cross, descended into hell; returned to earth; and finally ascended to heaven. Maurice, II, 149 "The statue of Chrishna at Mathura is black; and the temple is built in the form of a cross " Crawford's "Researches," II, 18. His hair was woolly; and he is so depicted in all the Indian paintings and statues.

B. C. 1312, Chorasmia.—Foundation æra of the Chorasmians, or Kwar-Ismians, 980 years before Alexander the Great Albiruni's "Chronology," ed Sachau, p 39 The Chorasmii were a great and rich nation of Sacæ, who dwelt in Bactria, on the Oxus, south of the Aral and east of the Caspian sea They worshipped the Sun, to whom they sacrificed horses, says Strabo, XI, viii, 6 to 8. They also worshipped the incarnations of the Sun, especially Ies Chrishna, for whose æra this year is evidently meant. The principal city of the khanate was Khiva

B. C. 1311, China.—Conjectural original æra of Yao, the third Messiah of the ancient Chinese mythological scheme, the first being Fo-hi and the second Hoang-ti The various dates assigned to Yao by Chinese native authorities are B C 2411, 2337, 2334, 2331, 2326, 2303, 2264, 2145, 2145, 2132, 1965, the last being that of the astrologer Hwang-fu-mi From this date, which, though the lowest of any, is evidently far too ancient, we have ventured to subtract one Chinese "phen," or divine year, which appears to have been equal to 654 common years (See Chap VIII) Yao was assisted or supported in his reign by Chun, or John. Yao was a wise and virtuous (mythological) ruler, whom, together with his Twelve disciples, the Chinese converted into actual emperors, adding four or five more to the line, whom they probably took from the mythological followers of Hoang-ti to enrich Yao It was in the reign of this fabulous being that the Deluge, hung-shway, took place, as described in the "Shu-king" Between the native dates above given and some of those brought to Europe by Du Halde and other Jesuit missionaries, there is a difference of exactly 63 years. Compare B. C. 2474 and 2397 with 2411 and 2334. With other dates the difference is 73 years. Compare 2337 and 2218 with 2264 and 2145. This is an indication that some of the Chinese native dates have come to us through East Indian equivalents, between which and our chronology there is a difference of 63 years. Others have come through both Indian and Byzantine equivalents, media which widen the difference to 73 years. For details concerning Yao see "Middle Ages Revisited," Appendix Q.

B. C. 1306, India.—Institution of the solar year and of the festival of Durgha, Mother of God, and of Dennus, Dionysius, or Ianus, Son of God. Correction of the Indian Calendar, previously lunar. Head of the year, 1st Aswin (then 29th August). Greswell, "K. H." V, 87. See B. C. 1176. "The Indian Deunnus and Durga were absolutely the same kind of conceptions and impersonations in India, as Orisis and Isis in Egypt." Greswell, F. C., IV, 31. De Milloue identifies Durga with Parvati and Pritheri. See B. C. 1336.

B. C. 1300, India.—Æra of Chrishna Dvaipayana Jesa, according to Ramchandra Ghosha, a modern writer, who says that Chrishna "re-arranged" the Vedas and taught them to his disciples. The abbé Raynal writes this name "Christna" which he gives both to the Indian Messiah and the sacred river of India.

B. C. 1300, Peloponnesus.—Æra of the Dorian Conquest, when the rites of Ceres (and Bacchus) were suppressed by the Dorians, except in Arcadia. Herodotus, Euterpe, 171; Max Müller; Clinton, F. H., I, xii. Herodotus adds that these rites were brought from Egypt by the daughters of Danaus. This date forms an important link in the chain of evidence which connects the Indian Chrishna with the Greek Bacchus.

B. C. 1292, Troy.—Troja Capta. Did. Sic. and several other of the Greek chronologists count 408 years from the first Olympiad backward to Troja Capta. This has usually been counted backward from the Olympiads of Corœbus, B. C. 776, making Troja Capta B. C. 1184 or 1183; but if it is counted from the Olympiads of Iphitus, B. C. 884, as it properly should be, it will fix Troja Capta in B. C. 1292 or 1291. This agrees with the æras of Perseus, Ies Chrishna, Bacchus, etc., and is probably of the same mythological orgin.

B. C. 1291, Argos.—False æra of Medusa. Acrisius, K. of Argos, being told by the oracle that he would be killed by his grandchild, imprisoned his daughter Danae in a bronze tower, that she might have no issue. In spite of this precaution she was visited by Jupiter, the supreme deity, by whom she miraculously conceived a

son named Perseus. Whereupon Acrisius committed both Danae
and her divine infant to an ark, which was launched upon the sea
From this vessel they were rescued by the fishermen of Seriphus and
protected by Polydectes the K of this Ægean isle   This Indian
legend is also told, in various forms, of Ies Chrishna, Foh, Fod or
Bod, Osiris, Ericthonius, Bacchus, Nyssos, Adonis, Tennes, Cypse-
lus, Darius, Cleomedes, etc.   The story of Astyges, Mandane and
Cyrus, in Herodotus I, 107, is of similar origin   See also Madya in
the Vishnu Purana   Thomas, "Jainism," II, 3   Among the adventures of Perseus are his killing of Medusa, queen of the Gorgons,
who was the vanquisher and successor of Marina, queen of the Amazons, etc   Diod Sic   This legend of Ies Chrishna evidently
travelled from India to China and Scythia and from Scythia into
Greece and Egypt, where it was adapted to the Scythian raid under
Madyes, B C 548 q v   The commentator upon Booth's Diodorus
fixes the slaying of Medusa by Perseus in B C 1291, which is a few
years after the Augustan date of the birth of the first Buddha, B C.
1316, and one divine year before the sack of Ascalon   For Marina
see B C 1394   For the æra of Medusa and sack of Ascalon, see
B C. 548

   B C. 1290, Greece.—Aera of Inachus, or Bacchus, according to
Aretes, apud Censorinus, ch XXI   Following are the various other
æras of Bacchus cited by Censorinus, who gives them in years before
the consulate of Ulpius and Pontianus, (A D 238)   The equiva-
lents are made in years of the present calendar, which begins in the
Olympian year 776 or A U 754=A D. 1. Aera of Bacchus,
according to Timæus, B C 1193; Eratosthenes, B C. 1183, Sosibius,
B C 1171   When the 63 years which have been sunk from the calendar are restored to it, all these æras are seen to be derived from
Chrishna   See B C 1156, 1181, 1300 and 1306
   Among the many names of Bacchus were Iacchus, Iaccho, Inachus,
Iaku or Jaku, Liber Pater, Logou Pater and Dionysius   His celestial
father was Zeus, or Jupiter; his virgin mother was Maia, though according to others her name was Semele, Demeter, Cybele, Venus
Melainis (the Black) and Rhea, or Proserpine   Bacchus was born on
the winter solstice, either at Nyssa in India, or according to others,
Nysa or Nissa in Arabia, he was born in a cave, among shepherds:
his head was rayed, and according to Ovid, Pausanias and Anacreon,
his complexion was black and his hair woolly, though according to
others he was of florid complexion with auburn hair parted in the
middle and floating down in ringlets   Some of the extant images

are black; others white; in all cases he is portrayed as young and beautiful; the corpulent Bacchus striding a wine barrel being a mediæval invention. Bacchus was included in a slaughter of infants ordered by K. Cadmus, but he escaped. He performed numerous well attested miracles and invented or established many of the most useful arts known to man. His doctrines were contained in the Book of Petrouma. The number of his disciples was 12. For preaching levelling doctrines he was condemned to death by Cadmus and subjected to be torn to pieces, some say crucified, on a vernal equinox, at the age of 33 years. At his death the sun was eclipsed. To judge the dead he descended to Hades, where he remained three days and nights; some say a much longer interval. From Hades he rose again and finally ascended bodily to Elysium. His sacraments were the communion, baptism, the oscophoria and the thaumagoria; his emblematic plant was the ivy; his epigraphic symbols were the +, †, Ιες, the bee, and the mystic fan; his zodion was the Bull; and the attributes of his images, the Cross, Bleeding Heart, Cantharus, (or sacrificial Cup), the staff of augury, the thyrsus and the fawn skin mantle.

B. C. **1290, Troy** —Fall of Troy, according to Aretes, that is, if Troja Capta is assumed to synchronise with his Bacchic æra, q. v.

B. C. **1260, Arcadia.**—April 25. Aera of the "Lykæa of Arcadia." Greswell, Kal. Hellen., III, 373. Lykæa was a surname of Diana; Lykæeus was a surname of Pan, whom Greswell, III, 372, recognises as the Sun and identifies with Poseidon of Troezen, Osiris of Egypt and Janus of Rome. In his Fasti Cath. I, 552, Greswell gives June 25, B. C. 1260, for the epoch of the Calendar of Pelops.

B. C. **1258, Troy** —Siege of Troy deduced from Herodotus in Euterpe, 145. He computes it at above 800 years before his time. The siege lasted ten years and therefore ended B. C. 1248, q. v.

B. C. **1252, Ionia.**—Aera of Ancient Ionia. Either this year, or B. C. 1248 (q. v.) says Greswell, K. H. III, 373.

B. C. **1248, Ionia.**—April 25. Aera of Ionia and epoch of First Panionic cycle. The second cycle began April 25, B. C. 592. Greswell, K. H. III, 373. These Panionic cycles were 656 years apart, roughly equal to one astrological cycle, or Divine Year. Cf. Herodotus, Euterpe, 145.

B. C. **1248, Troy.**—Fall of Troy according to the deduction from Herodotus given under B. C. 1258. There are over 40 different ancient authorities who have given a date to this event, most of them derived from Eratosthenes, who said "408 years before the first

Olympiad." If the quadrennial Olympiads were meant, this would fix Troja Capta in B. C. 1183; if the quinquennial Olympiads, then Troja Capta would answer to B. C. 1291 or 1292, q v   The date of Troja Capta given by the remaining authorities is as varied as the æra of Chrishna or Bacchus, from whose advent the date (not the story) of the Fall of Troy is evidently derived   Aretes says B C. 1290: Herodotus (as above) 1248; Dicæarchus 1212 (to this date should be added the Augustan alteration of 78 years); while the Parian marbles say Thargelion 7th, 1209 (add 78).   The date from the Parian marbles is based on the assumption that Diognetus was archon of Athens in B C. 264 or 263, which, to the extent that the calendar has been altered, may be incorrect   Herodotus, Euterpe, 145, fixes Troja Capta before Pan.   Its most probable date is B. C. 1292.

B. C. 1235, Attica.—Æra of Theseus, according to Rev. Lemprière   The Rev E Greswell prefers B. C 1206   In point of fact the date should precede that of Troja Capta.   The name of Theseus is evidently a corruption of Esus, because the initial letter, Θ, theta, with which the name is spelled, was unknown to the Greek alphabet at the period assigned to Theseus; theta, xi, phi, and chi, having been invented by Palamedes, a reputed grandson of Neptune, at a later period.   Pliny, N H VII, 57   Theseus (or Esus) was the son of Neptune by Æthra; the putative father being Ægeus, King of Athens.   Theseus was born at Genethliam, *the place of the birth.* Among his *ten* famous exploits was his victory over Busiris.   See B C 1528.   Most of these adventures, as well as his return to Athens from Crete, took place on the eighth day of a month, the number eight having (once) been sacred to Neptune   Bell's "Pantheon " Hence the Athenian sacrifices to Theseus were made on the eighth day of every month.   Theseus was condemned to death by Ægeus, but saved through the recognition of the tokens he wore.   A sacred dance, called by the Delians the Crane, was performed at Delos in his honor.   The identical ship in which he had voyaged from Crete was preserved in Athens for over a thousand years!   He changed the the name of the city from Attis to Athens; he instituted the Panathenæa and the Synœcia; he coined money stamped with the figure of a bull, or ox; he established the Isthmian games to Neptune, he voyaged into the Euxine to wage war against the Scythian amazons; he saved Athens by marrying their leader, Hippolyta, who otherwise would have entered and destroyed the city; and his sons went into the Trojan war   He descended into hell to carry off Proserpine and afterwards rose again to life. Finally he was shown the riches of the earth by Lycomedes from the top of a high rock, from which he was treacherously thrown and killed. After the death of Theseus his bones were preserved by the Athenians as sacred relics and his tomb became a sanctuary for the poor and oppressed. The story of Thesues is evidently that of the Pelasgian Ischenou, distorted and embellished by Greek fancy.

B. C. 1225, Argos.—Year of the Argonautic expedition, according to Rev. Dr. Clinton. Rev. E. Greswell, K. H., II, 485, prefers B. C. 1230 and says that Orpheus took part in it. On the other hand, Geodfrey Higgins, Anacal. I, 344, and Dr. Daniel Rutherford regard the story as altogether fictitious. Rutherford says that the star Canopus which is said to have guided the adventurers, was in fact not visible from Greece. Higgins says it is an Indian tale.

B. C. 1225, Venetia.—Conjectural æra of Diomede, a surname of Jason (Myth. de Banier, t. VI), to whom a temple was erected in Timatum, at the head of the Adriatic Gulf, now San Giovanni del Carso, and after whom were named the Diomedean Islands, on the east coast of Italy. One of these islands was called Teutria, or Taat-ria, which, in the language of the Veneti, meant the city of Taat. There was also a city of Teate on the adjacent mainland. In the former, according to the Veneti, this divinity received his Apotheosis, and from this place he vanished, or ascended to heaven. The place-names are Buddhic. The victims sacrificed by the Veneti to Jason were white horses. Strabo V, i, 10; VI, iii, 9. The æra of this myth of Jason has been fixed with regard to the period ascribed to the Argonautic Expedition. There is no doubt that the ancient Veneti worshipped Jason, with probably a sacrifice of horses; but much of the rest is Greek fable and perversion. In the Odyssey XVII, 443, Diomede is changed to Dmetor, son of Jasus, king of Cyprus.

B. C. 1219, Rajputana.—Jain æra of the incarnation of Ies Chrishna, Son of the Virgin Mai (or Deoki), the Mediator and Saviour of mankind, to whose worship have been erected some of the most magnificent temples in India. Prominent among these are the shrines of Dilwara, or Diluara and Duarka, variously written Dwarka, Dwaraca, Dwarica, etc. Dilwara is situated half way up Guru Sikra (the "Saint's Steeple"), a lofty summit of the Aravulli Range in Rajputana. It consists of four temples arranged in the form of a cross, which, says Col. Tod, form the most superb structure in all India. The site was purchased at the expense of covering it com-

pletely with silver coins and the total cost of the buildings and site
fell but little short of $100,000,000 The dates of the structures
range from the 11th to the 15th centuries of our æra Dwarka is
situated on the promontory at the southern entrance of the Gulf of
Cutch. Here splendid shrines are erected to Chrishna and Deoki
It is this location and the surrounding topography and place-names
from which Pococke drew the famous parallel with the temple of
Crissa, on the shores of the Crissean Sea, near the Gulf of Salona,
in Greece. The coincidences are certainly very remarkable.

The Jains trace the establishment of their religion on its present
basis to Parsavanasa, about B C 800 They are divided into two
sects, whose tenets, a mingling of Brahminism and Buddhism, do
not essentially differ. To them the creation is eternal, but not so
the heavenly incarnations of the Deity, who, at the beginning of
each Divine Year, are sent to restore peace on earth and re-establish
the affairs of mankind These avatars return to the bosom of the
Eternal into which they are absorbed for a time to again and again
issue forth in the metempsychosis. The most eminent convert to
Jainism was Asoka, B C. 263, who at first professed himself a worshipper of Ies Chrishna, but finally went over to Buddhism pure and
simple Thomas, "Jainism," p 8 That form of the cross called
the svastika was the symbol of Supárswa, the seventh Ticthankaru
of the Jains The following table supplies the various Jain, or
Janus æras; those in brackets being regarded as erroneous:

B C   SWETAMBARA JAINS.

1219.—Incarnation of Ies Chrishna, 1156 years before the Vicrama-
        ditya of B C 63. Col Wilford, Asiat Res IX, 209

1207 —Birth of Jain, the Disciple, 12 years later He lived 257
        years and died B C 950

545-4.—Re-incarnation of Ies Chrishna Duff Rickmers This date
        is one pseudo-Brahminical Divine Year, or 675 common years
        after B C 1219

533-2 —Second appearance of Jain, the Mahavira, one Divine year
        after B C. 1207, or 470 years before the Vicrama of B C
        63 Gen Cunningham calls this a nirvana of Mahavira

528-7 —Mahavira, 470 years before the Vicrama of B C. 57. Cunningham.

B C   DIGAMBARA JAINS

1219 —Incarnation of Ies Chrishna, 1297 years before the Vicrama-
        ditya of A. D. 78

1178.—(Incarnation of Ies Chrishna. Variant date.)

1108.—(Incarnation of Ies Chrishna. Variant date.)

1078.—Incarnation of Ies Chrishna, 1156 years before the Vicrama-ditya of A. D. 78. Col. Wilford, op. cit.

1036.—Jain, the Disciple, born 42 years later. He lived 86 years and died B. C. 950. Wilford.

662.—(Mahavira, 605 years before the Vicrama of B. C. **57.** Cunningham.)

629.—(Jain æra. The Pandits' "Chronology.")

569.—(Jain Mahavira. The Pandits.)

528–7.—Re-incarnation of Ies Chrishna, one Buddhic Divine year, 550 common years, after B. C. 1078 or 605 years before A. D. 78. Gen. Cunningham has discovered monumental proofs of Jainism at this date. Thomas, "Jainism," II, 80.

A. D.

800.—Æra of Avarsha, son of Govinda, a Digambara rajah of Guzerat, in the year of Salivahana 736, which, being computed from A. D. 63-4, is equal to A. D. 800.

The Jain æra of Ies Chrishna must not be mistaken for the Jain Anno Mundi, which is far more ancient. The confusion into which some of these æras are thrown is largely due to the alterations of the Roman calendar. For example, the incarnation of Ies Chrishna is fixed by the Swetambaras in the equivalent of B. C. 1219 and by the Digambaras, in the equivalent of B. C. 1078; a difference of 141 years. This is precisely the difference between the Salivahanna or Vicamaditya of B. C. 63 and that of A. D. 78. The Indian accounts are chronologically correct and harmonious: it is our own thrice altered calendar that makes them appear discordant. The Jain colossal statues of Iswaru (Ies) at Bellagolla and other places in India have woolly hair. Davis, in Asiatic Researches, IX, 256-64.

B. C. 1219, Rajputana.—Swetambara æra of the Calijoga. Wilford, op. cit.

B. C. 1219, Elis.—Æra of Ischenus, or Ischenou, Ισχευου, whose holy sepulchre stood in the middle of the stadium of Pisa, a city situated on the river Alpheus in Elis. See Lycophron, in "Cassandra," circ. B. C. 260 and the Commentary of Tzetzes. This sepulchre was successively called the tomb of Pelops, of Poseidon, etc. Pindar; Pliny; Dio Chrysostom. At the mouth of the Alpheus stood the promontory of Ichthys, the Fish. Pliny, N. H. IV. 6. The date

when this name was given it is unknown Ischenus, (evidently a corruption of Ies Chrishna), was the god of the Veneti, who, after his
adoption by the Greeks, was affected by the priests to be the grandson of Mercury and of Hera "our Lady," a sobriquet of Juno
There was an annual festival to Ischenus, called Ischenia, also a quinquennial one, the celebrated festival, which successively bore the
name of Ischenia, Cronia, Pelopeia, and Olympiade The fable that
Pelops was the son of Jupiter and that he came from Phrygia, also
the fact that he was worshipped as a god, belongs to a later age than
the worship either of Ischenus, or of Cronos. Pliny, N H XXVIII,
6, says that the ivory rib of Pelops was preserved at Elis Pausanius,
V, xiii, 3, says that the relic was the shoulder-blade of Pelops, which
had been miraculously recovered from the ocean It had no doubt
been previously venerated as a relic of Ischenus Both this and the
colossal foot of Hercules, which measured the course of the stadium,
are legends of the first Buddha and are doubtless of Pontine and
Oriental origin · The sacred festival and exercises successively
called Ischenia, Cronia (in Latin, Saturnalia) Pelopeia and Olympiade, took place every five years and lasted for five days, occupying
the epagomenæ, or interval, which distinguished the year of 360
from that of 365 days; a proof that the Ischenia were instituted before the discovery of the Julian year of 365¼ days As such discovery (so far as it related to the Occident), is attributed to the 6th
century B C , while the quinquennial Ischenia, even after they came
to be known as Olympiades, are assigned to the 9th century B C ,
it might seem to be superfluous to mention this deduction But it
must be borne in mind that the assignment of the Julian year to the
6th century is a fact, or at all events an approximation to the truth,
while the celebration of the Olympiades in the 9th century B C , is a
fable The Babylonians had a similar five-day festival to Anaitis, which
was approximately called the Sacaen or Sakaen; the Phrygians had a
similar one to Attis and Cybele, mother of the gods In Elis, at
the end of five years, the five epagomenææ were made up into an
intercalary month called Cronia Plutarch in Theseus assigns this
month by name and dedication to this hero, whose æra, it should be
stated, coincides with that of Ischenus In the Greek states the
Olympiads—if this familiar name may properly be used in alluding
to their archaic phrase—were celebrated every five years; and as
these periods were universally employed for the computation of time,
a correct knowledge of their origin cannot fail to be of interest to
the chronologer and historian

The classical story is that the five-year Olympiads were instituted by Jasius, B. C. 1406; revived by Iphitus king of Elis, and Lycurgus king of Sparta, B. C. 884; and altered to four-year periods and named after Corœbus, in B. C. 776; the first and last of these attributions and dates being fabulous. The five-year festivals or pentaeteris cannot be historically traced back farther than the festival and æra of Ischenus, nor was this earlier than the Indian æra of Ies Chrishna, of which it is doubtless an adaptation. Its epoch, therefore, is about B. C. 1219, concerning which we have the explicit testimony of Valleius Paterculus, I, 7: "Hoc sacrum eodum loco instuisse fertur abhinc annos MCCL, Atreus cum Pelopi patre funebris ludos faceret," that is to say, 1250 years before the consulate of of M. Vinucius, A. U. 783, or A. D. 30. This is equal to B. C. 1220.

The altar at Olympia which was common to Cronios and Helios; the name of Elis itself, which is probably a form of Helios (the Sun); and the testimony of Pausanius III, 61, that a stated or regular sacrifice was there annually made on the vernal equinox, suggest that, following the Indian Houli, the annual Ischenia were originally celebrated at this period of the year. However, the festival was afterwards, date unknown, transferred to the full moon following midsummer, and eventually to midwinter. The quinquennial Ischenia like its original in India, was always celebrated at midsummer. "Story of the Gods," IV, 4.

Among the attributes which were common to both Ies Chrishna (the Indian Dionysius) and to Ischenus (the Greek Dionysius), were the cross, the sacerdotal cup and the mantle of fawn-skin with white spots, mentioned in Pliny, N. H., VIII, 31. The Tanagra terra cottas in the British Museum may belong to the same cult. Among these are No. C. 293 (39) a bearded and rayed Figure entitled "Dionysius holding a cantharus" (sacerdotal cup); the rayed Virgin holding a Bleeding Heart; No. C. 278, Holy Mother and Child; and No. B. 412, Ischenus (?) with a Lamb upon his shoulders. All of these attributes, not the figures, are shown to be both oriental and Dionysian, in the cuts published by Rev. Alex. Hislop, in his "Two Babylons" and in Maurice's "Indian Antiquities."

The Olympiads as four-year intervals are not referred to by Homer or Hesiod. Herodotus frequently mentions the Olympian games, but he does not state their interval nor employ them as dates. Between Herodotus and Timæus there are no writings from which it can be deduced that they were regarded as four-year intervals.

Acusilaus and Hellanicus, for all that can be shown to the contrary, may have meant them for five-year periods. Cf Africanus and Eusebius, (Prep Evan X, 10) Nor is it certain that Timæus meant them for four-year and not for five-year periods Had Cæsar ordered the Olympiads to be reckoned as four-year instead of five-year periods, the difference which this would have made in ancient chronology, which is 108 years, is fully represented in the discordant dates of Troja Capta What is certain about them is that the Olympiads even after the name of Olympiads was taken from them, never lost their name of five-year periods; to the last they were always called pentaeteris, or quinquennales, both of which terms relate to five and not four years.

Phlegon or Tralles, (tempo Hadrianus), says that the olive crown was instituted in the 7th olympiad after Iphitus, and won by Daicles, of Messina This event is commonly assigned in chronological works to B C 752; but the computation is without warrant For all we know to the contrary, Daicles may have won his prize in B C 854

Turning now to the four-year olympiads, they could not have been earlier than the Julian year, because the only event they celebrated was what we now call the leap-year, which is peculiar to that cycle There are many reasons for believing that the four-year olympiads are not earlier than the Roman imperial period. After the institution of the four-year periods, in chronology, the quinquennales were called Cæsar's Games and they ceased to be known as Olympiads This was in the Augustan age. In the reign of Tiberius they were called Augustan games. See B C 63 for further mention of them. Ischenou had ten disciples; his earlier zodion was the Bull; afterwards the Lamb and the Fishes

B. C. 1206, Attica.—Death of Theseus, according to Gresswell, K H , IV, 513

B. C. 1200, Egypt.—Æra of Rhampsinitus, according to Blair Variants of name, Ram-Ies, Rhempsis Bryant identifies him with Orus, or Horus, Thammuz, Adonis, etc He was miraculously born of a Virgin, died at the winter solstice, descended to hell, rose again and ascended to heaven, etc Herodotus says that the resurrection of the Messiah was celebrated in his day by a solemn festival

B. C. 1193, Southern India.—Æra of Parasurama, according to one of the calculations in Bentley's "Hindu Astronomy" This is sixteen years earlier than the common reckoning, which is B C. 1177

B. C. 1193, Argos.—Inachus, according to Timæus, in Censorinus XX.   See the Hebrew Inachus, or Enoch, under B. C. 1188.

B. C. 1188, Judea.—Conjectural æra of Enoch.   According to Rev. Wm. Hales, author of " Chronology upon scriptural and scientific principles . . . tending to obviate the cavils of Sceptics, Jews, and infidels," London, 1830, p. 36, "The apochryphal Book of Enoch states that the ' Archangel Ariel, president of the stars, discovered the nature of the month and of the year to Enoch, in the 165th year of his age and the year of the world 1286.' " On p. 101 Dr. Hales follows the Greek Church and assigns the Creation to B. C. 5411; hence, by his reckoning, Enoch's revelation of the month and year was in B. C. 4125.   According to the Hebrew calendar this was 365 years before the Creation.   But as the Book of Enoch was presumably a Hebrew (or Hebraicised) work and as the Anno Mundi of the Hebrews was fixed in B. C. 3760 it follows that Enoch's revelation was intended to be fixed in B. C. 2474, which is the period of the Chinese Jove (Yao) to whose regulation of the calendar this legend appears to bear some resemblance.   If from this starting point the 1286 years of Enoch are again deducted, the product is B.C. 1188, which is approximately the æra of the Indian Parasurama and the Greek Inachus.   Higgins says that the Book of Enoch was quoted by Eupolemos, about B. C. 200.   Anacal. I, 545.   Both the name, the date and the story are of astrological origin.

B. C. 1183, Greece.—Æra of Inachus, also of Troja Capta, according to Eratosthenes.   Censorinus XXI; Clinton, F. H. I, 139, *et al.*   Callimachus fixes the æra of Inachus in a year equal to B. C. 1127; both of these computations being reckoned backward from the four-year Olympiads.   Here it is to be remarked that between all the dates of Eratosthenes and Callimachus there is a difference of just 56 years until they come to the four-year Olympiads (of Corœbus), B. C. 776, when they agree.   This variance may be due to a difference in using a starting point for both previous and subsequent dates, namely, at the five-year Olympiads of Iphitus, whose æra Eratosthenes fixes in B. C. 884, while Callimachus fixes it in B. C. 828. On the other hand, it may be due to the alteration of the calendar by Augustus Cæsar.

B. C. 1183, Troy.—Troja Capta, apud Eratosthenes, Apollodorus; Dion. Hal.; and Dio. Sic.   Computed from the four-year-Olympiads.

B. C. 1182, Southern India.—Incarnation of Parasurama, according to another calculation of Bentley, op. cit.   This is five years earlier than the common reckoning.   Another European calculation says B. C. 1181.

B. C. 1181, India.—Festival of Durgha celebrated this year. Owing to more correct astronomical data, which were obtained B C 945, the date of the Festival of Durgha was put back to B. C. 1192. Brennand, op. cit, 61.

B. C. 1181, India.—Æra of the Indian astronomer Parasara and of the Mahabharata wars. Brennand For Parasara see also B C 1391 and 596

B. C. 1181, Troy.—"Fall of Troy," according to Greswell. K.H , I, 303

B. C. 1178, India.—Digambara variation of the æra of Ies Chrishna See B. C 1219

B. C. 1177, Southern India.—Æra of Parasurama and his ten disciples Common reckoning Greswell, F C IV 31. By some writers this incarnation is called Dennus Parasurama was the eighth incarnation of Iesnu or Vishnu, as Ies Chrishna was the ninth; yet the followers of the latter have attributed a greater antiquity to their divinity than the followers of the former have given to theirs. The epoch was Aswin 1st, agreeing with our August 29th Cowasjee Patell regards this as the period (Aswin 1st, B C 1176) when the solar calendar was adopted in Southern India The discovery of the planetary character of Jupiter, the basis of the Jovian cult is also to be ascribed to (about) the same period It is rather singular that the worshippers of Augustus Cæsar should have changed his ascension day in the calendar from February 26th to the birthday of Parasurama, August 29th In the Roman ecclesiastical calendar it is still called the day of "Saint Augustine."

B. C. 1176, Southern India.—Parasurama, or Quilon, or Kollam (western) æra confined to Malayana, i e , Mangalore, Malabar, Cotiote, and Travancor to Cape Comorin This year, says Cowasjee Patell, the Indians changed from a lunar to a solar calendar, beginning with 1st Aswina=29th August. Gen Cunningham, op cit This was the birthday of the Indian Dennus. It was also connected with the worship of the Virgin Mother It was long afterward adopted for the alleged ascension day of the Roman Augustus. It is still the day of "Saint Augustine " See B C 1306 and 63; and A. D. 14 and 825 Cf the Pandits' "Chron "

B. C. 1176, India.—Most probable date when the orbit of Jupiter was determined and the Jovian cycles were commenced to be used for computing time This conjecture is based in part upon the periods when side cal or else sola, years (Pan cycles), instead of lunar ones, were begun to be actually employed in India and in the Greek states, both in Asia and Europe.

B. C. 1171, Greece.—Æra of Inachus, according to Sosibius, cited in Censorinus, XX. See B. C. 1290.

B. C. 1169, India.—The various æras which cluster around this period, viz., B. C. 1193, Parasurama; 1193, Inachus; 1183, Inachus; 1183, Troja Capta; 1182, Parsurama; 1181, Troja Capta; 1178, Ies Chrishna; 1177, Parasurama; 1176, Dennus; 1171, Inachus; and 1156, Ies Chrishna, are drawn variously from Indian and Greek sources, a conjunction which when they are corrected by the addition of 78 or else 108 years points to this period as the date of some actual event of world wide importance. The statement of Cowasjee Patell that this year the Indians changed from a lunar to a solar (sidereal) calendar; the adoption of the 1st Aswin (our 29th August) as the head of the calendar; the connection of the Indian Ies Chrishna, Dennus, or Dionysius with the Greek Inachus or Bacchus of this period; the æra of the worship of Zeus-pitar, Jupiter or Jove in Asia Minor and Greece—these and the other considerations alluded to elsewhere in this work point to this period as that of the reconstruction of the Brahminical, Chaldean and Greek astrologies.

B. C. 1156, India.—Æra of Ies Chrishna, according to Col. Tod. See B. C. 1315 for details concerning this favorite incarnation of the Orient.

B. C. 1144, Thebes.—Conjectural date of the Nativity of the Scythian or Indian messiah known to the Greeks as the Indian Bacchus, or the Bearded Bacchus, or Dionysius, who was born in Nyssa, near Mount Meroe, a mythological location, which Alexander the Great pretended to identify, on his march to the Indus. Here, at Nyssa, his soldiers sacrificed to the great oriental Conqueror of the World, whose footsteps the Macedonian declared he was retracing. Pliny, N. H. VI, 23; Justin, XII, 7. The Zendavesta places Nyssa, or Nissa, between Bactria and Merv. Duncker's "Persia," 31. But indeed there were Nissas and Meroes in all countries which laid claim to the honour of having given birth to Ies Chrishna or Bacchus. Before issuing from his Scythian birth-place Bacchus made a covenant with Lycurgus, King of Thrace, son of Dryas, one of the Seven great leaders who went with Eteocles and who perished in the Theban war, B. C. 1120. Eteocles was brother to Polynices, who had married a daughter of Adrastus, King of Sicyon, another of the Seven who went against Thebes. Lycurgus proving false to his covenant, the god caused him to be nailed to a Bacchic cross,

upon which he perished in agony   Dio Sic , p 119   In the shrine
excavated in the island of Milo in 1819, and which contained the
celebrated image misnamed the Venus di Milo, now in the Louvre
of Paris, were also found images of the Bearded Bacchus and the
Youthful Bacchus, one on each side of the goddess   The year B C
1120 marks the foundation of a republic in Thebes.   The city was
destroyed by Alexander the Great, B C 334, before he went to India.   To make the date given above harmonize with Indian dates, 63
years must be added, thus 1144 plus 63=1207 B. C.

   B. C. 1128, India.—End of the Tenth divine incarnation of Ies
Chrishna, or Vishnu.   Augustan date   See Table A.

   B. C. 1122, China.—First year of Tcheou or Chow dynasty employed for computing time by the Chinese Jews   See B C 509

   B. C. 1108, India.—Nativity of Jaina, or Mahavira   See B C.
1207.

   B. C. 1106, Chaldea.—August 8   Epoch mentioned by Greswell, F C , III, 475.

   B. C. 1106, Egypt.—Conjectural date of the Hycsos invasion,
couched in terms of the Christian calendar   To harmonize it with
oriental dates 63 years must be added, making it B C. 1169.   The
date is based upon the conjunction of the various æras and calendar
changes shown under B C 1169 and the civil and religious changes
and shifting of populations which appear to have taken place in the
Pontine and Greek states at about the same period   According to
Manetho, the Hycsos were driven out of Egypt after a residence of
511 years.   The Assyrologists say that the Scythians were driven
out of Assyria by Sargon II , who defeated them at Carchemish, in
B C 717 Another band was driven out in 605 (See 633) Egyptologists have commonly assigned a higher date to the Hycsos, because they have permitted themselves to be guided by an Egyptian
chronology that is based not only upon myths, but upon isolated
myths and myths of comparatively recent construction, not one of
them having regard for the division of the year into ten months,
which was universally established in the occident until it was changed
to 12 months during the æra of the second Buddha   Their date for
the Hycsos invasion is about the 15th or 16th century B. C., which
is far too early.

   Josephus on Appion argued that the Hycsos were Jews   Biblical
scholars have attempted to identify them with the Hittites of the
Bible   Rev Dr Sayce identifies the Hittites with the almond-eyed
pig-tailed race sculptured on the rocks of Hamath and other places in

Syria and Mesopotamia   Mr John D Baldwin and others have written what Prof A Schwartz calls historical romances on the Hittite race   In truth, the facts thus far known do not warrant the inferences of these writers   Pococke, 198, identified the Hycsos with the Hucsos or Scythic tribes of the Oxus   The 511 years of Manetho (if indeed there is any truth in it at all) may simply mean the interval between the Hycsos invasion, circ B C 1169-06, and the Scythic withdrawal, circ B C 633   The monuments of Egypt afford no corroboration of the assertion that any foreign race dominated the land for so long a period as 511 years

B. C. 1104, China.—First recorded observance of winter-solstice festival, worship of Joss or Josh, in China, B C 1104-1098, reign of Wu-wang, Chow (Tcheou) dynasty   Fergusson, 96

B. C. 1100, China.—Astronomical observations at Loyang in Laplace, "Connaissance des Temps " Probable date of the first introduction of Brahmo-Buddhism into China

B. C. 1078, Rajputana.—Alleged Digambara æra of the Calijoga   Wilford   Probably a blunder

B. C. 1076, Persia.—Æra of Zoroaster, according to Xanthus, who places him "600 years" before Xerxes   See B C 947, 590, etc

B. C. 1036, India.—Swetambara Jain æra of Ies Chrishna, son of Maia   See B C 1219 and 1036, China   The Benedictines have lowered this incarnation down to A D 65'

B. C. 1036, China.—Æra of Fod, son of Maya, who was born in India, according to an alleged account of the Chinese, viz , "28th cycle, 41st year, or B C. 1036 " Asiat Res ,vol II   Fod is the Chinese name of Buddha   Volney says there was no F sound in Chinese and that this name was pronounced Bod.   The 28th cycle and 41st year given in Asiat Res. is a Chinese date.   It agrees, not with B C 1036, but with B C 677.   This is a Jovian cyclical date adapted to Buddho-Brahminical purposes.   B C. 1036 is a Swetambara æra of the first Buddha

B. C. 1027, Cashmir.—Æra of Fod, who was born in Cashmir De Guignes, Asiat Res , vol II

B. C. 1027, India.—Æra of the first Buddha, according to Sir Wm Jones, Klaproth, Volney and others, evidently from De Guignes "The Buddha of 1027 B C is identically the same as the one who died 554 B. C   As far as real chronology is concerned, the recent date is alone in use "   The Pandits' "Chron." p. xiii   That Buddha died B. C. 554 is a religious belief; not an historical fact

B. C. 1000, Japan.—Æra of Buddha, Buddhso, Budz, or Siaha, possibly derived from Mat-sya, a surname of Ies Chrishna, the incarnation of Iesnu or Vishnu, whose zodion is the Fishes. He was born at Sicka (the country of the heavens) about B C 1000 At the age of 19 he became a hermit and taught the doctrines of immortality and of future rewards and punishments He prescribed five precepts Thou shalt not kill, steal, commit adultery, lie, nor drink strong liquors He wrote upon palm leaves the materials of a sacred book called Fodekio (pronounced Bodekio) which his disciples venerated as we do the Bible. A gigantic gilded image of this Buddha, seated on a lotus flower, is erected in the temple of Kata-isi Bell's Pantheon It should be added that in this image, as in most other images of Buddha, he is represented with woolly hair; a peculiarity that enables this divinity to be traced under all disguises of name and caprices of art Bell's date for the Japanese Buddha is far too ancient This is evidently the second Buddha, whose æra fell in the seventh century B C. See B C 712 and 660

B. C. 1000, India.—Approximate æra of the original Hindu code of Manu. The variants, Manu, Manou, Mani, Muni, Manes, Manis, Mannus, Menes, Menu, Minas, Munnoo, etc., represent the name of an ancient oriental god, lawgiver, hero, or mythos, whose alleged institutes are still observed by the Brahmins of India and whose imaginary æra stands at the head of the false chronologies both of that country and of Egypt The Hindu Code of Manu has been frequently altered, the last time apparently about A. D 500 It was translated from Sanscrit into Persian and thence into English in 1775 An English translation was made direct from the Sanscrit in 1794 The work in its present form has evidently undergone many alterations, some of which are regarded by Buller (ed 1884) to be as recent as the date above mentioned. But there can be little doubt that the bulk of the work belongs to a remoter antiquity Colebrooke ascribes it to the 16th century B C ; Vivien de Ste Martin, 13th to 12th century B C , Sir Wm Jones, to some period after the 10th century B C , and H H. Wilson, to the 9th century B C. For the more extreme views of Muller and of Cowell, consult Marsden's "Num Orient," ed. 1874, p. 5 In the Greek mythology of the republican period Manes was multiplied and degraded into a plurality of gods, spirits or genii, whose common mother was Mania and whose beneficence is first invoked in the alleged poems of Orpheus This would assign the Greek conception of Manes to a period prior to the Fall of Troy But Aristotle's doubt concerning the reality of Orpheus and of the genuineness of his hymns deprives these dates of any certain historical basis. We can only conclude with safety that the Greek knowledge of Manes ascends to and probably beyond the age of Solon, and coincides with that of the second Buddha; while in the Orient, his code was in vogue several centuries earlier.

B. C. 977, China.—Aera of Fod, who, according to the Chinese, was born in India, "23rd cycle, 41st year," or B C. 977. Father Du Halde, Hist China, I, 317   A Jovian date

B. C. 959, Tartary.—Aera of Barkhan or Buddha, who was born in Tartary. A Jovian date.

B. C. 959, Tibet.—Aera of Fod, who was born in Tibet   Cassini, Asiat Res., II, 27   This is really a Jovian date, or a date arising from the Jovian cycles, and as such is really not connected with the chronology of Buddha.

B. C. 955, America.—Aera of Votan, the Messiah of Yucatan, who descended from Imos, of the race of Chan, or the Serpent Votan introduced the religious Mysteries and after having appointed Zamna as his successor, he died and was buried in Isumal, to his sepulchre, in which town, pious pilgrimages were still made by the natives at the period of the Spanish conquest. It was Zamna, his disciple, who conferred upon the country the name of Maayha   Am. Encyc Brit   His followers erected the temple at Palenque on which is sculptured in gypsum an immense Latin cross with a figure on each side of it   Doane, 348   It is not difficult to recognise in the hero of this legend the Cashmirian, Tibetan and Mongolian Wotan, Woden, Barkhan, Fod, Buddha, or Quichena, son of Maia, whose æra in those countries is variously fixed in B C 1036, 1027, 977, or 959, (q v), these variations being probably the result of defective or altered calendars   It should be stated, however, that the æra of Votan appears to be Jovian, and not Buddhic   The name Imos, or Jamos, also belongs to the Jovian cult.   Cox's "Aryan Myth ," II, 81   The following dates relating to America, are, with one exception, given by the same authority, which, however, does not vouch for their correctness   (Cf A D 700 and 722)

    297 B. C —Quetzalcoatl, Cukulcan or Bacob, the Messiah, appears in Yucatan   This seems to have been a re-incarnation of Votan   The date is supplied by conjecture, being one Hindu divine year after the native æra of Votan   The name Quetzalcoatl may be a corruption of Quichena

  174 A D —Yucatan, dispersion of the followers of Quetzalcoatl

  174 —Guatemala, arrival of four Tutul-Xius people from Tulapan

258 —Guatemala, others of the same sect arrive.

488 —Hwui Shan, together with a party of other Buddhist missionaries from China (by way of Japan), land on the coasts of
America and travel southward to the land of "pointed plants,"
(the maguey?) which may be Mexico or Yucatan This date,
unlike the others herein, is from a Chinese account

635 —The Chichimecs (literally maguey-suckers, equivalent to
barbarians), invade Mexico from the north, that is to say,
from Chicomoztoc, which some have identified with the valley of the Gila

686 —The Chichimecs established the Toltec empire of Mexico,
with Nauhyotsin as their first king

895 —Re-appearance of Quetzalcoatl, as king of the Toltecs Dissatisfied with his subjects he establishes a new empire at
Huitzilapan (now Puebla), after which he mysteriously dis-
appears (This is the æra of Quichena at Delhi. See A. D.
890)

945 —Nauhyotl, one of his disciples, reigns until this year as king
of Huitzilapan; then dies.

990 —(Circ) Advent of Cukulcan in Guatemala He appears to
have been regarded as the same with Quetzalcoatl

1041 —Irruptions of savage Chichimecs from the North, who, in 1047,
destroy the Toltec power

1070 —Death of Huemec Atecpanecatl, the last king of the Toltecs

1090.—The Aztecs start from what is supposed to have been Lower
California. (See A D 1090).

1116.—They reach Chicomoztoc.

1177 —They enter the Valley of Anahuac

1325 —They found or establish the city of Mexico

1352.—Aera of the Mexican monarchy, of which Montezuma, who
died 1521, was the eighth king.

1464 —Guatemala.   The empire of the Tutul-Xius is overthrown

B. C. 947, Persia.—Aera of Magianism and of the "First Zoroaster " Greswell, F C , III, 178 This date is deduced by Dr
Greswell from no other testimony than the Persian custom, observed
in a recent age, of painting paschal eggs¹ If there were any valid
evidences, either of a "First Zoroaster" or of a belief in one, we
should be rather more inclined to look for them at an interval of a
divine year before the "Second" or principal Zoroaster This
would fix the first one in B C 1046 instead of 947   See B. C 1076,
590 and 389

B. C. 927, Greece.—Aera of Homer, B. C 962-27 Clinton, F. H., I, 362. Mr F A Wolf in his "Prolegomena," 1795, proves pretty conclusively that the epics of Homer were collected and "arranged" by Pisistratus about 550 B C In the present state of our knowledge it is impossible to say how far this revision extended. Clinton fixes the æra of Hesiod a century later than Homer

B. C. 895, Aegina.—Silver coined into money by Pheidon of Argos. Parian Marbles, sub anno But see B C 748 herein

B. C. 884, Attica.—Five-year Olympiads--pentaeteris--revived or else established in the reign ot King Iphitus; epoch, the summer solstice This great festival is incidentally said to have been originally established by Jasius B C 1406 According to Callimachus, it was revived by Iphitus, whose æra, in the equivalent of B C 884, is fixed by Erastosthenes. As the festival appears to have been intended to commemorate the discovery of the equable year (the year of 365 days) or else the establishment of an equable calendar, the attribution to Jasius, or rather to the period of Jasius, may be correct, yet we have no positive reference to the pentaeteris earlier than Iphitus This occurs in Callimachus Both Aristotle and Pausanias state that the terms (establishment or revival) of the Olympiads were sculptured on the Disk of Iphitus, a monument of a remote period to both of these authorities The pentaeteris or quinquennial Olympiads were probably in Rome altered by Cæsar to four-year (quadrennial) intervals, in which form they served to celebrate the Julian year which was instituted B C 48 Thereafter the pentaeteris took the name of Cæsar's games and finally that of Augustan games until they were abolished by Theodosius A D 394 In Athens the quinquennial was changed to a quadrennial festival and games, in tempo Augusto Josephus, Wars, I, xvi, 12.

B. C. 884, Sparta.—Apotheosis of Lycurgus according to Eratosthenes Epoch, the summer solstice Aristotle said that Lycurgus was "contemporaneous with Iphitus and joined him in settling the cessation of arms during the Olympic games " (Plutarch, in vita) This determination of his æra agrees with Herodotus, Thucydides, Cicero and Strabo Thucydides I, 18, dates the legislation of Lycurgus 400 years before the end of the Peloponnesian war To this date should be added 63 years This will make it about B C 867. Lycurgus was a king of the dynasty of Procles; his mother's name was Dion-assa; he pretended to have obtained his code of laws from the god Apollo, the priestess of Delphi said that Lycurgus was the beloved of Jupiter and more God than man, Plato say - ..a the Third

Book of his Laws that Lycurgus was a divine spirit residing in a human body; among other religious rites he introduced flagellation at the altars of Diana Orthia Cicero, Repub II, 10, says that Lycurgus was a contemporary of King Iphitus and lived 108 years before the first (quadrennial) Olympiad This is equal to the first year of the quinquennial Olympiads. Both Thirlwall and Grote regard Lycurgus as a real personage of the ninth century B C

B. C. 880, Chaldea.—Ragosin's date for the 8-rayed Disk of Shamash (the Sun) found at Sippara, by Rassam, in 1881

B. C. 876, Rome.—Aera of Romulus, according to Ennius See B. C 814

B. C. 841, China.—Winter solstice Beginning of the 60-year cycles calculated by Sze-ma-ts'ien, the astrologer, who lived in the reign of the divine Woote, B C 86, q v , Freret, XIII, 303-4 B C 841 is indeed a Jovian date, but it does not appear to be connected with the avatars or avataras of that sacred personage (Woden) whom Woote seems to have personated

B. C. 835, Tibet.—Aera used at L'hassa. Pandits' "Chronology."

B. C. 828, India.—Parasuramic cycle; more properly, B C 825, q v According to one astrological system, these cycles begin B C 4825, q v. According to another system, they begin B C. 1176 The cycles are millenial See Ch VIII, under cycles of 1000 years.

B. C. 828, Athens.—Revival of the five-year Olympiads, by Iphitus, according to Callimachus

B. C. 827, China.—According to Liu-shu, A D 1068, in his book called 'Wai-ki,' the "certain" or strictly historical æra of China, began this year. Fergusson, p 110

B. C. 816, Etruria.—The Etruscan æra, according to Varro. See "Middle Ages," Appendix S See also B C. 814

B. C. 816, Alba.—Aera of Procas Henry Dodwell, "De Veteribus Græcorum Romanorumque Cyclis "

B. C. 816, Rome.—Aera of the Foundation, according to Timæus. See B C 814 for a variant date.

B. C. 814, Carthage.—Aera of Carthage, according to Timæus, in Dio Hal I, 74. Niebuhr says B C 826

B. C. 814, Rome.—Aera of Romulus, according to Timæus, in Dio. Hal I, 74 This æra is corroborated by Ennius's expression of "about 700 years ago," by Cicero's æra of Carthage, by Cato, in Greswell, F C , I, 8, by the Alban, Etruscan and Carthaginian vulgar æras; b. . . . . and by th . . . . evidences furnished in chapter II. This year, or more likely B. C 816, seems to have been the correct æra of Romulus, as was believed during the Commonwealth, and down to the time of Augustus, who altered it to the equivalent of B. C 738. At a subsequent date it was altered by the Latin Church to the equivalent of B. C 753 For two years of the discrepancy, see B C 307

B. C. 776, China.—Eclipse of the Sun recorded in the Shu-king, sixth year of Yeu-Vang, dynasty of Tsheou. Bunsen, III, 381; Hales, I, 202

B. C. 776, Attica.—Vulgar æra of the four-year Olympiads (named after Corœbus) which are said to have commenced at the summer solstice, which then agreed with Hecatombion 1st, our July 15th or 16th It is alleged that they were afterwards altered to the first moon after the solstice and subsequently to the Roman July 1st, the first of a month nearest to the anniversary of the Apotheosis of Lycurgus These Olympiads were supposed to have been cited in Greek literature or monuments, about B. C. 260. Sir Isaac Newton, "Prophecies of Daniel" This is a deduction from the Parian Marbles, which were supposed to have been sculptured in the archonship of Diognetes B C. 263; but they are now known to be spurious See the (five-year) Olympiads, under the years 1406, 1219, 1183, 884 and 828 The four-year Olympiads were last used in existing literature A. D. 440

B. C. 770, Scythia.—Scythian or Tartar Invasion of China; subjection of the Northwestern provinces, removal of the Chinese Imperial Court from Shen-se to Honan; death of the Emperor Yeu-Vang; succeeded by his son Ping-Vang, who reigns over the distracted Empire until B. C 719. The Nirvana of Buddha, which Fa-Hian places in this reign, 770-19, probably marks the Tartar Invasion The history, Tchun Tsion, composed by Confucius, begins with the same period Cunningham, op cit ; Du Halde, I, 323

B. C. 769, Sabinia.—Aera of Tat, or Tatius (a name of Buddha), legendary king of the Sabines Tat reigned at Cures, which derived its name from the Curetes, the Cretan priests of Maia and conferred it upon curates, curés, etc. (Cf Homer, Il , ix, 529; Adams Rom Ant.) In B C 742 Tat (so runs the legend) became, with Romulus, joint-king of Rome, and, as such, he reigned six years, when, upon going to sacrifice at Lavinium, he met with a violent death in his 33rd year, A. U 18 His daughter espoused Numa Pompilius Echard, Rom. Hist I, 15, Lempriere, Dic Biog. It was long ago observed by Dupuis, Higgins and other mythological critics, that a period of 33 years was commonly attached to incarnations. This was an astrological conceit, founded upon the difference between the equable solar year of 365 d and the lunar year of 354 d, the interval being about 11 days; so that it takes about 33 years to carry the beginning of the lunar year through all the seasons to the same solar point and conjunction again. The interval between such conjunctions determined the earthly sojourn of the incarnation. This interval can be observed by comparing the Mahometan cycles with our own, the former being lunar and the latter solar

B. C. 753, Rome.—Anno Urbis Conditæ, the Year of the Building of Rome, according to Varro, hence called the Varronian date A number of other determinations are mentioned in chapter III hereof. See also B C 816, 814 and 750 The epoch is universally fixed in Palalia, 11 Cal May, translated April 21st The date of the Building, or Foundation, also marks the incarnation of Romulus, or Quirinus, who was born of the god Mars and the vestal virgin, Rhea Silvia (sometimes Ilia, sometimes Romana, sometimes Roma). Romulus was a ten months' child of florid complexion and auburn locks; who soon after his birth, which occurred in a lowly cottage in Rama or Rome, was condemned, together with his twin brother Remus, to be drowned. The water shrank back from the odious crime and the infants were saved by a she-wolf, who reared them on her milk until they were rescued by shepherds During his active career he was guarded or accompanied by 300 Celeres or Selecti. Not only his birth, but his death was miraculous, for being condemned by the tyrant Amulius, he was torn to pieces, died, rose again and was seen by Proculus Julius walking after his demise, which occurred in his 33rd year Cicero, de Legibus I, 2, 3; Ovid, Fasti, III The Sun was eclipsed when Romulus expired.

B. C. 750, Rome.—Anno Urbis Conditæ, according to one MS. of Cicero's "Republica," II, 10. But see 814 and 753

B. C. 748, Assyria.—Deification of Tiglath-pil-Esar II. Vernal equinox? Altered in Babylon to the 27th year of Nebu-Nazaru, says Ptolemy This modernization of date rendered the æra less ancient than that of the Babylonian Nebu-Nazaru, whose epoch was fixed at February 25th and afterwards at February 26th, B C 747. Albiruni calls this the "Anno Astronorum Babyloniæ " According to the Greek writers, the Babylonians called it their First Aera It was used in Egypt until the Augustan period, when the head of the Alexandrian calendar was shifted to the Roman August 26th, (See " Middle Ages," Appendix L, note 2), and finally to August 29th, corresponding with

both Aswin 1st and Thoth 1st   The Babylonian alteration from 25th
to 26th February was evidently made because the latter fell on
Wednesday   This difference of one day is carefully noted by Rev
Dr. Greswell, F C , II, 403, but without explanation   Gesenius
says that the Babylonian Nebu is Mercury, which is the same as
Buddha, Bacchus, etc   Rodwell in " Records of the Past," p 201,
says the same thing   Nebu is Mercury, or Dionysius.   Among the
variants of this Messiah's name were Nabon-Assar, Nabon-Issa, Nad-
Ius, Nebo-Sabesio, Nebo Nissa, and Nebo or Nebu-Nazaru, the last
being from Censorinus   He is identified with the Hebrew Thammuz
and Greek Bacchus   Nebu was foretold by the Babylonian prophets;
his celestial or else his putative father was Asshur, his mother was
the Chaldean Mylitta, or Greek Venus, he was born at Nazaru (?) near
Babylon; the Messianic star stood over his birthplace; flowers and
music attended his nativity, he was worshipped by the Magi; a
divine effulgence issued from his person, after many trials and sufferings, endured in his mission to disenthrall and elevate mankind,
he was condemned to a violent death   His disciples were 12; they
fasted 40 days   When, on the vernal equinox, Nebu suffered the
inevitable end, the sun was eclipsed and the earth rent with internal
commotions   Nebu descended to hell to judge the dead; he rose
again and ascended bodily to heaven   His principal sacrament was
baptism, his emblematic plants or woods were the fir-tree and yule-
log, his epigraphic symbols were the $+$, $+$, $\frac{?}{}$ and mystic fan and his
zodion was the Lamb

B. C. 748, Messenia.—Beginning of the " Third Age " or Aera;
revolt of the Messenians in the "fourth year of the twenty-third
Olympiad "   Pausanias, Messenics, xv   This year by the five-year
olympiads was B C 771; by the four-year olympiads and our present
calendar, it was B C 685   Add the 78 years sunk by Augustus and
subtract the 15 years added by the Italian chronologists, leaves 63
years, which, when added to 685, makes 748 years B C   The First
Aera of Pausanius was evidently the Brahmo-Buddhic-Chaldean æra,
commencing (by our present calendar), B   C 2064.   Herodotus
(Euterpe, 145), calls this the æra of Bacchus   The Second Aera of
Pausanius was the first " Brahmo-Buddhic-Chaldean," or Bacchic,
B C 1406, and the Third Aera of Pausanias was the Nebo-Nazarene,
or second Brahmo-Buddhic-Chaldean, B C 748   " After the revolt
of the Messenians " . . . "iron began to be used in battle "   Pausanias, Laconics, iii

B. C. 748, Aegina —Clinton, F H , I, 248, prefers this date for the æra and coinages of Pheidon   See B C. 895

B C 747, Babylon —Aera of the birth and incarnation of Nebu-Nazaru, or Nabon-Assar Both Hipparchus and Ptolemy employ it in their works. The epoch of this æra was fixed, as noted by Ptolemy, on the Roman February 26th, B. C 747, at noon, afterwards changed in Babylon to December 25th, B C 748 Both of these days were determined by the Roman astrologers to have fallen on the fourth day of the septuary week, which is the Hindu Buddha-war, or the Gothic Wednesday, the natal day and name day of Buddha, or Woden It is rather singular that after the advent of Augustus the Roman writers, (Censorinus, for example), should have employed or even have referred to this foreign and antiquated æra of Babylon; but if the difference between this æra and that of the olympiads of Iphitus, (which must anciently have been employed in Magna Græcia), be computed, it will be found that such difference closely corresponds with the number of years sunk from the Roman calendar by Augustus In other words, there is reason to suspect that the 78 years sunk by Augustus from the chronology of Rome were 78 of the 80 years between B C 828 and B. C 748.

B. C 747, Argos —Reputed æra of Phoroneus the Emancipator, who sacrificed to Juno, yet was himself worshipped Lutatius Placidus, in Stat Theb lib , IV, v , 580 Bryant, III, 65 Greswell, K H , IV, 191, believes that neither Inachus nor Phoroneus ever existed. This is quite possible. Pausanias, I, xxxix, 4; xl, 5, II. xxii, 12; II, xxv, 3, 4, 5, XV, 5; XVI, 1.

B C 747, Greece —Aera of the worship of Adonis, the Saviour, also called Iao, Thammuz, Hes-Iris, Osiris, etc According to one account Adonis was miraculously born of the Holy Spirit and the virgin Myrrha, his putative father being King Theias He was born in a cave in Syria Doane 365, citing St Jerome, says Bethlehem According to another account Adonis was the son of the mortal Venus, Mother of God, her progenitor being Julus, the son of Æneas Hence she was also called Julius Cæsar Dionæus, or Dionæus Mater This account preserved the name of the Indian Houli, of which more below Adonis was born on the Winter Solstice In Rome this was the occasion of the great festival of the 25th December, called Natalis Solis Invicti (Birthday of the Sun, the Invincible) "All public business was suspended, declarations of war and criminal executions were postponed friends made presents to one another, and the slaves were indulged with great liberties ' (Rev Dr Gross)

During his infancy Adonis was enclosed in an ark and committed to
the waves, with the object of destroying him. In this vessel he remained a year and a day before he was providentially rescued   Adonis
was killed by a wild boar (Typhon) whom he had rashly wounded
while hunting   This occurred on the Vernal Equinox.   After being
laid in his sepulchre, in which he remained several days, he rose from
the dead and ascended bodily to heaven. The Death and subsequent
Resurrection of this god were made the occasion of the most elaborate ceremonies both in the Greek states and colonies, in Ptolemaic
Egypt and afterwards in Rome   The lights in the temples were extinguished or turned down and an image of the god, bleeding from
his death wounds, was placed upon a bier and bewailed in sorrowful
hymns, the presiding priests anointing the mouths of the mourners
with oil and saying: "Trust ye in the Lord, who by the pains he
hath suffered hath procured our salvation." Plutarch, in Alcib and
Nicias says that the streets of Athens were filled with images of the
dead Adonis, borne to the sepulchre by trains of women, who were
weeping, beating their breasts and exhibiting all the outward marks
of grief   Says Calmet in "Fragments". "In these mysteries, after
the attendants had for a long while bewailed the death of this just
person, he was at length understood to be restored to life, to have
experienced a Resurrection; signified by the re-admission of light.
On this, the priest addressed the company saying: 'Comfort your-
selves, all ye who have been partakers of the Mysteries of the Deity
thus preserved, for we shall now enjoy some respite from our labours;'
to which were added these words, 'I have now escaped a sad calamity and my lot is greatly mended ' The people answered by the
invocation 'Hail to the Dove, the Restorer of Light!'" According
to Pindar, B C 522, an image of the typical Dove was exhibited
stretched upon a cross.   Doane.   Says Dupuis. "The obsequies of
Adonis were celebrated at Alexandria with great ceremony.   His
image was solemnly borne to a sepulchre which served the purpose
of rendering him funereal honors.   Before welcoming his return to
life, mournful rites were performed in memory of his sufferings and
death.   The great wound which he had received was shown, just as
afterwards was shown the wound which Christ received from the
thrust of a spear   The feast of the Resurrection of Adonis was celebrated on the 25th March " Says Rev. Dr Taylor: This festival,
identical with our Easter, was called Hilaria and was celebrated on
or shortly after the vernal equinox   Its name was afterwards transferred from the religious festival to the term of the law courts, which

began with the first day of the year, formerly March 1st, now January 1st   Hence the January term is still called hilary.   From the rejoicings which attended this festival we have the word hilarious with its cognates.   This word, together with Yule and others, is the progeny of the Indian Houli   The rites of Adonis were publicly celebrated at Antioch and Bethlehem (St Jerome, in Doane, 220), so late as the 4th century (arrival of the Emperor Julian) and at Alexandria down to the 5th century (time of St Cyril). Cf. Pindar; Plutarch; Julius Firmicius, St Jerome, Rev Dr Adams, "Rom Ant."; Rev Dr Gross, "Heathen Idol"; Rev Dr Taylor, "Diegesis"; Dunlap, "Myst of Adonis"; Murray, "Mythol"; etc   Although the pretended pedigree of Adonis connects his name with the æra of Troy, the materials of his worship cannot be traced further back than the 8th century B C , and even this date is suspiciously remote As a matter of fact, the cult in the Greek States could hardly have originated more than a century or two earlier than the time of Pindar   Somes of its features are of a period several centuries later.

B C 742, China —Chinese æra, according to Greswell, F C., I, 561

B. C. 738, Rome.—Nativity of Numa Pompilius.   In B. C. 715 Numa was elected king (Greswell, F C., I, 354, prefers B C. 714, or 713, but in IV, 156, he says B C. 715).   Numa afterwards erects a statue of Janus, the position of whose fingers indicated the number 365; in B C. 705, Numa institutes the festival of Rubigalia; and in B C 672 he dies, after a reign of 43 years   Livy, I, 21; Pliny, XVIII, 69, 5; XXXIV, 16, 1.   According to Livy, Numa was elected king in A. U. 39   He had espoused the daughter of Tat, the king of Sabinia, and was then a widower   He must therefore have at least attained the age of manhood.   The year assumed for his birth makes him 23 years old when he was elected king   The year also agrees with the false æra of Romulus adopted by Divus Augustus   It does not follow from this that Numa was a myth, yet such is the opinion of several historians   As with most of the demi-gods, his epoch was purposely antiquated in order to procure for him and his ordinances increased veneration   Pliny states that Numa was, (whilst Livy says he was reputed to have been,) a contemporary of Pythagoras   Pliny's view of his æra is corroborated by the character of the astrology of Numa and Pythagoras, which, in both cases, was that of the Second Buddhic age   Pliny says that Pythagoras discovered the movements of the planet Venus in either Olym 32, 33, 42, or 62, such being the variance of the Mss.   The equivalents in A. U are given variously in the same MSS , at 109, 113, 142 and 222   These discrepancies of dates hardly warrant Niebuhr in doubting (as he does) the existence either of Numa or Pythagoras   Rather do they bespeak the use of an altered calendar and an object of superstition removed backward in time, without also removing his contemporaries and other environment.   See B C 533

B. C. 736, India.—Pre-Augustan or Indian date of the Nativity of the Buddhic Ies Chrishna, Vicramaditya, Salivahana, or Buddha See chapter VI, table B   According to Gen. Cunningham, the Chinese missionary Fa Hian (fourth century) fixed the nirvana of Buddha at this period, namely, in the reign of Ping Vang, B C 770-19; but this appears to be a mistake of the nirvana for the nativity. The practice of substituting the æras of mythological, for those who are assumed to have been real, personages and *vice versa*, has led to great confusion in the identification of Indian divinities   The æra given by Fa Hian for Buddha is really that of the Brahmo-Buddhic incarnation, known as Ies Chrishna, the Salivahana, or the Vicramaditya; but since it has been also assigned to Buddha, there is no alternative but to accept it in that sense   See B C 78

B. C. 721, India.—Aera of the Nativity of Buddha, son of Maya He was born on the eighth day of the second month, the year beginning with the culmination of the Pleiades   This culmination occurred on Nov 17, or Martimas (Haliburton)   Hence the "eighth day of the second month" was Dec 25. Lillie, "Buddha and Early Buddhism," 73.   Among the many names of this, the second or principal Buddha, (who may have been in some respects historical,) are Iswar, Ies Chrishna, Gautama and Sakya-Muni   The Scythians and Goths called him Woden and the Greeks, Dionysios   His advent was foretold by prophets; his celestial father in India was the Holy Spirit, or in Burma the god Phralaong; his putative father was Suddhodana (India) or Thoodandana (Burma) who in India was a shepherd of the royal line of Maha Sammatu, and in Burma, a king   His virgin mother was Maya, or Maia. The Messianic star stood over the place of his birth, which was assigned to various localities, the favorite one being beneath a tree in or near the town of Kapilavasta in Nepal.   But in recent years (1896) a monolith of Asoka has been excavated which marks or pretends to mark the exact spot of Buddha's nativity   This is at Manza Poderiya, in Nepal, about 18 miles south-east of Kapilavasta   London "Times," Dec 26, 1896   Haliburton's date for the birth-day apparently belongs to the First Buddha and the ten months' year, when the birth-day itself was Martin mas, afterward changed in respect of Sâkya Muni to December 25th, both of these days having synchronised at one time or another with the winter solstice.   Buddha was born among shepherds, to the accompaniment of flowers, music and perfumes   He was recognized as the Expected One by the seers or Magi; his head was rayed; his complexion was black and his hair was woolly   A slaughter of Innocents was ordered by the tyrant Bimbasara, from which Buddha happily escaped, to perform his appointed mission of bringing peace and happiness to the world.   The proofs of his legitimacy or identity were his transfiguration and numerous miracles   His favorite disciple, of whom there were 12, was Arjon.   The duration of his long fast was 40 days, some say "many days"   He was tempted by the Evil One, Mara, but resisted his advances and devoted himself to the saving of souls   His doctrines are contained in the Baghavat Geeta, the Pittakattayan and other scriptures.   "He preached to all mankind the mystery of suffering"   Address of Supt. Gen. of Shway Dagon Pagoda of Burma, in Trubner's Record, 1880. After a life of great toil, austerity and voluntary sacrifice, Buddha was condemned to death and he partook of a Last Supper with his disciples. (Bishop Bigandet, II, 36.) Buddha was cruelly murdered on the vernal equinox in the 80th year of his age, upon which occasion the sun became eclipsed and earthquakes and meteors shook the earth   He descended to hell to judge the dead; remained there three days and nights; rose again and ascended bodily to heaven   His principal sacrament was baptism; his flower the lotus; his epigraphic symbols the †, + and mystic fan; his zodion was the Lamb, the sign of his future coming is the White Horse; and his images sit cross-legged, with a button on the forehead and a svastica on the naked breast

B. C. 717, Assyria.—Sargon II defeats the Scythians at Carchemish or Karchemich

B. C. 712, Japan.—Nativity of Sin-mu, Iva-sikono-mikotto, or Sin-mu-ten-oo, the first mikado, or sovereign-pontiff.   Posthumous title, Jimmu.   His reign began B. C. 660 (q v) and lasted until B. C. 585   His reputed age at death was 127 years   The Burmese Buddha (who is probably the same with Jimmu) died in the 128th year of the Eetzana æra   (This æra began B C 701) Bishop Bigandet says the 148th year   See B C 552.

B. C. 710, Media.—"Herodotus says that in Ol 17,2 Cyaxares was elected king by the Medes"   Diod. Sic., p 71 The passages in the extant copies of Herodotus relating to Cyaxares no longer contain a · .¹   Ol 17 2 is equal to 66 years after the year B C

776, therefore B. C. 710. Picot's date for the accession of Cyaxares is B C 635; Haydn's is B. C. 632, which is just 78 years later than that of Diodorus, an interval equal to the alteration of the calendar made by Augustus after Diodorus wrote his history.   But this is not all   Herodotus, I, 106, says that Cyaxares reigned 40 years, which according to Diodorus would be B C 710-671, yet it was in the reign of this same Cyaxares, as Herodotus explicitly informs us, and in the sixth year of his war with the Lydians, that "in the heat of the battle, day was suddenly turned into night," and that "this phen. omenon, Thales, the Melesian, had foretold to the Ionians, fixing beforehand this year as the very period in which it would take place "   Herod. I, 74, 103.   Apollodorus says that Thales was born in Ol. 35, 1 equal to B. C 639, while Phlegon of Tralles, according to Suidas, places the acme of Thales in Ol. 37, say 37, 2, equal to B. C. 630   The former of these dates would not make Thales the contemporary of Cyaxares, if the latter lived so early as the date given by Diodorus   In order to agree with Diodorus, the date given by Phlegon renders it necessary to regard Thales as being over 60 years of age before he reached his acme.   As according to Lucian he lived to the age of 100, this is not impossible; but it does not agree with Herodotus, I, 75 and 170, who represents Thales as diverting the river Halys to enable Crœsus to ford it during his expedition against Cyrus, circ B. C. 547, or with his being in Ionia when Cyrus reduced the Ionic cities, circ B. C. 546   See B C 585 for further remarks on the date of the eclipse predicted by Thales.

B. C. 703, Persia.—Reputed æra of Giemshid, Gjemschid, Djemschid or Jumsheed, the heaven-born king of Persia, who is said to have abolished misery and death during his reign, invented wine, performed numerous miracles and reconciled an equable and Julian calendar, by intercalating, every 120 years, one month of 30 days Hales, 42, apud Hyde, 205; Fraser, Hist Persia, 103 and 149, Greswell, F C , II, 81   This last statement implies that Giemshid was familiar with a Julian solar year of 365¼ days; also that at his epoch the year was divided into 12 months of 30 days (average); assumptions which barely and suspiciously come within the limits of probability.   In point of fact the Persian calendar was reformed not in B. C 703, but about B C 590, during the period ascribed to Zoroaster   The 120-year cycle of the Persians may have been devised, as we know was the case in China, not to harmonize the equable and Julian year, at a time when the latter was unknown, but to regulate the church festivals of a year which had originally consisted of eight months each of 45 days, afterwards of ten months each of 36 days, and finally of 12 months each of 30 days   Rev. Dr Hales' view of the antiquity of the 120-year cycle in Persia has been recently adopted by Prof Flinders Petrie with respect to Egypt, concerning which see cycles of 120 years herein   D'Herbelot says that although since the Moslem conquest the Persians have used the lunar calendar of their conquerors, yet they still keep the Neuroz at the vernal equinox, as it was established by Giemshid of their first dynasty   Although this is quite credible, it is not explained how it is carried out in practice   Giemshid is probably the same as Buddha, Jimmu, etc

B. C. 701, Burma.—Eetzana æra, in the 68th year of which Buddha was incarnated   Bigandet.   See B C 632 and 552

B. C. 694, Iesygia.—Aera of the Iesyges of Tarentum. After the Messenian war, B C. 743-24, the Lacedæmonian youths, called Partheniæ, were expatriated and sent to the Iesyges, a tribe (of the Veneti?) who occupied Tarentum, in the district of Iesygia, or Messapia, on the southern coast of Italy   These Iesyges came from Illyria, or Venetia. The place-names are those of their god Ies, or Taras, the Messiah. The Iesyges (sometimes Iazyges, Jezides, etc) of Italy had their own khans so late as B C. 480, and perhaps later   We hear of their settling Heraclea, in Lucania, in B C. 436   Strabo VI, iii, 1 to 3   The Iesyges, or Messapians, had the following settlements· 1, In Bosphorus, on the north coast of the Palus Mæotis, (Sea of Azof,) between the Tanais, (Don,) and the Chersonesus (Crimea); 2, In Thracia, on the northern coast of the Euxine, near the mouth of the Danube, whence they conducted the overland trade to the East   Ovid, Tristia, II; 3, On the west coast of the Ægean sea, near Tanagra; 4, In the auriferous district on the Marissus, a Pannonian affluent of the Ister (Danube); 5, At the head of the Adriatic gulf, near Aquilæa and the auriferous district of the Taurici Norici, 6, In Messapia, or Apulia, on the south coast of Italy; 7, At Cape Finistere in Spain and at the mouth of the Loire, near Cape Finistere, in Gaul; 8, In Menapia   They probably also had an emporium in Britain. With respect to the Iesyges of Bosphorus, Thracia, Illyria and Cape Finistere, they all tattooed their bodies   Herod v 6, Ency Brit , art. "Khazares," Strabo, VII, v 4   This may also be true of the others, though we have no records of the fact. Tattooing is still a common practice along the shores of Illyria, France, Britain and Germany   The word itself suggests the name of Taat or Buddha   At Cape Finistere they were known both as Veneti and Picts, or "painted men "   At about the

æra given above there were settlements or factories of a similar character on all the coasts of Europe, such factories being probably
united by a sort of Hansa, but with the exception of the tribes mentioned above, we are not yet warranted in regarding the other trading settlements as connected with the Iesyges The latter are probably the same people as the White Huns, the Leuco-Syrians, etc.
See the æra of Chersonesus and Santa Maura, B C 36, which is exactly one divine year after this date.

Iesides, Jezides, or Jezideen, is a name which to the pious and
uneducated Mahometans of the present day merely means heretics,
but which as we have seen has a far more significant origin   The
Moslem authors allude to the Jezides of Turkey as a peculiar people
who speak a language different from the Turkish or the Persian, yet
somewhat similar to the latter   They say that there are two kinds
of Jezides, black ones and white ones, they distinguish the white
ones by remarking that they have no collars to their shirts, there is
only a round opening for the head to pass through; and they say
that this opening is made in imitation of the circle of gold and rays
of heavenly light, to be seen in the pictures of their supreme khan,
or spiritual leader. The black Jezides are mostly fakirs or monks

The Turks and the Jezides cordially hate each other, and the
greatest insult that can be offered to a Turk is to call him a Jezide
On the contrary, the Jezides are very partial to christians, because
they believe that Jezide, their spiritual Master, was Ies Chrishna,
whom they confound with Jesus Christ.

They drink wine even to excess, they eat pork; they receive circumcision only when forced to do so by the Turks; their ignorance
is extreme, they have no books; they believe, however, in the christian evangelists and in the sacred books of the Jews, without being
able to read or possess them, they make vows and pilgrimages; but
they are not permitted by the Moslems to have either churches, temples, oratories, public festivals, or public ceremonies   Their rites
are limited to singing sacred hymns in honour of Ies Chrishna and
the Virgin

When they pray they turn towards the east, while the Turks turn
towards the south; they believe in the Devil and look upon him as
God's agent in the other world   One point of their religion is never
to curse; for fear of the Devil's vengeance

The black Jezides are regarded as holy men and it is not customary
to lament their death, on the contrary, the custom is to rejoice
For the most part the blacks follow a pastoral occupation They do

not kill their own meat; but leave this to the white Jezides All the
Jezides march in troops like the Arabs, often changing their habita-
tion, and living in tents made of goatskins. They arrange their tents
in a circle, with their cattle in the middle. They purchase their
wives, who ordinarily cost 200 écus each This was also a custom of
the ancient Veneti. Herod Clio, 196 They are allowed to divorce their wives, if it is in order to become a monk It is a crime
among them to shave or cut their beards, no matter how little may
be cut Ovid in Tristia, says the same of the Getae of Pontus Certain of the Iesidian customs bear a curious resemblance to our Christian rites, for example, at one of their sacred feasts, their priests
present to each a cup full of wine, saying to him "Take thou this
chalice of Ies Chrishna's blood " The other then kisses the hand of
him who presents the cup and drinks from it

B. C. 692, Egypt.—True æra of Thoth (pronounced Tot or Taat).
The Egyptian priests, in order to extort that veneration for the Buddhic god which is due to superior antiquity, carried the æra of Tot
back to B C. 1350, which is exactly one Brahmo-Buddhic divine year
prior to this date Greswell, F. C , III, 138

B. C. 691, Burma.—Sacred Æra or Grand Epoch, said to have
been established by An-ja-na, the grandfather of Gotama. The
Pandit's "Chron " This is probably identical with the Eetzana
æra

B. C. 677, India.—Æra of Fod, or Buddha See B C. 1036 and
A D 65

B. C. 673, Syria.—Æra of the Syrian Thammuz Several computations fix the date between B C. 673 and B C 659 in the Vulgar
æra Among the various names of this Messiah were Thamocz,
Adonai, (Greek, Adonis) Adonissus, (Gi Dionysios), Nazaratus, and
Nizzuz, (Psalms xxiv, 8, Hebrew ed); the last being evidently the
same as Nissus The worship of this incarnation, which may have
come from Pontus and Babylon, extended during the sixth to the
fourth century B C from Syria to Egypt and Greece Thammuz
was foretold by prophets; engendered by the Holy Spirit; conceived
by the virgin Maya or Mylitta, and born on the winter solstice among
shepherds He was recognised by the Magi, had 12 disciples, performed numerous miracles, strove for the enfranchisement of man,
fasted forty days, was grievously persecuted, and finally condemned
to a violent death, upon the vernal equinox, on which mournful occasion the sun was eclipsed and the people "wept for Thammuz " He
desce   ll   ude l to Heaven, there

to join the Father. His sacrament was baptism; his epigraphic symbols were the + and †; and his zodion was the Lamb. The Lord's Prayer (in Hebrew, the Kadish) appears to have been borrowed from this cult. It is given in full by Massey, in his "Genesis," II, 469.

B. C. 667, China.—Æra of Lao-kiun, or Lao-tsze, who is said to have been born in the third year of Ting-Vang of the Chow dynasty. The date given in T. W. Doane's "Bible Myths" is B. C. 604. The present date is attained by adding the 63 years still lacking in the Roman calendar. Lao-tsze was "a divine emanation incarnate in a human form." He was "born of a virgin, black in complexion and as beautiful as jasper." He was "antecedent to the birth of the elements in the great absolute, the pure essence of the Téen, the original ancestor of the prime breath of life," who "gave form to the heavens and the earth." Thornton, Hist China, I, 134, 137. Chamber's Encyc, art. "Lao-tsze." Both "king and people honor him with divine worship." Le Compte "Lao-kiun believed in One God, whom he called Tao, and the sect which he formed is called Tao-tse, or Sect of Reason." Doane.

B. C. 662, India.—If the Digambara æra of Mahavira's nirvana, which is "605 years before Vicrama," is reckoned from B. C. 57, it will make this date; and, as such, it has been adopted by some writers, but this is not the æra of Vicrama as meant by the Digambara Jains, who reckon from A. D. 78. According to this sect, a Mahavira's nirvana falls in B. C. 527, q. v.

B. C. 660, Japan.—Aera of Jimmu, according to some chronologists, among them Rev. Dr. Greswell, who fixes the epoch on February 19. Jimmu is none other than the second Buddha, or Ies Chrishna, who is incarnated every 658 years and was due to appear 658 years after the first Buddha. There are no historical records of Japan earlier than the third century of our æra. See B. C. 1000 and 712.

B. C. 658, Scythia.—Aera of Ies-anara, or Zanara, virgin spouse of God (Jupiter) and mother of the miraculously conceived Scythes (or Iesythes), the Messiah of the great Scythian nation, which included the Sacæ, Massagetæ, and Arimaspians. "Their vast and glorious empire extended from the river Araxes and the Caucasus mountains to the Euxine sea. (It therefore included the Colchians, Khazarians and Getæ). It also extended from the Indian ocean to the Caspian sea and even (at times) to Syria and Egypt. The Scythians established colonies in Paphlagonia, Pontus and Sarmatia, (Germany and the Baltic coasts). The r sacrifices to Mass an I i a (cythes

and Iesnara) were called *tauribolia*   They conquered as far (westward) as Thrace   In the Island of the Hypoboreans they observed the
cycle of 19 years (the Metonic).   Their year begins with the vernal
equinox   Zanara civilised Scythia, built numerous cities, enriched
the people and extended the empire   Upon her death the Sacæ
erected to her memory an enormous pyramid, crowned with her
image in gold and worshipped her as the Mother of God " Diod Sic.

B C 658, Crimea.—In this year the Heracleotes crossed the
Euxine and established a colony in the Crimea, near the present Se-
bastopol, which they called Cherronesus, or else Chersonesus, the
Greek word for a promontory, and there they lived, under free institu-
tions, for more than a thousand years   Encyc Brit , art "Khazares "
Herodotus represents the Heracleotes, or Heraclidæ, to have been a
Greek colony of Lydia, which descended both from Hercules, a
Greek god, and from Belus and Ninus, who were Babylonian gods.
(Cleo, 7)   Probably the truth, behind this evidently mythological
account, is that the Leucosyrians and Dionysian Greeks of Amisus,
in southern Pontus, having been driven away, either by Tiglath-pil-
Esar II, or else by Assur-bani-pal II, founded or else reinforced
a colony in the great Scythian peninsular, which they named Crimisus, since corrupted to Crimea.   Near Amisus in Pontus were
Heracleam, Sebastopolis, Eupatoria, and other places whose names,
like Crimisus, the colonists transferred to the shores of Scythia.
Here they met and intermingled with Ugrian traders, whose racial
name was conferred by the Greek mythologists upon Agron, the
fabulous progenitor of the Heracleotes.   "For the Geloni were
originally Greeks who, being expelled from the trading ports, settled
among the Budini; where they use a language partly Scythian and
partly Greek " Melpomene, 109   They worshipped a Messiah, or
Mediator, known to the natives as Ies Chrishna, to the Greeks as
Bacchus, or Dionysios, and to the Egyptians as Hesius, or Osiris.
The people of the Crimea also worshipped the virgin mother of
God   "The Tauri sacrifice to the Virgin all who suffer shipwreck

The Budini are a great and populous nation   The Geloni
adorn their temples after the Grecian manner, with images, altars
and wooden shrines   They celebrate the triennial festivals of Bacchus
and perform the Bacchanalian ceremonies . . .   By the Greeks the
Budini are erroneously called Geloni " Melpomene, 103-108.   This
form of worship may not have been in vogue when the Greeks first
invaded the Crimea, yet the foregoing extracts leave but little doubt
of its prevalence in the time of Herodotus, which was about B C

450   The Dionysian cult subsequently extended along the shores of the Euxine until it eventually embraced both of the extensive provinces known to the Occident as Bosphorus and Pontus   When the Greek colonies of the Crimea had fully established an overland trade with the Orient, which they did by way of the Palus Mæotis, and the rivers Tanais (Don) and Volga, this commerce encouraged the settlement in the intermediate countries of tribes of Armenians, Caucasians, and Scythians, who, together, formed that mixed and very remarkable race, the Cæsars, Chozares, or Khazares, whose history stretches from Ies Chrishna to the period of the crusades, A D 1106; and the emblems of whose religion are stamped upon the coins of Bosphorus and Pontus. That religion was Bacchic and Buddhic   See A D 64   The term "Greek," as used in this connection, is from Herodotus and may be misleading   It implies that the Greek Asiatic colonies were settled from Greece and therefore after Greece itself was settled by the Greek race or races, whilst the contrary may be the fact   The so-called colonies may have been first settled by this race and Greece proper may have been settled afterward   Such indeed is the opinion of Pococke, and apparently also that of Jamesion, Buchanan and other writers on the subject   Moreover, they all agree with Niebuhr in the opinion that most, if not all, of the history of Greece, prior to the age of Solon, is either fabulous or else greatly perverted   Herodotus himself says that the Phrygians, whom we moderns have been led to regard as Greek colonists, were older than the Egyptians   Euterpe, II, 2   This of course makes them older than the Greeks of Europe   In another place (Mel 33) Herodotus affirms that a complete line of communication existed in his day from the hypoborean regions in north-eastern Scythia, through Scythia, Thrace and Greece to the Adriatic gulf, (Istria and Illyria), along which line offerings were sent by the hypoboreans to the shrine of Delos, and in Terp. 3 he says that "the nation of the Thracians is the greatest of any among men, except the Indians "

B. C. 658, India.—Augustan date of the birth of Buddha.   See B C. 662, 660, 656, etc.

B. C. 657, China.—Aera given by Greswell, I, 582   Epoch, February 16

B. C. 656, India.—Nirvana of Buddha, B C 656-33, according to an inscription cited by Gen Cunningham and his translation of the years into the Christian reckoning.   The year 656 is the Indian or pre-Augustan date of Buddha's death.   The post-J   a an or Christian date of Buddha's birth was B C. 673 and his death l t 50 .

B. C. 656, Thracia.—Aera of Buddha or Mercury observed by the Chrestonians and other Gothic tribes of the Balkan Peninsular. "Their kings reverence Mercury most of all the gods; they swear only by him and claim to be descended from him " Herodotus, Terpsichore, 7   The same custom prevailed in England down to the reign of Henry II , whose pedigree, traced from Woden or Buddha, will be found at length in Palgrave's " Eng Com ", p 613 Among the customs of the Thracian Goths was the suttee. Herod , Terp , 5. This is clearly Oriental   The Buddhic or Bacchic cult is mentioned by Herodotus as the prevailing one among those tribes who occupied the Peninsular and the littoral of the Euxine, including the Crimea, where Justinian found it practised in the seventh century of our æra

B. C. 656, Chorasmia.—Conjectural æra of Kutaiba, who destroyed the ancient literature of Chorasmia and eatablished a religious schism Albiruni. The various places named after this Chorasmian khan indicate the line of his conquests   Among these are Kutais in the Caucasus 60 m east from Poti and Kutaiak, Kutaya, or Kiutapia (anc. Coteæum) on the Pursak, an affluent of the Sakaria, the ancient Sangarius   The last named place was the seat of the worship of the Piscenian Mother   See B. C. 645

B. C. 645, Assyria.—Æra of Nana-Sab-Esia, mother of the gods A cylinder of Assur-bani-pal, of a year which is believed to correspond with 645 B C relates that he captured the image of Nana in Elam, "a place not appointed for her," and restored it to " Urukh in Bitanna," from whence it had been taken 1635 years before (Ragozin's " Chaldea," 195) It is related by the Greek writers that, during the Trojan war, the date of which varies between 1334 and 1129 B C., the king of Assyria drove the Venetians out of Pontus and Cappadocia This was not 1635 years, it was at the most about 635 years before Assur-bani-pal.   The Venetians were probably allied to the Urtuki Turcomans of Pontus and Bithynia, worshippers of Nana-sab-Esia It was a common practise of the ancients after ravaging a hostile country, to bear away its gods and display them in the ensuing triumph. a custom which survived to the æra of Napoleon Buonaparte and which was certainly not neglected by the sovereigns of Assyria   At a later æra, Assur-bani-pal restored an image of Nana to the " Urukh in Britanna," from whom (not whence) it had been taken   Meanwhile the goddess had been doing duty in Elam, where the Chaldean priests had carved a false date upon it, a species of pious fraud, which, as the Rev Mr. Sayce shows ("Assyria", 189), Assur-bani-pal himself did not disdain to practice.   Nana's shrine in Bithynia was at Piscenus, and her image, or symbol, could scarcely have been older than the period assigned to the Trojan war. Similar to this is the fable of Orestes, himself a Scythian god, who was instructed by the Delphic oracle of Apollo to remove the image of Diana, mother of God, from the Taurica-Chersonesus to Greece. Pausanias, III, 3. The Greeks and Romans employed the same practice See B C 297 and 205.

B. C. 645, Persia.—Approximate æra of the worship of Mithra in Persia This cult may be traced backward to India Maurice, II, 204 Vestiges of it in that country may reasonably be assigned to nearly a century and a half earlier than in Persia, say to about B C 780 It was introduced into Rome during the first century of our æra Lajard Another name for Mithra or Mithras is Nanaia, or Nana, although contrariwise Langlois and others hold that Nana was a female god, the divine mother of Mithras. Ragozin says that Nannan was the Chaldean name for the moon; therefore the name of a female, an opinion which is greatly strengthened by the feminine appearance of all the Mithraic images now extant. It may be that Mithra and Mithras were the female and male embodiment of the same divinity Assuming (in deference to common opinion) that Mithras was a male, he was, according to Dupuis, Doane and others, the son of the virgin Nana; foretold and welcomed by the Magi; miraculously born in a cave, on the winter solstice (Mirgan, Pers , Natalis Solis, Rom); head rayed; complexion fair, tresses flowing; number of disciples, ten, afterwards 12 After a life of suffering, endured for the sake of mankind, Mithras died a violent death on the vernal equinox, descended to the nether world; remained three days and nights, rose again and ascended bodily to heaven Sacraments: eucharist and baptism, plants palm, cypress, pine and lily. Epigraphic symbols ♀, †; zodion, the Bull. Attribute. Phrygian cap Mithra is usually represented slaughtering the Bull

B. C. 644, India.—Death and Ascension of the Buddhic Ies Chrishna. He was born in the tribe of Yadu (Vishnu Purana, V, 23) at Gorakpore in Rajputana and was the issue of Ies-Saca the Sungod and the virgin Vasudeva His complexion was black; his hair woolly At the age of 29 he became an ascetic and preached social equality, charity, meekness, and faith in immortality He performed many astonishing miracles, declared that he had created himself, died in Kusinara at the age of 80, descended to hell, rose again and finally ascended bodily to heaven These dates and some of the details are from Ramchandra Gosha, while others are true Wilson and

Sir Wm Jones, the last of whom, however, alludes to the Brahminical Ies Chrishna, whose æra he fixes during the Mahabharata wars.

B. C. 644, Rome.—Aera of the re-incarnation of Ianus Quirinus. This is the name given to him by Ovid, Fasti, I, 69, and others Virgil calls him " Father Iasius, from whom our race is descended " Aeneid, III, 168 The name of Quirinus is probably a Roman corruption of Chrishna, or Quichena, as Iasius is of Ies The date is that of the nirvana of Chrishna. The earliest bronze ace, or eis, or ies of Rome, upon which the effigy of Iasius or Ianus is cast, and which, according to G. Feuardent and M Garrault, derived its name from the effigy, is of about the date B. C. 450. Its symbol, which accompanies the effigy of Ianus, is the Cross The statues of Ianus represented the hands raised, with the fingers expressing the number of days in the equable solar year, viz , 365 Pliny, N H , XXXIV, 16 (7) The earliest explicit mention of the equable year in the Occident is connected with Thales of Miletus, who is said to have " discovered it," though in fact it was probably known ages previously both to the Hindus and the Iesiges The adoption of a solar year in Rome is of a later date than Thales, therefore, historically, the worship of Ianus or Janus in Rome and the emission of coins with his image cast or stamped upon them, cannot be assigned to an earlier date than the fifth or sixth century B C According to Cato, Janus was a Scythian divinity. He was the son of the virgin Crissa, or Creusa, by the god Apollo To avoid the displeasure of her father, (Ericthonius,) Creusa entrusted her infant to an ark, which being transported to the temple of Delphos, the priestess of that sanctuary reared it tenderly and eventually restored it to its mother. Janus was a ten months' infant, born in an humble cottage; and among shepherds He was the patron of peace, of commerce and the vine In virtue of his divine origin he became the Prince of Peace and the Doorkeeper of Heaven We here have the mythology of several ages jumbled together Plutarch, Fabius Pictor; Virgil; Ovid, Fasti, I, 33, 122, 141, 199, 254; Noel, " Dic Fable " The attributes of Janus were the same as those of Dionysios and Osiris Faber, " Pagan Idol " He was also Bi-frons (two-faced) and held the keys of heaven. Diodorus and Macrobius state that the temple of Janus in Rome was built by Romulus; probably a fable. This temple had four sides, each with a door and three windows, representing the four seasons and twelve months Such a division of the year in Rome was in fact much later than the period assigned to Romulus Says Ovid: " When the Founder of the City divided the periods, he provided that there should be twice five months in the year " Fasti, I, 28   According to Livy, I, 19, the temple of Janus was built by Numa   But Numa's year was a lunar one and it consisted of (at the most) 354 days, which does not fit the 365 days represented by the fingers of Janus   These considerations fix the erection of his temple at Rome at a much later period   The real æra of Janus probably coincides with that of the Jain æra of Ies Chrishna and his worship was most likely introduced from the Orient by way of Pontus   See B. C. 1219   Janus died a violent death at the age of 33 years

B. C. 641, Syria.—Death or nirvana of Thamoez or Thammuz (Buddha), as fixed by the post-Augustan or Christian reckoning   The nirvana of Thammuz was celebrated on the last day of the month Thamoez.   The æra began on Ab 1st   The division of the year into 12 months and the week of seven days probably followed the introduction of this worship into Syria   See Maimonides, under B C 582   The alteration of the calendar possibly synchronises with the Armenian æra of B. C, 552, q v   The two intercalated Syrian months were evidently Teshrin II and Canoon II.

B. C. 639, Athens.—Birth of Solon, who died at the age of 80 years   Greswell, K H , I, 8, n

B. C. 638, China.—Chinese and Peguan æra of Buddha   Prof Wilson

B. C. 633, Pontus.—Invasion of the Sacæ, according to Herodotus and Ctesias   The Sacæ invaded Asia Minor in the reign of Cyaxares of Media and Psammitichus of Egypt   To these, as a contemporary monarch, has been added Sardanapalus, who is identified with Esar-banipal, of Assyria, B. C 668-626   Rodwell, in "Records of the Past," p. 287, prefers B. C 625 for the date of this invasion of the Sacæ.   They continued in Western Asia for 28 years before they were driven out   See B C 548

B. C. 633, Burma.—Buddhic æra   According to Bigandet, the birth of Buddha occurred in the 68th year of the Eetzana æra, which commenced B. C 701, q v.

B. C. 630, Persia.—Death of the first Zoroaster, according to the Abbé Foucher   Mem Acad Ins , vols 27, 29, 31, 39   He says that Zoroaster was born in Media, established his religion in Bactria under Cyaxares I and was put to death by the Scythians in B. C. 630   Hence he was born about B. C. 710.   The second Zoroaster appeared in the reign of Darius.

On the other hand, M. Anquetil du Perron maintains that there never was more than one Zoroaster, born about B C 589 and put to death by the Scythians in 512 To this view Mr Hyde and Dean Prideaux both assent M du Perron believes that the first Zoroaster of Pliny was no other than Hom or Hoomo, who flourished in the reign of Gjemschid Mem Acad Ins , vols. 31, 37. For Pliny's views see B. C 6369 For other opinions see B. C. 590. Niebuhr regards both the Zoroasters as mythical.

B C. 629, India.—Jain æra of Mahavira The Pandits' "Chron." See B C 1219

B. C. 619, Ceylon.—Cingalese æra of Buddha. Prof. Wilson.

B. C. 612, Rome.—Approximate date of the birth of Servius Tullius See B. C. 578

B. C. 610, Sicyon.—Approximate æra of the deification and worship by his subjects of Adrastus, son of Talaus, and son-in-law of Polybus This worship consisted of prayers, sacrifices, sacred dances, the observance of festivals and the performance of tragic choruses A shrine was erected to Adrastus in the forum or market-place of Sicyon, which shrine was still standing in the time of Herodotus. The Sicyonians had previously worshipped Bacchus Herod , Terp 67

B. C. 604, China.—Aera of Lao-tsze See B C 667

B. C. 600, Dioscurias.—A city of Colchis, at the mouth of the Charus, on the eastern shore of the Euxine, was founded about this time by the Milesians Koehne, II, 437. The interest in this event arises from the corroboration it may afford to the colonisation of the Crimea by the Heracleotes, B C 658

B. C. 598, India.—Birth of Buddha, according to Taylor's "India," p 44

B. C. 592, Attica.—Aera of Solon and the Republic. But see B C 582. Down to this period the government of Athens was an unmitigated oligarchy. Aristotle Until the period of Solon the Athenians "displayed no signs of that intellectual superiority which they were destined to assume " Clinton, F. H., I, viii. From this æra may be dated the rights of citizenship and suffrage, representation in the legislature, juries, (discasts,) habeas corpus, marriage laws, and many other institutes of freedom and civilisation, since become familiar to the states of Europe and America, but wholly unknown to them previous to the age of Solon.

B C. 592, Attica.—Lunar-solar octæteric calendar of Solon, beginning Gamelion 1st=January 18-19th at midnight B. C 592, the year which followed the archonship of Solon (Greswell) January 18th is still the Athenian New Year day This was anciently the period of the Halcyon Days, but various alterations of the calendar have shifted them about and finally shuffled them off altogether

B. C. 592, Ionia.—April 25 Beginning of the second Panionic cycle Greswell, Kal. Hell, III, 375.

B. C. 590, Persia.—Aera of Zoroaster: viz, 258 years before Alexander and 3000 years after the Creation Albiruni, op cit, 17. Greswell treats of the "first" and "second" Zoroaster, as the Hindus spoke of the first and second Buddha, the Macedo-Egyptians of the first and second Hermes and the Greeks, of the first and second Mercury Stanley ("Chaldaic Philosophy") translated Zoroaster, "Son of a Star." Others called him Zara Suidas says he was also called Nazaratus. This is the same as Thammuz or Buddha Plato, who calls him the son of Oromases, or Or-om-esus, or Son of God, says that he wrote a book called "Revelations," that after his death he rose again and lived ten days more, etc ("Lives of the Ancient Philosophers," [Anon,] pp ii-iv) Xanthus says that Zoroaster flourished 600 years before Xerxes' expedition into Greece, which occurred in Olym lxxv, 1, or (B C. 476), a reckoning that would fix Zoroaster in B. C 1076. This is the æra of Ies Chrishna. Cf. Anonymous "Lives of the Ancient Philosophers" London, 1702, 8vo. Br Museum Library No 275, g 8 But see herein B. C 389 Zoroaster was foretold by the Magi: his celestial father was Ormuzd, otherwise Or-om-esus, or Iesdan; he was born in Bactria on the vernal equinox (hilaria) to the accompaniment of flowers and music; he was recognized by the Magi as the Expected One and presented with flowers and perfumes; from his visage shone a divine light and his Messianic character was proved by numerous miracles Though tempted by Ahriman, the Evil One, he pursued his beneficent mission, which was to bring true religion, peace and happiness to mankind; these principles being incorporated in his Avesta, or as it is commonly called, the Zendavesta He had 12 disciples. His doctrines required or caused him to suffer a violent death, which occurred upon the winter solstice and was commemorated by the ceremonies of the Megalenses, or Mourners. His descent to hell and his sojourn there of ten days (some writers say three days and nights) appear to be of comparatively modern invention So may also he his bodily ascent to heaven His principal sacrament was baptism, his epigraphic symbol, the cross; his zodions the Lamb and Fishes; whilst his second (or third) advent was to be after three divine years These have since expired

B. C. 584, Ionia.—Augustan date of the solar eclipse said to have been predicted by Thales of Miletus, the Christian date being B C 601. Says Herodotus in Clio 74: "In the sixth year (of the war between the Lydians and Medes, the latter being commanded by Cyaxares), it happened that in the heat of the battle, day was suddenly turned into night   This phenomenon Thales the Milesian had foretold to the Ionians, fixing beforehand this year as the very period in which it would take place " Greswell, K. H , VI, 653, declares that in the western world no eclipse was ever calculated from actual observations before the time of Hipparchus, B C 160-45; and that the prediction of Thales was based upon the cycle of the eclipses, or Divine Year, which determines the round of eclipses once in 6586 days, without reflecting that a knowledge of the cycle itself could only have been derived from actual and oft-repeated observations previously made and therefore many ages before the time of Hipparchus   Sir G B Airy, and F Partington, in Brit Cyc 1835, art "Astronomy," fix this eclipse, Sept 30, B C 610; Calvisius and Father Petau, July 30, 607; Mayer, Costard, Stukely, Montucla, Kennedy ("Scriptural Chron ") and Hales, 603; Pingré and Bishop Usher, 601, Petavius and Larcher, 597, Pliny (Nat Hist II (ix), xii, says A U 170, which is equal to B C. 584   Scaliger, Newton, Riccioli, Des Mignoles, Kepler, Strauchius, Manfredi, De Brosses and others say B C. 585   Rev. Wm Hales ("Scriptural Chron ") says the eclipse of 607 was only visible near the equator; that of 601, north of the Euxine; that of 597, north of the Caspian; while that of 585, "followed the course of the Mediterranean Sea and did not touch Cappadocia " Though this is not impossible, it is difficult to see how it could do one without the other   If the story is true, Kepler, Newton, Riccioli, and Manfredi should be decisive as to the date of the eclipse; but in fact the date really belongs to mythology and not to astronomy.   Thales predicted the eclipse, not from the appearance or movements of the heavenly bodies, but by means of the Divine Year   Add the 78 years sunk by Augustus, to B C 584 and it becomes the Indian date of the death of Buddha, or Ies Chrishna, the god of the Khazares, who at this period were the masters of the so-called kingdom of Media   The name of " Cyaxares, son of Phraortes " sounds so much like a Greek corruption of the "Khazares, sons of Prototh-Ies," that it is to be feared that this portion of the history of Herodotus is confused and unreliable

B. C. 584, Khazaria.—Æra of Mad-Ies, son of Prototh-Ies, king of the Scythians   Herod I, 103   F Dubois de Montpereaux, in his "Voyage autour du Caucase," 1839, IV, 354, says that according to the Georgian historians, these "Scythians" were the Khazares or Ghazares of the Cimmerian Bosphorus

B. C. 584, Ascalon.—Aera of the fable of Medusa. The first regnal year of Cyaxares, (son of Phraortes,) king of Media, the Irruption of the Scythians and the Plunder of Ascalon, all occurred in B C. 633. The Scythians (Montpereaux calls them Khazares), under Madyes, entered Asia Minor and marched through Syria to the conquest of Egypt. Upon the frontier Psammitichus met them with presents and turned them away. On reaching Ascalon a portion of their number plundered the temple of the Celestial Venus, or Venus Urania, the oldest and probably the richest temple erected to the worship of this mother of the gods. "Upon the Scythians who committed this profanation and upon all their posterity, the goddess visited the punishment of effeminacy." (So is this difficult passage in Herodotus, I, 105, construed by Prof. Ch G Heyne, in Com. Soc Reg. Gotting., anni 1770, II, 28-44.) During the following 28 years the Scythians ravaged the whole of Asia Minor, but were at last driven out by Cyaxares, who inveigled and destroyed their leaders. In B C 548, Cyrus of Persia conquers Asia Minor, and in keeping with his tolerant attitude toward the Jews, as shown in the Bible, he restores the temple of Ascalon to the worshippers of Venus We have here all the elements of the fable of Perseus, which was probably invented by the priests of the plundered temple Madyes, upon being effeminated, becomes Madyesa, whom the Greeks call Medusa. The detachment who plundered the temple, being effeminated, become Amazons Their ferocity is symbolized by the horrid aspect and serpent hair of Medusa and their ravages are compensated by the valour and generosity of Persia, or Perseus. The Persian priests did more than this; they deified Cyrus himself See B C. 1291.

B. C. 582, Babylon.—Aera of Thammuz. Probable date when the Chaldean calendar was altered. This is believed to have been done by Nebo-Chadn-Izzar, whose father, Nebo-Pol-Izzar, had been appointed by Saracas, king of Assyria, as his viceroy, in Babylon. Pol-Izzar betrayed his master and plotted with the Medes, and in 606 Nineveh was captured and the Assyrian empire overthrown After a reign of two years as king of Babylon, Pol-Izzar was succeeded by his son, who had already defeated Necho of Egypt, at Karchemish and who subsequently (in 582) invaded and ravaged Egypt itself. It was probably after his return from this enterprise that Nebo-Chadn-Izzar made those alterations of the calendar which have been attributed to the mythical Nebo-Nazaru, or Thammuz The changed divi-

sion of the year from ten to 12 months, the invention of the myth
of Nebo-Nazaru, and the establishment of his æra, by dating back
to B C 747 or 748; all appear to have been effected during this
reign.   On the subject of Thammuz (or Tammuz, or Tham-Ies)
Maimonides has the following: Thammuz was a false Messiah who
appeared before the king of Assyria and proclaimed to him that he
had brought into the land the worship of the Seven planets and the
zodiac of Twelve Signs   The king, indignant at his boldness, ordered him to be put to death   On the following night all the statues
of the gods from every part of the world assembled in the Temple
of the Sun at Babylon.   The statue of the Sun, which stood amidst
them all, was hurled to the earth, whilst those who surrounded him
began to weep for Thammuz, and this weeping they continued until
he arrived.   Upon the following day, at dawn, each of the gods returned to his proper temple; in memory of which (strange occur-
rences) the Sabians (Crestos) weep for Thammuz on the last day of
the month which goes by his name   Noel.   Weeping for Thammuz
is mentioned as an idolatrous rite in Ezekiel, viii   Greswell, II, 554,
says the rite was observed on the first day of Thammuz, which he
tallies with August 28th in the Julian calendar, but in his zeal to
maintain a Hebrew Primeval Year of 12 months, Dr Greswell, although a most learned and industrious writer, has closed his pages
to the reception of almost all evidences that fail to harmonise with
this theory.   August 28-29 is a sacerdotal day of great antiquity connected with the worship of Ies Chrishna.   It is also that to which the
Romans assigned the death of their god, Augustus Dionysius   It is
still the day of "Saint Augustine" in the Roman calendar   For the
day of Thammuz, see B C 641

B. C. 582, Attica.—Most probable date of the archonship and
legislation ascribed to Solon and described herein under B C 592
Suidas says in one place, Ol xlvii, which is B C. 588, Aulus Gellius
says the 33d year of Tarquinius Priscus, which is equal to B C 582,
Demosthenes intimates an equivalent date; "Eusebius" and "Jerome" date the previous legislation of Draco in Ol xxxix, or B C
624-620; while Diod. Sic., as quoted by Ulpian, says that the legislation of Solon was 47 years later, which is B. C. 577-73; Cicero, in
Brutus, 10, 39, regards Solon and Pisistratus as contemporaries or
Servius Tullius, who reigned B C 576-33, finally, Suidas, in another
place, says Ol lxi, which is equal to B. C. 554.   The mutilated
Parian marbles do not give the æra of Solon, but they fix the "tyranny"
of Pisistratus in the archonship of Connas, which was 297 years be-

fore that of Diognetus This is equal to B. C 561. The mutually corroborative dates of Demosthenes and Aulus Gellius are regarded as furnishing the most reliable information on the subject

B. C. 578, Rome.—Accession of Servius Tullius. He was born about 612, the son of a captive woman of Corniculum, his father unknown. While yet a youth he was found asleep in the palace of Tarquinius Priscus, his head surrounded by a divine flame Both the king and his queen Tanaquil having witnessed this prodigy, Servius was adopted by them and educated as one who was destined by the gods to fill an exalted station Tarquinius betrothed his daughter to the youth, who, upon the death of his patron in 578, was called by Tanaquil to the vacant throne. During his reign, "the temple of Diana at Ephesus was universally venerated" and Servius, in order to foster the worship of this goddess, encouraged the building of a temple to her in Rome, among the principal rites of which was that of baptism in running water The ambition of Tarquinius Superbus and the favours which Servius bestowed upon the lower orders of citizens led to his assassination by the nobles in the Via Cypriana, close to the temple which he had erected to Diana, B C 534, aged about 78 years Livy, I, 18 to 48; IV, 3 Higgins, Anal , II, 393, regards the story of Servius Tullius as mythical and as resembling that of the Hindu incarnations. With this opinion, the present writer cannot altogether agree.

B. C. 576, India.—Aera of Parasara, a celebrated Indian astronomer, according to the scriptural astronomer, Bentley. See B. C. 1391 and 1181

B. C. 569, India.—Jain æra of Mahavira "The Jains in some parts of India follow the æra of Mahavira, their last Jain, whom they regard as the preceptor of Gotama, placing him in the year 569 B C., and thus a few years prior to Gotama Others call him the Disciple, twelve years later than Gotama. He was the 24th teacher of the Jain religion No Jain inscriptions show traces of an exclusive chronology. They bear invariably, the Sumbat date of Vicramaditya." The Pandits "Chron." As the Sumbat æra coincides with B. C. 57, the 24th teacher and the date of 569 B C , both appear to be afterthoughts. See B C 1219 The Pandits' statement with regard to the chronology of the Jains does not agree with Col. Wilford, Gen Cunningham, or Mr Edward Thomas' work on "Jainism"

B. C. 567, India.—Augustan date of the death of Gotama, the Buddha, as given in Asiatic Researches. Duff Rickmer's "Indian Chronology" fixes Buddha's birth in B. C 557 and his death in B. C.

477. Rhys Davids assigns his death to about B C 412; Westergaard and Kern to between B. C. 388 and 370   These dates are entirely out of harmony with what is known, beyond question, of Buddhic laws and institutes.   The lowest admissible date for the death (nirvana) of the Second Buddha is B. C. 578.   The Cingalese date of B C. 543, though commonly used in works of reference, is 35 years wrong.

B. C. 552, Burma —Death of Buddha in his 80th year.   The 148th year of the Eetzana æra and commencement of the Religious æra   The world convulsed by earthquakes.   Bishop Paul A Bigandet, in his " Life or Legend of Gaudama," furnishes the following account from Burmese sources.   Buddha was a ten months' child, miraculously born of the queen Maia, impregnated by the god Phralaong, his putative father being king Thoodandana.   Immediately after his birth Buddha was recognised as of divine origin and was worshipped by the wise and powerful, among others by his putative father.   He preached a Sermon on the Mount, converted the courtesan Apapalika, performed numerous miracles, partook of a Last Supper with his disciples and died in the " 148th year of the Eetzana æra, in the full moon of Katson, on a Tuesday, a little before daybreak."   He was conceived in the year 67 of the Eetzana, born in 68, on a Friday; retired to meditate in solitude in 96, on a Monday; and became a Buddha in 103, on a Wednesday   After his ascension king Adzatathat abolished the Eetzana æra and substituted the Religious æra beginning in the 148th year thereof, or that of the Buddha's death

B C 552, Armenia.—Aera of Armenia, which about this year was colonised by a mixed race of Khazares and Greeks, worshippers of Ies Chrishna or Dionysios.   See Gotland, B. C 90, and Armenia, A D 552

B C 551, China.—Birth of Confucius, according to Rev C Hole.   But see 511.

B. C. 548, Magna Graecia.—Apotheosis of Aesculapius, this being his 33rd year.   He was born at Samos, some say Epidaurus, in the 50th olympiad, B C 580, his celestial father was Apollo; his virgin mother was Coronis; his putative father was Mnesarchos; he was exposed, when an infant, on a mountain, but saved by goatherds; he was recognised by the sages as the Expected One, "the Saviour"; rays of glory encircled his head, he had 12 disciples and 300 selecti, he performed innumerable miracles, and after many sufferings which he underwent for the sake of saving humanity, he was at last snatched up to heaven The principal scene of his activity was Croton, in Magna Græcia Grote says that Aesculapius established a select aristocracy; Pococke says that his religion was Buddhic-Lamaism Both of these views seem far-fetched According to Ovid, (Metam.) Aesculapius, after suffering death for mankind, rose again before his final disappearance He was worshipped in Greece, Ptolemaic Egypt, Rome and several other countries of the ancient world His zodion was the Lamb, and at the temple erected to his worship at Mendes in Egypt, this zodion was employed to represent the god One of his statuesque attributes is the serpent. He is sometimes referred to as Aesclepiades.

B C. 547, Egypt —Real date of an Egyptian calendar in the British Museum, which, according to Greswell, is falsely and fraudulently dated in the "56th year of Rameses the Great," whom he regards as a personage "who never had any real existence, except in the chronology of the monuments." F C., III, 411, n. Judging from the calendrical alteration which seems to have been effected in Babylon B C 582, (q v) this year, B C. 547, appears to mark the date when a similar alteration was effected in Egypt

B C. 545, India —Vira æra of the Jains. Duft Rickmers, p. 23. For Vira, read Mahavira. See B. C 1219

B. C. 544, India.—Sakya (æra) or nirvana of the Second Buddha. This is only one of many dates accorded to this æra in the Orient It is deduced in the following manner The Nirvana occurred 196 years before Kandra Gupta, (the contemporary of Alexander the Great), B. C. 348. Hence 348+196=544 B C The Pandits "Chron "

B. C. 544, Siam.—Nirvana of Buddha, December 25th Marsden, op cit and Stokvis Greswell, I, 583, says B C 545.

B. C 543, Ceylon —Nirvana of Buddha, Son of the Virgin Maia Massey, "Genesis," 550. The favorite name of this incarnation is Sakya Muni. Taylor's "India," p. 44, says that Buddha was born B. C 598

B. C. 543, India.—Sacred æra of India, Ceylon, Ava, Siam, etc. Pandits' "Chron "

B. C. 543, India, Burma and Ceylon.—The nirvana of Buddha occurred 214 years before Asoka, according to the Indian records Cunningham. But see B. C. 263. If the christian date of Asoka's accession is correct, viz , B C 263, this would place the nirvana of Buddha in 477, whereas the common (christian) date in Ceylon and Burma is 543 The difference of 66 years is noticed, but not accounted for, by Gen Cunningham. An explanation is offered herein under the year B. C 814, "Rome" The puranas date the accession of Asoka in 311 or 312 of the nirvana. If we add the oldest date of Asoka, B. C 266, and the 63 years dropped from the calendar, this would place the nirvana in B C 641

B. C. 534, Rome.—Calendar ascribed to Numa. See B C 452.

B C 533, India.—Nirvana of Mahavira, according to the Swetambara sect of Jains, who date it 470 years before Vicrama, who was born, by the christian calendar, B C 63 This reckoning throws Mahavira into B. C 533. The Digambara Jains fix the nirvana of Mahavira 605 years before the æra of a Vicrama, who is 141 years later than him of B C. 63, hence his date is A. D. 78. This computation throws Mahavira into B C 527 Both of these dates are from Gen Cunningham

B. C. 533, Persia.—Persian æra Deification of Cyrus the Elder He was the son of god, miraculously born of the virgin Mandane, the daughter of Astyges, his putative father being Cambyses. (Herod Clio , 107, 204) Owing to the prediction of the Magi, his grandfather issued orders for his destruction while he was yet an infant. In pursuance of this cruel decree Cyrus was given out to be put to death, but was providentially saved by a shepherd After some years of service as a pastor, Cyrus was recognised as the predicted heavenborn prince of the world, and as such was invited to ascend the throne of Persia The name of his mother, as it appears in the extant MSS of Herodotus, may be a corruption of Mania, Mariana, etc This name appears in Mariandynia, a province and people of Asia Minor under the sway of Cyrus, probably named after Maryamma or else her namesake, the Pescenuntian mother See B C 205 Rome The Mariandynians were apparently the same people alluded to in Polymnia 76, whose name is effaced in the MSS . and who, like the Carians, or Leleges, wore peculiar crests upon their horned helmets Herod. Clio, 171; Strabo, voc Leleges. Cf Abbé Halma, on Ptolemy, p 208. Cyrus was born about B. C 594, ascended the throne 569, was deified and worshipped in 543 or 533, and died in 529 According to Mirkhond, Cyrus did not die at all; he disappeared supernaturally. Diodorus says that he was crucified

B. C. 533, Crotona.—Pretended advent of Pythagoras and his twelve disciples, whom the Benedictine monks of a recent age adroitly alluded to as the "Twelve Spheres" These numbers were obtained from an anonymous biographer whom Sir Geo. Cornewall Lewis discredits. Instead of 12 the Pythagoreans held that the number 10 was alone perfect. They had ten (not 12) celestial bodies, viz , the five planets, sun, moon, earth, heavens and the antichthon, the latter an invisible body that sometimes caused eclipses Roth regarded Xenophanes, Anaximenes, and Pythagoras as exact contemporaries, fixing the æra of the latter B. C. 569-470. Pauly fixes his birth, 580-68 Meiners fixes his birth in Olym. xlix, 2 and death in Olym. lxviii, 3, or lxix, 2 In the quadrennial olympiadsthis would be 583-506 or 503, while in the quinquennial olympiads it would be 643-547 or 543 See B. C. 738. Lewis regards the account of the travels of Pythagoras in Babylon and the East as "too suspicious to fulfil the conditions of historical credibility." The 300 Selecti of Pythagoras and Pisistratus appear in the 300 Celeres of Romulus and Tamerlane.

B. C. 527, India —Nirvana of Mahavira, according to the Digambara sect of Jains See B. C 1219

B C. 527, Athens.—Death of Pisistratus, who had been worshipped during his lifetime as an incarnation of the deity and had reigned absolutely 33 years, during which time he altered and published the poems and theogeny ascribed to Homer Herodotus, Cicero, Pausanias He was guarded by 300 Selecti Polyænus.

B. C. 525, Egypt.—Conquest and plunder of Egypt by Cambyses, k of Persia, who for his disrespect to the native gods, was loaded with infamy by the priests. Diodorus says that the Persians reigned in Egypt 135 and the Macedonians 276 years, but as this does not agree with the received chronology, it has yet to be seen which is right

B. C. 521, Persia.—Aera of Darius, son of Hystapses. He was born about 547; ascended the throne and was deified about 521; conquered Babylon, 517 (Greswell prefers 520-19); reconnoitered the valley of the Indus, 515, and in or about the same year proclaimed himself and demanded to be worshipped, as a Manifestation of the Deity Revolt of the Ionians, 499; suppression of the revolt by Darius, 498; revolt of the Scythians (Goths), 499; Scythic invasion of Asia Minor, 495, ineffectual invasion of Scythia (Thracia) by Darius, 495; his Retreat, 494; Darius defeated by the Greeks and allies at Marathon, 490; conquers Egypt, where he is worshipped as god; (Diodorous, book I;) and dies in 485 The Greek writers in suppressing some of these particulars and concealing the fact that Darius was their lawful suzerain, have greatly perverted the meaning of ancient history.

B. C. 521, Lydia.—Aera of Lydia Humphreys' "Coin Manual," p 548 It is quite possible that this is identical with the æra of the Ionian revolt given above as having occurred in 499

B. C. 512, Attica.—Institution of the ten tribes and prytanies. Grote, "Hist. Greece," IV, 219-20. The Athenians had previously consisted of four tribes. Herod. Terp. 66-9.

B. C. 511, China.—Confucius, (Kung-fu-tsu) born B. C. 511. De Milloué, "Guide au Musée Guimet," Paris, 1894, p. 96. Rev. Ch. Hole fixes his birth in 551 and death in 479; but De Milloué's date is preferable. Confucius was the author of a moral code, which, though recognising the existence of a Supreme Creator, (Kang-ti) taught that true religion embraced not man's relation to the gods, but to his fellowmen. Praying, on the part of individuals, is dispensed with; this act of piety being relegated exclusively to the Emperor, who, upon the solstices and equinoxes, is required to pray for the entire nation. Veneration, not worship, is enjoined for ancestors, who should be regarded as though still living. This constitutes "la seule veritable religion des Chinois Confucéens." De Milloué.

B. C. 510, Athens.—After the expulsion of the Pisistratidæ, Isagoras, the son of Tisander, whose ancestry is alluded to by Herodotus in a mysterious manner, supposedly because it pretended to be derived from Bacchus, was worshipped (for a brief period) until he was deposed by Clisthenes of Athens. Herod. Terp., 66-72.

B. C. 510, Rome.—Aera of the Republic, the first consuls being Lucius Junius Brutus and Lucius Tarquinius Collatinus. Lenglet says B. C. 509. These consuls began their offices on August, 1st, our Lammas. See B. C. 156. The Fasti Consulares, or Lists of the Consuls, from this date onward, are given by Livy, Gothofredi, Lenglet, Lempriere, Greswell, Babelon and Cohen; the two last being the most complete.

B. C. 509, Chorassan.—Aera of Moses, according to an ancient marble inscription erected by the Jews of Cai-fong-fou, the capital of Honan, 150 leagues from Pekin, China. The Jews in this place were a colony which came from Chorassan and Samarcand, about A. D. 73. The inscription relates that "Moses lived 613 years after the beginning of Tcheou." This reign began B. C. 1122. According to this account Moses lived B. C. 509. This is two Divine years later than the period assigned to the Moses of the Bible. See Zalmosis, B. C. 495.

B. C. 495, Thracia.—Appearance of Gebel-Eisis, or Zalmosis, "a native deity among the Getæ " of Thracia, who taught the immortality of the soul, gave laws to the Getæ, (Diodorus, book I), disappeared in a subterranean abode for three years, was lamented as dead, and yet was resurrected and returned to life again. Festivals with human

sacrifices were offered to him every fifth year   Herod Mel , 93-96
Herodotus rather diffidently expresses the opinion that Zalmosis, or
Eisis, was earlier than Pythagoras, son of Mnesarchos, but if this
was true he has mentioned Eisis out of his chronological order, for
such mention occurs during his account of the Scythian expedition
of Darius The worship of Eisis in Thracia, Scythia and the Crimea,
was continued to a much later date.   He is probably the same with
the Hesus of the Gauls, one of whose altars was recovered in 1726
from beneath the Roman foundations of Notre Dame and is now in
the Cluny Museum of Paris   Dupuis, I, 22   See Moses, B.C 509

B. C 495, Rome —Aera of the Roman Habeas Corpus Act.   On
the ides of May (this is now Whitsuntide) A. U 259, a temple to
Liber Pater was erected near the Circus Maximus, probably to commemorate the passage of an act which resembled the modern Habeas
Corpus   Down to that time the Roman creditor had the right to
seize and imprison the person of his debtor   In that year, owing to
certain affecting circumstances related by Livy, the consul issued an
edict that "no person should hold any Roman citizen in bonds or
confinement, so as to hinder his being brought before the consuls,
that no person should take possession nor make sale of the effects of
a soldier while upon service, nor detain in custody either his children
or grandchildren " Livy, II, 24   A similar edict was issued by
Solon. See B C. 325 and 592

B. C. 485, Spain and Gaul.—Aera of Hesus. son of God and of
Maria, the Virgo Paritura   St John Chrysostom, in a sermon which
he is asserted to have preached on December 25, A D 386, said that
the observance of this day as a religious festival had not been clearly
known to "them " (his hearers) longer than ten years, "but that it
had been familiar, *from the beginning*, to those who dwelt in the
West " London "Chronicle," December 25, 1897.   In this connection, those who dwelt in the West could only have meant the Celts
or Gauls, who worshipped Hesus, as mentioned in Ovid and Lucan
In France, on Christmas Day, so late as the reign of Louis XIV.,
the monks used to go about with a box, crying, "tiré-lire," and begging for alms for "a Lady in labor " This was said to have been a
custom derived from the Druids, who practiced it before the Christian æra.   Dr Robinson (of Edinburgh), in his ' Natural Philosophy," pp 200-210, cited in Rev Wm D D Hales' "Chronology,"
p 50. See B C. 495 and 470.   For authorities concerning Hesus,
the son of Maria, consult Higgins' "Celtic Druids "

B. C. 480, Bosporus.—Approximate æra of the kingdom of Bos-

porus Humphreys, p 169. This date probably marks the emancipation of Bosporus from the suzerainty of Persia   At a later period
Bosporus was added to Pontus.   See B C. 301.

B. C. 479, Argos.—Aera of Chrysis, priestess of the Pelasgian
Juno at Argos.   This æra is used by Thucydides in his history of
the Peloponnesian war, at the beginning of the first year of the war,
which was the 48th of Chrysis   This answers to B C 431

B. C. 472, Rome.—Beginning of the Roman lustra, or five-year
cycles   Haydn   Contrariwise, Censorinus, XVIII, attributes them
to the reign of Servius Tullius, about a century earlier   Epoch. August 1st (now called Lammas), at that time the New Year day in
Rome

B. C. 470, India —Brahminical æra of Ies Chrishna

B. C. 470, Gaul.—Conjectural date when the Druidical 30-year
cycles began.   They are mentioned by Pliny, N H , XVI. 95   The
Gauls (Gallaicans) are mentioned by Herodotus, VII, 108, as having
"anciently" occupied Samothracian Greece, near the river L'Issus.
Their sea-port (now inland) was Issmarus   The next historical notice is in 390-85, when vast bodies of Gauls overran Italy and Greece,
plundered the temple at Delphos and marched in a sort of crusade
to their holy land of Maryandynia, where many of them remained
Simon Pelloutier, in his " Histoire des Celtes," V, 15, says that the
Virgo Paritura was worshipped in the district of Chartres more than
a century before the Christian æra.   Cf Dupuis, III, 51   A similar
statement appears in Rigordius, cited by L'Escaloperius de Théologia Veterum, Gallorum, cap. X, and in André Duchesne, Les Antiquitez et Recherches des Villes, ed 1609, pp 292-6   Of a possibly still more ancient date is the Druid altar, on which is carved a
representation and the name of their god, Hesus, cutting the sacred
mistletoe   This stone was found in 1726 beneath the Roman foundations of Nôtre Dame de Paris and is now in the Cluny Museum
Hesus is alluded to in Ovid and Lucan   Rev G S Faber, in his
"Orig Pagan Idol ," says that Hesus, Esa, Ma-Hesa and and Har-
Esa are the same, and were known to the Latin writers as Mercury
Higgins, Anacal , I, 154   Arrian, ch VIII, alludes to the same god
as Herichiishna   The Druidical reverence for the samolus, or passion
flower, is mentioned by Pliny, N. H , XXIV, 63.   It must be gathered with the left hand, while fasting; the person who gathers it
must not look behind him, etc   The samolus and passion flower are
identified by Anguillara   Certain Druidical rites were forbidden by
decree ('   '   '' 97 (\   ,   it our-

ished B C 44, says (V, 2) that the Gauls wore gold crosses on their breasts The 30-year cycles were employed in ancient Greece as a sæculum, or " age," by which to compute time

B. C. 463, Rome.—Consular year begun August 1st Livy, III, 6 This New Year day, belonged, in fact, to a much earlier period

B. C. 453, Judea.—Ezra writes the Chronicles Putnam

B. C. 452, Rome.—" In this year the Decemvirs changed the order of the months and placed February after January." Am Encyc. Brit., art. "Calendar." According to this authority, when "Numa" divided the year into 12 months, instead of ten, as it stood more anciently, he placed January at the beginning of the " year " and February at the end If the same "year " is meant in both cases this would place January between February and March; and it would follow that the reform of the Decemvirs simply consisted of changing the places of January and February—one for the other But this is probably not what took place "Numa" is more likely to have been the Decemvirs themselves, who placed February at the end of the Consular year, which began with Lammas, and January at the beginning of what has since become the Julian year, in other words, they placed one of the new months at the end of each of the two sets of five months in the ancient year of ten January was, therefore, between December and March, while February was between July and August The essential point is the admission of the Britanica that the existing order of the months was established by the Decemvirs. John of Nikios hints that under Augustus, February was made to change places with August. See chap. II of the present work.

B.C. 432, Athens.—Metonic "euneakaidecæteric" lunar-solar calendar, commencing Hecatombion 1st, July 15th, invented by Meton Adopted by the state, B C, 425, to supersede the Solonic calendar, which began on Gamelion 1st. Although itself erroneous and although the measure of the error was calculated and offered to be remedied by Calippus, B C 330, the Metonic calendar was not superseded until it was absorbed in the Julian, B C 48 Meton retained Solon's three decads to the month and left unchanged the intercalary month at the end of Poseidon; but he changed the New Year day to first Hecatombion, whose position he also altered making it equal to our 15th July. Greswell, Kal Hell , I, 507. Parker says July 16, B C. 432.

B. C. 415, India.—Ctesias a Greek physician of Cnidus, resided, between 415 and 388, at the court of Darius II of Persia He wrote

"Indica," the earliest western work on India, an "abridgment" of which by Photios still exists   Duff Rickmers

B. C. 395, Sparta.—Death of Lysander, a Spartan commander, who, after destroying the Athenian fleet in the Hellespont, sailed to Athens, obtained its surrender and thus ended the Peloponnesian war, B C 404   The glory of this achievement, coupled perhaps, with the reading of Ctesias' account of the Indian incarnations, turned his head   He set himself up for a god, and, as such, accepted worship from the terrified and servile inhabitants of Asia Minor   His pretensions were resented by the Spartans, who, charging him with embezzlement, consigned him to opprobrium, neglect and poverty   His attitude and history were curiously repeated two centuries later by Scipio Africanus   See Rome, B C. 201

B. C. 389, Persia.—Aera of Zoroaster, according to Avicenna, who says Zoroaster was born 372, 660 days (i e., about 1020¼ solar years) before the æra of Iesdigerd, which makes Zoroaster's birthday equal to March 3, B C 389   The Pandits "Chron " See ante, B C 590, for another account   Zoroaster is assigned by Persian writers to the reign of Gustasp, whose name is mentioned in the Zendavesta.   Zoroaster himself is mentioned by Plato, B C 427-347   In these dates no account is taken of the 78 years dropped from the calendar by Augustus, nor of the 15 years restored (probably) after Justinian II.   In adopting Avicenna's opinion of Zoroaster's æra, the Pandits, p. xxiii, refer to Troyer's translation of Dabistan; Sir W. Ouseley's "Travels in the East" (who cites Agathias), Shea's translation of Mirkhond ; Conder's "Persia and China," Clement of Alexandria (who says that Pythagoras was the "forerunner" of Zoroaster) ; and Jamblichus' "Life of Pythagoras " See also works of Walter Moyle.

B. C. 389, Phoenicia.—Persian æra of Tripolis, comprising the cities of Aradia, Sidon and Tyre, on the coast of Phœnicia   This æra was found by Cardinal Henry Noris, on several coins of Elagabalus (years "531, 532 and 533 ") and by him mistaken for the æra of Seleucus   Diodorus Siculus says that in Olym cvii, 2 (B. C 351), Tripolis rebelled against and repelled the Persians   See A D 220 for other dates of Elagabalus.

B. C. 380, Europe, etc.—The Sun left the sign of Aries and entered Pisces in the 12-sign zodiac   It takes 2160 years to make the precession of each sign   Higgins, Anacal , I, 194   Hence the entrance of the sun into the next sign occurred A D. 1780, q. v   Elsewhere Higgins fixes the first-named event in B C. 360, his year for Alexander's birth   Anacal , I, 777; II, 346

B. C. 365, Gotland.—Aera of the Scandinavians, British and Icelanders Epoch. December 25 Greswell, F. C., I, 575 This epoch is based on the assumption that the Gothic winter solstice fell on the Roman Brumalia or Christmas, whereas it really fell on Martinmas

B. C. 351, Phoenicia.—Revolt of Tennes, king of Sidon, against the suzerainty of Persia Picot, "Tablettes chronologiques, après l'abbé Lenglet du Fresnoy," 1808.

B. C. 350, India.—Panini, the Indian grammarian, from whose work numerous data have been gathered relating to chronology, is assigned to this date by Bohlingk; while Goldstucker and Bhandarker place him earlier than the second Buddha.

B. C. 332, Egypt—Apotheosis of Alexander the Great, the conqueror of Egypt and afterwards of India, who, it was subsequently pretended, died aged 33 years Scene, the Temple of Jupiter Ammon, time, the winter solstice, zodion, the Fishes Quintus Curtius; Censorinus, D N , ch XXI The same year was afterwards adopted for the "Coptic" æra Ten years are sometimes wrongly subtracted from this æra by disregarding the difference between the Anno Mundi of Greece and Rome (See B. C. 5502, 552 and 323). According to Mirkhond, Alexander frequently declared that his conquests were made for the glory of God and to propagate the true faith. Shea's trans , 396, 405 This was also the pretence of Cæsar, Mahomet, Cortes, and others. Higgins, Anacal , II, 347, says that Alexander's conquests were facilitated by the popular belief that he was the Expected One, Al-Ischa, the Saviour; hence also his name of Isskander. This belief could only have been founded on the eleventh incarnation of Brahma, or Iesnu, due, by the Augustan chronology, B C 470 and by the Indian chronology, B. C 548 In such case Alexander was born two centuries too late . There is no other incarnation year which fits his chronology so nearly, unless it be the Lokkal of B C 377. The following are the dates of the principal events connected with the history of Alexander:

B C CHRONOLOGY OF ALEXANDER THE GREAT.

356 —Alexander born, 21st July.

335 —Philip assassinated by Pausanias.

335.—Alexander begins to reign over Macedonia

334.—Alexander destroys Thebes in Bœotia and advances against the Persian satraps in Asia.

334.—Battle of the Granicus. Submission of Asia Minor

333.—Defeat of Darius and the Persian forces at Jassus

332 —Alexander destroys Tyre, July.   Takes Egypt   Is deified on
the winter solstice   *Beginning of the Alexandrian Æra*

331.—Alexander takes Babylon.

331.—Conquers Persia   Begins his Persian reign.

327 —Departs from Nicæa, October 23

326 —Crosses the Indus and conquers Hither India. Arrives at Pat-
tala (mouth of the Indus) in August

326 —Departure of the fleet from the Indus, October 2.

324 —Erects altars to the twelve gods on the Hyphasis and returns
Townsend erroneously gives this year for the Aera of Alexander.

323 —Alexander dies at Babylon, November 12.   The Rabbins say
B C. 308, a difference of 15 years.

322.—Is buried near Memphis in Egypt.

298.—Serapion built, and Alexander's remains removed thither   For
some of these dates see Vincent's notes to Strabo, III, 122, 141.

B. C. 330, Punjab —Æra of Kandra Gupta, the sacred king of
the Punjab and Magadha, the Sandrocottus of Magasthenes and of
Justin, XV, 4.   The Pandits fix his æra in B C 348   (See B C
554)   While Bunsen fixes his death in B C 256   (See. B C 6658)
Dunker, Lassen, and the numismatists fix the æra of Sandrocottus in
B C 315, q v.

B. C. 327, India.—Year of the Invasion of India by Alexander
the Great, according to Albiruni, who evidently regards this as *his
æra*, par excellence   This year is also adopted by the Abbé Lenglet
de Fresnoy, Dr. Greswell, Haydn, Townsend and other chronologists.   Diodorus also regards the invasion of India as the æra of
Alexander; for he says, book I, that the Egyptians count 23,000
years from the reign of the Sun to Alexander's "passage into Asia";
although he does not give its date.   Some chronologists date the invasion of India in B C 326

B. C 325, Rome.—Æra of the Paetelian law, A. U. 429, by
which it was made a misdemeanor to detain any person in custody or
confinement, unless as a punishment for crime and after lawful conviction   Livy, VIII, 28   This was substantially a re-enactment of
the Habeas Corpus act of A U 259, or B C. 495.   It constitutes
one of the greatest monuments of human liberty and progress   See
B. C. 495 and 132

B. C 323, Macedonia —Æra Philippica (Philip III).   Epoch,
November 12 (Martinmas) Clinton, F R., II, 217, says B C 324

B C 323, Egypt.—False Alexandrian æra, dated from the death of Alexander, which occurred at Babylon, November 12, B C. 323, his reputed age being 33 years. "In A. D 285, ten years were discarded from this æra " Hadyn, voc. "Alex." and "Mundane," and Abulfeda, in Gibbon, V, 193, *n*. This is all wrong The common Alexandrian æra was not dated from the death, but from either the apotheosis of that prince or else from his invasion of India. The ten years were not discarded in A. D. 285, but in the reign of Justinian II , or else at a still later period "Middle Ages Revisited," ch VIII. The æra of B C 323 is that of Philip III , Alexander's successor. Censorinus, XXI. See B C 323 (324).

B. C. 322, Egypt.—"Incarnation" of Ptolemy Soter. The Ptolemaic æra began on Thoth 1st or August 29th

B. C. 322, Egypt.—Phenix, or Phœnix period began, the 215th year (some MSS say the 225th) year, of which, fell in the consulate of P Licinius and Cneius Cornelius, A U. 657 Pliny, N H , X, 2 Harduoin says that the Phenix was a period or cycle of 532 years. If so, it was the same as the Paschal cycle of Dionysius, q v.

B. C. 315, India.—Accession of Kandra Gupta, according to Duncker's "India," p. 74; and Lassen His "divine mission" is mentioned by Justin See B C 330 His reign lasted 24 pears

B C. 312, Antioch —"Incarnation" of Seleucus Nicanor, or Epiphanes, Son of Apollo, and conqueror of India. Autumnal equinox Some chronologists place this æra (the Seleucidan) in B. C 311 and the epoch on September 1st The Arabs say October 1st. The Pandits' "Chron ," p xxxi Stokvis says October 4, B C 312 The miraculous conception and birth of Seleucus and his treaty with Sandracottus, or Chandra Gupta, are related in Justin, XV, 4 The Seleucidan æra is believed to have been employed in the Syriac version of the New Testament, mentioned in Marsh's Michaelis, II, 31. At the end of the book was written, " This sacred book was finished on Wednesday the eighteenth day of the first month, Conun, in the year 389, by the hand of the apostle Achæus, a fellow labourer of Mar Maris " Michaelis supposed this date to agree with A D 78 and the month with December. Conun was not the first month of the Seleucidan, but of the Alexandrian calendar. This colophon is probably a modern forgery

B. C. 311, Edessa —Æra used by Hieronymous, probably derived from or identical with the Seleucidan. Clinton, F R , I 317. Greswell, F. C , III, 238, calls it the " Æra Græcorum " Appleton says it was used by the Jews of the Middle Ages.

B C. 307, Athens.—Deification and worship of the living Dem-

etrius Poliorcetes, whose æra dates from this year, the epoch being
the vernal equinox in the month of Munychion.

Demetrius Poliorcetes, born B C 337, died B. C. 283, was king of
Macedon, 294-287.   He was the son of Antigonus, who, in the first
division of Alexander's empire, received for his share several provinces of Asia Minor   After taking part in his father's wars in Syria
against Eumenes and Ptolemy, Demetrius sailed to Greece, and in
307 took Athens without resistance   Anarchy, civil wars, and fear,
had now brought the Greeks so low, that they hastened to greet and
worship both the absent Antigonus and the present Demetrius, as
gods and "god-protectors"   Temples were erected or altered to
their honour, priests were appointed to conduct a worship which was
profanely addressed to these divinities, an altar was erected upon
the spot where Demetrius first landed, and it was consecrated to
Demetrius Cantabates, his portrait was wrought in the peplum or
holy veil, and the Greeks changed the number of their tribes from
ten to twelve, calling the new ones Antigonis and Demetrias; thus
increasing the senate from five hundred to six hundred members
But adulation did not stop even here   Led by Stratocles, Dromoclides,
and other sycophants, the senate decreed that the messengers who
should be sent on public business to either Antigonus or Demetrius
should be called theori, a sacred title, hitherto reserved for the holy
officers who on solemn festivals carried the sacrifices to Delphi and
Olympia, that the same worship should be paid to Demetrius as to
Ceres (Maia) and the infant Bacchus, that the festival of Bacchus,
previously called Dion-Issus, should be called Demetrius, that the
month of his apotheosis, Munychion, should be called Demetriou,
that the last day of every month should be called Demetrias; that
sacrifices should be made to Demetrius as to a god; that Demetrius,
as the god-protector, should be consulted as an holy oracle and be-
sought to reveal to mankind the most pious and acceptable method
or ritual of consecrating an intended offering of shields to Delphi;
that the temple of the Parthenon, sacred to the virgin-goddess Minerva, should be consecrated as a palace for the sacred Demetrius,
that his word and act were Infallible and should be accounted holy
in respect of the gods and just in respect of men, that he be invited both to the lesser mysteries and the greater, that the office
of archon and the custom of giving the archon's name to the year,
be abolished, and that a new æra should begin, with the advent of
the new god Demetrius   Demetrius wore "a double diadem, a robe
of purple interwoven with gold, and shoes of gold cloth, with soles

of fine purple   There was a robe a long time in weaving for him, of most sumptuous munificence.   The figure of the world and of all the heavenly bodies were being displayed upon it, but it was left unfinished "   He became difficult of access and either declined to grant an interview to those accredited to him, or else treated them in a distant and haughty manner.   Though he favoured the Athenians more than the other Greeks, their ambassadors waited at his court (of Pella) two years for an answer   For an ampler account of this scandalous worship, see "Middle Ages Revisited," II, 8

B. C. 307, Athens—In this year, according to Greswell, the Prytanes were increased from 10 to 12, the two new tribes being named after Demetrius and his father Antigonus   Greswell, K H., I, 84, *n*, citing Diodorus, Plutarch, Pausanias, etc.

B. C 307, Rome—The years A U. 446 and 447, answering in Baker's edition to B. C 306 and 305, appear to have been inserted into the Roman annals by Livy   There was no account of them in Piso, as he himself states (IX, 44) and it is quite possible that the annals of the years inserted were taken from other years, so as to make the reckoning of time agree with the calendar alterations of Augustus, to whom Livy personally submitted his History of Rome, before committing it to the public   According to Lenglet, the years inserted were A U 447 and 448, corresponding with B C 307 and 306, in the earlier one of which the consuls were Ap Claudius Cæcus and L Vulumnius Flamma, and in the later, Q. Marcius Tremulus and P Cornelius Arvina, the dictator being L. Papirius Cursor, I   The two years of discrepancy may be identical with the two years mentioned in chapter II herein

B. C 305, Rome—A U 449   Upon the motion of Caius or Cneius Flavius, curule ædile, the Roman calendar (hitherto announced verbally) was now first required to be posted up in writing, probably to prevent further jugglery   This was "203 years after the consecration of the Capitol "   Livy, IX, 46; Pliny, XXXIII, 6   In this year, or in the previous one, B C 306, the first sun dial was erected in Rome by Papirius Cursor   Both of these events imply a return to the use of a solar calendar.

B. C. 301, Pontus.—Reputed æra of the kingdom of Pontus, it having been previously a satrapy of Persia   (See Bosporus, B.C 480)   Perisades, who reigned B C 289, struck gold coins with the legend "Perisades Basileus "   The coins of this kingdom commonly bore Dionysian emblems; and for this reason were held in great veneration by the pious Greeks and Romans.   The kingdom of Pontus was alone permitted by the Romans to strike gold coins   M A R

B. C. 300, Antioch.—Artemisius 22nd   Date of the Foundation of Antioch and Seleucias by Seleucus, according to Greswell, Kal Hell , III, 437.

B. C. 298, Bosporus.—Reputed æra of the kingdom of Cimmerian Bosporus   This kingdom having become united to Pontus, the æra, which differs from the Pontine by only three years, is probably of the same origin   Both of these æras are deduced from extant coins (Humphreys, Coin Manual, 164-8); but this deduction should be accepted with caution   Stokvis and Kœhne fix the æras of both kingdoms in A U 457, or B. C 297

B. C. 297, Pontus.—Approximate date when the image of Dionysius, Mercury, Hermes, Osiris, or Serapis, was carried in state from Sinope, in Pontus, to Rhacotis, the ancient name of Alexandria, in Egypt   Ptolemy I , surnamed the Saviour, dreamt that a godlike Youth appeared before him and entreated that His image and shrine might be brought from the temple of Sinope, in Pontus, promising that if this were done Egypt's power and the City's prosperity would be assured   Having spoken thus, the bright Vision ascended to heaven in a column of fire.   Upon consulting Timotheus of Athens, a Dionysian priest and a lineal descendant of the Eumolpides, (High-Buddha-priests; Pococke,) the king sent an embassy to consult the oracle at Delos.   They received this reply: "Continue your voyage   carry off the image of my Father; but let that of my Sister remain "   The ambassadors next sailed to Sinope, from whence, after three years' persistent entreaty, backed by rich presents, King Scydrothemis gave them permission to remove the sacred image to Egypt.   However, the image itself somewhat anticipated these tedious negotiations by walking aboard the ambassadors' ship, which soon afterwards sped to Alexandria, where the god was received with great rejoicings and enshrined in a gorgeous temple, (Serapion,) especially built for his accommodation and that of Isis   Tacitus, Hist , IV, 83-4   The relation of this prodigy by so respectable an authority as Tacitus, corroborated, as he is, in the main by Plutarch and Clement Alexandrinus, affords no slight proof of the partiality of the Romans, for whom this account was written, for the cult of Dionysius, and that, too, at a period (that of Tacitus) when the worship of Augustus had been established by law for more than a century   The locality assigned to the miracle is corroborated by the coins and other monuments of Pontus, which assure us that, from the earliest to the latest period of its autonomy, its religion was

Dionysian. As to the identity of Dionysius, Osiris and Serapis, see M. Gaignant's Dissertation at the end of the fifth volume of Burnouf's Tacitus; also Plutarch, De Isis et Osiris Jerome fixes the removal of the shrine of Serapis in B. C 286 and Eusebius in B C 278; a difference from the date above assumed of 11 to 19 years. Greswell says B C 281. Dionysios, Mercury, Hermes, or Serapis, who was foretold by the angelic vision which appeared to Ptolemy, had for his celestial father, Jove, the Supreme; his virgin mother was Maia (in Egypt, Isis); the Messianic star indicated his birthplace, which, in the case of Hermes was on the Kyllemian Hill; he was born on the winter solstice and was recognized by the "bishops of Chrestos" His head was rayed, his complexion florid; and his hair, auburn. He performed numerous miracles, fasted 40 days, was tempted by the Devil and, in the case of Hermes, embodied his doctrines of salvation in a book that went by his own name His apostles were 12; he was persecuted for his religion and condemned to death by crucifixion He was executed on the vernal equinox; rose again and ascended bodily to heaven; yet the serapion at Alexandria was exhibited as his sepulchre and at the base of it was deposited a cross. His principal sacrament was baptism and his epigraphic symbols were the †, ♀ and ☿ the last one being the well-known symbol of Mercury, still used as a trade sign by chemists and apothecaries

B. C. 293, Rome.—In the dictatorship of L Papirius Cursor II , (B. C 293,) the "year of 12 months was introduced instead of the old Roman year of ten; and the first sun dial was set up " Mrs Alfred Gatty, per H K F Gatty, in Archeol Jour , January, 1889, p 188. No authority for this statement concerning the calendar appears in Livy's Annals of this year See chap. II herein

B. C. 288, Bithynia.—Erroneous æia of Bithynia, deduced by Humphreys, 102, from the coins of Nicomedes II., (Epiphanes,) B. C. 149-93, Nicomedes III., (Philopater,) B C 93-75 and Nicomedes IV., B C 75-65, which are respectively stamped 160, 205 and 223 years, evidently of the Seleucidan æra of B C 312 To hide the 14 or 15 years' alteration in the christian æra which these dates disclose, an imaginary æra has been imputed to Zissetes or Zipœtes, a Persian satrap, the father of the first king of Bithynia.

B. C. 283, Pontus.—Æras of Apamea, Bithynium, Nicæa, Nicomedia and Prusa ad Olympam, found on coins of those cities. Reinach, Rev. Num , 1887, W. Wroth, "Cat. of Greek Coins," 1889, ed Poole.

B. C. 282, Antioch.—Regnal æia of Antiochus I the "Saviour," king of Syria, son of Seleucus Nicanor and father of Antiochus Theos, or "The Living God "

B. C. 263, India.—Æra of the accession of Asoka, son of Bindusara, son of Chandra Gupta, which is variously dated B. C. 266, 264, 263, 232, 231 and 226, all of these dates being in the vulgar æra If 63 years, the difference between the vulgar and the pre-Augustan æra of Rome, are added, these dates become B C 329, 327, 326, 295, 294 and 289 None of these dates synchronise with the Divine years either of Brahma or Brahma-Buddha. B. C. 263 is from Duncker, p. 525, who calls it that of the Eleventh incarnation of Iesnu, Ishnu, Vishnu, or the Matsya. (Zodion of the Fishes) B. C. 232 and 231 are from the Puranas, which date the accession (reign) of Asoka, 311 or 312 years from the nirvana of Buddha, yet Gen Cunningham dates the nirvana 214 years before Asoka B. C. 226 is assigned for the death of Asoka As the æra of Asoka is employed for the starting point of many Indian dates, it is to be regretted that it cannot be fixed with more precision The date above selected, B. C. 263, seems the most likely, for it is asserted in the Journal of the Asiatic Society of Bengal, LII, 36, that the third Buddhic ecleastical council was held in Southern India, B C 246; and this, if correct, was almost certainly during the reign of Asoka Nevertheless, the subject is not without difficulty See B. C. 255. Senart fixes the accession of Asoka in B C 273.

B. C. 263, Athens.—Assumed year af Diognetus, the archon inscribed in the Parian marbles and the year from which all the dates are calculated by Abbé Lenglet de Fresnoy Both Rev J Robertson and M Gibert have proved that the important date in Marble XLV has been altered and the archon's name defaced Rev Wm. Hales says that some of the marbles were used to repair a chimney in Arundel House Rev. J Robertson says the dates are all false. Selden detected that the marbles embrace two methods of computation, with a difference of 25 years between them; this difference running along without variation from Cecrops to the Fall of Troy; after which they agree If this difference were followed down, it would fix Diognetus in B C 238

B. C. 255, Egypt and Syria.—"Christ, as Ichthys, the Fish, dates from B C. 255 " Gerald Massey, in " The Natural Genesis," I, 455. Mr. Massey means by this that the Messianic symbol, which, from the sixth century B. C , down to this year, was the Lamb, was superceded by the Fishes, or Pisces The year B C 255 (or B C 254) is that of the Apotheosis of Alexander, namely, B C 332, al-

tered 78 years by the Augustan chronologists The zodion assigned
to this "incarnation" was the Fishes See the zodion of Asoka, under B C 263 See also B C 24

B. C. 254, Cyprus.—Æra of Citium, deduced by the authorities
of the British Museum from a stone monument now in their "Religious" collection. They say that the 57th year of this æra corresponds with the 31st regnal year of Ptolemy Philadelphus. This
reign began B. C. 284: hence the æra of Citium would be B. C. 310
On another stone monument in the same collection the 52nd year of
Citium is said to correspond with the 25th year of Ptolemy Soter,
whose reign began B C. 322. Hence the æra of Citium was B C.
349 There is evidently some confusion here.

B. C. 250, Parthia.—"Incarnation" of Arsaces I , King of
Kings.

B. C. 247, Parthia.—Æra of Arsaces I , deduced by Geo. Smith
from a cuneiform tablet dated "year 108 of Arsaces." Cunningham.
Thomas, "Jainism," p. 14, says, B C 248

B. C. 238. Athens.—Possible year of Diognetus See B. C. 263

B. C. 235, Rome.—Six years after the end of the first Punic War
the Temple of Janus was closed, and it remained closed for 17 years.
Adams, 553.

B. C. 206, Syria.—Antiochus III invades India and concludes a
treaty with Sophogasenos

B. C. 205, Rome.—Æra of the Matrem Deorum in Rome. Her
statue, or symbol, supposed to have been a mass of meteoric iron,
like that of Mania, in the Caaba, was brought this year (B C. 205-4)
from Piscenus, in Mariandynia (Galatia) by order of the Senate.
The ceremonies were both solemn and magnificent Livy. "Between the Mater Idæa Piscenuntia, or Phrygia, whose proper name
was Cybele, and her co-mate Attes, Attis, or Attia and Isis, there
was absolutely no difference except in name It must have been the
height of inconsistency to recognize or to tolerate the former and
yet not to recognize, or to refuse to tolerate, the latter " Rev. Edw.
Greswell, Fasti Catholici, II, 443, *n.* The same may be said of
Maryamma (see B. C. 1332 and 533) and of Mania, Mother of the
Lares, or household gods, whose festival, the Compitalia, is connected with so early a period as the reign of Servius Tullius. Bell's
Panth. ; Noel, Dic Fable Hislop, "Two Babylons," 206, makes
the same remark of Cardea, the mother or wife of Janus, mentioned
in Ovid, Fasti, VI, 101 For the cognate fables of Nana and Diana,
see B C. 645 About this time, B C 191, plus 5 years, the Lex

Acilia resigned the intercalation of the calendar to the pontiffs. Smith's Dic. Rom Ant   See B C 191 herein

B. C. 205, Numidia.—Æra of Massin-Issa, King of Massylia, in Numidia, this being the year in which, after defeating Scylax, he recovered his kingdom   Livy

B. C. 204, Egypt.—Æra of Ptolemy IV., Philopater, B. C. 221-04, who, after putting to death his mother, Berenice, and taking to wife his sister Arsinoe, (whom he subsequently murdered,) pretended to be the Son of God and demanded to be worshipped as such. His pedigree began with Bacchus and Althea (daughter of Thestius), and was carried through *their* daughter, Dejanira, and the line of the Heraclidæ down to Arsinoé, the wife of Lagus, the father of Ptolemy I , Soter.   From the latter to himself (Philopater) the descent was matter of notoriety   Upon his return from Syria to Alexandria, after defeating Antiochus III , at Rhaphia, B C. 217, Philopater caused all the Jews in Egypt to be assembled in Alexandria and branded with the *Chrissophyllo*, or symbol of Bacchus (the cross), a mark that he himself wore   Satyrus, in Theophilus ad Autolycum, ii, 7, 8, III Maccabees, ii, 29

B C 201, Rome—Æra of Scipio Africanus, who attempted about this time, (the 5th Ludi Sæculares fell in A U 550), to get himself recognised by the Romans as the Son of God   Aulus Gellius; Censorinus; Herbert

B. C. 200, Rome.—Cicero de Legg , lib ii, says that the ancient year of ten months was changed to 12 months, during the consulate of Dec Brutus, or A U. 616   If we accept the Varronian date of the Foundation of Rome, this corresponds with B C 138.   If we adopt the Timæan and Ciceronian computation, it corresponds with B. C. 200.   Cf R T Pothier, Pandectæ Justinianeæ, Parisis, 1818, I, clxvi   See above B C 452.

B. C. 199, Epirus—Æra of Titus Quintius Flamininus, a Roman general, who, while in Epirus and in the year of Rome 555 (the fifth Ludi Sæculares fell in A U 550) impiously assumed the title and authority of God on Earth   Plutarch

B. C. 191, Rome.—Lex Acilia.   Intercalation of the calendar resigned to the pontiffs   See B C 205.

B. C. 190, India.—Millenium of Parasurama, *i e.*, when the Christian 15 years alteration are added to the Augustan chronology

B. C. 190, Khazaria—Æra of the Khazares, according to the Encyc. Brit.

B. C. 175, India.—Millenium of Parasurama   See B C. 1175 and 190

B. C. 165, Bactria.—The Hiang-nu drive the Yueh-ti westward into Sogdiana; while the latter drive the Sacæ into Bactria. Specht, according to Duff Rickmers, p. 15

B. C. 156, Rome.—Date of the latest change in the Epoch of the Roman consular year. The consular day at the outset of the Republic, A U 244, B C 510, was in all probability the calends of Sextilis, afterwards known as August 1st, now called Lammas Because Tarquin was expelled on Regifugium (the King's Flight) February 23rd or 24th, Dr Adams believes that the first consuls (A U 244 or B C 510) were elected and went into office on this day But aside from the doubtfulness or there having been any February in the Roman calendar at the outset of the Republic, it does not follow from Livy that the new consuls entered office on the very same day that Tarquin was expelled It would be more reasonable to suppose that they began their term a few months later, say on the Middle Day of the ecclesiastical year. Livy says of the year of Rome 291 or B. C 463 (corrected by the Abbé Lenglet to 289 or B. C 465) that "the elections were then held, and Lucius Æbutius and Publius Servilius being chosen consuls, they began their office on the calends of August, which was at that time considered the beginning of the Civil year" This is the most exact definition of the Roman new year in any ancient author There is reason to believe that the custom of beginning the civil year with the day now called the first of August went back to the foundation of the Republic As the first of March (the epoch of the ecclesiastical year) was called Messo, (from Mesotheus, a surname of Bacchus, Janus, or Mercury), so the first of August was anciently called Messa, a surname of Ceres. The Goths called the first one the Mess or Mass-day par excellence and the second one (by way of distinction) the Latter Mass, corrupted to Lammas (Dr Johnson) Several metonyms of these terms will be found in chapter II, herein. Although we are informed that so late as A U. 291 or B. C. 463 the consular day was still Messa, or Lammas, yet in A U. 299 or B C 455 it was changed to the day now known as Whitsuntide Livy, III, 36 In A U 331 or B. C. 423 it was changed to the ides, the middle or mass-day, of December Dio. Hal , XI, 15; Livy, IV, 37; V, 11. In A U. 363 or B C 391 it was changed to July 1st Livy, V, 32, VIII, 20 In A. U 530 or B. C. 224 it was changed to the calends of March Furgault, "Recueil Hist d'Ant ," mot "Calendrie" Finally, in A U 598 or B. C 156, it was changed to 	ry st Ovid F. ti 1 8 ; Lil, 147; Livy, Ep 47; Adams, Rom n latia

B C. 146, Achaia —Macedo-Achæn æra. Stokvis. In this year Achaia became a Roman province

B. C. 143, Judea.—Maccabean or Asmonean æra November 24 Townsend says B C 166   The Abbé Lenglet says "Kislev 25, our November 24, B C. 165, when Judas Maccabæus purified the temple and re-established divine worship." Humphreys says the earliest Hebrew shekels, those of Simon Maccabæus, were stamped "Year I" and issued about B. C. 144.   Lenglet commences the pontificate of Simon in B C. 143, which is the year herein adopted for this æra

B. C. 125, Sidon and Tyre—"Incarnation " of Antiochus VIII., (Gryphus), the conqueror of Sidon and Tyre.   It commenced with the first day of Hyperberetacus, or 19th October. Hieronymous, in Clinton, F. R., I, 317   Humphreys, p 548, says, B C. 126.   See B. C. 110.

B. C. 122, Rome.—Æra of the Sempronian law, A U. 632, which provided that no sentence should be passed upon a Roman citizen unless by virtue of law or warrant of the Comitia   Cicero, pro Rabir., 4.   See B C 495 and 325.

B. C. 110, Sidon and Tyre.—Variant date of the "incarnation" of Antiochus Gryphus, according to Stokvis   (See above, B C. 125)   The difference which now appears between this and the previous date is probably due to the fact that the change of 15 years in the calendar was effected during the interval when the translation of each date severally was made into the Christian æra

B. C. 103, Ascalon.—Aera mentioned by Hieronymous, in Clinton, F. R , I, 317.

B. C. 100, Rome.—Birth of Caius Julius Cæsar, a descendant of Venus (the mother of gods, who was called Julius Cæsar Dionæus, or Dionæus Mater)   He was a ten months' child; born miraculously (from the side); he laughed at the moment of his birth; and over his cradle a star appeared to announce his advent to the world   At the age of 17, in B. C 83 he became a priest of Jupiter   His first public service was in Bithynia and Cilicia, where he doubtless imbibed that Oriental theogony which he afterwards so effectually employed as a political instrument.   In B C 73 he became a cardinal, or member of the Sacred College; B. C. 64, Pontifex Maximus; B C 60, Consul for five years, afterwards extended to ten years;]3 C 48, battle of Pharsalia, conquest of Egypt, acquisition of the Oriental trade, command of the world; B C 48, deified in Egypt in the temple of Jupiter Ammon. B C. 47, reform of the calendar, B C. 46, deified [...] of Rome March 25 (10) monument found at

Evora, in Portugal, inscribed "Divo Julio," or the living god Julius, a fastigium, or steeple, a mark of ecclesiastical sanctity, was placed upon his house; a coin was struck with his effigy holding a sword in one hand and a book in the other, with an inscription importing that he governed both spiritually and temporally (Du Prez); his face was concealed by a peplum or veil, and the custom of kissing his foot was introduced at court   These practices were suddenly arrested by his assassination, which occurred March 15, 44, the day afterwards called "parricidium"   Upon his death the earth was convulsed; six hours of darkness supervened; and a comet arose in the afternoon which appeared for a week together and was believed to be Cæsar's spirit in heaven.   (Suetonius)

B. C. 98, Arabia.—Death and æra of Kab ben Luayy, according to Albiruni, Sachau's trans., 1879, p 39.   It has been suggested that Kab ben Luayy is possibly a corrupted Roman name

B. C. 97, Rome.—A U. 657, Cneius Cornelius Lentulus and P Licinius Crassus, consuls   A decree of the Senate was passed forbidding human sacrifices.   This appears to have been aimed at the worship and rites of Hesus, both in Scythia, Persia, Antioch, Gaul and Britain   A similar decree appears to have been issued by Tiberius   Pliny, N. H , XXX, 3; Tacitus, Annals, II, 69.   The Brahmins of India very anciently had a similar interdict; also the Egyptians; (Herod , Eut., 45;) also the Jews

B. C. 90, Gotland.—Æra of Woden, or Odin, the Buddhic god of the Scythians and Norsemen.   This æra began on the first Thor, which coincided with the winter solstice   The Norse Woden is probably identical with the Mongolian-Chinese Woote   (See B C 86)   This æra of Woden is one Divine Year after Nebo-Nazaru, B C. 748, and two Divine Years after Jasius and the Ten Dactyles, B C. 1406; there being an interval of exactly 658 years between each of these three dates.   Allowing for the 12 years inserted in the calendar by the Chaldeans (See chapter III) the æra of Woden was exactly three Divine Years after Ies Chrishna, Bel Issus, Cres, etc., with all of which incarnations it was evidently connected   There can be but little doubt that these cycles and the myths concerning them were carried from India into Asia Minor and Europe, by the Scythians and Goths.   The great festivals of the Norsemen during the earlier centuries of our æra appear to have fallen on what are now known as the Cross-Quarter Days, which, in fact, are relics of the ancient ten months' year   According to Brady, II, 353, the Yule festival of the Norsemen commenced on Hokunott, or Holy Night, which agreed with the beginning of the month Thor. Du Chaillu says that Yule fell in the "middle" of our month of January. This may mean the 18th, or the ides (the ides in the 36-day month) of January, which is still the Christmas and New Years' day of the Armenians, namely, 18th January. If correct, this belongs to a different period from that alluded to by Brady According to the Landnama, V, 15, Yule was changed to our 25th December during the reign of Hakon, king of Norway and foster-son of Athelstan, king of England, who had converted Hakon to christianity, about A D 940, but we are not informed on or about what day it was previously kept As Yule (now our Christmas) falls at midwinter, the changes alluded to, did not necessarily alter the solar period of the festival, but merely the nominal date of it; in other words, what took place (dates uncertain) was one or more alterations of the calendar. The fact that the English kings down to the reign of Henry II traced their royal pedigree down from Woden, by just as many generations as would suffice to fix the æra of this heaven-born personage in A U 664, or B. C. 90, affords reason to suspect that the history and æra of Christ was not known in England until a later period than that assigned by the Romanised Landnama to the proselyting efforts of Athelstan

B. C. 90, Rome.—Æra of Minius Ieus, who led the insurgents in the Social War of A U 664; he adopted a sacred name (Ieus); and struck gold coins stamped "Italia," some of which are still extant. Del Mar's "Hist Monetary Systems"

B. C. 88, Rome.—"In the year of Rome 666, the haruspices announced that the earthly day of Etruria was drawing to a close." This prediction was probably based upon the knowledge that the cycle of Eclipses, or Indian cycle of the Incarnation, or Divine Year, would soon recur Higgins' Anacal, I, 181 See B C 78

B C 86, China—Death and posthumous deification of Woote, possibly named after Buddha, Wooten, or Woden, as he was called by the Baltic Goths The Chinese Woote, by avoiding war, earnt the sobriquet of the "Prince of Peace" He ordered that upon the death of a noble, his estate should be equally divided amongst his lawful children, thus abolishing primogeniture He restored the Buddhic literature, which had been destroyed a century previously by Chi-hoang-ti. Woote ordered the doctrines of Confucius and Mencius to be publicly taught He drove the Tartars beyond the Great Wall, conquered Pegu, Siam, Cambaia and Bengal, appointed kings over these states, and thus himself became a king of kings Felted paper was invented in the reign of Woote's grandfather; paper money was first used in Woote's reign, while printing became common in that of his grandson.

B. C. 84, Athens.—Æra of L Cornelius Sylla, who was deified this year in Athens and hailed as Epaphroditus, the son of Venus, mother of gods The date is derived from inscriptions, (Rev J. B Lightfoot, "The Apostolic Fathers," I, 494,) the Apotheosis appears in Plutarch Two years later, Sylla was created Perpetual Dictator in Rome, the first instance of the kind, says Plutarch, in 120 years As the last instance was that of Q Fabius Maximus, B C 537 (Lenglet), the present difference is 135, not 120 years; indicating an alteration in the Christian calendar of 15 years In B. C. 89 Sylla married the daughter of Metellus, the Pontifex Maximus. About B C. 84 he was initiated into the mysteries of Ceres, at Athens Plutarch. The Syllan æra, A. U. 670, which, according to the Christian calendar, is B C. 84, was adopted by numerous urban communities in the eastern provinces, for the reason that being brought, after the close of the Mithradatic War, under direct Roman administration, they then first received city rights Mommsen, Hist. Rome, 1886, I, 327.

B. C. 82, Pontus.—Æra of the union of Pontus and Bosporus, B C 82

B. C. 78, India.—Augustan date of the Nativity of Ies Chrishna, or Salivahana, which some translate as Son-of-a-Virgin, and others as Cross-borne The æra is also assigned to Vicramaditya, the Holy Vicar of God. a Buddhic re-incarnation, according to native astrologers Greek sign of the Fishes This was the 11th incarnation, or avatar; it was also the period when, according to the Hindu theory, the world was to come to an end; an event that was confidently looked for by the pious, in every portion of the earth into which the astrology of the orient had penetrated The real date of Salivahana or Vicramaditya—for according to Col Wilford, they are practically the same—was that of the Apotheosis of Augustus It is the sinking of 78 years from the Roman calendar, which makes it appear 78 years older than it really is Moreover, by sinking these 78 years from the latter instead of from the former part of the calendar, the æra of Salivahana is sometimes thrown into A D 78 The identity of the Salivahanic and Augustan æras was asserted by Nicoli di Conti; and repeated by Higgins, Anacal , I, 763, who noticed that "since the Romans have entered India, the Hindus accepted the birth of Augustus Cæsar for the æra of Salivahana " These statements have been confirmed by the discovery of the identity of Nurguti Tirounal and Augustus Quirinus   See Rome, B. C. 63   Thetranslation of "Cross-borne" is from Maurice, "Brah. Fraud Exposed," p 161

B. C. 78, Egypt.—Deification of Ptolemy IX as the god Dionysios, whose coming had been foretold by the priests of Osiris, and whose mission upon earth was to restore peace and happiness to mankind.   His assumption of the *rôle* of Dionysios is mentioned by Diodorus Siculus, who visited Egypt during his reign.

B. C. 78, Mecca.—Aera of the Caaba temple, whose linen or silken veil "was first offered by a pious king of the Homerites, who reigned 700 years before the time of Mahomet " Hence, 622 (year of Mahomet) from 700 leaves 78   Abulfeda in vit Mahomet, c. 6, —ested by Gibbon, V, 191   The Caaba is not mentioned by Agatharcidc?, who wrote A U 650, but it is mentioned by Diodorus, who wrote A. U. 746; hence it was probably erected during the interval It is again mentioned, together with its venerated Black Stone, by Maximus of Tyre, in the second century   Gibbon, V, 192 *n*   The Black Stone is held by Higgins to typify the Messianic Buddha; by others, the virgin mother of Buddha.   The epoch of the Caaba æra appears to have been midsummer   Gibbon, V, 186 *n*   Yet Stanley, (Hist Phil Ldn , 1687, p 1066,) says the Arabians celebrated the birthday of the Lord on the 24th day of the tenth month   Hislop, T B , 94.

B. C. 78, Rome.—Æra of Quintus Sertorius, who, it is pretended, was born in Nursia, near the headwaters of the Arno in Italy, in the year B C 125, exactly one sæcular interval before the Apotheosis and the wrongful celebration of the Ludi Sæculares by Augustus; a circumstance that leads to the suspicion that the latter may have been anticipated in his alterations of the calendar by either Sylla or Sertorius, both of whom set themselves up for gods Sertorius took sides with Marius in the civil war.   After the defeat of the latter, he went to Spain, where he raised a force of rebellious Romans and native provincials, with which he kept the field for several years, successfully resisting the arms of Sylla, Metellus and Pompey.   It is alleged that in order to augment his influence with the Spaniards, Sertorius pretended that he was the miraculous progeny of the Deity by the Virgin Rhea and that a white fawn which always accompanied him was the agent of communications vouchsafed to him from heaven.   He appears to have been a Dionysian and an initiate of the Eleusinian mysteries.   He had been allied with King Mithradates of Pontus, where the Dionysian cult was in universal esteem. (Florus III 5)   Sertorius was treacherously stabbed to death B C.

73 by the members of his council or "Senate" who had invited him to supper with that object and who doubtless were rewarded for their services by the aristocratic party in Rome

B. C. 70, Sinope.—Æra recovered from coins. W. Wroth, Gr Coins, ed. R. S Poole. Wroth also uses the Sinopian æra of B. C. 45, q. v.

B. C. 64, Antioch.—Æra discovered on coins by Cardinal Henry Noris, "Annus et Epochæ Syro-Macedonum," Lipsæ, 4to, 1696, p 156   He says that this æra agreed with Olym. clxxviii, 4   He supposes that it commemorated the action of Pompey, who in that year drove Tigranes out of Syria   In reality, it marks the Christian year of Salivahana, whose æra Augustus lowered by 78 years and the Sacred College afterwards increased by 15 or 16 years, making it fall in B C. 63 or 64, whereas its true date is A D. o or A D 1 The Cæsarian æra of Antioch, which was in common use throughout the West, down to the seventh century, commenced B C 48, q v

B. C. 64, Rome.—Year of the miraculous Conception of Atia, or Maia, the mother of Augustus Cæsar, who was worshipped during his lifetime as the Son of God, the Living God, the Sacro-sanct, Dionysius, Mercury, etc   Suetonius, in vita; Pliny, Tacitus; Virgil, Ovid; "Middle Ages Revisited," Appendix V; Rushforth, "Latin Inscriptions," ch. V; "Monumentum Ancyranum"; Duruy's "Hist. Rome," etc.   The Conception occurred at Martinmas.

B. C. 63, India.—Aera of Salivahana, or Vicramaditya, the reincarnation of Ies Chrishna, these deities being evidently one   Col. Wilford (Asiat. Res vol IX) says that· "In general the Hindus know but one Vicramaditya, but the learned acknowledge four; and when at my request they produced written authorities, I was greatly surprised to find no less than eight or nine   .   Every Vicramaditya is made to wage war against an antagonist called Salivahana, Salavan, and often denominated Nrishina, Nagendra, etc , except one, whose name was Maha-Bat, and that of his followers Mahabbata-dicas, that is to say Mahomet and the Mahometans."   Vicramaditya was granted sway over the entire world for 1000 years; after which Salivahana, "a divine child born of a virgin and the son of Tacshaca, a carpenter," would deprive him of his kingdom.   In the Cumarica-c'handra it was predicted that this would happen after the expiration of Calijoga 3100.   Toward the end of his millenial term Vicramaditya sent out to find the Expected One, that he might destroy him; on the contrary, he was himself destroyed by Salh, the ivine Child, then but five years of age   Col Where rs Major

Mackenzie's "Vicrama-charitra" and believes that this legend is
"derived from the apochryphal gospel of Christ," an opinion which
is at variance with the conclusions of the same author in vol V of
the "Asiat Researches" It is also at variance with the monuments
Wilford repeats that to every Vicramaditya there was a corresponding Salivahana, so that virtually the æra of one is that of the other;
indeed "originally," _i e_, in the chronological lists in the Puranas,
they were considered but as one individual. That they were the
same is also the opinion of Di Conti, Marsden, Prinsep, Tod, Cunningham, Higgins, Massey and other orientalists and critics   The
æra which the Cumarica-c'handra predicted, when Vicramaditya or
Salivahana would appear, originally tallied with that of the apotheosis of Augustus. The Augustan alteration of the calendar put the
æra of Salivahana back to B C 78 and the subsequent alteration by
the Latin Sacred College has put it forward to B C 63 By deducting and adding the sunken and restored years from and to the wrong
end of the calendar and by other arithmetical means, this æra has
been cast into B. C. 58, (Sewell's "Ind Cal ," 1896) B C 57, B C.
56 and A D. 78   The 141 years of difference between the two
Jain æras mark the extreme limits of these variants, _i c._, B C 63
and A D 78, and while it proves that one is post-christian, it implies that the other is pre-christian Mr Sewell (op cit.) also shows
that an Indian sidereal year, or the beginning of a new series of
Jovian cycles, dates from A D 78 a circumstance that must have
added to the confusion which has been made to surround the æra of
Ies Chrishna or Salivahana

Cunningham says that the æra of Salivahana or Vicramaditya is
commonly used in all Northern India, except Bengal, where it is
only partially employed   In different parts of India the head of the
Vicrama calendar is either the first day, or the first day of the full
moon of Chaitra, or Ashadha, or Addi, or Assar, or Kartika   (Sewell)
In the Hindu Panjangam for 1897 the year begins with Chaitra 1st
(our April 13th) and Houli (Yule) falls on April 17th, which is the
first day of the full moon following the vernal equinox. Rickmers prefers the full moon of Chaitia   This corresponds with the Persian New
Year day, or Neuroz. Houli or Yule is sacred to Ies Chrishna and
is celebrated in most parts of India by persons of both sexes and
all ages, even by the Moslems The ceremonies are gay and joyous
Coloured balls made of the red flour of Juba are thrown about, as in
the confetti carnival of the Italians   It is a festival of universal
rejoic .., in which a   women join with great hilarity and pleasantry,

shouting Houli! Houli! Houli! Houli! When Chrishna descended to earth
he encountered the nine Houlis (Muses) and danced with them Noel
citing Turner's "Ambassy to Thibet" The number of the Houlis
probably stood for the nine days of the ancient week, or nundinum,
of the solar calendar Like the other oriental incarnations Salivahana's advent was foretold by the astrologers and it appears in the
Cumarica C'handra, his celestial father was Ies-nu, his putative father
Taishaca, the carpenter, his virgin mother, Maia; his star, the Messianic Originally the nativity of Salivahana was fixed at Easter
B. C 1; it now stands, owing to the alteration of the Roman calendar, at the winter solstice, B C 63 Salivahana was born in a cottage,
among shepherds, but was immediately recognised by seers as the
Expected One. His head was rayed, his complexion black, his hair
woolly. He performed numerous miracles, fasted 40 days, had 12
disciples, was persecuted by Vicramaditya and overcame him At
length he was condemned for his doctrines and died upon the cross,
(Higgins' Anacal, I, 662) at the vernal equinox, upon which, the sun
was eclipsed. He descended to hell, released the condemned, remained three days and nights, rose again and ascended to heaven,
an event which is celebrated by the Indian Houli. His principal sacrament was baptism, his symbol the ✝ and his zodion, the Fishes

B. C. 63, Asia Minor.—Christian equivalent of the year stamped
by Pompey as his own æra upon the coins of the numerous cities
which he conquered in Asia Minor, cities which probably yielded to
his supernatural pretensions as much as to his valour. Noris, op cit.
Humphreys, 548

B. C 63, Rome.—Elevation of Caius Julius Cæsar to the office
of Pontifex Maximus Greswell, F C, II, 42

B. C. 63, Rome.—Sept 23 Nativity of Caius Octavius Cæpias,
afterwards called Caius J. C Octavius, and afterwards Augustus, of
the gens Maria, the putative son of Caius Octavius, a tradesman and
the son of a baker, by his wife, Atia, or Maia, who was niece to Julius Cæsar. In B C 59 Augustus was adopted by L Philippus and
in B C. 47 he was adopted by Julius Cæsar, as his own son. Augustus was born in A. U 691, in the consulship of Cicero and in the village of Velitre, near Rome Its walls having been blasted by lightning, the sacred oracle was interrogated, and replied that the future
Ruler of the World would arise from the spot By this was meant
the Advent of the god Augustus His advent was also predicted in
the Sibylline books and by the astrologer, Figulus. Julius Marathus
reported that five or six months before the Nativity of ... istus, it

was predicted by a public miracle that Nature was about to bring
forth a Prince to rule the World   Upon this, the Senate enacted that
no male child born that year should be suffered to live; yet Augustus escaped   His father had designed to sacrifice him   From this
danger he also escaped   (Dion Cass)   In the Theologoumenon,
written by Asclepiades of Mendes, it is related that Atia (or Maia)
having fallen asleep in the temple of Apollo, a sacred serpent slipped
close to her, and afterwards left her   Upon awakening, she seemed
to know what had happened, and purified   When the mark upon her
person could not be concealed, she ceased to frequent the public
baths   In the tenth month (*mense decimo*) after this miracle she was
delivered of Augustus, who, for the reason stated, was known as the
Son of the god Apollo, or the Sun   The Conception, therefore, occurred on the winter solstice, now known as Christmas   Before Maia
was brought to bed of him she dreamed that her body was scattered
to the stars and encompassed the Universe   Octavius, her husband,
also dreamed that from within her shone the bright beams of the
Sun.   In the Curia, Augustus, having told P Nigidius the hour of
his Nativity, the latter proclaimed him the Lord of the Universe.
Afterwards Octavius (the putative father) consulted the oracle of
Liber Pater (Dionysius) in Thrace, and when wine was poured upon
the altar, it blazed into a flame that enveloped the steeple (fastigium)
of the temple and ascended to heaven, a miracle that had occurred
but once before, when Alexander the Great had sacrificed upon the
same altar   On the following night, Octavius dreamed that his
heaven-born Son grasped the Thunderbolt and Sceptre and wore the
triumphant robe of Jupiter, his head surrounded by a radiance of
glory, his chariot decked with laurel, whilst yoked to it, were six
steeds of purest white   C Drusus relates that while yet a babe, Augustus, being left in his cradle, was found next morning upon the
turret of the mansion, facing the rising Sun   So soon as he was old
enough to speak, he reproved a troop of clamorous animals, and
from that moment they were hushed to silence   Q Catalus dreamed
that Augustus was Jupiter Optimus Maximus   Marcus Cicero dreamed
that Augustus was let down from heaven by a golden chain   Dio ,
xlv, 2, says that at the precocious age of 12, Augustus was familiar
with Greek and made a funeral oration in public.   At 16 he went to
study at the temple of Apollonia, in Epirus   When Augustus went
with Agrippa to the studio of Theogenes at Apollonia, and divulged
the hour of his Nativity, Theogenes, who was one of the wisest men
of his age, fell down and worshipped him as the Almighty (*adora-*

vitque eam). In memory of this circumstance, Augustus afterwards
struck a coin with the Capricorn, that being his natal zodion Ovid,
in the Pontine letters, which are still extant, addresses or alludes to
Augustus as God, or, the Living God, (Theos) He built a shrine
to this god in his house at Tomis and there worshipped him, both
during the life-time of Augustus and after his Ascension to heaven.
In the Fourth Eclogue Virgil addresses Augustus as the divine Son
of God, the Son of the Immaculate Virgin and Prince of Peace; and
in the Æneid, VI, 789-93, as Augustus Cæsar, Son of God. Horace
calls him "Maia's wingéd Child," "Father and Guardian of the human race," "The Living God" (*praesens divus*), etc , while Manilius
invokes him as "the colleague of Jove, thyself a God; all of these
writers being contemporaries of this divinity. Pliny and numerous
others of a later age allude to him as God (Theos, or Deos), or the
Son of God (Divus filius) The Senate recognized him as the long
predicted and expected Sacrosanct, or Messiah, a fact that Augustus
mentions in his will, which is carved on the temple of Ancyra, still
standing with the inscription upon it The year of his Apotheosis
was B C 15, when a tax was laid upon the Roman world. The name
of one of the months, Sextilis, was changed to Augustus, an honor
accorded only to gods. At first Augustus only claimed to be the Son
of God, afterwards he accepted the title and prayers due to the Creator and, as such, was addressed in the temples which were dedicated to his worship He erected near the Tarpeian Rock in Rome, a
temple, which was inscribed, "to Augustus, the First Born of God "
Baronius, App , XXVI, p 447. Frickius, cap X, p 98, says that the
inscription proclaimed him to be the Son of Apollo and the Virgin
Mother. Many of these temples, called Augusteums, are still standing, and one of them, in Vienne, Dauphiny, has the nail holes of the
original block letter dedication cut upon it In the inscriptions of
the recently exhumed public edifices of Ephesus, Augustus is addressed as Τίος Θεου, the Son of God. A special corporation of
priests, Collegium Sodalium Augustalium, was instituted to conduct
this worship, and 11 cities of Asia contended for the honor of erect-
iug a new Augusteum As the supreme pontiff of the Roman Empire, Augustus lawfully acquired and exercised authority over all
cardinals, priests, curates, monks, nuns, flamens, augurs, vestal virgins, temples, altars, shrines, sanctuaries and monasteries, and over
all religious rites, ceremonies, festivals, holidays, dedications, canon-
izations, marriages, divorces, adoptions, benefices, wills, burying-
grounds, fairs and other ecclesiastical subjects and matters Altars

have been found at Ancyra, Lyons, Leon (Spain) and other places, inscribed to him as the Son of God, and numerous coins are extant bearing the same title   Says Tacitus   " The reverence due to the gods was no longer exclusive.   Augustus claimed equal worship Temples were built and statues were erected to him, a mortal man was worshipped and priests and pontiffs were appointed to pay him impious homage."   Even the emperors who succeeded him, among them Tiberius, Nero and Hadrian, built altars and offered sacrifices to Augustus   The common people wore little images of Augustus suspended from the neck   Great images and shrines of the same god were erected in the highways and resorted to for sanctuary   There were a thousand such shrines in Rome alone   Augustus wore on his head a pontifical mitre surmounted by a Latin cross, an engraving of which, taken from a coin of the Colonia Julia Gemella, appears in Harduini, de Nummis Antiquis, plate I   The number of prodigies and miracles related of or concerning him is endless; among others, that the ghost of Julius presaged his victory at Philippi; that fishes leapt from the sea to do him homage, that a thunderbolt struck the letter C from the title of "Cæsar" upon his statue, and thus made it " Æsar," or " Æsus," which, in the Etruscan language, signified the deity (deus)   The image of Augustus upon the coins of his own mint-age, or that of his vassals, is surrounded with the halo of light which indicates divinity, and on the reverse of the coins are displayed the various emblems of religion, such as the mitre, cross, crook, fishes, labarum, and the Buddhic and Bacchic, or Dionysian monogram of P.   His heavenly character was also attested by the miracle of his touch, which was sufficient to cure deformity or disease   So univer-sally were his divine origin and attributes conceded, that many peo-ple, in dying, left their entire fortunes to his sacred (personal) fisc, in gratitude, as they themselves expressed it, for having been per-mitted to live during the incarnation and earthly sojourn of this Son of God   In the course of 20 years he thus inherited no less than 35,000,000 aurei, each containing as much gold as the modern Eng-lish sovereign   Many potentates bequeathed him not only their pri-vate fortunes, but also their kingdoms and people in vassalage   Not only was his godship accepted, it was exacted, both during and after his life-time   The senator Afidius Memla, for refusing to take an oath in the name of the god Augustus, was heavily punished; and the ancient city of Cyzicus, for neglecting the worship of Augustus, the Son of God, was deprived of its privileges   For removing the head from an image of Augustus, several persons were put to the torture and others executed. For changing one's clothes in the presence of his image, the penalty was death For whipping a slave near a shrine of Augustus, the penalty was death For defacing the effigy of Augustus upon a coin, the penalty was death For defacing his effigy upon a ring, the penalty was death For accepting honours in a distant province on the same day that somewhat similar honours had been decreed to Augustus, the penalty was death Caius Silanus, pro-consul of Asia, for "irreverence to the divinity of Augustus," was excommunicated, and banished to the desert isle of Cythera (Cerigo) and forbidden fire or water Even Apuleia Varilla, a niece or grand-niece of Augustus, for alluding to him irreverently, barely escaped a capital sentence In B C 9, Herod, who, after the battle of Actium, had acknowledged and worshipped Augustus as the Son of God, went so far in his homage as to celebrate the panageia of Jasius, or the pentaeteris, or five years' sacred games, and to call them Cæsar's games These games were celebrated by Augustus as Cæsar's games and were afterwards kept up by a decree of Tiberius, which named them the Augustan games At a private feast which became known as the Supper of the Twelve Gods, twelve intimate friends of Augustus were attired as gods and goddesses, himself personating Apollo His favorite titles, however, were Janus Quirinus and Dionysius, and as he had been initiated in the mysteries of Ceres, he was commonly worshipped as Augustus Dionysius, a statue of him in this character being depicted in Duruy's "Rome." He gave evidence of his humility and charity by publicly begging alms for the poor once a year, on the New Year day, holding his own hand forth to receive what was offered. As he approached his 76th year his coming demise was foretold by the sacred oracle, and when he sank at last to a peaceful rest, he was mourned by the whole empire A stately funeral bore his remains to the mausoleum, his dirge was chaunted by the children of the nobles, the Senate decreed him divine honors, and the Senator Numericus Atticus swore that he saw his effigy ascend to heaven. A splendid representation of the Ascension, carved upon a huge cameo, was presented by the Emperor Baldwin II. to Louis IX. of France, and is now in the cabinet of France. It is depicted by Duruy, op cit. Suetonius says that Augustus died on the 14th calends of September For sacerdotal reasons and in order to make it agree with a certain ancient festival, both of India and Egypt, his death and Ascension day has been fixed to August 29th, still dedicated to "Saint Augustine." For a similar reason his Nativity had previously been altered by transposing the months of February and August, as mentioned by John of Nikios. This, or like tamperings with the calendar, evidently arrested the attention of Dr. Clinton and Sir Cornewall Lewis, the former of whom reproves Archbishop Usher for venturing to make precise calculations as to the position of the months prior to and after the Julian correction, "a precision," says he, "for which we have no authority" Fasti, Hell, III, xi. Nicoli di Conti, who travelled in Bengal and other parts of India during the early part of the 15th century, declares that in the orient, Augustus and the Indian Vicramaditya (or Salivahana) were regarded as the same. "De Comitibus," published in A D 1444. A famous holiday is still observed in India which may have furnished a date (Aswin 1st, or August 29th) to the Augustan cult of Rome. See B C 1176 This is the festival of Aurguti Tirounal, which is celebrated in the month of Pretachi, or Bhadra, (Buddha,) and lasts nine days, to Aswin 1st, answering to our August 20-29 It commemorates the birthday of Quichena For Aurguti Quichena read Augustus Quirinus, and consult Nicoli di Conti The festival is especially observed by shepherds, from the tradition that Quichena, whose emblem was the Lamb, was born in that class. The ceremonies include a procession, in which is borne the statue of Ies-nu, or Chrishna, or Quichena, or Quirinus, for these names are all one A cocoa-nut shell, containing some small silver coins (formerly half-denarii, now fanams), is suspended from the porches of the houses When the procession arrives opposite to them, the shells are smashed and the coins scattered Tirounal is the Indian word for a chariot, which was the emblem stamped upon the reverse of those Roman quinarii whose export from Rome to India is so much deplored by Pliny The obverse was stamped with the image of Augustus Brugsch (Materiaux, 17), thinks that August 29th was celebrated as a feast day in Egypt so far back as the VIth dynasty of Egypt, while Dr. Greswell, with ample warrant, regards the dates on Egyptian monuments as anachronical forgeries. The Indian Parasurama of B C 1176, which celebrated the birth of Dennus (Dionysius) began Aswin 1st, which coincided with our August 29th Beside the authorities incidentally mentioned in this account the reader is referred to Seutonius, in "Aug ," the Monumentum Ancyranum, Bundell Lewis on the Antiquities of Vienne, Lanciani, "Pagan and Christian Rome," Rev A Herbert, "Nimrod;" Dion Cass ; Lucretius; Pliny, N H , Macrobius, Allmer, "Les Gestes du dieu Auguste;" Mommsen ' Res Gestæ di i Augusti;" Du Choul; the Corpus Inscriptionum Latinorum et Græcorum; Rushforth, "Latin Inscriptions;" Manigan, "Worship of the Emperors," Josephus, Babelon, "Moneys of the Roman Republic," Cohen, "Coins of the Republic and Empire," John Penn, "Fourth Ecologue;" and the Dizionario Epigrafico de Ruggiero, art. "Augustus." In the last-named work nearly one hundred sacred titles, given to Augustus, are cited from marble and bronze monuments still extant. Among them are Jupiter Op. Max., Apollo, Janus, Quirinus, Dionysius, Mercurius, Volcanus, Neptunus, Liber Pater, Savus (Saviour), etc. The epigraphic symbols of the Augustan cult were the † and ♀.

B. C. 58, India.—Æra of Vicramaditya, according to Stokvis and other chronologists. Sewell places it in B C 57; possibly a variation of B. C. 63

B C 57, India.—Samvat or Sumbat, according to Sewell and the Pandits, the latter fixing it at the expiration of the 3044th year of the Calijoga and giving it also the name of Vicramaditya, of whose æra it is evidently a perversion. Of the various Indian æras connected with the lunar-solar year, this has now become the principal one. It is chiefly used in Telingana, Hindostan proper and Nepal, but not much in Bengal, and scarcely at all in the Peninsular. As the festivals and religious observances of the Hindus and Buddhists have been made to depend on the lunar reckoning (c'handra-mana) the Samvat, which is a luni-solar division of the year, has been adapted to æras which once were on a solar basis. The Samvat "begins with the Hindu luni-solar year." The Pandits "Chron.," p xxix. This is Easter, or the first full moon after the vernal equinox. Duff says the new moon. Dr Hales fixes Samvat in B. C 56 and says that a copper plate has been found in the ruins of Mongeer (Monghyr) in Bengal, on the Ganges, dated Samvat 33, which he makes equal to B. C 23. The place mentioned was anciently called Mudgalpur and once possessed a handsome Brahminical temple which the Moslems converted into a mosque. The river at Monghyr is still used by the Hindus for ritual bathing (baptism) and pilgrimages. Thornton

B. C. 57, Gaul.—Aera of Divitiacus, sovereign-pontiff of Gaul, for so is he regarded by Higgins, in his "Celtic Druids," p. 12. This view is founded upon various passages in Cæsar de Bell Gall and one in Cicero de Div., I,41, in which Cicero ascribes to Divitiacus the gift of prophecy. This was common to every augur and haruspice, not only among the Druids, but also among the Etruscans and Romans. The supernatural pretensions of Divitiac were probably

greatly modified by the victorious Cæsar   The æra is possibly a variation of B. C. 63

B. C. 53, Pontus.—Deification of Deiotaurus, tetrarch of Galatia,
whose city of Piscenus or Pesinus was the seat of the worship of
Maia, Mother of the Gods   As a reward for his services to the Romans in their Asiatic wars and especially the one against Midthra-
dates, king of Pontus, the Senate conferred upon Deiotauras the
title of king of Lesser Armenia; whereupon he declared himself to
be the Son of God and began to build a new city in which his worship was intended to be conducted   "What do you mean," said M.
Crassus to him, "by proceeding to build a new city when the Twelfth
Hour, (meaning the Divine Year), is at hand"?   Deiotaurus alternately embraced the causes of Pompey and Cæsar and by the latter
was confirmed in his title of king, but probably warned at the same
time, to drop his impious pretensions.   In B. C. 46 the grandson of
Deiotaurus is said to have instigated Phillip, his physician, to accuse
the king of desiring to poison Cæsar, while the latter was on his way
from Egypt to Rome   From this accusation Deiotaurus was successfully defended by Cicero and Brutus, the discourse of the former
being still extant.   Cicero, Letters, III, 225, and Orat. pro Deiotaurus.

B. C. 49, Antioch.—Aera of Antioch.   See B. C 48, Antioch.

B. C. 48, Rome.—Apotheosis, æra and calendar, of Julius Cæsar
At the Winter Solstice of this year (December 25) Julius Cæsar was
publicly acknowledged and proclaimed in the Temple of Jupiter
Ammon as the Son of God.   Like the various pretenders to divinity
who had preceded him, Cæsar was of divine origin, the offspring
(somewhat distantly removed) of the Celestial or Virgin Venus and
Anchises   He was a ten months' child and, like Salivahana, he was
cross-borne and issued from the side of his mother, of whom he was
delivered by an operation that still bears his name. he was born
laughing, while a Star appeared over the place of his birth to announce the auspicious event to mankind   Upon being officially
recognised as the expected Messiah he secluded himself from the
public view, became difficult of access, clothed himself in a pontifical
robe, wore a sacred veil upon his head and rich slippers upon his feet,
which those who approached his throne were required to kiss (Suetonius). "Julius Cæsar ordered a coin to be struck with his effigy,
holding a sword in his right hand, and a book in the other, with an
inscription that imported he was Cæsar both by one and the other "
Du Pre Notes on Horace, in Usum Delphini   This was the origin

of the Roman pontifical claim to both "temporals and spirituals "
It was evidently for these pretensions that Cæsar suffered death at
the hands of the Roman nobles and not for the inferior offense imputed to him by the Poet, of having aspired to be a king; for he was
already, and by the sufferance of the entire nation, much more than
a king   But Shakespeare wrote at a time when the truth of these
matters dared not be discussed; and it must be admitted that he
made the most of the only motive which he could safely venture to
assign for the assassination of Rome's transcendent hero   Violent
commotions of the earth and six hours of darkness followed his
death.   He was not only deified by decree of the Senate, but worshipped as a god by the people.   "When his heir, Augustus, first exhibited those sacred games which had been consecrated to his memory there arose a comet in the afternoon which appeared for a week
together and was believed to be Cæsar's soul in heaven; for which
reason there was always a Star placed upon the vertex of his statue "
(Suetonius, in vita).   The date of the assassination was the ides of
March, B C 44   Picot   Among the changes effected in the Roman
state by this greatest of men none is of greater interest at the present distance of time than his reform of the calendar   He adopted
what is now known as the Julian solar year of 365¼ days, appor-
tioning 365 days to the year of twelve months and intercalating the
remaining quarter of a day into every fourth year, known to us as
the leap year   He began this new solar calendar of Rome with January 1st in a year that, according to Smith's Dic. of the Bible, corresponded with A U 707, or B C 47   Furgault says January 1,
B C. 46   Greswell says December 30, B C 46   Picot says January 1, B. C 45   Dr Smith's date was selected by him perhaps because it corresponds more nearly with the Cæsarian æras of Antioch
and Laodicea.   As for the day, January 1st, it was already the beginning of the consular or civil year; and it appears to have been so
ever since B. C 156, q. v   There is every reason to suppose that
Cæsar did not alter it; yet Dr. Greswell, in order to complete his
theory of a primitive Hebrew year, has attached the Julian calendar
to the epoch of December 30th   Assuming Dr Smith's date to be
correct, Cæsar's calendar commenced one week after his deification
at Alexandria.   The date in Censorinus corresponds with B C 46
Stokvis says January 1, B C 45   Dr Hales says that the first day
of Cæsar's calendar began a lunar cycle; but unless he means that
Cæsar's calendar was a lunar one, which it certainly was not, the remark appears to lack significance.

B. C. 48, Thessaly.—Battle of Pharsalia, at which Julius Cæsar defeated Pompey   In the time of Lucan, which was about a century after this famous battle, its date was not known.

> Tempora signavit leviorum Roma maiorum
>
> Hunc voluit nescire diem   Luc vii, 410.

Modern chronologists usually fix it on August 9, B C 48. Greswell, F C , I, 254 *n*, says "Sextilis 9," which he makes equal to June 5, B C 48. Lucan's expression possibly refers to the alteration of the calendar by Augustus

B. C. 48, Tyre.—Cæsarian æra of Tyre, Tishri, 1st, B. C 48 (Syrian), or Gorpiæus, 1st, 49 (Greek)

B. C. 48, Antioch.—Cæsarian æra of Antioch. Greek epoch, Gorpiæus 1st (as in Tyre); Syrian epoch, Sextilis (or August) 9th The Syrians, however, fix the æra in B C 47   Evagrius, III, 33, fixes it in B. C. 48-9. Woolhouse and Stokvis say September 1st, B C 48. Cardinal Henry Noris attempted to prove by means of two coins that the æra of Antioch was in B C 49   One of these is of Tiberius, with "Tiberius Augustus, sub Flacco Antiochensium, Anno LXXXII," in Greek. He says that as Flaccus was pro-prætor of Syria, A. D. 33, it follows from this inscription that the æra of Antioch was B C. 49   Naturally; but the year of the pro-prætorship is by no means certain   The other coin, which is ascribed to Galba, is without his name and only says "sub Muciano   Antiochensium   Anno CXVII," in Greek   Noris takes this Muciano to be Publius Licinius Mucianus, mentioned in Tacitus, Hist II, whom he supposes was pro-prætor in A. D. 68. The validity of the deduction depends upon the years when these men were pro-prætors in Syria, of which there appears to be no certainty   Upon a comparison of all the evidence on this subject, the year B C. 48 has been determined as the most likely one

B. C. 48, Pontus.—Cæsarian æra of Neo Claudipolis, recovered from coins   W. Wroth (R. S. Poole), "Cat Gr. Coins." See also B C. 7 and A D 64

B. C. 47, Laodicea.—Æra mentioned by Hieronymous. Clinton, F R , I, 317   Also recovered from coins. Picot, I, 470.

B. C. 45, Sinope.—Aera recovered from coins   Picot, I, 470 See B C. 70.

B. C. 44, Rome.—Assassination of Julius Cæsar on the ides of March   " chronologists say B C 45   Cf " Middle Ages Revisited " App. V

B. C. 42, Rome.—Battle and æra of Phillipi Epoch, September 9 Greswell, K. H., II, 114; V, 228

B. C. 42, Rhodes.—Roman æra of Rhodes, as deduced from coins. The principal dates relating to this once foremost maritime state, which have survived the wreck of time, are as follows: After the Persian war, about B C 470, Rhodes became tributary to Athens; B C. 412, Rhodes joins the Peloponnesians; 408, the three Rhodian cities of Ial-Yssus, Lindus, and Camirus, unite to build or improve the great port of Rhodes; 394, Rhodes becomes subject to Athens; 357-5, during the Social War Rhodes defies Athens and achieves her independence; 351, Rhodes sues for Athenian protection, and through the influence of Demosthenes, she obtains it; 331, Rhodes is conquered by Alexander the Great and receives a Macedonian garrison; about B C 320, Rhodes again achieves her independence and now enters upon the most glorious period of her career, during which she establishes the Maritime Code which still goes by her name; 285, Rhodes is besieged by Demetrius Poliorcetes who is defeated and leaves behind him such a vast number of bronze engines, implements and weapons that the Rhodians are enabled to erect a trophy from them; 280, this trophy, an immense bronze statue of the SUN, familiarly known as *the Colossus*, is erected near the port, not straddling it, as is represented in popular engravings; 224, the Colossus is overthrown by an earthquake, 48, Rhodes espouses the cause of Julius Cæsar; 43, in revenge for which, the city is attacked, captured and plundered by Cassius; 42, but in the following year it is succoured and protected by the troops of Augustus, after which time the island becomes an appanage of Rome

B. C. 41, Sicily.—Aera of Sextus Pompeius, the real son of Pompey the Great and the pretended son of Neptune, or Taras He demanded to be worshipped as a god on earth Born B C 75 Defeated by Augustus and killed B C 35

B. C. 40, Judea.—After the assassination of Cæsar several provincial rulers impiously set themselves up as gods on earth and demanded to be worshipped as such. Among these were Herod, Marc Antony, Sextus Pompeius and Augustus, the last one destroying or subduing all the rest Herod was born in B. C 73, (Hole), or B. C. 66, (Hales). He assumed the godship in Olym clxxxv, B C. 40), when Cn Domitius Calvinus II, and C Asinius Pollio were consuls. Upon his coins appeared the sacred symbol of the cross, in several forms, mostly with "Year III" His employment of the cross on his coins was probably interdicted by Augustus and Antony, who, however, subsequently confirmed him in his kingdom, but not in his godship. After the battle of Actium he paid a relief of 800 talents to Augustus Herod rebuilt the Jewish temple to Yaova, but'erected a larger one to Augustus, called the Cæsareum. The City of Samaria he re-named Sebastos, and throughout his life he erected numerous temples to Augustus, which he named after him and in which the worship of Augustus, as god upon earth, was enjoined and conducted   Herod reigned 37 years and died B C. 4   Josephus, Ant. XIV, xiv, 5; XIV, xiv, 15; XIV, xvi, 4; XVII, viii, 1; Wars, I, xxviii, 8

B. C. 40, Rome.—Aera of the sacerdotal Advent of Augustus and (as it afterwards proved, of the temporary) closure of the temple of Janus, which occurred after the treaty with Marc Antony, in the consulship of Cn. Domitius Calvinus II and C Asinius Pollio, A U 714   This is the Advent and the æra sung by Virgil in the Fourth Eclogue "The great months shall then begin to roll," etc   See Penn's elaborate Treatise on this subject   But Antony broke the Peace, the temple of Janus had to be reopened, the contest was re-newed, and, after the battle of Actium, a new æra, that of the Apotheosis of Augustus, B. C. 15, had to be substituted for the one thus prematurely glorified by the court poet   An Augustan coin of this year, A U. 714, is stamped "Imp. Cæsar Divi F," (Penn's "Fourth Eclogue," 153)   The word æra itself is derived from this epoch, A, meaning anno; E R, erat, A, Augusti. Vide Isidore ("Origines" V, 36), Sepulveda, and Vossius This æra of Augustus is used by the monk Polydore Vergil (15th century) in his De Rerum Inventoribus, ed. 1868, p 124

B C. 38, Rome —So-called Spanish æra, January 1st   For ex-ample, a Spanish charter dated 1292 agrees with our A. D 1254. Archeol. Jour., XLVII, 26   This is the Julian (Cæsarian) æra, whose equivalent in Anno Domini has been altered ten years   Rev E C Brewster, "Dic Phrase and Fable," and Appleton's Encyc , say the Spanish æra began with the year when Spain fell under the dominion of Augustus   In such case it began B. C. 40.   The Pan-dits fix it in A. U 715, or B. C. 38, and regard it as "fictitious." It was only abolished in A D 1415, or 1422, down to which year it was used in Africa, Spain, Portugal and the Southern provinces of France   The Pandits' "Chron ," p. xxix.   The months and days of this æra are those of the Julian calendar

B. C. 36, Pontus.—Aera of Cherronesus, or Chersonesus, in the Crimea, deduced from dates on coins Kœhne, I, 169   "Cher-sonesus, a town f the Heracleota," (Pliny), on a small peninsular about the middle of the Crimean shore, is said to have been founded by the inhabitants of Heracleium, a city situated near the mouth of the Amisus in Pontus This is probably just the reverse of the truth   The town of Kosleve, or Eupatoria, is supposed to stand on the site of Chersonesus   The æra of Chersonesus is astrological. It possibly also marks the date when "its freedom" was granted by Marc Antony   Pliny says the town was anciently called Megarice and afterwards Heraclia Chersonesus.

B. C. 36. Leucas.—Aera of Leucadia, one of the Ionian Islands, now called Santa Maura   (See "Middle Ages Revisited," App V) This æra, whether from Leucas, the White Horns, or from Leucadius, a surname of Apollo, is significant, because it appears to be exactly one astrological cycle after the æra of the Khazares and one cycle before the Hegira of Mahomet   See B C. 694, and B C 36, Pontus

B. C. 36, Asia Minor.—Marc Antony pretends to be an incarnation of the deity and calls himself "the new Bacchus, the husband of Minerva and the lineal descendant of Hercules."   Herbert (Nimrod)   The time was ripe for this.

B. C. 31, Rome.—Battle of Actium, fought September 2 (Dion Cassius), B. C. 31.   This was altered afterwards to August 29, to make the day tally with the festivals of the Augustan chronology. "Middle Ages Revisited," ch. VIII, note 18.   It was employed by Josephus, Ant. XVIII, ii, 1.   It is said that amongst the Greeks of Antioch it was used so late as the ninth century, under the date of September 1, B. C. 30; but this was probably the epoch of the First Indiction.   The Actian æra was altered at a later period to December 25, B. C. 31, and finally to January 1, B. C. 30

B. C. 30, Rome.—Aera of the First Indiction   The Indictions are alluded to in Malala, the Paschal Chronicon, and in the letters of Pliny the Younger to the emperor Trajan, during the first century of our æra, yet Gibbon II, 62, did not trace them higher than Constantine

B. C. 30, Egypt.—Augustan æra, first regnal year in Egypt Epoch, January 1st.   Censorinus, XXI.   This author, from his own year, namely, the consulate of Ulpius and Pontianus, which, according to the Christian calendar is fixed in A D 238, reckoned as follows· From the origin of man to the Deluge of Oxyges, unknown; Oxyges to Inachus, about 400 years; Inachus to first Olympiad, about 400 years; Olympiad to present year, 1014 years; Foundation of Rome to present year, 991; calends of January in calendar of Julius Cæsar, to present year, 283, Augustan æra in Egypt, commencing with calends of January, to present year, 267; same in Rome, (Augustus VII and Agrippa III, Coss,) 265 years   Assuming the Christian equivalent of his starting point to be correct, the deductions given herein must follow   Greswell fixes the epoch of the Augustan æra in Egypt on Thoth 1st, then August 31st; yet Censorinus is explicit as to the calends of January

B. C. 28, Rome.—First Augustan regnal year in Rome, two years later than his "æra" in Egypt, because "the Egyptians at this date had been for two years under the power and authority of Rome" Epoch; January 1st.   Censorinus, XXI.

B. C. 28, Rome.—Year of the Nativity of "Issus, son of Mariam," namely, "Anno Alexandro, 304," as fixed by the Jews and Christians   Albiruni, op cit., 21.   This date, if reckoned from the Apotheosis of Alexander, which took place in his 24th year, is equivalent to B C 28; if reckoned, as Albiruni reckons it, from the 27th year of Alexander, it is equivalent to B. C 25, which is the year of the Lex Regia and accession of Augustus.   In another place Albiruni says that the Christians of his time (tenth and 11th centuries) fixed the Nativity of Jesus in Anno Augusto 43, which, he contends, is erroneous   Nicephorus Gregoras fixed it in Anno Augusto 42   See B. C. 5506.

B. C. 27, Rome.—Augustan regnal æra, commencing February 14   Woolhouse, op cit   This is a curious combination of errors. The year results from deducting Censorinus' 238 from 265 and omitting A D. 0; the day results from Censorinus' remark that although the Augustan æra dated from the calends of January, the bill establishing it was not enacted until the 16th calends of February   This is not February 14th, but January 17th   Haydn gives this year for the beginning of Augustus' reign   Stokvis says the same and gives two epochs, viz , February 14 and September 1.

B. C. 25, Rome.—Lex Regia and Accession of Augustus Cæsar, according to some chronologists

B. C. 25, Alexandria.—Æra of the Nativity of "Issus, son of Mariam," according to Albiruni, who says that in his time it was so fixed by both the Jews and Christians, namely, in "Anno Alexandro, 304"   This last-named æra he commences with the 27th year of Alexander's life.   The year B. C. 25 is given by some chronologists as that of the Lex Regia and the Accession of Augustus   It is also the date of the Augusto-Egyptian calendar, according to Massey, "Gen" II, 400.

B. C. 24, Southern India.—Beginning of the Grahar-parivritti 90-year cycles, whose epoch is fixed in the 3078th year of Calijoga. The year is "solar" Pandits' "Chron ," p. xxix See A. D. 1777 Other authorities say that the year is sidereal

B. C. 24, Syria.—According to some authors this year, instead of B. C 28 or 25, marked the Accession and First Tribunitian year of Augustus, when the latter struck or permitted to be struck a coin in Syria stamped "Aug. Tr Pot ," and the year "230," in an æra which was unrecognized by Cohen ("Mon. et Med. Imp ," 2d ed , I, 164) When the 78 years are restored, which Augustus sunk from the calendar, this becomes the æra of Alexander, thus 24+230+78 =332 B. C See B C 255 It corroborates the computation herein under B. C 25.

B. C. 21, Samos —Indian embassy received at Samos by Augustus. Duff Rickmers

B. C. 18, Cilicia.—Aera of Anazarba, the metropolis of Cilicia, according to the Abbé Belley, cited in Barker's " Lares and Penates," p. 55, *n.*

B. C. 15, Rome.—Apotheosis of Augustus Cæsar, as Lord of the World and Prince of Peace, and the official date of his æra, viz , A U 738 Augustus was the Son of Maia, (Horace, lib. I, ode ii, line 43,) by the god Apollo. (Suet. in Aug. 94) This year marks the permanent closure of the temple of Janus and an epoch of universal peace By assuming that the æra of Romulus Quirinus began 738 years before, that it was that of his Apotheosis, and that his Apotheosis occurred when Romulus Quirinus was 33 years old, the Augustan astrologers brought the beginning of the eighth cycle of 110 years, celebrated by the Ludi Sæculares, precisely to this year, and the Ludi were actually celebrated in accordance with that reckoning Thus, seven cycles=770 years, less 33=A U 737 This ended the seventh cycle The eighth began with A U 738, or B. C 15 Suetonius, Aug 100: Censorinus, De Die Natale, XVII; " Middle Ages Revisited," App S From this time forward the worship of Augustus as the Son of God became the official religion of Rome. Aera 1, or Anno Domini, 1, meant the first year of our Lord Augustus All these dates were afterwards altered to the extent of 15 years. (For the word "æra," see B C. 40) From the chronological evidence furnished by coins, some of the most important institutes of the empire have been traced to this date Thus, Lenormant, II, 218, shows that the re-organization of the monetary system, the division of the prerogative of coinage between Augustus and the senate, and

the granting of coinage authority to the pro-consuls, all date from
this year   The æra of Augustus can be shifted backward or forward
to the extent of 30 years, at pleasure of the chronologist, by applying the 15 years' interval, since made between the Christian and
pagan Roman calendars, either to the last year before, or to the first
year after, the interval, and by confusing the regnal year of Augustus
with his Apotheosis   By these means the "æra" of Augustus has
been variously thrown into A D 15, 14, B C 8, B C. 10, B C 15,
B. C. 28 and B. C. 30.   "Middle Ages Revisited," ch VIII, *n*, 18.
It is evident that Livy, Pliny, Censorinus, and other ancient authors
have been tampered with by thus shifting the Augustan æra, so that
now every date is either a puzzle or a battle ground   A brief chronology of Augustus appears under A D 14

B. C. 10, Rome.—Shifted year of the Augustan æra employed by
some chronologists. Censorinus shows that there were only 18 years'
difference between the Julian æra (B. C. 46) and the Augustan regnal
year in Rome

B. C. 8, Egypt.—Year of the Augustan Apotheosis in Egypt,
where he was worshipped as Thurinus, or Thoth   Epoch, January
1st   After the death of Augustus the epoch in Egypt was reckoned
from the 29th August, a day with which the Sothic and Ptolemaic
æras both agreed   See above, years B C 1322 and 322   With regard to the transposition of February and August in the Egyptian
calendar, consult Ovid and John of Nikios, ch. 64   For the name
Thurinus, consult Suetonius

B. C. 7, Pontus.—Aera, probably Augustan, of Neo Claudiopolis,
recovered from coins. W Wroth (R S. Poole), Cat Gr Coins   See
also B C. 48 and A D 64

B. C. 7, Pontus.—Aera, probably Augustan, of Germanicopolis,
recovered from coins   W. Wroth (R S. Poole), Cat Gr. Coins   See
A D 64

B. C. 2, India.—The Cumarica-c'handra says. "After 3100 years
of the Calijoga expire, king Saka, or Salivahana, will appear, to remove wretchedness from the world " Salivahana was to be a Divine
Child, born of a Virgin, and the son of Tacshaca, the carpenter
Col Wilford's "King of Magadha," in Asiat Res , IX, 435, as cited
by Rev Wm. Hales, I, 197   This is within three years of the death
of the third Buddha, (11th Chrishna) by the Indian calendar, or of
his birth by the Augustan.

B. C. 7, Pontus.—Aeras of Amasia and Sebastopolis Heracleopis,
recovered from coins   Renier, Rev. Arch , 1877, Ramsey, Jour

Phil. II, 151; Wroth, (Poole,) Cat Gr. Coins. (The æra of Amasia is printed as of B. C 7, but corrected in Mr Wroth's copy at the British Museum to B C. 2 See A D 64.

B. C. 1, Tyana.—Apollonius of Tyana was a youth of between 16 and 20 years of age at the time of the death of Archelaus Philostratus, in vita, I, 7, 12, 13 Archelaus died A D 17. Hence the birth of Apollonius was coincident with the Christian æra Clinton, F. R , I, 8 This is also the opinion of Gibbon, I, 369 Hole says he was born B. C. 3 and died A D. 98 Priaulx says that Apollonius visited India about A D 45 See the hebdomadal cycle in chapter VIII hereof The mother of Apollonius was informed by a god who appeared to her, that "he himself should be born of her," and the divine Apollonius was the result Doane, 128, citing Philostratus Apollonius, while yet a mere youth, abjured the pleasures of life and became an ascetic He lived upon the simple fruits of the soil, wore only linen clothing, went bare-footed, suffered his hair to grow long and slept on the bare ground. He observed the Pythagorean five years of self-imposed silence, and being filled with the Holy Spirit performed innumerable miracles, testifying to his divine origin and mission upon earth But the universal worship of Augustus throughout the Roman world soon put an end to the pretensions not only of Apollonius, but also to those of the many other aspirants for divine honours who appeared at this period

A. D. 1, India and China—Nativity or re-incarnation of the Indo-Chinese Buddhic Ies Chrishna, or Joss. Most of the following details are from Father Du Halde's "History of China" In A D 51, Ming-ti, a legitimate sovereign of the Han dynasty, ascended the throne of China In the fifteenth year of his reign, A D 65, there appeared to him a gigantic and godlike apparition, whose effulgence covered the entire earth, reminding him of the prediction of the prophetic Confucius, namely, that in this year the Holy One, would re-appear in the West. Upon awakening from his pious vision, Ming-ti immediately dispatched an embassy of venerable and learned men to India, where the Divine Incarnation was expected to appear These magi, having arrived at the principal place in India celebrated for the worship of the Buddhic incarnation, (probably Gorakpore in Rajputana,) took part in the solemn rites of the religion founded by Ies Chrishna, familiarly known in China as Jess or Joss, and they adored His sacred image; after which, accompanied by a number of bonzes, or Buddhic priests of India, they returned to China So soon as the report of their mission was conveyed to the emperor, he

issued a proclamation recognizing and authorizing the practice of
Buddhism and the worship of Joss, as one of the three great religions
of the state. The epoch of this incarnation is the first moon after
the vernal equinox, which corresponds with our Easter. If, in order
to make it correspond with the beginning of the Christian year, the
fifteenth year of Ming-ti is reckoned from the 1st of January, then
the incarnation of the Indo-Chinese Ies Chrishna took place in A D
64 But as this year is deduced by Father Du Halde from the years
of the Chinese Jovian cycle, which are 63 years older than the
Christian æra, 63 years have to be deducted in order to reduce the
year of the Indo-Chinese incarnation æra to the Christian reckoning
Hence the incarnation took place in A D 1; in other words, it occurred, or was believed to have occurred, 1899 years before the
present year, 1900. This is evidently the same Ies Chrishna, who,
according to Ramchandra Gosha, was previously incarnated B C
724, (apotheosized B C 657,) and ascended to heaven B. C 644
In such case the putative father of the Indo-Chinese Ies Crishna was
of the royal race of Ies-saca, and he was the son or husband of Vasudeva. Ies Chrishna's mission on earth was antagonism to the phar-
isaical religion of Brahm; the rejection of his ritual, sacrifices,
puranas and institutions of caste and slavery and the inculcation of
justice, meekness, and faith in salvation He aided with the multitude against the few and with the poor against the rich, claiming
equal rights for all men who accepted the faith According to Du
Halde's Jovian chronology and the Buddhic years of the apotheosis
and death, Joss was apotheosized in A. D. 130 and died A D 144;
according to the Christian chronology Joss was apotheosized A D
67 and died A. D. 81.

A. D. 1, New Granada.—Approximate æra of Chinzapagua
(Sent by God) which, according to the archæologist Señor Gonzalo
Ramos Ruiz, must be placed "at about the beginning of the Christian æra" Chinzapagua was the Messiah of the Chibcha or Muiska
Indians, a nation of more than a million souls, who inhabited the
elevated region of Lake Guatavita, about eight leagues from Bogota
in New Granada Chinzapagua was born of the Sun and one of the
daughters of an earthly king or zaque. Having ascended a hill to the
eastward of her father's palace, the young virgin encountered the
rays of the Sun and, in consequence, gave birth to an emerald, which,
being wrapped in cotton and carried in her bosom during five days,
at length developed into a beautiful Youth, who was univerally acknowledged as the Child of the Sun After beginning a magnificent

temple to his heavenly father—of which, it is said, there are ruins at
Tunja—this Messiah predicted the coming of a strange and cruel
race, who would conquer the country   Subsequent to the making
of this prediction he mysteriously disappeared in Suamoz, the present town of Sogamoso   "At the time of his disappearance he was
an old man with a long white beard and of a different race from the
Chibchas, whom he taught agriculture and how to spin and weave
and to build cities "   His footprints were to be seen in the solid
rock in various parts of the country   One of his images (of gold)
shows a large cross behind the head and ears, another one exhibits
the Sacred Heart of the messianic myth   Señor Paravey, who has
compared the language of the Chibchas with the Sewa dialect of
Japan, finds many philological analogies "with almost complete
identity of their respective numeral characters "   The Chibchas
counted by scores, had a zodiac of ten signs, divided the year into
twenty months and had a cycle of twenty years, "which was marked
by the sacrifice of the Guesa "   The ten zodions were Ata, Boza,
Mica, Muihica, Hisca, Ta, Cuhupcua, Suhuza, Aca and Ulchihica.
These are supposed to be the names of Chinzapagua's disciples   The
Guesa rite consisted in sacrificing a youth once in twenty years to
the god of harvests   Cf   Century Magazine, October, 1891

A. D. 1, Rome.—The Christian æra, which, as now used, began
at midnight between December 31, B C 1, and January 1, A D 1.
The year (not the day) of this æra is attributed to Dionysius Exiguus,
a Scythian monk and astrologer, who, it is claimed, flourished during
the reign of Justinian I , and computed this year from the paschal
cycle which began B C. 8 and ended A D. 524, but who is much
more likely to have flourished during the reign of Justinian II , A D.
705, because no evidence has been adduced to prove that the æra
was employed before December 1, A D 781, during the pontificate
of Hadrian I   Bury's ' Later Roman Empire," II, 504 Cf Brady,
II, 343, who claims, though not upon equally convincing grounds, that
the Christian æra was used so early as either 730, or 742, that is to
say, during the reign of Pepin, A D 714-68 Cf. Scaliger, de
Emend Temp   The Christian æra is based on the Nativity of Jesus
Christ at Bethlehem in Judea, which, according to the gospels, occurred during the procuratorship of Cyrenius, or Quirinus, and the
reign of Herod, while the Roman tax levy of Augustus was in progress
and at a period of the year when the flocks were feeding in the
fields   Numerous attempts have been made to synchronize these
dates, but with so little success that Scaliger regarded the determin-

ation of the Nativity as beyond the skill of man.   The Natal Day has been celebrated in various ages on Martinmas, Whitsuntide, Jesus Day, Palalia, Easter, the Vernal Equinox, Cæsar's Day, the Feast of Tabernacles, and Brumalia, or Christmas, the last one now superceding all the others   Clem Alex ap , Putnam, Chron., 252; Massey, Gen., II, 399; Bower, vita Bon VIII; Cassini, op. cit ; Brady, II, 121, 341, 343, Matthew Paris; and Zonaras.   Greswell, F C , I, 536, says the Nativity occurred April 5th, but he does not say that it was ever celebrated on that day.   In order to bring the Nativity within the reign of Herod, Archbishop Usher computed that it occurred in B. C 4, that being the year in which Herod died On the other hand, Waddington (Fastes Asiat , Paris, 1872,) proves that neither this year nor A. D. 1, fell in the procuratorship or governorship of Quirinus, which occurred eleven years earlier   The census appears to have been taken under Augustus in A. U. 723 and 738.   Mon Ancyc , VIII, Cohen, Rom Fasti   It is amost certain that the tax levy was made in the same years

A. D. 8, Abyssinia.—So-called Anno Christo of Abyssinia   Prinsep, "Ind Antiq ," ed. 1858   This is really the year of the apotheosis of Augustus in Egypt, B. C. 8, shifted to A D 8, as explained under B. C. 15.   See also A. D 14, 284 and 524, also cycles of 532 years in chap. VIII, herein.

A. D. 14, Rome.—August 29th.   Death and bodily Ascension to heaven of Augustus Divus Filius (Son of God), this having been his official title, which is stamped on his coins and is employed by Horace, Ovid, Virgil, Manilius, Suetonius, Pliny, Tacitus, Censorinus, and indeed all the writers of the Augustan period   The Ascension was sworn to as having been actually witnessed in effigy by Numericus Atticus, a senator and noble of the Praetorian order   Suetonius, Aug , 100

Following are the principal dates relating to Augustus .

63 B C —Nativity, 9 cal. October
40 B. C —Advent Virgil, Fourth Eclogue   Premature closure of temple of Janus   Title "Son of God" stamped on coins of this year.
30 B C —January 1   First regnal year in Egypt.   Censorinus.
28 B. C.—January 1   First regnal year in Rome Censorinus   "Middle Ages Revisited " says B C 27; other authorities say B C 25, 24, etc   Augustus acknowledged by the Senate as the Sebastos, or Sacro-sanct   Mon Ancyr.
25 B C —Imperial accession   Second closure of Janus.

15 B. C —Apotheosis in Rome. Ludi Sæculares. " Middle Ages Revisited " says B. C. 16 Third and permanent closure of Janus.

8 B. C.—January 1, afterwards August 29. Apotheosis in Egypt. " Reform " of the Egyptian calendar.

8 A. D.—So-called Anno Christo of Abyssinia, really the apotheosis of Augustus in Egypt of B C 8, shifted to A. D. 8, as ex-explained under B C 15 Epoch, August 29.

14 A. D —August 29 Death and Ascension to heaven of Augustus. An ampler chronology appears in " Middle Ages Revisited," App T.

A D. 14, Egypt.—Shifted æra of Augustus employed by some chronologists; really that of his death and Ascension. Cf. " Middle Ages Revisited," App. V.

A. D. 35, Pontus.—Aera of Comana, recovered from coins W. Wroth, op cit. The æra is printed as of A D 38-39 but corrected to A. D 35 in the author's copy at the Br. Museum See A. D 64.

A. D. 40, Ceylon.—Nirvana of the Third Buddha Noel

A. D. 40, Mauretania.—Moorish æra according to Stokvis, who, however, gives no explanation of it. Mauretania was divided by the Romans into two provinces, A D 42 Perhaps this date and the æra are connected

A. D. 64, Pontus.—Aeras of Cerasus (Cer-Iasus) Neo Cæsaria, Trapesus and Zela, recovered from coins W Wroth, op cit Printed as of A D 63, but corrected in the author's copy at the Brit Museum to A. D. 64. It requires but slight examination of the process by which this date has been computed to perceive that it belongs to the æra of Augustus. The usual type of the coins issued by the Greek colonies of the Euxine, before the period of Augustus, was the bust of Dionysius, encircled by a fillet of ivy, sometimes wearing the Phrygian cap of Liberty; the Cross, sur-mounted by a Ser-apis, or head of Bacchus (Koehne calls it the head of Osiris); the plain cross, the ☧ or so-called Christian but really Bacchic monogram; or else the svastica Koehne, Pl VIII, figs 4, 7; XXI, 2, XXXVIII, 4. With the advent of Augustus these sacred emblems were swept away and replaced by the head of the new Messiah, whom Rome had accepted as the object of its religious devotion. Ovid's letters prove that even in Pontus the worship of Augustus was supreme

A. D. 65, China.—Aera of Fo, Tod, or Bod App Cyc., X, 264 See B. C. 1036

A. D. 65, India.—Beginning of the Jovian or 60-year cycles of the Jyotistava The Pandits' "Chronology" See A D 1025.

A. D. 68, Rome.—Dionysian æra of Rome "Upon the news of Nero's death (June 9, A. D. 68) many people, adopting for the emblem of their hopes the Phrygian cap of Liber Pater, ran widely through the streets, uttering revolutionary cries, and fomenting an excitement that ended by involving the Senate in their design and the issuance of an act proclaiming a republican government Among the measures of the short-lived administration was the coinage of money designed to announce the restoration" . . . "A common type of these coins was a citizen clad in a toga with a cap of Liberty on his head and the legend LIBERIATI." Others had "LIBERTAS RESTITUTA," etc Within a single year the ephemeral republic was succeeded by no less than four emperors, to wit, Galba, Otho, Vitellius and Vespasian. Del Mar's "Hist Monetary Systems," chap on "Rome"

A. D. 74, Java.—Saka, deduced from the Roman year The Pandits, p xix, citing Sir Stamford Raffles and Crawfurd. See A D 78

A. D. 78, Madras, etc—Shifted Saka of Salivahana, or Vicramaditya, the real epoch of which was Easter Day, A. D 1 See also B. C. 78 and 63 This saka was shifted 78 years by being computed from the Roman dates that had previously been altered by Augustus Cæsar The migration of Indian families from one province to another and the resulting commingling of Indian customs and dates alluded to by Sankara Balkrishna Dikshit, in the "Indian Calendar," may have assisted the blunder. Unaware of such shifting, the Pandits date the Nativity of Salivahana from the Nauroz, or beginning, of the Hindu luni-solar year, Baisack, 1, Calijoga 3179, the Roman equivalent of which is now March 14, A D 78 Stokvis repeats the same error. Other authorities make Baisack 1, equal April 13 Sewell also fixes the Saka of Salivahana in A D 78; Wilford says A. D. 79; Cunningham also says A D 79; yet in dating Gupta in A. D. 167 (Saka, 241,) he fixes Salivahana in B. C. 75. The earliest actual inscription yet found with "Saka" is dated 725; the earliest with "Samvat" is dated 33, equal to B. C 23, according to Rev Wm. Hales, I, 198.

A. D. 78, India.—Re-establishment of the Indian Jovian cycles of 60 years, which Cunningham admits "must have been in use before the Christian æra" This epoch was probably shifted like the Saka of Salivahana. The Indian Jovian cycles originally began on the vern. . . . . p 15 . . . . began

March 14. Sewell, in "South Indian Chronology," p. 10, says March 15

A. D. 79, Burma.—Prome æra established by King Samandri This is evidently the same as the Saka of A D 78 and was doubtless deduced in the same manner

A. D. 81, Balli.—Saka deduced from that of Java See A. D. 74 Cf. The Pandits' "Chron ," p xix

A. D. 121, Athens.—Christian equivalent of the Attic-Hadrianic æra, referred to in Corpus Inscrip No 281, as that of Hadrian, archon of Athens and sovereign-pontiff of Rome In this inscription he is styled "Theos," or the living God. Cf. Phlegon, de Mirabilibus, XXV, 93; Corsini, Fasti Attici, IV, 173-5 Hadrian enlarged and beautified Athens, called the new portion after his own name, completed and dedicated the Olympian temple to Jupiter, which had been 560 years in course of construction, presided at the Dionysia, gave Athens a new Code of Laws and was recognised in the inscriptions as its Second Foundei. Corp. Inscrip , 520 Cf. Spartianus, in vita; Scaliger, De Emend., etc.; Gruter, cclxxvi, 4 Basing his conjecture on certain remarks in Galen, Dr Greswell, K H , II, 155, thinks that this year marked for Athens the adoption of a solar calendar, to supersede the Metonic luni-solar, and that the New Year day was changed from 1st Hecat., to 1st Boedrom ; but whether this change took place in 121 or 136, or some other year, seems doubtful. The dated coins, "A U. 874," of Hadrian, point to the date last named as the true one.

A. D. 136, Egypt.—Appearance of Osiris, the Redeemer, in the form of Apis, the Bull Life of Hadrian, by Ælius Spartianus This is exactly one Divine Year (658 common years) from the Apotheosis of Darius Hystaspes, who ruled both in Persia and Egypt and was worshipped in the last-named country as the Creator Perhaps this Apis miracle is connected with the Annus Magnus of Censorinus. See below, A D 138, Rome.

A. D. 136, Judea.—Æra of Barco-cheba In 131 Hadrian rebuilt Jerusalem, gave it the name of Ælia Capitolina, erected in it a temple to Jupiter, placed his own image in it and commanded it to be worshipped. The indignity offered by this ordinance, the near approach of the Brahminical Divine Year, the prediction of a solar eclipse and the exciting harangues of the Rabbis, raised up a national champion in the person of Barco-cheba, or Barkobab, who in A. D. 134 proclaimed himself to be the Promised One and bade defiance to the Roman arms In two years' time the Romans slew 580,000 Jews, including their ill-starred Saviour, and reduced Judea to a desert, in which condition it has remained substantially ever since

A. D. 138, Rome.—Accession and æra of Antoninus Pius, consulate of Antoninus Pius and Brittius Præsena, when the 18th Thoth corresponded with 12 cal. August, whereas, a century later, it corresponded with 7 cal July. This æra appears to have been called Annus Magnus; but no explanation is given. Censorinus, Die Natale, ch. XXI The reason is probably that the Brahminical Annus Magnus, or Divine Year, fell in A. D. 188, and that the alteration of the calendar, occasioned chiefly by the action of Augustus, resulted in a dislocation of many years between the Eastern and Western æras See A D 78, A D 136, Egypt, and A D 187, Rome

A. D. 166, India.—Gupta æra, according to Stokvis.

A. D. 167, India.—Æra of Gupta. Cunningham. But see A. D. 78, 206, 318 and 319.

A. D. 187, Rome.—Brahminical Divine Year, Table A Reign of Commodus Dr Greswell, F C, I, 525, says that in this reign the calendar was "wantonly tampered with and deranged;" but furnishes no particulars Commodus, who reigned 180-192, gave great encouragement to the worship of Isis-Osiris.

A. D. 195, Persia.—Birth of Mani, or Manes, founder of the Manichæan religion and author of the "Shabarkan" Albiruni Barkan, or Barkhan, is one of the names of Buddha, whilst the æra of Manes is Brahminical. Manes styled himself both Messiah and Paraclete, and was attended by Twelve Apostles. Herbert, "Britannia after the Romans," II, 155 Manes received divine revelation in his 13th year (mitsva), the 2nd of Ardishir, King of Kings He was cruelly put to death by Ormuz I, about A D 271. According to Albiruni, if we reckon from the anno astronorum Babyloniæ (B C 747), Manes was born A. D. 220, whilst if we reckon from the regnal period of Alexander the Great, Manes was born A D 206 and died A D. 271 to 273 Here is a discreancy of 14 or 15 years Some Manichæans still existed in the time of Albiruni, the 11th century

A. D. 205, Persia.—Æra of Ardishir ben Bebek, King of Kings and founder of the Sassanian dynasty Albiruni says "from Alexander to Ardishir is 537 years" Title assumed, "Shah-in-shah"

A. D. 206, India—Aera of Gupta, A D 206-9, according to Dr Bühler But see A D 78, 167, 318 and 319

A. D. 211, Rome.—Beginning of the reign of Caracalla, who died in 217. Yet this monarch, according to Eckhel, (Doc. Num Vet, II, 63, 111,) issued coins in Macedonia with the head of Alexander the Great, radiated, stamped in an unknown æra with the Greek letters denoting the year 275. By the received chronology this date cannot be explained; but if allowance is made for the 15 or 16 years' alteration of the Augustan calendar, effected by the Italian Sacred College, the year was reckoned from the æra of Julius Cæsar; thus B. C 48 plus 16 plus 211=275

A. D. 220, Rome.—Establishment of sun-worship, or Mithraism, as the official religion of Rome, under Elagabalus See "Middle Ages Revisited," Appendix R. See also B. C. 389 for dated coins of Elagabalus

A. D. 223, Persia.—Sassanian æra. Epoch September 27 Stokvis Lenglet and others say A D 225 See 205

A. D. 250, Central India.—Chedi, Chesh, or Kalachuri samvat, or æra of Central India Cunningham It is fixed by Robert Sewell in A. D. 248 and called Chesh, or Chedi, its epoch being Aswin 1st. "The Indian Calendar," Table III Stokvis and Duff Rickmers say Calijoga 3350, or A D 249 This æra is now obsolete

A. D. 262, Ephesus.—Destruction of the temple of Diana in Ephesus by the Goths, Gallien being emperor of Rome. Townsend When the ruins were excavated by J T. Wood, 1865-70, the following inscription was found upon the peribolus wall Augustus Cæsar, Son of God, emperor, consul XII times, tribune XVIII times, pontifex maximus, restored the fane of Diana and repaired the fortified wall of the Augusteum. G Asinio Gallo, pro-consul, Sextus Lartidio, legate Middle Ages Revisited, App. T.

A. D. 271, Persia.—Death and Ascension to heaven of Manes, the Messiah, the most noted of whose followers was Augustine of Hippo, fifth century See A D 195. Clinton, F R., I, 317, fixes the death of Manes in A. D 278; Eusebius says A. D 282

A. D. 279, Rome.—Æra of the ordinance of Probus, permitting the cultivation of the vine in Champagne (Gaul), Germany and other northern provinces. Gibbon, I, 67, thinks that the vines of Burgundy may be as old as the age of the Antonines, the evidence upon which this opinion rests being that of Eumenius, in the fourth century. Dio Sic. V, 2, said that Gaul did not produce wine; yet Pliny alludes to the culture of the vine in Gallia Narbonensis, Vienne, Spain and Egypt. Book III, Nat. Hist It was the policy of Persia, and afterwards of Greece, Rome and Spain, to monopolize the culture of the vine in the Mother country, and to forbid or discourage it in the provinces. The date when this rule was relaxed or abrogated often marked the dawn of provincial independence and the rehabilitation of the popular cult of Dionysius.

A. D. 284, Eastern Empire.—Æra of Diocletian. In the Asiatic provinces of the Roman Empire this æra took for its epoch the New Year day of the Seleucidan æra and began on the autumnal equinox; in Egypt and Abyssinia it took for its epoch the day of the Augustan Apotheosis, namely, Thoth 1st, our August 29th. Stokvis and Cunningham. The latter says it was extensively used. See B C 8 and A. D 8 and 14.

A. D. 312, Byzantium.—Æra of Constantine. Autumnal equinox. Some chronologists assign to this year, or else to A D 313, the beginning of the Indictions; others hold that they were established long before the æra of Constantine. Scaliger and Lenglet begin the Indictions from the æra of Julius Cæsar. They were really of oriental and Pelasgian origin and were re-established by Augustus, B C 30. From the inscription on a coin of Constantine (No 463), representing a section of a zodiac with "Rector totius orbis," Cohen infers "a change of calendar" in this reign, but we have no details. "*Description historique des Monnaies frappées sous l'empire Romain,*" 2nd ed, 1880.

A. D. 318, Guzerat.—Gupta, or Balabhi, or Valabhi æra, according to the Pandits, op. cit., who derive it from an inscription found at Somnath, and who date it Vicramaditya, 375. Prof Cowell says A. D 318-19; Dutt says A D 319; Dr. T. Block, Asiat. Soc of London, Dec 11, 1894, says A D 329.

A. D. 319, Guzerat.—Gupta, or Balabhi, or Valabhi æra, "241 years after Saka," commencing with the month of Kartika. Sewell. It was discontinued A D 802, when the city of Balabhi was destroyed. See A. D. 78.

A. D. 348, Abyssinia.—Æra of Maherat (or grace). See A. D 1348.

A. D. 377, Arabia.—Saracenic æra. In this (?) year (fifth consulate of Valens) Mavia, or Mania, queen of the Saracens, at the head of an army, invaded the Roman province of "Arabia," lying between the Red Sea and the Nile, demanding, among other things, the liberation of Moses, a Saracenic priest, who had been condemned by the Romans to the Bisharee mines, and who, though a worker of miracles, was unable to effect his own release. After Mavia had defeated the Roman army, "an occurrence still held in remembrance among the people of the country and celebrated in songs by the Saracens," (? men,) the venerated Moses was liberated. In A D

379, the year following Valens' death, Mavia sent a contingent of Saracens to assist the empress Dominica in her defence of Constantinople against the Goths   Confused accounts of these transactions, mingled with circumstances impossible of belief, appear in the pages of Sozomen and Socrates   The æra of Mavia extends 320-92   She is mentioned by Rufinus, who died in 410   Mania, Mavia, Maria, Mary, Mæra, Maia and Maha are regarded as the same by Higgins, Anacal , I, 308, and La Loubère, III, 136

A. D. 389, Rome.—First triumph of Theodosius   Supposed official change of the Roman state religion   Gibbon, ch XXVIII

A. D. 393, Rome.—Re-consecration of Roman temples   Lanciani's "Pagan and Christian Rome," p 39   The usurper Eugenius re-consecrates them to the ancient state religion   "Ancient Britain, chap. VI.   The date seems astrological   After deducting the 63 years' alteration of the calendar, it remains one-half of 658 years, or of a Divine Year

A. D. 394, Rome.—Second triumph of Theodosius, death of Eugenius, re-consecration of the temples; final official adoption of the new religion.   Zosimus, (Vatican MS)   Mendelssohn.   (1887), fixes the history of Zosimus in A D   450-501

A. D. 397, Gaul.—Æra formerly used in Gaul and Britain; epoch, November 18, since changed to November 11, and now called Martinmas   This festival, once known as Brumalia, was celebrated in Scythia and Greece in very remote times as the natal day of Dionysius   It constituted one of the four great Dionysian holidays and was observed for ten, afterwards seven, days, before and after November 18th, an interval once known as the Halcyon Days and subsequently as St Martin's Summer.   After the decline of emperor-worship, it was revived in Rome, from whence it probably made its way, together with the other Dionysian festivals, to Gaul, some time during the fourth century   The date of November 18, 397, possibly marks the revival of the Dionysian cult in Gaul   The medieval monks, to hide this fact, invented St Martin, who, as they allege, was born at Sabaric, in Pannonia, in 316, became bishop of Tours in 375, and died on November 18, 397, in whose memory they pretended that this day was kept   The festal ceremonies which are still observed at Martinmas by the people of Gaul, Britain and Scotland, and which closely resemble those of the ancient Greeks, do not support this theory. Cf. Picot, "Chron "; L De Mas Latrie, "Chron "; Bell's Pantheon, voc. "Halcyon Days", Brady. op. cit.

II, 274; Potter, I, 443; Putnam, 252, Townsend, voc "Martinmas"; and Chapter I, hereof.

A. D. 406, Mecklenburg.—Death of the Gothic leader Rada-Gaisus, who had proclaimed himself an incarnation of the Deity and who, as such, was worshipped or venerated by the Obotrites of Mecklenburg   The last incarnation of Woden was fixed in a year equal to B C 90 According to the Dionysian astrology this incarnation was due to recur after an interval of 532 years, that is to say, in A D 442   However, it is by no means certain that the Goths of the Baltic employed a Dionysian divine year   In 406 Rada-Gaisus invaded Italy with a large force, expecting to capture Rome and inaugurate a new Empire, but in this enterprise he failed   He was defeated before Florence and barbarously put to death by Stilicho. Mascou, Hist Goth   Gibbon, who follows De Guignes, ascribes the Gothic invasion of Italy to the Hunnish invasion of Tartary and the latter to the displacement of population in China; but the chronology of the period does not support this theory   See A D 421

A. D. 410, Rome.—Death of the Gothic leader Alaric, who set himself up for an incarnation of the Deity. He was born about A D 375   In 397 he ravaged the whole of Greece, and although checked by Stilicho, his actions were approved, or condoned, through the weakness of Arcadius, who appointed him Master-general of the provinces he had desolated   Alaric besieged, captured and ransomed Rome in 410 and afterwards marched into Apulia, where he died the same year.   He was buried in the channel of the river Busentinus, near Cosentia

A. D. 412, Arabia.—Year of Treason, which, according to Al-biruni, was 110 years before the "Year of the Elephants," which nevertheless is fixed herein at A D 532, q v

A. D. 421, Bactria.—First regnal year of Baharam Gur, (Gur meaning Holy, or Saint), King of the Iesha, (these people were so named by Sung-yun, A D 520), or the White Huns, (so named by Col Francis Wilford, in Asiat Res , IX, 206), or the Indo-Scythians, (so named in Duff Rickmers "Chron of India," sub anno, 460) Their rule extended from the borders of Persia to the Punjab.   The date is from Wilford, who deduces it from the Augustan year of the Calijoga   It would therefore, together with the dates derived from it, differ 15 years from the Christian dates   In A D 376 (Christian date) the Huns of the Caspian drove the Scythians back from Pannonia into Thrace (Sozomen); about 420 the Iesha are persecuted and driven from Merv by Varanes, or Baharam V., the Sassanian k of Persia, 430, the Iesha are attacked by Kitolo of Peshawar; 434, accession of Attila; 446, Attila's treaty with Theodosius; 448, Priscus, who was born in Attila's capital of Ieshelburg, now Buda-Pesth, learned this year of the conquest of Bactria by the White Huns The æra of Vicramaditya, a son of Baharam Gur, is 20 years after the first regnal year of his father, or A D 441 (Wilford) In A. D 458 (deduced from an oriental date) Balkh was the metropolis of this people It is presumed that the coins (which are still extant), struck by their king Toroman, near the beginning of the fifth century, stamped "52" in an unknown æra, refer to the advent of this Vicramaditya. Duff Rickmers begins Toroman's reign in 460 and continues it to 510 It is more likely to have commenced in 441 + 52 = 493 and to have lasted until 510 Toroman erected a temple at Mooltan in the Punjab, which is said to have been dedicated to the Sun In 600 the Iesha were peaceably settled in this portion of India Wilford, op. cit ; Cunningham, in "Numis Chron ," 1894, and "Anc Geog India," pt I, Specht, "Asie Central"; Rawlinson, "Seventh Monarchy " See A D 441.

A. D. 422, Arabia.—"Year of Treason," 520 years after the death of Kab ben Luayy Albiruni Kab ben Luayy's æra roughly synchronises with that of Salivahana

A. D. 441, Bactria.—Æra of the ninth one of the various Vicramadityas discovered by Col Wilford in the Indian annals This Vicramaditya was the putative son of Baharam Gur, k of the White Huns. From his æra, which was Calijoga 3543, to the Hegira, the Indians reckon 196 years, yet according to the Christian dates there is an interval between them of only 181 years, a discrepancy of 15 years. Col Francis Wilford, in Asiat Res. IX, 302

A. D. 444, Rome.—Restoration of the Ischenian quinquenalles, or quinquennial games, by Theodosius II Lenglet; Picot II, 279; Lempriere

A. D. 493, Rome.—Theoretical Gothic period in Italy It began after the close of a Dionysian paschal period of 532 years from the Advent of Divus Augustus, B C. 40, coinciding with the first year of Theodoric, who reigned just 33 years, A. D 493-525. All these features are astrological This Gothic æra was followed by a Gothico, or Lombardo-Byzantine period, 553-752, when Ravenna was taken by Pepin; the imperial exarch retired to Byzantium; and the temporal kingdom of the Italian popes was founded The Roman coins and marbles of this period, 493-525, indicate the prevalence of the Ischenian or else Dionysian cult in Rome down to near the beginning of the temporal power

A. D 524, Rome.—Year when it is pretended that the Canon of Dionysius Exiguus was constructed   Greswell, F C Intro., 192, reluctantly admits that this canon might not be earlier than "the end of the seventh century " It really belongs to a period later than the Restoration of Justinian II. The year A D. 524 completes one Dionysian divine year commencing with the Egyptian apotheosis of Divus Augustus, B C 8   It is therefore astrological, and as such is open to the suspicion of having been connected with the name of Dionysius Exiguus in after times and for theoretical purposes.   Bury says that the Christian æra was not used anywhere until 781, q. v

A D. 530, Byzantium (Constantinople) —"An embassy, said to be Indian, bringing gifts to the Emperor Justinian, reaches Constantinople " Priaulx, "Ind. Emb to Rome," 126, Duff Rickmers.   As this event was of an extraordinary character its date may be conjectured not to have been wholly unconnected with the Dionysian cycle and expected re-incarnation of Ourgouti Tirounal, or Augustus Quichena.

A D. 531, Persia —Æra of Meshdak, the Messiah of God on earth, his advent coinciding with the last year of Kobad ben Feroz, the shah-in-shah of Persia. Albiruni.   The advent of Meshdak (sometimes Messdak, Machdak, Mashdak, or Mazdac), occurred one Dionysian cycle after the Apotheosis of Augustus, when, according to a belief long entertained throughout the Roman world, that divinity would again visit the earth to restore it to peace and happiness Meshdak taught a community of wives and property.   He was executed this year by Chosroes   Fraser's "Persia," p 132.

A. D. 532, Armenia.—Æra Armeniacum Augustorum, the completion of which was one Dionysian cycle after the Apotheosis of Augustus, when this Messiah was confidently expected to re-visit the earth   The new cycle was to begin Navasardi 1st=August 11, which is the Augustan ascension-day, as shifted by an equable calendar that continued in use down to very recent years   The head of the calendar belonging to this cycle was January 1   The Christian Armenian æra was invented in the 13th century and attributed to A. D. 552, q v

A. D. 532, Arabia.—Augustan æra of Arabia, exactly one Dionysian cycle from the Apotheosis of Augustus, son of God and Lord of the World   In order to conceal the origin of a cycle whose long

continued use and significance they could not at once suppress, the
pious Mahometans of the following century entitled this æra the
"Year of the Elephants," and alleged that it commemorated the defeat
of the Abyssinians and their elephants by the tribe of Koreish, under
Abraha; events whose inconsequential character mark the fictitious
character of the commemoration.   Albiruni fixes this victory of the
Koreish 110 years (this is equal to one Ludi Sæculares) after the
"Year of Treason," and 90 years before the Hegira.   Gibbon, V,
198, assigns the "defeat of the Abyssinians," which is evidently the
same event, to the year of Mahomet's birth.   This he fixes in A. D.
569.   It will be observed that there is no such uncertainty about the
æra as there is about the occurrence assigned for its observance.
But the mollahs probably did the best they could with the obnoxious
out-growths of the monstrous and degrading religion of emperor worship which they inherited from Rome.

   A. D. 548, India.—Magi San, 548-9, which is 45 years before the
Bengali San. Sewell.

   A. D. 548, Scythia.—Conjectural year assigned by Genghis Khan
to the incarnation of Budantsar, who was miraculously conceived of
a Mongol widow and from whom he claimed descent, through Yesukai, or Iesu-chri.   See A. D. 1206.

   A. D. 552, Armenia.—Æra Haicana, or so-called Christian æra
of Armenia, invented probably in the 13th century and dated back
to July 9, 552.   Stokvis says July 7.   This year is one Dionysian
cycle from the Apotheosis of Augustus, while the epoch is that of
the Greek Olympiads.   The æra is attributed by Cardinal Pagi, (a
Roman papal secretary,) to the mission of Julian of Halicarnassus
and the schism it wrought in the Armenian religion; but this pious
legend of the church cannot be reconciled with the light which archæology and numismatics have thrown upon the history of religion
in Armenia.

   A. D. 552, Japan.—In this year, according to Klaproth, the religion of Buddha was introduced into Japan from Corea.   But see
B. C. 712 and 660.

   A. D. 567, Byzantium (Constantinople).—Greek cycle of the
re-incarnation of Ies Chrishna.   Greek zodion of Aquarius, the Water-
man.   This cycle may have facilitated the advent of Meshdack, Mahomet, Musailima, etc.

   A. D. 569, Mecca.—November 10th. (Martinmas.) Birth of Mahomet, according to Gibbon.   The Benedictines, also Hole and
Townsend, fix this event in 570; while the Penny Encyp. prefers 571.

Following Townsend, who follows the Benedictine monks in the remaining dates, Mahomet begins to preach in 609; is Summoned by the angel Gabriel, 610; is opposed by the Koreishites, 613; flies to Medina (Hegira), 622; of which place he is appointed Prince; defeats the Koreishites, 623-25; captures Mecca, 630, dies at Medina, Monday, June 8, 632, after having founded one of the greatest empires of the world. See A D 610 and 622

A. D. 570, Mysore.—Tippoo Saib, (A. D 1783-99,) besides employing the Hindu æra of the Calijoga, (See B C. 3102,) established an æra dating not from the Flight, but from the Birth of Mahomet, and at the same time re-introduced the 60-year Jovian cycles These regulations did not survive him He died in 1799, at the age of 52 They are partly explained in Kirkpatrick's " Select Letters of Tippoo Sultan." For birth of Mahomet, see A D 569.

A. D. 583, India.—Shifted year of the Hegira The Pandits, xix

A. D. 591, Southern India.—Fasali, or Fuslee æra of Southern India Sewell It was established in A. D. 1638. The Pandits.

A. D. 592, Northern India.—Fasali æra of Northern India Sewell About this period, A D 592, Amsuvarman of Nepal ruled in the name of Siva-deva Hiuen Tsing, in Beale, II, 81 n This æra was established by Akbar in A D 1556. The Pandits

A. D. 592, Upper India.—Fasali æra of Akbar. "This and the Sumbat years are both current in the provinces of Bahar, Benares and the ceded and conquered provinces " The government revenue is collected by the Fasali, or Fuslee, (or harvest, or revenue,) year and the common affairs of life are reckoned by it The Sumbat year is chiefly used by the native merchants and bankers " The Fuslee (sometimes Fussily), or harvest, and the Vilayuty, or country year, 1197, began in September, 1789; the Bengal year 1197, in April, 1790 " (This seems to be the year used by Sonnerat and Noel) " These æras appear to have been introduced in the reign of Akbar, who ascended the throne of Delhi on Rub-us-sanee 2nd, A H 963, or February 14, A. D. 1556." (For a different translation of these dates, see A. D. 1556) "A solar year for financial and civil transactions was then engrafted on the current lunar year of the Hegira, or subsequently adjusted to the first year of Akbar's reign But the Fuslee year 963 having expired in September, 1556, the commencement of it must be reckoned back to September, 1555, whereas the Bengal year 963 did not commence till April, 1556, and extended to April, 1557 The difference between the Fuslee and Christian æras is 592 years from the commencement of the Fuslee year, Aswin 1st, in September, to the end of December, and 593 years from January to the Fuslee year's termination on Bhadoon 30, corresponding with a variable date in September. Thus, Aswin 1, 1197, plus 592=September 5, 1789, when the Fuslee year 1197 began, and Bhadoon 30, 1197 plus 593=September 23, 1790, when it ended The Vilayuty, or Amli year, current in Orissa, differs from the Fuslee in a few days only, by adopting the Bengal method of reckoning the months The Christian exceeds the Bengal æra 593 years from April 11 to the end of December, and 594 years from January to April 10 Thus, Iesaac or Bysaack 1, the commen⌐ ient of the Bengal year 1197, plus 593 =April 11, 1790, an⌐ ₒ termination, Cheyt or Chittere, 31, 1197, plus 594=April 10, 1791. This furnishes an easy (?) rule for ascertaining the corresponding years of the Fuslee, Vilayuty, Bengal and Christian æras respectively " Harrington's "Analysis," vol. II, p. 176 and 5th Report, p 38

A. D. 592, Bengal and Orissa.—Vilayuty San, A. D. 592-3 The Amli San of Girísa-Chandra's "Chron Tables" (Pref , xvi) differs from the Vilayuty San only in details Sewell

A. D. 593, Bengal.—Bengali San, or Meshadi (Messianic) æra Sewell, in "Indian Cal ," p 42, says A D 593-4.

A. D 593, Orissa.—Amli San, commences from the birth of Indradryumna, or 12th day of the light half of Bhadra Each month commences when the Sun enters a sign of the zodiac. It is used in the law courts of Orissa and in business transactions. The Pandits.

A. D. 593, Orissa.—Vilayuty, or Vilaity San, commences Aswin 1. Used in collecting government revenue in Orissa In the Bengal Presidency it is customary to insert all of the following æras at the head of every regulation enacted by the government. 1, The Bengali San; 2, the Vilayuty or Amli year of Orissa; 3, the Fuslee year of the Upper Provinces; 4, the Fuslee year of the Peninsular The Pandits.

A. D. 600, India.—Æra of Mahratta Sur-San Sewell says 599-600

A. D. 603, India.—Harsha æra. Sewell Duff Rickmers says October 22nd, 606 See A D. 607.

A. D. 607, India.—Sri-Harsha æra of Kanauj. Epoch: March 3rd Cunningham See A D 622

A. D. 609, Arabia.—Advent of the impostor Musailima, who pretended that he was the Paraclete. Albiruni.

A. D. 610, Arabia.—Year of the Summons Mahomet is summoned on the 27th of Ramadan by the Angel Gabriel, to redeem the evangelical promise of the Paraclete This year is exactly one Divine Year, or one astrological incarnation cycle, (658 years,) from the deification and æra of Julius Cæsar It is evident that this æra was intended to replace the Julian (Cæsarian) which was in use in the Greek provinces, whilst the year of the Hegira, an afterthought of Omar, was invented to supplant that of Iesdigerd, used in the Persian provinces, which fell under the sway of the Moslems Mahomet's birth was also made to tally with the re-incarnation of Ies Chrishna. His miracles, his twelve apostles and the other astrological features of his religion, are noticed by Gibbon, ch I; Boulainvilliers, book III, and Higgins, in the " Anacalypsis "

A. D. 622, Tibet.—Srong Tsau Sgampo, Grand Lama, an "incarnation" of the deity L A Waddell, "Buddhism of Tibet," 1895, places his æra in 641; Appleton's Cyc., X, 261, and Duff Rickmers say 632.

A. D. 622, Tibet.—Æra of the Lama Teshi-lunpo, an æra employed within the last two centuries The Pandits' "Chron "

A. D. 622, Tibet.—Æra of Mckha-gya-tsho, a symbolical name for the number 403, such being the mode of reckoning in Tibetan mediæval works It indicates the employment in Tibet of the Hegira, or the æra of Mekha, or Mecca "The Tibetan writers, indeed, ascribe the destruction of the Buddhist religion in the North to the Mahometans " If 403 be deducted from the Tibeto-Jovian æra of A D 1025, the quotient is 622, the year of the Hegira The The Pandits' "Chron "

A. D. 622, India.—Harsha Kala, or Harshavardhana, of Kanouj, or Kanauj A. D. 606-48. This æra varies, in different authorities, from 603 to 635 Calcutta Review, April, 1891. Sewell says 603 and 606-7, Cunningham says 607

A. D. 622, Persia.—IesdigerdI II , deified 26 June, (29 August), A D. 632 (Prinsep) By sinking ten years of the calendar, this has been altered to 622. (See Anno Mundi B. C. 5502) The alteration from June to August made the deification of Iesdigerd agree with the day of the Augustan æra in Egypt. Woolhouse says 16 June, 632 Albiruni says "from Alexander to Iesdigerd's accession is 944 years " This would make the latter A. D. 617, thus 944 less 327=617

A. D. 622, Arabia —Hegira, or the Flight, from Mecca to Medina, or æra of Mahomet, Friday, July 16. This day is said to have been instituted by Omar, but Albiruni says the Moslem calendar was reforn i l b 1 ⸱ ⸱aliph Al Mutadid, tenth century This year, 622, is that of Iesdigerd, (see Persia, A. D. 632 and 622), while the day is that of the Greek Olympiads   The year is astrological, while the day is ecclesiastical   (See Elis, B C 1219).   The Arabian astronomers date the Hegira from Thursday, Moharran 1st, (July 15,) 622. This difference of one day may be due to the fact that the Moslem mollahs begin the day at sunset, whilst the astronomers, with more precision, begin it at noon   The Moslem year is substantially lunar. The civil months are adjusted by a cycle of approximately 30 years, 19 of which consist of 354 and 11 of 355 days, in all 10,631 days, or 29 years and 39 days, Julian.   The 12 months of the Moslem calendar contain alternately 29 and 30 days.   The last month of the intercalary years has 30 days.   The intercalated years are the 2nd, 5th, 7th, 10th, 13th, 16th, 18th, 21st, 24th, 26th, and 29th of the cycle   The month commences from the evening on which the New Moon is seen; hence its duration depends on the weather and it may differ in places not far apart.   (This was formerly the case also with the Jewish lunar calendar.   Lyons, 14)   But in the Moslem calendar no month may contain less than 29 nor more than 30 days   In legal deeds dated by the Hegira, the day of the week should be inserted   The Pandits "Chron "

A. D. 632, Persia.—Æra of Iesdigerd; epoch, June 16, Stokvis. See A D 622

A. D. 634, Arabia.—The Koran was published by Abubeker in A D 634 and revised by Othman in 652 and by other princes at subsequent dates. See A. D. 622 and cf Blackie's Pop Encyc , art "Literature."   The English translation by Sale is said to be merely an adaptation of Maracci's Italian translation which was made under the direction of the Italian papal censorship   It is greatly perverted, a fact which has in its turn influenced other translations   The Moslem World, 1893

A. D. 637, Siam and Burma.—Siamese and Burmese incarnation æra. Marsden, op cit , calls it "the astronomical year " and says the æra was deduced from a letter written A D 1769, by the king of Pegu to the French commander at Pondicherry, dated "12th of the month Kchong, year 1132."   Robertson, "India"; Cunningham, "Indian Æras," and Stokvis, "Chronology," fix this æra at Saturday, March 21st, A D 638, for India and Burma   It is mentioned by Cassini and by Higgins, in his "Anacal " I, 168.   Sewell calls it the æra of the Magi and fixes it at A D 638   The Pandits call it the Muggee San and fix its epoch in A. D 639   The days and months in this æra correspond exactly with those in the Bengalee San of

A. D 593-4, the difference between them being 45 years   The Pandits "Chron." Duff Rickmers calls this the Arakan æra and fixes it in 639.   "Joannes Moses, collector of the land tax for the province of Pegu, said that whenever the king thought the years of the æra too many, he changed it "   The Peguan æra was derived from the astronomers of Siam who fixed it in 638   Francis Buchanan, M D., in "Asiatic Researches," VI, 171.

A. D. 638, Pegu.—Æra mentioned by Dr. Buchanan.   See 637 Siam and Burma.

A. D. 639, Ceylon and Ava.—Pouppa-Azan San of Ceylon Established by Pouppa-chan-ra-han   Bishop Paul A Bigandet   Year begins with new moon of solar month, Chittere.   The division of months is the same as in the luni-solar system of India   The Pandits.

A. D. 657, Siam.—The re-incarnation of Salivahana, due in the Orient A D. 579, was (owing to 63 years difference between the Eastern and Western astrological calendars), not due until A D 642 in the Occident.   (Table B).   Between these two dates fell the In-carnation of Salivahana marked by the zodiacal sign of the Water-man, the Summons of Mahomet, the Hegira, the Incarnation of Srong Tsau Sgampo, Kanouj, and Iesdigerd, and finally the Siamese incarnation, all of which, except that of Salivahana, evidently re-lated to actual historical personages.   This—among other rea-sons—accounts for their not having taken place in the proper astrological year, according to the Western, or Roman, calendar In this interval, A D 579-642, were also completed the Twelve Ages of Etruria, according to Varro   Thus 12x110 (the period of the Ludi Sæculares)=1320, less 738, (the year of Romulus by the Augustan calendar used by Varro), equals 582   "Middle Ages Re-visited," App S

A. D. 700, Europe.—Approximate æra of Gothic architecture in Europe

A. D. 700, Mexico.—Toltec æra, according to Greswell, F. C., I, 361.   The astrologically correct date is A. D 722, q v.

A. D. 705, Constantinople.—Restoration of Justinian II to the throne of the Roman Empire, assisted by the Goths, an event marked by the issuance of a gold solidus, stamped with the earliest valid effigy of Jesus Christ known to exist.   The legend is "d. N. Ihs. Chs. REX REGNANTIVM "   The requirement of Justinian, that his tribute should be paid in coins of the imperial stamp, had caused the war with Abd-el-Melik and led to the complete independence (rather an extension) of the Arabian Empire, and the coinage of pieces with monotheistic legends, to which this coin was a reply. Theophanes; Cedrenus; Zonaras; "Hist of Monetary Systems," p. 171. Brady, "Clavis Calendaria," I, 403, says that the earliest effigy of Jesus Christ is of the year 707; but in this respect the learned author appears to be mistaken to the extent of two years

A. D. 712, Spain.—Conquest of Spain by Tarik, a lieutenant of Mousa-ben-Nosier, the commander of the Moslem forces at Ceuta After Tarik had defeated the army of the Gothic king Roderic, A D 709, he advanced to Toledo and in a short space of time nearly the whole of Spain fell beneath his arms "The fame of this extraordinary exploit aroused the jealousy of Mousa, who, crossing from Africa, hastened to complete the conquest of Spain and share the vast spoil of Tarik. By A. H 94 (A D 712), the conquest was completed and Mousa, like Cortes at a later period, found himself master of an empire greater and richer than that of the caliph, his master" "Hist Mon Sys," ch IX. "When Mousa arrived in Andalusia, one of the bishops of that country said to him, 'Oh, Mousa' We find thee mentioned in one of the prophets, who predicted an illustrious Prince, answering exactly to thy description, who is to enter this country'" (and conquer it, by the will of God) Ibn Dhahan, in Al-Makkari, Appendix lxxvii. Jaddus, the high-priest of Jerusalem, had the same welcome for Alexander and the Aztec priests in Mexico the same for Cortes they said he was the Expected One

A. D. 722, Mexico.—Conjectural æra of Quetzalcoatl, or Bacab, or Bacob, the Messiah, Son of God (Iesona), begot by the Holy Spirit (Echiah), upon the earthly virgin Sochiquetzal Quetzalcoatl was foretold by prophets, the place of his birth was indicated by the Morning Star; he was born at Tula, on the winter solstice, to the accompaniment of flowers and music; he was recognised as the Messiah by seers and astrologers; his head was rayed; his complexion was black; his hair was woolly, he performed numerous miracles; he fasted 40 days; he was tempted by the Evil One; he resisted, was persecuted and eventually crucified on the vernal equinox, by order of the tyrant Eupaco; on which occasion the sun was eclipsed. He descended into hell to judge the dead; was absent three days and nights; he rose again, and finally ascended bodily to heaven. He had 12 disciples; his sacraments were the communion, eucharist and baptism; his emblematic plant, the maguey; his epigraphic symbols were the † and svastica; and the sign of his second coming was the White Horse More curious than any of the above details, all of which according to Doane will be found in Lord Kingsborough, VI, 164, 180, and in Humboldt, is the fact that while the horse was unknown in any portion of America, yet the Second Advent of Quetzalcoatl was depicted in the Mexican picture-chronicles with a figure of what the astonished Spaniards had no difficulty in recognising as a White Horse Quetzalcoatl's other name of Bacob suggests the Buddhic Barcan and Hebrew Bacocheba See A D 700

A. D. 752, Rome.—Temporal kingdom of the Pope founded. See Rome, A D. 493 and A D. 1870.

A. D. 771, Baghdad.—An embassy from Sindh to the caliph Al-Mansur is "supposed to have given the Arabs their first knowledge of Hindu astronomy " Duff Rickmers, 68

A. D. 781, Rome.—In this year, 1st December, Pope Hadrian "ceased to use the years of the Emperors as dates and adopted the formula, ' Under the reign of the Lord Jesus Christ, our God and Redeemer!' " Bury, " Later Rom. Emp ," II, 504. This date controverts the reputed adoption of the dates ascribed to Dionysius Exiguus Cf. also Massey, "Genesis " I, 443.

A. D. 786, Arabia.—Death of Almukanna, who impiously pretended to be the Son of God, A H , 169 Albiruni, p 188, says that this impostor affected to be the Creator himself

A. D. 790, Tibet.—Fisher, "Hist Siberia," assigns this year for the æra of Dalai-Lamaism, which he supposes to be a mixture of Buddhism and Nestorianism Malte-Brun, II, 104. But Fisher is mistaken, both as to date and inference Dalai-Lamaism is much order than Nestorianism Its sources are Shamaism and Buddhism. Lama is the name of the sea-god of the Tibetan lakes Kara, Dsida, Eldzighen, Buka, Teugri, etc , which in ancient times were probably united The same sea-god was named by the Hindus, Varuna; by the Babylonians, Oannes; and by the Tarentines, Greeks and Romans, Taras, Poseidon, or Neptune.

A D 800, Rome.—In the Italian pontificate of Leo III , 795-816, one year of an "Indiction was left out, or (else) a year of the world counted twice over." Bury, op. cit , II, 425. Heimbach, in "Ersch und Gruber," p 215, holds the latter, whilst Bury adheres to the former view The year thus "tampered with " (Bury) belongs to the eighth century. Perhaps it was dropped by Gregory VII. in order to bring the coronation and æra of Charlemagne, which is dated in this year, to a round number of years after the Nativity of Christ (See below.)

A. D. 800, India.—Coronation, first regnal year and æra of Amogavarsha I., son of Govinda III , rajah of Gujerat. (Salivahana, 736, is equal to the Christian year 800, or the Augustan year 815; hence, Duff Rickmers says A D 814) Amogavarsha was a Digambara Jain, who having conquered many of the Western countries of India, set himself up for a god and was worshipped as such by the lords of Vanga, Anga, Magadha, Malava and Vengi.

A D. 800, India —Sergius, a Manichean, appeared and preached at Lha-dac, (near Canacor,) the metropolis of the Gangeatic provinces, about the beginning of the ninth century Col. Wilford, in Asiat Res , IX, 217.

A. D. 800, Rome —Brumalia, now Christmas Day, December 25. Coronation and æra of Charlemagne and of his adoration by Pope Leo III Chronicle of Moissac; Bury, op. cit ; Bryce, op. cit See A D 790

A. D 825, Southern India —Kollam, or Parasurama, (Simha; Kanya) Sewell's " Indian Calendar " Because he can find no extant record of its use earlier than A D 825, Sewell believed this year to be the epoch of the Kollam æra. Such a conclusion is hardly warranted of a country whose antiquities are as yet so little understood in the Occident as those of India Indeed, Sewell contradicts himself in saying further on that the Kollam is divided by the Hindus into cycles of 1,000 years, of which the present period is deemed the fourth, and therefore, that according to them, this Kollam began in Calijoga 1927, or B C. 1175, or in 3528 of Scaliger's Julian period As the latter corresponds with B. C. 1185, either the calendar, or Mr Sewell, is, in this instance, ten years wrong The Pandits say that the fourth cycle of the Parsurama commenced in September, A D 825. This is a mistake for A. D 1825. Duff Rickmers calls this year, beginning August 25th, "the epoch of the Kollam Andu, or sidereal reckoning, of North Malabar, dating from the sun's entering Kanya on the 1,434,160th day of the Calijoga. There is a Southern Kollam, which begins a month earlier Thirty days are intercalated in 116 years, making the average year 365d., 6h , 24.8s." See B. C. 1176.

A D. 845, India.—Augustan date of the re-incarnation of Brahma, the sixth Divine Year since the Calijoga Table A.

A D. 845, Tartary.—Æra of this empire, according to Genghis Khan, 12th century, who declared that he was the re-incarnation of that Deity who was due to appear, and who had appeared, in Tartary towards the beginning of the ninth century of our æra. Major R. D. Osborn's "Islam," p 371.

A D 849, England —Alfred the Great, b 849, r. 871, d Oct 28, 901.

A. D. 870, Nepal —Newai æra. The Pandits' "Chron ," p xix

A. D. 879, Nepal. —Newar æra Sewell and Duff Rickmers.

A. D 880, Nepal —Nepal, or Newar æra, recovered from coins In 1768, when Nepal was conquered by the Goorkhas, this æra was discarded for that of Salivahana, or the Vicramaditya, or else for the Jovian Saka, which was re-established in A. D. 78 Cunningham The Pandits state that the Nepal æra has been superceded by the Vicramaditya Sewell fixed this æra (the Nepalese) in A. D 879 and its epoch on Kartika 1st Stokvis says October, 880 For a similar change of æra at same period in Mysore, see B. C 3102 For a like change in China, see B C 2632

A. D 880, Tibet —Æra of Khri 1 De Ssrong b Tsan, an "incarnation" of the Deity App Cyc art "Lamaism"

A. D 890, India. —Toward the end of the ninth century another Salivahana "manifested himself at Delhi " Col Wilford, op cit. The date 890 is conjectural

A D. 909, Egypt —Æra of Abu Mohammed Obeidallah, the first Fatimite caliph of Egypt He announced himself as the Mahdi, or Messiah, foretold in the Koran His successor, Ahmed, A D 929, struck gold coins, whilst another of the same line, A D 974, struck glass coins; both in defiance of the prerogatives assumed by the caliph of Baghdad

A D. 914, Arabia —Death of Al Hallaj, A H 301 This impostor pretended to be the Messiah, or Son of God Albiruni, 188, says he affected to be the Almighty himself.

A D. 922, Baghdad. —Æra of Mansur, or Huseyn Ibn Mansur, called also Abul-Mughith He was born at Beyza in Fars, and "after a life spent in teaching the most exalted mysticism," was put to death by command of the Mahometan mollahs for impiously declaring himself to be the Almighty. His execution took place at Baghdad, on the 24th of Zil-Kada, A H 309, or March 26th, A D 922 Note on p 242 of Browne's "History of the Bab " It is not known how many, if any, of Mansur's followers survive at the present day.

A. D 930, Iceland. —Establishment of the Republic of Iesland by the Norsemen

A D 931, Arabia —Death of Ibn Abi-Zakariyya, A H 319

This impostor pretended to be the Messiah, and Son of God. Albiruni, 188, says that he impiously proclaimed himself as God

A. D. 936, Granada.—Secession of Granada from the Caliphate of Baghdad, which was declared and effected this year by Abd-el-Raman III , "Son of Maria," (Calcott, I, 200,) the first Moslem sovereign in Spain who struck coins of gold.

A. D. 937, Peru.—Supposed date and correction of the native calendar, deduced by Greswell from his hypothesis of a Primitive Hebrew Year.

A. D. 965, Northern India.—Rise of the Kalachakra system of Buddhism in Northern India, Cashmir and Nepal. Csoma, "Grammar," p. 192. Duff Rickmers.

A. D. 965. India.—Re-establishment of the Vri-haspati cycles of 60 years. According to the Joyotistava, this year completed the 15th cycle. The Pandits. But see A D. 78, 1024, 1025, 1027 and 1807.

A. D. 978, Turkestan.—Æra of Seljuk, son of Alankavah, the Virgin Mother. Mirkhond, cited by Gibbon, V, 654, *n* Year uncertain; varying from 971 to 978 See æra of Roum, A D. 1078.

A. D. 982, America.—Discovery of America by the Norsemen from Iceland, which, since A. D 930, had been an independent Republic, whose populace, history and religion removed it entirely beyond the influence of the Roman empire. After America was discovered Christianity was introduced, A. D. 1008 The dates and leadership of the various expeditions which sailed to and explored the coasts of America are given by Mallet as follows:

982 —Eric the Red, lands near Cape Farewell.

986.—Eric the Red; East coast of Baffin's Bay.

986.—Bjarni; Herjulf-ness, Greenland.

998.—Leif, son of Eric, East and West Bygd, Greenland, where colonies were planted, 280 farms were cultivated and 15 Christian churches and 83 monasteries were erected before 1121, when the first bishop was ordained

1000 —Leif; discovers Helluland (Newfoundland), Markland (Nova Scotia), Leifsbooths (Nantucket Bay) and Vine-land (Martha's Vineyard).

1002.—Thorvald colonises Leifsbooths

1003 —Thorvald discovers coasts of the Carolinas

1004 —Thorvald sails inside Cape Cod and lands at Keel-ness

1005.—Thornstein, East coast Baffin's Bay.

1007.—Thorfinn and Gudrida his wife, together with 160 persons provided with live stock and other supplies visit Cape Sable Island,

. Cape Cod and Stromfiord, Buzzard's Bay, at which last place they settle Here in 1008 was born Snorri Thorfinnson, the progenitor of Thorwalsden, the famous Danish sculptor

1008 —Thorfinn, Mount Hope Bay

1011.—Helgi and Finnbogi, Leifbooths.

1014 —Thorfinn returns with his wife and child and a valuable cargo to Iceland. There leaving his family, he sails to Norway and Bremen, where he disposes of his cargo and again returns to Iceland, where he dies The widow then performs a pilgrimage to Rome, where, had they not been already known through other sources, she would scarcely have failed to mention the American discoveries. At all events, they were published in the reign of Sveyn II , by Adam of Bremen, about 1067, who wrote "The king also made mention of another region discovered in the Northern Ocean, which had been visited by many people and was called Vineland, because grapes that produce a very good wine grew there spontaneously; corn also grows there, without sowing, in great abundance We know this, not by fabulous hearsay, but from authentic accounts furnished by Danes " (Adam Brem. de situ Dan c 246) The narrative of Thorfinn's colony, published about 1123 was probably written by Tholak Runolf's son

1121.—Eric, first Christian bishop of Greenland, appointed this year, visits the colony of Vineland, which he probably persuaded to return to Iceland, for except in the sagas, we hear no more of it.

1264 —Iceland becomes subject to Norway and loses its republican constitution Before this date all further exploration to the westward had ceased

1285.—Athalbrand and Thorvald discover a new land west of Iceland, but no results follow.

1290.—Eric III , king of Norway, called the "Priest-hater," dispatches Rolf, the Discoverer, to explore the coasts of America In 1291 the Genoese send a ship to the Westward with the same object. Anderson, sub anno

1295 —Assassination of Rolf the Discoverer The exploration of America again dropped In 1299 a voyage was made from Bilbao to Greenland. Anderson

1347 —A Greenland bark which had visited Stromfiord reports that she had rescued 17 men from a boat or wreck at sea. They had attempted to reach Markland, but had failed.

This appears to have been the last of the Norse voyages to America Indeed, they ceased substantially about the period that Iceland lost its autonomy; an event that followed closely upon the conquest of Constantinople by the Latin papacy and its assumption of entire control over the Western Kingdoms This prompted its legates and bishops to discourage any further exploration of America, for fear that it might result in the discovery of a sea route to India and so ruin the trade of the Levant. Many runic monuments and other remains of the Norsemen have been found in Greenland, but none of an unquestionably valid character in Markland or Vineland; the rude characters engraved on the Dighton rock being of doubtful origin. Among the Greenland remains is a runic monument discovered in 1824 at Kingiktorsoak, Baffin's Bay, the inscription upon which is thus translated " Erling Sighvats-son and Bjarni Thordarsson and Eindridi Odds-son, on Laugarday (Saturday) before Gangday (Whitsuntide), raised these marks and cleared the land, 1135 " Mallet, North Ant. 248; "Ancient Britain," chap. II, *n* 13; Sagas of Eirek the Red and Thorfinn Karlsefni, in the Codex Flatoiensis, published A D. 1387 to 1395; Ant Am. Copenh 1837 See also A D 1453, herein

A. D. 999, Ghazni.—Mahmoud of Ghazni declares his independence of the caliphate of Baghdad and separates Balkh, Herat, and other districts of Caubal, (the Greek Bactria), from the Arabian Empire

A. D. 1000, Europe.—The Millenium The Brahmo-Buddhic date of Buddha's birth was B C 6000 (Table B). The second Buddhic, Bacchic, or Dionysian Cycle from Salivahana, or Ies Chrishna, ended with A D 1000 (Table D). Upon these materials the medieval astrologers built a new mythos which is thus described· As the world had been created in six days, which were followed by a seventh day of rest, it was argued by "analogy" that the 6000 years of the Septuagint, which closed with the birth of Christ, would be followed by 1000 years of Sabbath, which would terminate with the second coming of the Saviour Gibbon, I, 562*n*. "It was a universal belief in the Middle Ages that the world was to finish with the year 1000 of the Incarnation. . . Donations to the churches were multiplied. . . . A terrible plague raged in Aquitaine; the churches were besieged and all the roads leading to popular shrines, or places of pilgrimage, were crowded with the plague-stricken population " Morell's Hist France, 107. For a long period previous to this year no public buildings were erected, no basilicæ, temples, or monuments, but when the dreaded year was safely passed numerous structures were commenced Encyc. Brit , "Architecture." Voltaire I, 265, declares that two crusades to Jerusalem were attempted at this period, and he intimates that their object was to reach the Holy City before the end of the world approached. According to this opinion Peter Hermit, Joachim the Prophet, St Barnard of Clairvaux and St Norbert were all imitators Cf Baronius, XII, 51, An 1106. It is rather singular both of this year and 1492 that while the Romans were looking for the destruction of the old world, the Norse pagans and Moslem heretics took part in discovering a new one.

A. D. 1002, England.—Massacre of the Danes by order of King Ethelred, on Hokeday, afterwards called St Brice's; not St Bride's, nor St Bridget's, as in some works. Grafton and Holingshed fix this event in the year 1012 In medieval hagiology St Brice was a bishop of Tours, the successor of St. Martin and the putative father of a miraculous infant, which, when only 30 days old, testified regarding its own paternity and whose mother was the bishop's laundress Brady, "Clavis Calendaria," II, 276 The festival day of St Brice is fixed by Brady on November 13th, which is so near Martinmas as to excite the suspicion that these festivals may have anciently been connected Sebastiano de Covarruvias Orosco, in his "Tesoro," Madrid, 1611, says that Hoguera was anciently a Feast of the Dead. This was the Sothic festival marking the heliacal rising of the Pleiades, which has been elucidated so fully by Haliburton The massacre seems to have been incited by the millenium.

A. D. 1009, Egypt.—Æra of Hakem, a Fatimite caliph, "the tenth manifestation of the Most High," upon whose advent the religion of the Diuses is supposed to be founded See A D 909 This "incarnation" styled himself Hakem-biamr-Allah, which was shortened to Bemrillah Higgins identifies his followers with the Assassins Anacal I, 699, and authorities cited. But this is doubtful. See A. D. 909 and 1090.

A. D. 1024, China.—First year of Jovian cycle 57; birth of Tchin-tsong, who, in A D 1035, picked up the book of Tao, which had fallen from Heaven (See A D 1035) The year A D 1024 marks the establishment of the Kia-tse, or Jovian cycles of 60 years, says Cunningham, who, however, in admitting that the Jovian cycles of India "must have been in use before the Christian æra," implies a somewhat like antiquity for those of China The Jesuit astronomers, cited by Father Du Halde, admitted, without reserve, a far greater antiquity for the Kia-tse, holding that they had actually been in use in all strictly historical time See B. C 2717 and A D 1025 and 1027 The fact seems to be that the Kia-tse were used in

China many centuries before our æra, the Chinese fixing their beginning in B C 2337, though this date is much too ancient. The Kia-tse were abandoned in favour of other methods of computing time, and were finally revived by the Taoists of the 11th century. This revival is what Cunningham, Bentley and others, have mistaken for the origin of these cycles and æras.

A. D. 1025, Tibet.—Re-establishment of the Vri-haspati-chakra, or method of counting time by Jovian cycles of 60 years. The Tibeto-Moslem writers on the Kali-chakra claim that the Jovian 60-year cycles in India are not older than about A D 965-6, nor in Tibet than about 1025-6 (See A D 622) Mr. Bentley, the ecclesiastical astronomer, used this evidence to invalidate the antiquity of oriental astronomy, and in this respect Gen Cunningham followed him. The Pandits, remembering that Bentley and Cunningham were English, and fearful of offending their English readers, have followed these writers; yet elsewhere in their " chronology" they represent this cycle as "one of the most ancient in all Asia," and begin its use in B C 3185, 3174 and 3114. The true cycle of Jupiter is approximately 12 years; the 60-year cycle being merely one of its multiples; so that in speaking of one, the other is implied; and both are represented in our divisions of the zodiac, the clock, etc., which in Chaldea are certainly as old as Nebu-Nazaru, and in the orient very much older The Chinese begin these cycles in B. C. 2717, (q v). Says Rev Dr. Greswell, F. C , III, 361 "The existence of this dodecæteric period of antiquity is an acknowledged fact." Brennand and Lewis are more explicit and assign the Jovian cycle to a high antiquity. Such cycles are mentioned in the fragments attributed to Orpheus Censorinus, who wrote during the third century, attributes a dodecæteris to the ancient Chaldeans (D. N , xviii.) A dodecæteris, which appears to have been formed on the Jovian cycle, is recognized in the Surya Siddhanta, the Geoponica and many other very ancient works and systems The oriental nations have evidently exaggerated the antiquity of this cycle; but it was certainly known and used at the period of the second Buddha, and probably at that of the first Buddha The Pandits furnish formulæ for computing the years of this cycle by three systems, the Surya Siddhanta, Jyotistava, and Telinga Each year of the 60 has a different name, both in India, China and Japan In Tibet they use both the Chinese and Indian names The astronomical year of Tibet begins with Iesaac, or Baisack 1st, on the vernal equinox The civil year is luni-solar, its epoch varying in the several provinces from December to February The

Hors, or Turks, keep their New Year some days after the winter solstice; the people of U'tsang at L'hassa begin theirs with the new moon of February. The year A D 965-6 is believed to have completed the 69th cycle of the Surya Siddhanta, 68th of the Telinga astronomers and 15th of the Jyotistava   The Pandits

A. D. 1027, India.—Re-establishment of the Vrihaspati-chakra, or Jovian cycles, of 60 years, a difference of three years from the Chinese reckoning of A. D 1024   Cunningham.   See A D. 1024, 1025, and A. D. 1807

A. D. 1035, China.—The Book of Tao falls from Heaven   See A. D. 1024.

A. D. 1038, Korassan.—The Seljuks annex Korassan in the name of Tugril Beg, A H 429   Some authorities date the Seljukian æra from this year; others from A H 431; and still others from A D 1076, q v

A. D. 1050, Rome.—Lanfranc, superior of the Benedictine convent of St Maur, afterwards Archbishop of Canterbury, and Nicolas, cardinal and librarian of of the Roman church, revise the text of the Scriptures   Gibbon, ch XXXVII, note 117

A. D. 1075, Persia.—Julah, or Jul-al-ad-din æra.   "The Julah begins from Shaban 5th, A..H 468, under Jul-al-ad-din.   The year begins with the Nauroz, (New Year,) or the day that the sun enters Aries "   The Pandits "Chron ,"p xviii   See A D 1079

A. D. 1076, Korassan.—Æra of the Chalukya, or Seljuka dynasty.   Cunningham   Gibbon, V, 654, says A D 1038   Stokvis says A D. 1077   Sewell says this æra was not used after 1162

A. D. 1076, Chalukya.—Epoch, 14th February, Salivahana, 997 Beginning of the Chalukya (Seljuk) Vikrama-varsha æra.   First year of the reign of Vikramaditya VI   Duff Rickmers

A. D. 1078, Roum.—Æra of the Seljukian kingdom of Roum, whose capital was fixed this year at Nicæa by Soliman, the Gazi. Gibbon, V, 675.   See æra of Seljuk, *ante.*

A. D. 1079, Persia.—Jul-al-ad-din æra, begins 15th Ma..ii, at noon.   This was the day of the vernal equinox at Ispahan   Duff Rickmers says March 24th.   Stokvis says March 14th   Jul-al-ad-din, or "Divine Glory," a Seljukian Sultan, was otherwise called Melek Shah.   He was the first "barbarian" to "become a caliph, or Emir-al-omra, Commander of the Faithful."   Gibbon, V, 670.   Greswell, F C., I, 682, who calls this æra the "Gelalæan," fixes its epoch in Phervandinmah 1st=March 15th, A. D 1079, and elsewhere says it was calculated with such precision that some astronomers have preferred it to the Gregorian correction of the Julian æra; and that the French Directory of 1792 contemplated its adoption for the calendar of the Republic. The author of the Persian calculations was the celebrated astronomer and poet, Omar Khayyam

A. D. 1081, Armenia.—Æra Armeniaca Azaraica Two or three years after the publication of the calendar of Omar Khayyam the Armenians dropped their previous method of computing time by Buddhic cycles of 552 years and, instead, adopted the Dionysian or Paschal cycle of 532 years. Cf. Greswell, F. C., Intro., xvii See A D. 552.

A. D. 1090, Persia.—Æra of the Assassins, under Nassan-ben-Sabah The leader of this murderous sect in Syria was known as the "Old Man of the Mountain " Yet, so late as the end of the 12th century the Assassins employed the æra of Alexander the Great.

A. D. 1090, Mexico.—Beginning of the native Aztec Julian æra, the previous calendar years having been equable Epoch, corresponding to our 1st January. Prinsep. Other authorities say 25th December of the same year In both cases the winter solstice of A D. 1090, may be meant. Humboldt dates the reform in A. D 1091. The Aztec Julian year consisted of 365d 5h 46m 9 3-13s , being only 2m 36 10-13s. shorter than the true time According to Newcomb this is 365d. 5h. 48m. 46s At the end of a cycle of 52 years the Aztecs added 13 days; and at the end of another cycle of 52 years they added 12 days to their calendar; thus 25 days in 104 years The Pandits' "Chron." Aztec tradition says that the Quinames were the original possessors of Mexico. Their records furnish the following dates A D. 544, the Toltecs leave their original seat; A. D 648, they enter Mexico; A D. 700, beginning of Toltec æra in Mexico (Greswell); A D 1325, foundation of the Aztec empire in Mexico; A. D. 1525, death of Montezuma and conquest of the empire by the Spaniards, under Hernando Cortes. For other dates relating to Mexico see B. C 955.

A. D. 1095, Europe.—Popular date of the first Crusade. **But** see A. D. 1000.

A. D. 1105, Bengal.—Lakshmana Sena æra, epoch, Kartika 1st. Cunningham. Stokvis says January, 1106 Keilhorn and Sewell **say** A. D 1119; a difference of 14 years from Cunningham

A. D. 1114, Simla.—Æra of Simla, beginning with the month of Ashadha Duff Rickmers says 1113 Sewell fixes the Simla Samvat used in Guzerat, in 1113-14 The Pandits fix the Siva-Sinha Samvat of the Gohils, in the island of Dee, in Vicramaditya Samvat 1169, or A D 1112.

A. D. 1119, Bengal.—Lakshmana Sena, according to Sewell, epoch, Kartika 1st. This æra was established by a Vaidya king of Bengal, named Laksmanasena.

A. D. 1145, Rome.—The alleged venality and corruption of the Roman pontifical court led to a movement for the separation of Church and State which was voiced by Arnold of Brescia   For this he was condemned at the Lateran Council of 1139 and banished from Italy   In 1145 the exactions of the papal See led to popular resistance; a Republic was proclaimed; the Senate was reconstituted; the temporal power of the pope was repudiated and the holy father was forced to retire from the city; coins were struck in the name of the Roman Republic, liberty was proclaimed; a secular magistrate was appointed, Arnold was sent for, and he returned to Rome to govern the new state.   In 1155 a counter-revolution of the fickle populace compelled Arnold to seek refuge in the country, the pope returned to Rome in triumph and Arnold was apprehended, dragged to Rome and crucified on the Piazza del Popolo. To hinder the degraded populace from worshipping his remains they were burnt and the ashes thrown into the Tiber.

A. D. 1154, Bengal.—Æra of Bengal: Marsden, op. cit.   It is based on the Divine Year of Salivahana, the variance being due to the Augustan alteration of the calendar and to the difference between the Moslem and Hindu calendars

A. D. 1163, Tartary.—Birth, of Genghis Khan, or Zinghis Khan. See A D. 1206

A. D. 1186, Europe.—End of the world in this year, foretold by astrologers   Encyc. Brit, art "Astrologers"

A. D. 1190, Persia.—Advent of David El David, a Jewish Messiah, during the reign of Laid Alladin.   Wm. a'Beckett, Univ. Biog. Year uncertain.

A. D. 1204, Europe.—Fall of Constantinople and termination of the Sacred Roman Empire

A. D. 1206, Tartary.—Æra of the Apotheosis of Genghis Khan, born 1163, deified 1206, started from Lake Baikal for the conquest of China, 1214, died 1227   This conqueror claimed to be a reincarnation of the Deity, who had formerly appeared upon earth, an event that had occurred, according to Maj R D Osborn's "Islam," p. 371, about the beginning of the ninth century   The incarnation thus referred to could only have been that of the 13th Brahma, or

Vishnu, due A. D 845, Augustan date. If so, it marked the rise of three other independent Moslem empires besides that of Tartary, viz , Egypt, Granada and Ghazni See A D. 845, 909, 936 and 999 Higgins, Anacal. II, 353, says that Genghis claimed to be the tenth avatar; and that his mother was a widow, who pretended she had been impregnated by the Sun In stating his claim to supernatural origin Genghis appears to have been badly advised by the astrologers, for his case would have been very much stronger had he pretended to be, not the relic of a Brahminical, but the hero of the Hindu incarnation due A D 1237 Cf Rankin, Hist. Mong , 177 As the reigning Chinese monarchs claim descent from this Son of Heaven, it is possible that Genghis permitted his astrology to be modified by the requirements of his new subjects The Encyc Brit presents what might be called the Chinese, or Buddhic, case for Genghis It says that he was the son of Yesukai, the eighth in descent from Budantsar. As it intimates that Budanstar is mentioned in the "History of the T'ang dynasty of China " (A D 619-90,) it follows that Budantsar's æra was of a previous date, say A D. 548, that being just one divine year before the deification of Genghis Khan. The names both of Budantsar and Yesukai, or Iesuchi, are significant

A. D. 1227, Tartary.—Death and bodily ascension to heaven of Genghis Khan, who was worshipped as the expected Messiah or God on earth, according to Higgins, Anacal , I, 356

A. D. 1237, India.—Pre-Augustan date of the Brahmo-Buddhic re-incarnation, or re-birth, or Divine Year, of the Hindu Brahma-Buddha, or Ies Chrishna,

A. D. 1260, Rome.—Second coming of Christ expected by the Sacred College Higgins, Anacal , I, 689

A. D. 1281, Tibet.—Ti-ssu, the Saca Lama. Exactly one Divine Year, or Astrological cycle, or phen, after Srong Tsau Sgampo and the deification of Iesdegerd, Kanouj, etc He was called "the Lama of Sakya " Appleton fixes his apotheosis in 1280

A. D. 1296, Delhi.—Æra of Ala, a Patan King of Delhi, during whose reign, A D 1296-1316, the particular year being uncertain, he set himself up for an incarnation of the Deity and affected the sacred name of Iss-kander (the name assumed by Alexander the Great) and Jul-al-addin (Melek Shah) See above, A D. 1079. Ala's impious pretensions were cut short by poison, administered by Kafur, grand vizier Garrett, Hist Ind , 63.

A. D. 1307, Switzerland.—Æra of the Republic. Declaration of Independence, November 4th.

A. D. 1311, Boeotia.—Thebes plundered and destroyed by the Catalan Grand Company of Barcelona. Encyc. Brit

A. D. 1317, India.—Nirvana of Buddha, Augustan date, Table B.

A. D. 1344, Tibet.—Æra of the Great Buddha's last re-incarnation, according to the information derived personally from the Grand Lama or Little Buddha, by Rev D W Le Lacheur "When we entered the Buddha's tent, he sat me on his mat and (in that sacred seat) I am sorry to say, I was worshipped (by his people) . . The Buddha was laughing all the time (at my confusion) . . Asked when the Great Buddha would return, he said: 'In 773 (years) from this Chicken year (1887) the Great Buddha will be upon the earth.'" "The Land of the Llamas," by Le Lacheur, South Nyack, N Y, 1887, p. 58 Adding 773 to 1887 makes 2660, the year of the Great Buddha. Deducting from this, three divine years each of 658 common years, carries the computation of the Great Buddha year back to A D. 1344 See A D 1281, 1347, 1355 and 1360

A. D. 1344, Southern Konkan.—Joor san, Shoo-hur, or Shahur (Shahur is the Arabian word for "months") There is reason to believe that this æra was established by one of the Moslem kings of the Deccan, subject to the sway of Tugluk Khan. It is founded on the Hegira and is distant from it one astrological cycle, plus 64 years, thus 622 plus 658 plus 64=1344. There is much confusion concerning its epoch In one place the Pandits fix this at June 6, 1342, or A. H. 743, and they add that "others place it a year earlier" In another part of their chronology they say Shahur 1313 equals A. D 1834. Their final figure for the epoch of Shahur is A. D. 1344, and they refer to Jervis' "Report on the Weights and Measures of Southern Konkan," or Concan, which is now included in the Presidency of Bombay.

A. D. 1347, Tibet.—Æra of Tasi, a Buddhisatva Appleton's Cyc

A. D. 1348, Abyssinia.—Æra of Maherat, (or Year of Grace). The Abyssinians pretend that they were converted to Christianity A D 348, and that when a thousand years from this period had accumulated they were cast off and a new reckoning of another thousand years was begun from the point where the previous millenium ended Gresswell, F C Introd, xvi.

A. D. 1355, Tibet.—Immaculate conception and miraculous birth of Tsong-K'apa Lama, the "incarnation of Makala." Ascended bodily to heaven in 1419. Appleton's Cyc

A. D. 1360, Tibet.—According to the "Century Magazine" for December, 1890, Tsong-K'apa was born A. D. 1360, near where Kumbum now stands   After performing his religious mission and ascending to heaven he was "transmigrated into the person of Gedun-drupa, who founded the Trashil 'unpo lamasery in 1446 and became the first of the series of incarnated gods, known as Panch'en rinpoché, although native works say that the first pontiff bearing this title was born in 1567, (a Brahminical date).   Becoming afterwards incarnate in Gedunjyats'o, he returned to L'hassa," etc.   Jyats'o means the sea; hence "Ged un Jyats'o," possibly, God of the Seas; a form of the Neptune Myth.   The Japanese conferred a similar title upon some of their deified emperors   At Samos, during the sixth century B C. the king threw into the sea a golden ring. Herodotus, Thalia, 41. "The prince of Mingrelia (Colchis) assumes the title of Dadian (Dar-dion?) or Lord of the Sea, though he possesses not even a fishing boat." (Malte-Brun, Geog I, 304)   In Venice the doge, or duke, annually weds the sea, by casting a ring into its waters   This custom is said to have been instituted by "the Pope" of Rome in A D 1177, a year in which there were five rival Popes, viz , Alexander, Victor, Paschal, Calixtus and Innocent.   In fact the custom is of far higher antiquity.   It appears to have been brought from the Orient' through Colchis, Pontus and Samos to Venice and perhaps also to Tarentum.   ~ (('.   '

A. D. 1370, Tartary, Zagatai.—Æra or first regnal year of Timur-Bec, (Tamerlane,) born 1336; died February 19, 1405.   His conquests, which began with the empire of Zagatai, (capital, Samarcand,) afterwards extended over Persia, Baghdad, Muscovy, Russia, India, Syria, and also, nominally, over Egypt and several other states He announced himself as the Paraclete and Deliverer, whose divine mission it was to proclaim the kingdom of God, punish idolatry and advance the cause of civilisation.   He was guarded by 300 Selecti Life by Sherefeddin Ali, translated by P de la Croix, London, 1723 Tamerlane pretended to be the Son of the Sun.   Higgins, Anacal , II, 353.

A. D. 1391, Corea.—Æra of "the Foundation," that is to say, the Mongol conquest of Corea, deduced from the Treaty between Corea and Japan, A. D 1894.   Sinensis, (Japanese Min. to England, 1896,) says the epoch of the Foundation was 1392.   "The 23rd day, sixth moon" of Corea agrees with the Japanese æra of Meiji, "25th day, seventh moon"   Sinensis also says that the 17th day of the 11th moon of the 504th year of the Corean monarchy, became, after

January 6th, 1896, the first day of the first moon, of the 505th year; the king having resolved to adopt the Gregorian calendar.

A. D. 1436, Abyssinia.—Æra of Abyssinia, according to Greswell, F C , I, 555

A. D. 1453, Constantinople.—May 29   Capture of Constantinople by the Turks under Mahomet II , and final dissolution of the Roman Empire.   Mahomet granted the subjugated Christians personal security and the free exercise of their religion.   Haydn, voc. "Eastern Empire."   In 1492, the Latins responded to this act of clemency by plundering and expelling all the Moslems and Jews from Spain   The fall of the Roman Empire had the effect to close the lucrative oriental trade to Venice, Genoa and the other Latinized states, and confer it entirely upon the Moslems.   This event induced the Latin Pontificate to moderate that hostility toward maritime exploration westward, which had marked its policy with the Norsemen (See A. D 982)   The removal of this discouragement was soon afterwards followed by Columbus' discovery of America and De Gama's opening of the sea-route to India.

A. D. 1469, Punjab.—Æra of Nanek, Nanac, or Baba Nanac, at first the leader and teacher, afterwards the Messiah of the Sikhs. " The belief of the Sikhs was originally, according to Malcolm, a pure deism, but it has so far degenerated that they now consider their founder as a Saviour and Mediator with God "   Thornton's Gaz , art "Punjab "   Nanac was born at Raypur, 60 miles west of Lahore, and was named Guru, or "Spiritual pastor" by his votaries, who called themselves Sikhs, or "disciples "   Nanac advocated the assumption of arms, the renunciation of caste, the elevation of woman, the protection and education of children, the admission of proselytes, the unity and incorporeality of God, and religious toleration to all   While he deplored religious disputes, he never ceased to preach against the Hindu trinity, polytheism, the worship of saints and images and the decoration of temples.   His justice was inflexible, his courage above suspicion; his reading immense.   His only weapon of proselytism was persuasion and simplicity of manners.   In 15 years he traversed the kingdoms of India, Persia, Arabia and Ceylon, preaching the unity of God.   After many adventures, the Rajah of Callanor, one of his disciples, offered him a retreat for his old age, where he died in tranquility A D 1539, aged 70 years , a term which is rarely attained by the founders of religions   The place of his burial became famous, and every year upon the return of his deathday an immense concourse of people gather to pay their respects to his remains. Noel, art "Nanac" Those Sikhs who adhere to the original doctrines of Nanac are called Khalasa; they are less fanatical than the Singhs (lions), a class of Sikhs who in resentment for the murder of Guru Govind, the fourth leader after Nanac, have never ceased to bear arms, even in times of peace To such an inexcusable extreme has this precept been carried that, as Barnes observes, it has rendered many of them insane; a disease which, it may be added, has not been lessened by their proclivity to renounce the purer doctrine of the Khalasas and relapse into image-worship. Thornton's Gaz of India, art. "Amritsu"

A. D. 1488, India.—Termination of the XIVth avatar of Iesnu, according to Christian chronology Table A It was possibly to dissipate the fears which this æra engendered concerning the destruction of the world that induced the learned Alfonso of Castile to construct a chronology based upon Dionysian divine years—which went back to B C 6994 and threw the incarnation periods into new forms. See B. C. 6984.

A. D. 1492, Byzantium.—Expected millenium and end of the World. Upon the assumption that the Creation took place September 1, B C. 5509, q. v., the present year was A. M 7000, when the world was to come to an end. Uranologium, 379, E. cap xvi While the Greek church were looking for this catastrophe, the Latin church, which enjoyed the advantage of a different Anno Mundi, employed its energies in persecuting the Moslems and Jews, several hundred thousands of whom were this year (March 30) robbed, tortured and driven out of Spain. Meanwhile, following the route laid down for him in 1474 by the Moor Toscanelli, Columbus, who indulged no theories of a millenium and was a mere navigator with a practical object in view, found a New World, the plunder of which enabled the almost extinguished torch of European progress to be lit afresh. See A. D 493

A. D. 1492, America.—Its discovery by Columbus, October 12 This great event, combined with De Gama's voyage to India in 1497, had the effect, eventually, to change the whole course of astrological and religious doctrine and political development However, before this occurred, Cortes advised the king of Spain by letter (in Kingsborough, VI, 111), to obtain a grant of the tithes of the Mexicans from Pope Alexander VI The royal application was refused, the Pope preferring to enfeoff the king in the lands of America and reserve the vectigals, which were payable in cash, for himself Higgins,

Anacal , II, 393. This and like reservations may have had no little to do with promoting the Reformation of 1517, q. v.

A. D. 1492, America.—Columbus, Cortes, Cabesa de Vaca and other of the Spanish conquistadores were guilty of the grave imposture of assuming either that they themselves, or their master, Charles I , of Spain, was that Messiah whom the Indians of the Antilles, Mexico and Florida all believed would soon make his appearance on earth. They were worshipped by the natives in so ample a manner that all the rights of property fell before their presence The Indians who guided Cabesa de Vaca did not take him to unfriendly tribes, because they were unwilling that their enemies should enjoy so great an advantage as to behold this divinity. Even when the Spaniards despoiled them, the natives begged their visitors not to distress themselves about it, assuring them that they held the loss of their goods as naught compared with the pleasure of having beheld them. So the Spaniards moved on in the accepted character of Children of the Sun, who had power to confer or take away life and from whom nothing could be concealed because everything was known to them. Until their real character was disclosed by their repeated crimes, the natives never stood before them without trembling and did not dare to speak or to lift up their eyes The Spaniards kept up this imposture by assuming great state and gravity with them and by speaking but seldom. Sir Francis Drake practiced a similar imposture upon the natives of California Some writers have assumed that what the Indians worshipped was not a Messiah, but strength, power, splendour, superior craft, the guns, the horses, the armor, the glittering trappings and brave array of the Spaniards; while others have ascribed it to the Spaniards' knowledge of letters, medicine, etc ; but these theories will not account for the explicit declarations on this subject which were made by Montezuma and conveyed by Cortes in his letters to the King of Spain Consult Helps' Conquerors of America, vols II and IV, Irving's "Columbus," passim, Naufragios de Cabesa de Vaca, c. 31; and U. S. Minerological Rep , 1867, p 271.

A. D. 1497, India.—Vasco de Gama opens the sea route to India, China and Japan This brought to Europe some knowledge of Indian literature and astrology, which was not without its influence in stimulating that resistance to the claims and exactions of the Latin papal See which formed the distinguishing event of the ensuing half century

A. D. 1503, India.—Brahminical Divine Year, Augustan date.

To make the true date, deduct the 78 years sunk by Augustus. (See ch. IX.) The Hindu date is A D 1425 (Table A).

A. D. 1504, Peru.—Approximate æra of Viracocha, the Messiah, who was due on earth during the reign of the twelfth Inca, Huayna Capac, who died in 1525. Pizzarro grimly announced himself as the Lieutenant of the expected Messiah and as such he was actually venerated by the confiding and deluded natives, whose king he had betrayed and murdered in cold blood   Garcillaso de la Vega; Prescott's Peru, I, 325, 330, 437.

A. D. 1510, Calicut.—In this year Alfonso Alboquerque, a Portuguese naval commander made his appearance off Calicut, or Kolikod, a seaport of Malabar, 560 m south of Bombay, and captured and plundered the city   The sovereign of Calicut was called by the Moplahs (a mixed race of Arabians and Brahmins) their Isamorin, corrupted to Zamorin, whom they worshipped as sovereign-pontiff and God upon Earth. He was suzerain to the kings of Cochin, Canamor and Coulao, none of whom could coin money without his authority. He appears to have descended from a line of Isamorins whose epoch went back to the ninth century of our æra

A. D. 1517, Europe.—On the eve of All Saints Day, the 31st of October, 1517, Martin Luther, a Saxon monk of the Augustine order, nailed to the door of the Schlosskirche in Wittenberg on the Elbe, his " Ninety-five Theses " denouncing the sale of indulgences by the See of Rome   This action is commonly taken to mark the beginning of the Protestant Reformation   But, in fact, the protest and movement against Papal simony began long before. It is much more convincingly condemned in the pages of Matthew Paris than in those of Martin Luther   However, in Matthew's time (13th century) the movement received no popular support   The people were so poor and miserable that they could only suffer   In the early part of the 15th century, when John Huss dared to brave the resentment of Rome, by denouncing its encouragement of religious imposture and its simoniacal practices, the populace, though in sympathy with its champion, shrank from his support and saw him burned at the stake without an attempt at rescue   But in Luther's time the case was different. A new world had been discovered, the cosmogony of the Church had proved to be false and its authority was much shaken. America had yielded during the first 25 years of its despoilment more gold and silver than Europe had possessed in coin and plate previous to the Discovery. This metal had been hastily coined and thrown into the circulation, first of Spain and afterwards of France, England and Germany   The resulting Rise of Prices threw all Europe into a ferment; a condition of affairs which afforded very substantial support to Luther's stand against the Church   ("Halcyon Age," p 14).

A. D. 1524, Europe.—Year of the predicted recurrence of the biblical deluge and destruction of mankind.   To avert this calamity floating arks were built by many persons, among others by President Aurial of Toulouse, who expected to be stranded on the Puy de Dôme, but the cataclysm failed to occur and indeed the season turned out to be unusually dry   Haydn, Dic. Dates, art. " Deluge."   Encyc. Brit , art. "Astrology "   In the *Miller's Tale* of Chaucer, A D 1340-1400, something of the sort is related of an earlier period

A. D. 1534, England.—April 21, (Palalia). Execution of Elizabeth Barton, the "Holy Maid of Kent " She was born in Aldington, Kent, about the beginning of the century, became a nun, and saw visions in which were revealed to her many forecasts of future events, some of them of a partly political character, as the consequences of the divorce of Henry VIII from Catherine of Aragon   Her parish priest, Richard Masters, and Dr Bockling, a canon of Canterbury, regarded these as divine revelations.   The chapel at Aldington became the centre of numerous pilgrimages and of many excited and tumultuous assemblages   Elizabeth's visions multiplied.   She received letters written in gold by Mary Magdalene   The emissaries of the Pope of Rome and the partisans of Queen Catherine encouraged these delusions   Even such men as Sir Thomas More, John Fisher, bishop of Rochester, and Warham, archbishop of Canterbury, lent their support to her ravings   In 1533, the king ordered her to be examined before Parliament, who found her guilty of treason, and in 1534 ordered her to the block

A. D. 1555, Bengal,—Ilah æra, according to some authors

A. D. 1556, Bengal.—Ilah, Ilahi, or Bengalee San of Akbar, a solar æra and calendar dating from the deification and first regnal year of Akbar in 1556, but not established until 1584   The apotheosis of Akbar is discussed by Col Van Kennedy in Bombay Trans , II, 242, and Higgins, II, 354   His æra commenced on Iesaac, or Bysaac 1st, which coincided with the entrance of the Sun into Aries. The month of Cheyt, or Chittere, began with Pisces and so on through the calendar, each of the twelve months beginning with a different zodion, in the customary Greek order of rotation   According to the Pandits' " Chron ," Akbar's reign began on Rubi-us-sani 2nd, A H 963, or February 14th, A D. 1556, which those writers regard as the true epoch of the Tarikh Ilali, or Bengalee San This is also the date adopted by Sewell and by Cunningham Amir Fatteh Ul-lah Shirazi, who corrected the calendar from the time of Ulugh Beg to Akbar, says Friday, Rubi-us-sani 5, A H 963, or February 19, 1556, N. S. Here is a difference of three days and a discrepancy of five days. The Pandits, in another place, also Poole, both say that the Ilali began on the vernal equinox, whilst the Pandits, in still another place, say April 11, 1556 These last named dates appear to be erroneous The names of the Ilali months are the same as the ancient Persian Most of them have either 29 or 30 days, although some have 32. There are no septuary divisions. The Ilali æra is used on the coins, inscriptions and records of the reigns of Akbar, Jehangir and other sovereigns In the reign of Jehangir and in subsequent reigns the Ilali date was usually coupled with that of the Hegira From Timur to Akbar the principal æras in use were the Hegira, A D. 622, the Turki, B. C 5054, and the Julal-ad-din, A D 1075, or 1079. To these Akbar added the Bengalee San, A. D. 1556, the Fasali æra, A. D 592, and the Vilayati, Vilaity, Amli, or Dakhani æra, A. D 592-3.

A. D. 1564, France.—New Year day changed by edict of Charles IX., from March 25 to January 1. See 1582.

A. D. 1580, Holland.—Aera of the Dutch Republic Declaration of Independence and foundation of the Seven United Provinces, September 29 The Roman names of the months were changed to others, which, like those of the Goths, were descriptive of the seasons, but they have since become obsolete. The same fate afterwards befell the months of the French Republic.

The following dates are connected with the Revolution: 1524 and, 1546, capricious monetary laws of Charles V , causing widespread commercial distress ; 1566, Confederation of Beggars , 1572, Resort to arms ; 1574, paper money issued at Leyden , 1576, Sack of Mechlin and Antwerp by the Spaniards; 1576, November 8, Treaty of Ghent; 1579, January 29, Union of Utrecht ; 1580, Establishment of the Republic

A. D. 1582, Rome.—Institution of the Gregorian calendar, which required that October 5, 1582, should be counted as October 15, thus altering and correcting the Julian (Cæsarian) calendar, ten days. This alteration was soon afterwards officially adopted in the Roman Catholic states, to the destruction of the Cæsarian aera. By the Protestant states of Germany it was adopted partly in 1700, and partly in 1774, and by Great Britain and her Colonies (including British America) in September, 1752, when the third of that month

was called the 14th.   These eleven days constitute one difference
between O S. and N. S.   Another, arises from the fact that with
the adoption of the Gregorian calendar, the New Year Day was
changed from March 25th backward to the previous January 1st.
Events which occured between these dates were at first assigned to
both: *e. g.*, the English Revolution of 1688, (William and Mary)
which occurred in February of that legal year, was for a time dated
February 1688-9   We now say February, 1689   Russia, although
she has adopted the Christian year, still employs the Julian day, between which and the Gregorian reckoning there is now a difference
of 12 days   The origin of the difference was in Julius Cæsar's
assumption that the solar year consisted of exactly 365¼ days,
which is not the fact.   Neither is the Gregorian mean year of 365d.
5h 49m 12s. quite correct, the latest and most exact determination
of astronomers being 365d. 5h. 48m 46s (Newcomb)   Nevertheless at the date of its adoption, the Gregorian year was supposed to
be correct.   See A. D 1564.

A. D. 1600, Europe.—Epoch January 1st (Gregorian) the "Æra
of Man," as employed by the modern Reformers, Agnostics, Free-
thinkers, etc , of Europe and America, many of whose periodicals
employ this one as well as the Christian æra   Its inventor was
Thaddeus B. Wakeman, Esq , of New York, who, in a brief
memoir on the subject explains that the first year of the æra ter-
minated January 1st, 1601, and that it marks the introduction of
the Copernican system of astronomy, "which put in end to the
previous geocentric fallacies and sounded the knell of its attendant
ignorance and superstition   It was also the year, February 17, 1600,
when Bruno sealed with his life his devotion to the new truth."
This æra likewise marks the Halcyon Age of Europe, when most of
the great discoveries and improvements in science, legislation, art,
and mechanics, which have distinguished the subsequent period,
had their origin   For a detailed account of these discoveries and
improvements, consult Del Mar's "Halcyon Age."

A. D. 1611, Japan.—Rising against the Portugese in Japan during
the shogunate of Iyeyasu, whose posthumous title was Gongen   In
1542 two Portugese were wrecked on the coast of Japan; in 1545
Mendez Pinto, a Portugese adventurer, was driven into a Japanese
port by stress of weather   Within a year after this event a regular
trade was established by the Portuguese between Ningpo and Naga-
saki   Trading was succeeded by mining and mining, by the ascendancy of the Portugese and the practical enslavement of the natives

The Portugese having discovered a great resemblance between the institutes and forms of Buddhism and Christianity conceived the plan of usurping the government through the agency of religion. Affecting to believe that Christ and Buddha were the same, they asserted that the period of his re-appearance was drawing nigh. "The very idols of Buddha served after a little alteration with the chisel for images of Christ" (Griffis.) They made converts of Bingo and other discontented daimios and employed them to betray and enslave their countrymen Okubo, the converted governor of Sado, was promised by the Portuguese to be made hereditary emperor "Fire and sword, as well as preaching, were employed as instruments of conversion." (Griffis) By these nefarious means they rapidly made a million of "communicants," including military leaders, officers of the fleet, and other persons of influence Documentary proof of their treacherous designs having reached the Shogun, measures were taken to defeat them. The ringleaders were arrested and their followers proceeded against. In the four years of civil war which ensued, more than one hundred thousand lives were sacrificed By the year 1615, the "communicants" were all suppressed, and in 1624 the last of the Portuguese were driven from the kingdom One of the consequences of these events was the renunciation of the Buddhic and a reversion to the more ancient Shinto religion, by vast numbers of Japanese Griffis, "Mikado's Empire;" Encyc Brit., art "Japan"

A. D. 1648, England.—Æra of the Commonwealth, which is usually dated from the flight of the king, Charles I , and the assumption of administrative powers by the Parliament. The following dates relate to this period: Oliver Cromwell born, 1599; member for Huntingdon, 1628, for Cambridge, 1640; rupture between parliament and king, when Cromwell is appointed captain in parl. army, 1642; lieut.-general, 1644; battle of Naseby, 1645; he returns to parl., 1646; parl army enters London and flight of king, 1647, parl. assumes government, 1648; king beheaded, January 30, 1649, Cromwell, as Lord Lieutenant of Ireland, concludes brief campaign in that country and returns to London, 1650; Charles II lands in Scotland, 1650, Cromwell's victories at Dunbar, 1650 and Worcester, 1651, cause Charles' flight to France, 1651; Cromwell forcibly dissolves Long Parl and is invested in Westminster Hall as Lord Protector, 1653, domestic tranquility and vigorous foreign policy, marked by great advance in British naval power, 1654-5; new parl , 1656; Cromwell dies, 1658, succeeded by Richard Cromwell, who is deserted by Monk, the commanding general of his forces.   The latter invites Charles II to return to England   Entry of the king into London and Restoration of the monarchy May 2, 1660.

A. D. 1650, Tibet.—Incarnation of Nag-wan Lo-zang   Waddell.

A. D. 1653, Brazil.—Pretended divinity of an Indian chieftain on the Orellana, who set himself up for the Fish-god, and as such was worshipped by his tribe   These people, or else others near them, wore jade ornaments, practised circumcision and the tonsure, affirmed the metempsychosis, etc.   They were first encountered during D'Acunha's survey of the Orellana (Amazon) in 1639, when the Fish-god was invited into the camp of Commander Teixeira.   Southey's Hist Brazil, I, xviii, pp 590-621, ed 1810.

A. D. 1656, Begapoor.—Jaloos san, an æra established by Adil Shah II.   The Pandits' "Chron."

A. D. 1664, Konkan.—Raj-Abhishek æra of Sivaji (Sevajee) the celebrated Mahratta chieftain, as stamped on his coins.   To get the Christian year, add 1664 to the coin dates.   The months "probably" accord with the Shaka system   The Pandits' "Chron "

A. D. 1673, India.—Rajasaka, beginning with the month of Iestha   Sewell.   (Obsolete)

A. D. 1747, India.—Cycles of 60 years ratified or confirmed   Marsden, op. cit.   See analogous confirmation of the Calijoga by Hyder Ali, under B C. 3102.

A. D. 1752, Travancore.—Æra of Martanda Varma, 28th rajah of Travancore   He succeeded his uncle, Nama Varma, in 1729   Like all the rajahs of Travancore, Martanda was a Nair, one of the inferior Brahminical castes.   Dissatisfied with his caste, Martanda caused himself to be regenerated, or re-created, by the following ceremony, which is described by the Abbé Raynal, in his "Hist. of the East and West Indies," II, 85: "In 1752 he caused a Golden Calf to be cast which he entered into by the muzzle and came out . . . Since that time his edicts were all dated from the day of this glorious regeneration and, to the great scandal of the remainder of Hindostan, he was acknowledged for a Brahmin by all his Brahminical subjects "   His full name was Vanji Martanda Varma Kulsek'hara Perumal   He died in 1758

A. D. 1752, England.—Adoption of the Gregorian calendar. This Year of Change had but nine months.   See A. D 1582.

A. D. 1752, America.—British Colonies   Adoption of the Gregorian calendar   This year had but nine months.   See A   D   1582 and England, 1752.

A. D. 1776, United States of America.—Æra of the Independence of the United States of America, July 4th. This æra, coupled with the Christian æra, appears in all the Proclamations of the President

A. D. 1777, India.—First year of the 21st cycle of the Graharparivritti, or 90-year cyles Pandits' "Chron ," p xxix This carries the beginning of these cycles back to Calijoga 3078, or B C. 24. The epoch begins with the Hindu solar year

A. D. 1780, Europe, etc.—The Sun left Pisces and entered Aquarius. See B. C 380.

A. D. 1792, France.—Æra of the Republic, Vendemaire 1, or September 22. This æra was established November 24, 1793, and abolished December 31, 1805

A. D. 1792, England.—Appearance in London of Joanna Southcott, a fanatic, from Exeter, where she was born in 1750. She announced herself as the Woman predicted in Revelations, xii, "clothed with the sun . . . being with child . and she brought forth a man-child who was to rule all nations," etc. In this delusion, or imposture, Joanna was supported by four divines, named Whitfield, Wesley, Southcote and Brothers. "A disease favoured the delusion that she would be the mother of the promised Shiloh She died December 27, 1814. In 1851 there existed in England four congregations professing to expect her return " Haydn.

A. D. 1796, India.—Vrihaspati: first year of the 84th cycle, according to the Surya Siddhanta The Pandits See B C. 3185.

A. D. 1804, China.—Vrihaspati: first year of the 76th Jovian cycle, according to the Chinese account. The Pandits. This makes the cycles begin with B. C. 2657, q. v.

A. D. 1807, India.—Vrihaspati first year of the 83rd cycle, according to the Telinga account The Pandits. This makes the cycles begin with B. C 3144, q v.

A. D. 1807, India.—Vrihaspati. first year of the 14th cycle, according to the Tibetan account. The Pandits. This makes the cycles begin with A. D. 967. See A D 966.

A. D. 1825, India.—Beginning of the Fourth millenial of Parasurama. See Kollam cycles under A. D 825.

A. D. 1827, Utah.—Mormon æra, church of Latter Day Saints. In this year Joseph Smith found the Book of the Law which had fallen from heaven into Westchester County, New York. In 1830 the first Mormon church was organised at Kirkland. Ohio, 1844, Smith killed at Nauvoo, Illinois; 1848, the Mormons emigrate to Utah;

1885, polygamy interdicted in the territory of Utah by the United States government

A. D. 1843, America.—The second coming of Jesus Christ foretold in the Apocalypse of John and as computed by the Adventists led by William Miller and hence called Millerites. Miller was born in Pittsfield, Mass , in 1781; died in 1849   At the period when the second advent of Christ was expected, Miller had a following of over 50,000 people, some of them in Philadelphia, where the present writer then resided.   Among the Millerites were many tradesmen, who being led to believe in the fast approaching day of judgment, abandoned their warehouses stored with valuable merchandise, to the depredations of the unbelieving rabble, who rapidly bore away their contents, while the owners looked on with unconcern and apathy, wondering why any people should be so simple as to burden themselves with goods at a time when goods could be of no further use to them.   After the predicted day had passed without any sign from heaven, the deluded votaries were buoyed up with further predictions and postponed dates, and even at the present time there are said to be 15,000 or 20,000 of the sect in America still looking for the momentous day of the second advent.   See 1898

A. D. 1844, Persia.—Bab æra   Mirza Ali Mahomet, or the Bab, (Gate) was born at Shiraz, in 1817 or 1818 and executed at Tabriz, July 8, 1850.   His Manifestation is dated Jemadi-ul-Ula, 5th, A H., 1260, May 23rd, A D 1844, but his æra is reckoned by his followers from the preceding Persian Nauroz, or New Year's day, Wednesday, March 20th, 1844   He claimed to be a lineal descendant of Mahomet, through Hescham, and to be the Sacred Personage foretold by Jabir, one of the twelve Imams of the prophet, as He who would appear on earth exactly one thousand years ("equal to the period of Noah's prophetic mission ") after the Minor Occultation of Mahomet, the 12th Imam, which occured A H. 260.   He was also foretold by another one of the twelve Imams, to wit, Jafar-i-Sadik, who said that the promised Deliverer would appear in the year " 60."   The Bab appeared in A H "1260 "   The Bab's predecessor (for he had one) in the pretension of divinity, was Hazrat-i-Kudduz   He was a six month's child, who called himself the " Lord Jesus," the " Kaim," and other titles pertaining to divinity For these pretensions Hazrat was executed May 22nd, 1849   It was not until after this event that the Bab announced himself as the Holy One, the Lord of the World, etc , and he took care to perpetuate the title by appointing as his successor, Ezel, or Subh-i-Ezel, the Morning of Eternity, a personage who in 1893 was still living in Adrianople Notwithstanding the tragic fate of the Bab and the exile of Ezel, the followers of the religion they founded are said to number at the present day between half a million and a million of persons. Browne's "History of the Bab;" Curzon's "Persia."

A. D. 1845, India.—Deification of Ghasi Das, about this time Sir Alfred Lyall, "Asiatic Studies," p. 108

A. D. 1845, England.—The Agapemone (Greek, "The Abode of Love,") was established this year at Charlinch, near Bridgewater Somersetshire, in pretended imitation of the Agapæ of the Bacchanals. The leader was a physician named Henry James Prince, born 1811, physician 1832, revivalist 1836 In 1845 he claimed to be an Incarnation of the Deity; and, attracting numerous followers, mostly women of property, they all lived in common and took public part in the perpetration of the grossest indecencies These were exposed in the trial of Nottidge v Prince, July 25th, 1860. The sect is still in existence. Cf "Spiritual Wives," by Hepworth Dixon, 1868; Haydn's Dic Dates, Story of the Gods, *vita* "Nebo-Nazaru," p. 2

A. D. 1848, Europe.—A revolution broke out in France, February 23rd, 1848, the immediate cause of which was the interference of the government with a popular banquet and demonstration which had been planned for Washington's Birthday, February 22nd The result of this rising was the flight of the king, Louis Philippe, to England, where he died shortly afterward Meanwhile the spirit of revolt rapidly spread to Germany, Hungary and Italy, in all of which countries popular governments were erected After a brief interval and chiefly through the influence of the clerical parties in each country, who were encouraged and actively aided by Pope Pius IX , the popular governments were suppressed, the leaders (this relates chiefly to the Italian states) were tortured and butchered, and the former regimes were restored

A. D. 1852, China.—First regnal year of Hun-seu-tseun, the leader of the Taiping rebellion and usurping "Emperor" of China. This person, who was born at Kuang-si or Quang-si about 1815, became a convert to Christianity in 1850, and as such was instigated to overthrow the established government and open the country to the benefits of a superior civilization However, he took a somewhat more independent attitude than had been intended by his mentors He announced himself as a descendant of the last em-

peror of the Ming, or only legitimate dynasty, the "restorer of the
worship of the true god, Shang-ti, . .   the brother of Jesus
and the second Son of God " Beside the name of Hun-seu-tseun,
he assumed that of Tien-teh, or Celestial Virtue, Tien-wang, or
Celestial King and many others Haydn In 1852 he captured
Nanking and issued silver coins with the legend, "Sacred Money of
the Tai-ping." During the next few years he acquired virtual control of the Yang-tse-kiang Valley and was materially assisted in his
design of conquest by the attitude of the European powers In 1857
England declared war against China and captured Canton, in 1858
the Taku forts were taken France also declared war against China and
in 1860 Peking was captured and looted. Harassed by internal foes
and threatened with overthrow by foreigners, China was induced to
sign the Elgin Treaty and pay an indemnity of eight million taels,
about eleven million dollars. The Imperial army, which had lately
been drilled by the American colonel Ward, was now placed under
the English colonel Charles G Gordon In June, 1864, the imperial forces led by Gordon besieged Nanking; on June 30th, Hun-
seu-tseun committed suicide; and a few days afterward Nanking fell
and, with it, the Taiping rebellion Gordon himself died in the defense of Khartoum (Egypt) January 26, 1885

A. D. 1868, England.—Advent of Mrs Girling, who claimed to
be "the Bride of Christ," and as such to be immortal She led a
community of Shakers, which survived until 1885; their immortal
leader dying in 1895 The date of the advent is uncertain

A. D. 1868, Japan.—Æra of Meiji, when the hierarchy and
feudalism both came to an end The Nengo, or aera, of Meiji was
originally in A D. 1867. In the 5th year of Meiji, 1872, the Japanese government abrogated its lunar calendar and adopted the
Gregorian system. In that year the 2nd day of the 12th month fell
on December 31st. The remainder of the Japanese month was
dropped from the calendar and the following day, or January 1st,
1873, was reckoned the first day, of the first month, of the sixth year,
of Meiji Wm Bramsen, "Jap Chronology," 1880.

A. D. 1870, Italy.—September 20th Capture of Rome by the
Sardinian forces, followed October 9th, by a Royal decree declaring
that "Rome and the Roman provinces shall constitute an integral
part of the Kingdom of Italy " This decree had the effect to absorb the dominions and terminate the temporal power of the Latin
Papacy, whose foundations had been laid by Pepin the Short, so
long ago as A D. 752. In 1850 the Siccardi bill, abolishing exter-

nal ecclesiastical jurisdiction, had passed the Sardinian Chambers, and in 1861 (the second period of Garibaldi's activity) this law was extended to the whole kingdom of Italy; so that the termination of the temporal power in 1870 was not unheralded. Upon the facade of an enormous theatre which is now (1898) being erected at Cosenza, in Calabria, is graven this inscription, "September 20, 1870 This political date marks the end of Theocracy in civil life. The Day which terminates its moral rule will be the Epoch of Humanity," —"sarà la data umana " London Daily Chronicle, May, 1898

A. D. 1872, Punjab.—Deification of Ram Singh. Lyall, op. cit

A. D. 1883, Soudan.—Manifestation of Mahomet Ahmed It being a widespread belief among Mahometans that the Mahdi will appear at the close of some century from the Flight, advantage was taken of it by this impostor, in the year A. H 1300 or A D 1882-3, to raise the standard of a holy war in the Soudan The terrible fate of the brave but misguided Arabians who followed the Mahdi is related under A D 1898 The burial place of the Mahdi was obliterated by General Kitchener in 1899

A. D. 1895, India.—Period when the reincarnation of Dionysius, Ies Chrishna, Salivahana, or Vicramaditya, was due Greek sign of the Archer, the Indian Dhanaus From this time forward was to begin a New Age. This belief threw the whole of India into a state of excitement and unrest

A. D. 1895, Punjab.—Manifestation of Mirza Ghulam Ahmad, who signed himself " Chief of Qadian, Gurdaspur District, Panjab." This personage pretended to be a prophet and messenger of God. A letter written by him in Pali was translated into English, published in 1886 or 1887, and addressed to the ministers of religion "everywhere." It offered to forfeit to them 200 rupees a month if he, Mirza, failed to perform miracles in proof of his divine mission A further proclamation from him in English and signed as above, with the date of March 23rd, 1894, the original of which is before the writer, offered to forfeit 5,000 rupees to any one who should write "an Arabic book equal to mine in beauty of language and size." His own composition (in Arabic and Urdu) is entitled " Nurr-ul-Haqq," (Divine Light) His pretensions were similar to those of the Bab (see A. D 1844) and, like the Bab's, they were based on the Koran. However, his æra, or the date of his Manifestation, were evidently based upon the Hindu æra of Salivahana B. C 78; for the year 1895 is exactly three Divine Years, of 658 years each, after that date

A. D. 1895, Messiahs.—Appearance in the United States of Francis Schlatter and seveıal other German fanatics, who pretended to be in communication with the Deity and to work cures or miracles A similar pretender named Antonio appeared in Brazıl and had numerous followers Other persons of similar pretensions appeared in the same year, one each ın India, Tibet, Sıcıly, Mexıco, and Mashonaland, South Afrıca. The personage last alluded to was named Ka-goo-bie, or Gumbar-ısh-amba, who called hımself the M'lenga, or the Deity and who ınstıgated the Mashona war of 1895-96. A full length portraıt of thıs "manifestation" (evidently from a photo) was publıshed ın the Illustrated London Graphıc of Decem- ber 25th 1897.

The following account of Schlatter's death ıs from the New York Sun of June 10th, 1897:

El Paso, Texas, June 6th, 1897 —A week ago on last Frıday two American mıne prospectors found ın the foot hılls of the Sıerre Madre on the Puentas Verdas Rıver, thırty-five mıles southwest of Casa Grande, ın the State of Chıhuahua, all that re- maıned of Francıs Schlatter, the "Dıvıne Healer" The prospectors' attentıon was attracted to hıs "camp" by espyıng a saddle astrıde a lımb ın a dead tree high up ın a gorge through which the rıveʳ runs Schlatter's skeleton was found lyıng stretched out on a blanket close up to the tree. Hıs bones were bleached whıte, and along- sıde was a copper rod and a mınıature baseball bat.

Pıled up besıde the trunk of the tree were saddlebags, a large memorandum book, a package of letters bound by a rubber band, some blankets, and sıx suıts of under- wear A Bıble and a canteen were ın the pıle, and a canteen half full of water. The saddle ropes and some extra clothing were dırectly over the skeleton on a lımb of the tree. In a knot hole ın the tree were found needle, thread and buttons In the ın- sıde cover of the Bıble was inscrıbed the name "Francıs Schlatter" Under thıs were two verses ın prayer, followed by the sıgnature "Clarence J Clark, Denver, Col" There were no sıgns of vıolence, and the prospectors belıeve that Schlatter dıed of self-ımposed starvatıon, as there were no cookıng utensıls of any kınd ın camp

The Jefe Polıtıco at Casa Grande was notıfied on May 30, and on June 2 the skele- ton and effects were brought to that vıllage, where the authorıtıes hold them awaıtıng a claımant. Casa Grande ıs sıtuated fifteen mıles from the present teımınal of the Rıo Grande, Sıerre Madre and Pacıfic Raılway—a new lıne for the past year under constructıon from thıs cıty to Casa Grande Amerıcans at Casa Grande examıned the letters and other effects and pronounced them undoubtedly those of Schlatter. An Indıan ınformed the authorıtıes that several months ago he came upon a gray horse ın the neighborhood where the camp was found The horse was hobbled A Mor- mon cowboy saıd that durıng the month of November last Schlatter rode up to hıs camp, fifty mıles west of Casa Grande, on a gray horse He was unarmed, carrıed no provısıons or cookıng utensıls, refused to eat anythıng, and saıd he was fastıng The cowboy saıd hıs vısıtor seemed strange and preoccupıed, and durıng the few hours at hıs camp, cured the cowboy's horse of a swellıng on the back and forelegs by rubbıng hıs hands over them He ıdentıfied the saddle at Casa Grande as that of hıs vısıtor ın November It bears the mark of a Denver manufacturer

Fıancıs Schlatter, three years ago, was a shoe-cobbler ın Denver, and earned a precarıous lıvıng at hıs trade. He began to hear "sılent" voıces, as he saıd, and ın obedıence to theır commands gave away hıs tools and began a pılgrimage toward the Pacıfic coast, He was arrested several tımes as a vagrant and thrown ınto jaıl He footed the entıre dıstance to Calıfornıa and returned to New Mexıco, where he was heard of among the Indıans as the Messıah The newspaper reporters dıscovered that he was followed by mobs of Indıans who worshipped hım and that he cured the sıck by touchıng the afflıcted with hıs hands He fasted for forty days, labourıng continuously, and went to Denver, where he was besieged daily by immense throngs of people from all parts of the country When some persons were arrested for selling handkerchiefs blessed by him, and against whom he was summoned as a witness, he suddenly disappeared He was soon afterward found in New Mexico, travelling through the most uninhabited parts, going southward He was last seen in the United States, by cowboys near Lordsburg, nine months ago, going toward the Mexican line

A. D. 1895, Tibet.—Re-incarnation of Mina Fu-yeh Wellby's "Through Unknown Tibet" 1898. This re-incarnated Buddha seems to have possessed a genuine charm of character and fascination of manner Captain Wellby really liked him:

"His explanation of how he came to be recognised as the re-incarnation of the previous Mina Fu-yeh shows how convincing the proofs of identity are to one who has been brought up to accept and believe in the theory. He relates how, when very small, various articles were laid out, from which he was to select those which had been his own in his previous life-time. Among these was a number of rosaries, from which he had no difficulty in choosing his own 'For,' he says, 'I had used it daily for years, how is it possible that I should not know it from among all the others?' Of course I knew it ' So on with other articles, his own identity was established without a doubt, and he became heir to the accumulated property of fifteen former life-times He talks freely of his last life-time, pointing out the site of the house in which he lived, and which was burnt down about two years before his death, it was, he says, a far finer house than the one he now occupies "

When he was not praying or writing or reading, the Buddha was quite willing to make himself useful.

"But early as we were, our host was before us, and when we left our room we found him making preparations for breakfast He explained that his steward and several of his servants were away, so he had to do a great deal himself It seemed strange to see an incarnate saint, who is held in the deepest reverence and worshipped by men, busying himself unlocking drawers producing sugar and butter, and generally attending to the most trivial and mundane matters, chattering away all the time like an ordinary mortal "

A. D. 1897, Kiao Chao.—Seizure of Kiao Chao, China, by the German forces, whose commander issued a proclamation dated "14th November, A D, 1897, or the 21st day, 11th moon, 23rd year of (the emperor) Huang Tsu, Chinese Reckoning " London "Chronicle," January 6th, 1898 This makes the first year of Huang Tseu agree with A. D 1875.

A. D. 1897, Austria.—In May, 1897, in the northern part of the Bukovina, near Gallicia, the peasant population was greatly excited by an eighteen-year-old prophetess named Jaryna Jeryernkowna The girl declared that she died and was buried four years ago, and went to heaven, and was sent by God to redeem mankind. Despite the parish priest's protests a procession was arranged, and hundreds followed her to the Church of Szerowce, where she prayed aloud and delivered a sermon The Mayor and councillors were convinced of the girl's heavenly mission The prophetess and the attendant crowds then made their way to Stara Zuczka, where she delivered another sermon in the church.   At Sadagora, a number of gendarmes, after a violent scuffle with the excited crowd, arrested the girl, and committed her to prison   London "Chronicle," May 26, 1897

A. D. 1898, Arabia.—September 3. "Battle" of Omdurman, at which 12,000 to 15,000 Arabians, under the leadership of the Khalifa Abdullah, successor to the Mahdi, or Messiah, were slaughtered by the British and Egyptian forces under Gen. Kitchener.   Said G. W Stevens, correspondent of the London *Daily Mail*

"It was not a battle but an execution   .   The Dervishes were not driven back, they were all killed in coming on   .   .   .   The bodies were not in heaps, they spread evenly over acres and acres   .   .   .   The honour of the fight must go with the men who died   Our men were perfect but the Dervishes were superb—beyond perfection   .   .   Their riflemen, mangled by every kind of death and torment that man can devise, clung round the Black Flag and the Green, dauntlessly emptying their poor rotten home-made cartridges   .   .   The last Dervish stood up and filled his chest, he shouted the name of his God and hurled his spear, then toppled with his face to his conquerors "   The Khalifa escaped to the White Nile

A. D. 1898, England.—Easter day   End of the Gentile times, to be followed by the second coming of Jesus Christ, according to the Second Adventis's   "If our predictions fail, the Sun will fall with us.   . .   The Gentile times end (Luke xxi, 24,) on the 20th of March, 1898, at 2 o'clock in the afternoon." London "Past and Future," February 2, 1898, p 71   See A. D 1843

A. D. 1908, England.—Beginning of the thousand years, at the termination of which, the world will be destroyed   Rev. M P. Baxter.

"On Thursday, June 9th, 1898, a meeting of the Court of Common Council was held at Guildhall, the Lord Mayor presiding   On the recommendation of the City Lands Committee, it was resolved that on the Rev M. P Baxter surrendering his present lease of premises in Tudor Street, a building lease be granted to him for eighty years, from midsummer next, at ground-rents varying from £90 to £424 per annum.   When his petition was before the court it was elicited that the lessee was the gentleman who recently predicted the immediate end of the world. The Prophet, however, has since written to explain that the end of the world, in the sense of the general conflagration, will not take place until the termination of 1,000 years from Easter, 1908 "   London Weekly Times and Echo, June 12, 1898.

A. D. 1928, England.—End of the thousand years when (on Easter Day) the world will be destroyed, the next Millenium of the Second Adventists.   "Past and Future," 1898, p 70.

CHAPTER VIII

CYCLES.

THE author has endeavoured to bring together in this chapter all the cycles, whether astronomical, astrological, or civil, which have come under his notice during several years of study. They are arranged in the order of their duration, beginning with one day and ending with 240 million years, one of those vast eons of time, if we may use such an expression with propriety, which practically represents eternity and which could only have emanated from peoples who believed in the immortality of the soul. Among these were the Indians, Egyptians, Chaldeans and Greeks The Chinese had no such vast ages; neither had the Jews, nor the Romans the Chinese cosmic cycle—an unique instance—being probably of Hindu origin and modern invention or adoption

---

1 day.—The period of the earth's revolution on its axis constitutes the most perfect measure of time The time occupied in this movement is called a day

7 day week, or the Hebdomadal cycle. This is not a natural, that is to say, an astronomical cycle, but an artificial one. It is not exactly, but only roughly, the fourth part of a lunar month, which consists of about 29½ days The seven-day wake, or week, might possibly have been employed by primitive tribes before any solar calendar was in use, though of such a circumstance no record survives the "Accadian" and Chaldean evidence on this point being unsatisfactory. The seven-day week had no existence during the many centuries when time was reckoned by solar years of ten civil months. Its present observance as a day of rest has not been traced further backward than the adoption of a twelve months year, which occured during the second Buddhic period Even during that period it was not used by the Greeks or Romans until those peoples adopted the Dionysian cult. On this point we have the explicit testimony of Dion Cassius, who, writing about A D 229, says of the septuary week. "It is not very long since this custom was introduced by the

Egyptians to other nations; for I believe the ancient Greeks had no
knowledge of it " The Rev Dr Hales, who could not refute the
innumerable evidences that the Romans observed a week of nine days,
nundinæ, said, in his Chronology I, 19, that the gentiles "dropped"
the seventh day, the Greek gentiles observing the tenth day and the
Roman gentiles the ninth   This is disingenuous and might be misleading The gentile Greeks never observed the seventh day; neither
did the gentile Romans; therefore they did not "drop" it.   Dion
Cassius says (xxxvii, 18, or Xiphilinus Abridg pp. 14, 15) that the
days of the septuary week were named by the Egyptians after the
seven planets, the Egyptians being the "first authors of it ; " that
the Romans and other nations now employ this week; that the first
day is Saturn's day, which the Jews celebrate as a holiday, upon
which they abstain from work; that the order of the days among the
Egyptians runs as 1, Saturn; 2, Jupiter; 3, Mars; 4, Sun; 5, Venus;
6, Mercury, and 7, Moon; or, as they are now named, 1, Saturday;
2, Thursday, 3, Tuesday; 4, Sunday; 5, Friday; 6, Wednesday, and
7, Monday   Although he does not give the order of the days in
Rome, it is quite evident from what he does say that it was not the
Egyptian order, but the Buddhic, or Dionysian order.   He says that
the first day was Saturday and that the fourth or middle day, like the
fourth string in the musical scale, was the foundation of the system,
"so that," to use his own words, "it will be found that the heavens
rule the days with a harmony which is analogous to that of music "
This influential middle or mess-day, (Gothic, mid-wik,) originally
Sun-day, was subsequently named after Dionysius, the Roman Mercurius, from whom the fourth day of the septimana still takes its name,
as in the French Mercredi, the Spanish Miercoles, and the English
Wednesday, because there was no such messianic influence over the
other days nor no such name of mess, mid, medial, or mediator, ascribed
to any other god except Dionysius   As to Dion's belief that the Egyptians were the first authors of the septuary week, or the first to give
these names to the days, though there is no reason to doubt its sincerity, it is evidently a mistake   The Hindu and perhaps even the Scythian septuary week appears to be older· in short, both the astronomy
and the astrology of the Seven days, like that of the Seven asterisms,
are Oriental   Apollonius of Tyana found the septimana, or septuary week, in use in India, when he visited it about A D 45; (Philostratus, in vita, III, xiii, 148, A), and the names then given to the
days were probably those which we find in the Code of Manou to-day,
though in this place they are of comparatively modern insertion.

They are as follows: Rabi-var, Som-var, Mangal-var, Buddh-var, Vrishpat-var, Gurn-var, Shukra-var and Sani-var In fact the septuary week is probably several centuries earlier than Apollonius and many centuries later than Manu

9 day week.—An artificial cycle precisely the fourth part of the 36-day civil month in the 10-months' solar year This cycle was called nundinum by the Romans and is still preserved in the novenas of the Italians, which occur in their church festivals and ceremonies On the ninth day the temples were thrown open for public worship. The peasants improved the occasion to fetch their farm produce and home-made wares into the cities and expose them for sale within the enclosures of the temples, which were thus converted into fairs For this privilege they paid a tax to the temples. This custom still survives in the smaller towns of France, Germany and other continental states, though now the fair-day is the first of the cycle of seven, instead of, as formerly, the last of the cycle of nine Nor is there now any tax The first day of the nundinum was called prima-feria, the second, secunda-feria, etc., whence we have the word fair Sunday fairs, a relic of the ancient custom, were only abolished in England by the act of June 10th, 1850. Townsend

10 days.—The Greek cycle of 10 days is sufficiently noticed under a previous head The days of the Chinese 10-day cycle are named Kia, Yih, Ping, Ting, Wu, Ki, Keng, Sin, Jen, and Kwei Gaubil, "Lettres Edifiantes," xxvi, 225, 228 The Greek custom of dividing the month into three decades each of ten days was revived by the French during the Revolution, but abolished by Napoleon I

30 and 31 days.—For months of 30 and 31 days, see " 36 days " and 10 and 12 months.

36 days.—Prior to the second Buddhic period the solar year in all the principal states of the world was divided into ten civil months each of 36 days, with 5 intercalary days, or epagomenae, to make the equable year. The period of the change from 10 months of 36 days to 12 months of 30 days, with intercalaries, is believed to have been as follows India, B C 662; China, 657; Miletus, 592; Athens, 582; Babylon, 582, Egypt, 547 and Rome, 451 The period of the " Second Hermes," or second Buddha, is recognized by both Strabo and Diodorus.

45 days.—There are reasons for believing that during the prevalence of the earlier form of the Solar worship in India, Scythia, Assyria and Egypt, the solar year was divided into eight civil months

each of 45 days, with intercalaries   The Sun god was typified by a
human figure holding an eight-spoked wheel, the Eight principal
gods of early Egypt, to each of whom one month of the year was
consecrated, are mentioned by Herodotus (Euterpe, 82, 145, 156);
ancient zodiacs have been discovered which are divided into eight
sections, while the dislocated features of the present calendar and
the odd days set apart for certain astrological festivals, also indicate
a remote subdivision of the year into eight parts

304 days.—Censorinus, (D N XX,) says that Philolaus reckoned
the natural year to consist of 364½ days, Aphrodisius, 365⅛, Calippus, 365; Aristarchus of Samos, 365 1-1623: Meton, 365 5-19,
Œnopides, 365 22-59; Harpalus, 365 13-24; and Ennius, 366 days
Moreover, he argues, that by the recession of Thoth 1st from July
20th to February 26th, ending with the Divine year A D 138, (namely,
144 days in 576 years of the Sothiacal cycle,) the Egyptians and
before them the Chaldeans, employed the Julian year of exactly 365¼
days   (Other ostensibly ancient authorities to the same effect, are
cited by Greswell, F C , I, 74, 75, etc.)   But see the 360-day and
especially the 365¼-day cycles given below.

After thus showing and arguing that both the Romans, Greeks,
Egyptians and Chaldeans were very accurately acquainted with the
length of the year in days, Censorinus informs us that in the Alban
calendar, from which the Roman calendar descended, there were only
ten months, with altogether 304 days, as follows   March 31, April 30,
May 31; June 30; Quintilis (now July) 31; Sextilis (now August) 30;
September 30; October 31, November 30; and December 30.   He
adds that when Numa, or else Tarquin, extended the year to twelve
months. it was done by supplementing January with 29 days and
February with 28, and that one day was taken from each of the six
months that had had 30 days, thus making four months each of 31 days,
seven months each of 29 days and one month of 28 days; total 355
days   Finally, that an intercalary month of 22 or 23 days was added
every two years between the last day of February and the first of
March.

Except as to the last sentence, this account is anachronical, confused and defective   It has every appearance of having been tampered
with by the custodians of the manuscript.   An intercalary month,
every two years, of 22 or 23 days, would add 11¼ days to 355, making
a mean year of 366¼ days, which is in excess of the fact by one day
But this is the least.   It is simply incredible that any calendar, we

will not say the Roman, but even the Alban, should have reckoned only 304 days to the year, whether the latter was divided into ten months, or any other number The merest child would not fail to observe that the year had many more days than 304. It is evident, from the confused condition into which the Roman calendar fell before the time of Julius Cæsar, as well from the lateness of the period when Censorinus wrote, (which was A. D. 238, or about seven centuries after the Roman year was divided into twelve months,) that all the details of the ancient calendars, both of Rome and Alba, were lost; and therefore that with respect to the number of days in the months, of which ten went to the year, the text offered for that of Censorinus, even if it has not been altered, is not to be altogether relied upon. But that it has been altered is the opinion of every critic who has examined it

Brady, (Clavis Cal., I, 15,) in repeating that the Alban year consisted of 304 days, furnishes the following details April 36 days; May 22; March 36; June 26, Quintilis 36; Sextilis 28, September 16; October 39; November 30; December 35; total 304. Here is one month with 35 days, three months with 36, and one month with 39 days, besides several small and unequal months, one of which contains but 16 days Such a calendar is preposterous. It is contradicted by common sense; by the Roman method of dividing the months into calends, nones and ides; and by the nundinæ; all of which indications and features point to four intervals of nine days in each month; a conclusion admitted even by Hales, (I, 19,) but still denied by the Sacred College of Rome and its apologists.

In order to account for a 304-day year, Greswell, F. C., I, 503, invents a nundinal cycle of 8 days and a lunation of 32 days, 19 of which imaginary lunations make 608 days, or two years of 304 days each! A 304-day year is bad enough, but a 32-day moon and an 8-day week are still worse. There is neither astronomical nor historical foundation for any of them. A 10-months' lunar year is simply impossible Whenever the year was thus divided the calendar must have been a solar one.

Sir George Cornewall Lewis, in his "Astronomy of the Ancients," London, 1862, examined this matter with great care. He showed that Macrobius, I, xii, 39, Scaliger, de Emend Temp , ii, p. 172, ed 1629, and Dodwell, all rejected the 304-day year as preposterous; and to the opinion of these chronologists he adds his own, which is that the 304-day year is impossible Moreover, he contends that both the Greeks before Solon and the Romans before Numa, had a 360-day year Finally, he shows, upon numerous ancient testimonies, that the Greek and Roman years were full years and that they were divided into ten months   Yet he shrinks from expressing the very palpable conclusion that if the years were full and had 365, or even 360 days and there were but ten months, the latter must have consisted of 36 days each.   The nundinum or week of nine days should have taught him better; but his superstition was evidently stronger than his reason. After labouring to prove with Greswell that a nundinum meant eight days, he declares himself unable to harmonise the conflicting testimonies on the subject of the ten months' year, which he leaves precisely where he found it.

The notion of a 304-day year seems to have arisen in this way· if 12 months now contain 365 days, how many days did ten months anciently contain? Answer, 304 days   It was a mere arithmetical result; a quotient in the rule of three; having no relation to history and merely suggested by the desire to avoid confessing that the septuary week is not so ancient as is pretended. The 32-day moons and 8-day nundines of Dr. Greswell and Sir George Cornewall Lewis are of the same arithmetical character   Plutarch in Numa says that so far back as the time of that demi-god, the Roman year had 360 days To these days may be added the five epagomenæ   The fingers of the statues of Janus, one of which is said to have been erected by Numa himself, commonly indicated the numbers 365   Pliny, XXXIV, 16; Macrobius, I, ix, 10; Lydus de Mens , IV, 1, and Suidas.   Macrobius even argues, Sat , I, 13, that Numa's intercalary cycle proves that he knew the year to consist of 365¼ days   In the face of such evidences, what is the value of an argument for a year of 304 days? Cf. Livy, I, 19, Macrobius, op. cit ; and the 24-year cycle, herein.

327 days.—Dr Greswell, F. C., I, 61, assures us that "chronology has little to do with any revolution of the moon but the synodic " This learned, but far too credulous writer, never seems to have suspected the sinister resources of lunar chronology, the cunning of the ancient priests, nor the significance of the Divine year   Albiruni explicitly informs us that the Hindus, not of his own time, but of some earlier age, used a year of 12 lunar revolutions, aggregating 327 days 7⅔ hours (Sachau's ed , p 15) This accords to each lunar revolution 27 d 6h 38m 20s. Consequently the Hindu lunar month was not the synodic. It was either the sidereal of 27 days 7h. 43m 11 54s or else the nodical, of 27d. 5h. 5m 35.6s., preferably the latter, on account of its superior amenability to intercalation

with the solar year The nodical month as the basis of a chronological system grafted upon the worship of the Sun, inevitably led to
the nodical cycle, the Divine year and the Brahminical system of
avatars or incarnations. The measurements of the nodical and sidereal months given above are those of Lockyer The ancient Hindu
measurements probably slightly differed.

354 days.—This is a lunar year, or a year of 12 lunations The
354-day year of Solon which followed the 360-day solar year of Athens
was of this character So was the year (whether instituted by Numa, or
Tarquin, or the Decemvirs,) which probably followed immediately
after the Roman ten months' solar year of 360 days A lunar year of
354 days is still used by the Hindus, Jews and Moslems. To make
up the 11¼ days (approx) of the solar year, an intercalary month is
added to this lunar year, at appropriate intervals Numa is said to
have added one day for luck and intercalated the remaining odd days
every two years, between the 23rd and 24th of February Pliny, N H ,
XXIV, 7, Livy, I, 19; Adams, "Rom Ant " It is now tolerably
certain that it was not Numa, but the Decemvirs

360 days.—A solar year of 360 days with 5 intercalaries (the
equable year, q v) was in common use in many ancient states, especially during republican periods Whenever the nobles and ecclesiastics regained their ascendancy, they invariably altered the
calendar to a lunar, or else to a luni-solar, year, so as to confuse the
computation of time and render themselves the arbiters of contracts
and sponsors of the festivals. A 360-day year was used in Babylon.
Berosus apud Josephus, Ant X, 11; in Egypt, Dio Sic. XVII; and
in Greece; Plutarch. For the epochs when this year was employed,
see below

365 days.—The equable solar year It is ascribed by Diogenes
Laertes (Thal. § 5) to Thales (circ B. C 585) which may mean either
that Thales discovered it or else that previous to that date the calendar
of Miletus was lunar But the authority is virtually anonymous and
worthless The equable year is mentioned by the Hellenicus in Plutarch and by Herodotus with reference to Egypt. Censorinus says
that the equable year was employed by Calippus in Greece B C 330;
but Lindenbruch has proved that Calippus used the Julian year
The equable year in Greece was much earlier than Calippus. See
chap VII, B C. 1219. The equable year appears to have been used
in Etruria so early as the time of Procas and in Rome so late as the
time when Cneius Flavius ordered the calendar to be affixed to the

public buildings, about B. C. 305, and was probably used down to the period of Cæsar's reform of the calendar Its employment seems to have begun in India during the first Buddhic period and thence radiated to China, Chaldea, Miletus, Egypt, Greece and Rome Euterpe, IV; Brady I, 15

The following dates are at present only to be regarded tentatively.

CHRONOLOGY OF THE EQUABLE YEAR

Date B C	Country	Authorities
1426	India	Bailey, Laplace, *et al* See Ch VII, herein, sub anno.
1306	India	Epoch, Aswin 1st Greswell, K H , V, 87
1176	Southern India	Epoch, Aswin 1st Cowasjee Patell. See Ies Chrishna, Parasurama, etc
?	Chaldea	Epoch, the festival of Anaites Cf Berosus in Josephus.
?	Phrygia	Epoch, the festival to Attis and Cybele
1250 ?	Egypt	Epoch, Thoth 1st. Hellenicus in Plutarch's Isis and Osiris Herod , Eut.
1219	Greece	Epoch, Vernal equinox, (Ischenia,) Valleius Paterculus. Plutarch in Theseus The equable year was abolished by Solon Sir G Cornewall Lewis, Anc. Astron
816 ?	Etruria or Rome	Plutarch in Numa Epoch, March 1st

The determination of the equable solar year, its incorporation into the law of the land, and its adoption in practice, constituted a veritable charter of freedom to mankind The previous employment of a lunar calendar had everywhere enabled the priesthood at their pleasure to lengthen or shorten the months, to precipitate or postpone important events, to accelerate or delay payments, to shift the holidays and festivals and to alter or destroy their significance, so as to give them new and false meanings and attributes. Actual instances of this sort are given by Livy, Censorinus and other ancient writers So flagrant did this abuse of privilege become, that in many states of antiquity it was demanded of each new monarch that he should swear before being crowned that he would not permit the calendar to be altered. The institution of the equable year swept away the lunar calendar and with it many of those mysteries and impostures, which, in the hands of an unscrupulous hierarchy, had become a potent means of deception, tyranny and oppression

Lunar calendars are still employed by the Brahmins, Moslems and Jews With regard to their practical effects among the followers of the two first mentioned cults, no details worthy of consideration have reached the Western world The Jews retain a lunar calendar in their prayer books and ecclesiastical almanacs, but in actual practice and in every day life they use the Roman solar calendar Indeed, without consulting an almanac, the laity would be quite unable to fix the New Year day, the Day of Atonement the Passover, the Feast of Tabernacles, or any other great festival to any particular day of the year.

In view of the synchronism between the institution of the equable solar year in India, Chaldea and Greece and the æra and festivals assigned to Ies Chrishna, Iesnu and Ischenou, it will hardly be questioned that the legends, mysteries and rites peculiar to these deities and their relation to the apparent course of the Sun, were originally intended to fix, celebrate and commemorate the institution of the Solar Year At a later period—that of the second Buddha—some of these rites, which meanwhile had been overthrown by the temporary ascendancy of the aristocratic and ecclesiastical party, were revived, in Greece, for example, by Solon, and piously ascribed to Bacchus; whose æra, that is to say the æra of the restoration of the Solar Calendar, was thrown back to and confused with that of Ischenou

365.242392 days.—The decimal expression of the "true solar year," as given by Joseph N. Lockyer, "Dawn of Astronomy," London, 1894, p 251.

365 1=4 days.—A year composed of this number of days is called the Julian, because it was first fixed and permanently established in the law of any country by Julius Cæsar, who incorporated it into the law of the Roman Empire, B. C 48. In some countries the Julian year was approximately known several centuries earlier than Cæsar. Herodotus only mentions the equable year of 365 days (Euterpe, 4); while Strabo and Diodorus believed that the year of 365¼ days was known to the priests of Thebes (Egypt) so early as the æra of the of the "Second Hermes " Although thus perhaps claimed too much, there is reason to believe that the Julian year was approximately known in Egypt much earlier than in Rome. As for Dr Hales' suggestion that the Egyptian rectification of the sidereal (Sothiacal) year, of one year in 1460 years, proves that a knowledge of the Julian year was as old as the use of the Sothiacal cycle in Egypt, it rather proves the contrary; for had the Julian year been known, the rectification could have been made once in four years and the calendar preserved from a confusing retrogression running through 15 centuries The Sothiacal cycle was employed to harmonize the sidereal and solar year and for that purpose only. The following table shows the oldest dates known of the Julian year or of any approximation toward it:

CHRONOLOGY OF THE JULIAN YEAR

Date, B C	Discoverer and Country	Authority
Uncertain	Indian	Bailly , Delambre.
"	Chinese	Delambre, Astron. Anc. I, 417
"	Siamese	Bailly , Cassini.
"	Chaldean	Bailly , Delambre , Freret.
547	Egyptian	Strabo , Diodorus. (Doubtful).
542	Œnopides of Chios	Censorinus, XIX, says 365d 8h 57m.
432	Meton of Athens	Censorinus says 365d 6h. 18m 57s.
——	Aphrodisius	Censorinus says 365d 3h.
480	Harpalus	Censorinus says 365d 13h
432	Meton of Athens	Greswell says 365d 6h 18m 56.8s
330	Calippus	Greswell says 365¼ days.
280	Aristarchus of Samos	Censorinus says 365d 0h 0m 53s
150	Hipparchus	Greswell says 365d 5h. 55m 12s.
80	Geminus of Rhodes	Delambre, Astron Anc , I, 298, says 365¼d
48	Julius Cæsar	His year was exactly 365¼ days

The æra of Œnopides of Chios is uncertain   He is mentioned by Diodorus (1, 96,) Stobæus and Sextus Empiricus, of whom only Stobæus makes him later than Pythagoras   The date adopted in the table is from Greswell, who, though a very learned man, too often enslaved his judgment to his theory of a primeval year and calendar   Could reliance be placed upon this date it would follow that the Greeks approximated the Julian year so early as the time of Pythagoras.   But the absence of the Julian year from the pages of Herodotus, is a serious obstacle to this theory.   Upon a review of all the evidence it seems hazardous to admit even a knowledge of the Julian year in the West earlier than the time of Meton.   As to its establishment in the law and practical use, there is no record earlier than Julius Cæsar With regard to its chronology in the Orient, we are without reliable dates.   We can only surmise that this knowledge, like most other knowledge of the kind, radiated from India to China and Siam, on the one hand and to Chaldea and Egypt, on the other   Nothing more can be said until Oriental archæology is able to add its testimony to our at present very slender stock of reliable information on this subject.   The determinations assigned to Meton, Callippus and Geminus are the deductions of modern astronomers

Whatever may be the real antiquity of the Julian year, when Cæsar established and supported it with the authority, the arms, and the literature of Rome, he conferred upon the world a boon of the highest value   Tedious as are the steps by which mankind has endeavoured to emancipate itself from hierarchical rule, none has proved of more practical importance than the recognition and adoption of a true year in place of a false one; a solar year in place of a lunar one   It rescued from the control of hierarchs the archives of the past and the framing of history   It laid the foundation of political and religious literature, which before that time could have had no stable existence, because before that time there was no certain date; no reasoning from experience, no science of causation. It inflicted a death-blow to lunar calendars, one of the principal supports of religious imposture Above all, it vindicated the holiness and majesty of scientific truth and its superiority over mere human contrivances to secure the freedom and happiness of mankind. Cæsar was a priest of Jupiter; he was the High-priest, the Pontifex Maximus of Rome; a man of great intelligence, the most comprehensive knowledge and the utmost refinement. It can scarcely be doubted that he was fully aware of the importance of his decree which established and enforced the Julian year; and much might be written to prove that this had more to do with the hatred which afterwards assailed him from noble and hierarch than the peurile charge of having set up himself for a king.

6585 2=3 days.—The Ecliptical Cycle, or Cycle of the Eclipses, of exactly 6585 78 days This is the most significant of all the cycles, and was well known to the Hindus at a very early date, "says Brennand." The Chinese called this number of days a Ven, Fen, or Phen, (which means ten), the Chaldeans, "The Period," and the Greeks, as many authors assert, a "saros," the root of the word being sar, meaning ten However, the terms sossos, neuros and saros have been explained by Polyhistor, Syncellus, Abydenus, Suidas, Vallancy, Dupuis, Greswell and other commentators, so variously, that in order to avoid a verbal dispute, they have not been used in the present work at all The Ecliptical cycle embraces the entire series of eclipses, of which there are usually 29 lunar and 41 solar. The priests employed it to awe the multitude and the commanders of armies to terrify the enemy Moreover, there was built upon it an astrology and a messianic theory which pervades all the religions of antiquity and which therefore renders a knowledge of this cycle and of its origin and the uses to which it was put, of essential importance to the study of religion and history.

Bailly fixes the discovery of this cycle in India and Tartary to the period when the vernal equinox was well within the constellation Taurus, in other words, over four thousand years ago This date for the vernal equinox in Taurus is based upon the erroneous assumption that the number of the zodions has always been twelve. It must therefore share the fate of the erroneous assumption Other writers have discerned evidences of this cycle in India so early as the Mahabharata wars, although it may not have been determined accurately until a later period.   It was only after the 12th century B. C that what appears to be distinct marks may be seen of the messianic theory to which the cycle gave rise, or with which it was connected This theory was that the Creator would appear upon earth to rectify the deranged affairs of mankind every 6585 months, or in as many months as there were whole days in the cycle As the year then consisted of ten months, the incarnations or avatars fell every 658th year. Continuing upon the same line of thought, the messianic theory foretold the destruction of the world in the same number of years 6585, from the Creation.   Grotesque as this theory may seem to us when set forth in sober terms, it actually forms the basis and it may be added the only basis, for some of the holiest and most tender beliefs in which humanity has found consolation for the wounds and havoc of injustice, misfortune and death.   The philosopher may allude to it with coldness and contempt: the worshipper can only remember the maternal sanctuary at which he learnt those exquisite allegories behind which lurks this skeleton of an astronomical truth. As the cycle is really not a diurnal, but a lunar one, it is treated more at length under 223 lunations and 6585 lunations, q v.   '

6660 days —The Ecliptical cycle, according to Berosus Higgins, Anacal , I, 180

6793 1=2 days.—Revolution of the moon's node Lockyer See 230 months   Brennand calls it the sidereal period of the moon's node and fixes it at 6793.39108 days.   The Surya Siddhanta made it 6794.443 mean solar days   Brennand, 43

19,756 days.—Exeligmos, a cycle consisting of three ecliptical cycles, which was used by the Greeks, Egyptians and Chaldeans to foretell eclipses Greswell, F C , I, 69 n, IV, 100   See 669 lunations.   The Hindus had the ecliptical cycle in the 15th century B C.

1 month.—A revolution of the moon, or a synodic lunation, consists of 29d 12h 44m 2 84s Lockyer, p 213 This is a month Eleven other determinations will be found in Greswell, F C , I, 69. The nodical, tropical, sidereal and anomalistic months consist each of 27 days and a fraction, such fraction of a day varying from 5 plus, to 13 plus hours.   The civil month has varied from 45 to 30 days.

10 months.—The ancient year consisted of ten civil months each of 36 days, with five intercalaries.   On this subject we have the testimony of Ovid, Livy, Censorinus, Aulus Gellius and other ancient writers   This testimony is corroborated by proofs from extraneous sources   There cannot be any reasonable doubt that previous to the period ascribed to the second Buddha, Bacchus, or Hermes, that is to say, between the eighth and sixth centuries B C , the year, among all civilised peoples, was divided into ten months each of 36 days and that in Rome, the day of rest, of worship and of fairs, was the ninth and not the seventh, as it became at a later period

It is a curious circumstance, which has not yet been satisfactorily explained, that in the mythos of the Brahminical or Brahmo-Buddhic avatars the incarnated god is often described as a ten months' child, and that in such respect, as well as in others, it differed wondrously from other children. Ten months of 30 days each would not differ so much from the ordinary period of gestation as to render it at all wonderful; whilst ten months of 36 days would. It is therefore suggested that the true explanation of this detail of the mythos is connected with the superior length of the ancient month

12 months.—There is no valid evidence extant to support a year of twelve civil months, that is to say, a solar or luni-solar year of 360, 365, or 365¼ days, divided into 12 months of 30 days each, or thereabouts, prior to the period of the second Buddha, or Hermes. There were, indeed, years of this number of days, but not of this number of months The year was divided not into 12, but into ten, and still more anciently into eight, months; the division into 12 months being apparently a product of this period. The testimony of the Bible, upon which Hales, Greswell, Kennedy and other scriptural chronologists rely so implicitly, does not touch the case at all; because there is no portion of the Bible which may not have been written after that period See 36 and 365¼ days

13 months.—An ancient year of 13 lunar months is mentioned by Gerald Massey (The Natural Genesis, II, 308,) who believes (though erroneously) that it gave rise to the superstitious notion of 1 l-luck which is attached to the number Thirteen. In A. D 1899 an American inventor, (State of Indiana), patented a calendar year of 13 civil months each of 28 days (with an intercalary day) in the belief that his invention was novel and was likely to be generally adopted throughout the world!

27 lunar mansions.—At a very early period (Bentley says between B C 1528 and 1371) the Hindus divided the ecliptic into 27 (previously 28) lunar mansions or nachshatras, giving to each one 13⅓ degrees, thus $27 \times 13⅓ = 360$. Each mansion, nachshatra, or asterism included a group of stars, whose principal one, the yogatara, gave to, or took its name from, the nachshatra. The Vedas called these the 27 daughters of Daksha, whom he gave in marriage to the moon, Soma The Chinese have a similar division of the ecliptic into 27 sieu, but they apportion it differently, giving to some of the mansions or sieu 30 degrees and to others but a few minutes The Arabians had 28 mansions, differing from both the foregoing, but with some analogy for the Chinese system The Egyptians adopted the lunar mansions at a comparatively late date, but made little or no use of them The lunar mansions had no place in Greek astronomy. The period when the Hindus changed their division of the ecliptic from 28 to 27 parts is regarded by Brennand as earlier than the composition of the Vedas, or indeed, of any historical record. These lunar mansions served somewhat the same purpose in Hindu astronomy as the solar zodiac in that of the Western nations Sir Geo Cornewall Lewis; Gerald Massey

99 lunations.—Approximately 2922 days. The octæteris cycle, so called, because it equalled eight Julian years, e. g , $8 \times 365\frac{1}{4} = 2922$ days In this period the lunar year and the Julian (but not the natural) solar year can be adjusted Censorinus, XVIII, ascribed the invention or discovery of the octæteris cycle to Eudoxus of Cnidus, who flourished in the fourth century before our æra. Boeckh, Ideler and Gotfried Muller believe that the octæteris is as early as Proclus, fifth century B. C This conclusion is derived from the festival of Chresto-mathia, which Proclus describes A large ball was fastened to the top of an olive stick and another smaller ball in the middle. To the latter were attached 365 smaller balls, by purple fillets The top ball represented the Sun, the middle ball the Moon and the smaller ones, the Stars; the corresponding fillets representing the course of the Sun in Days The objection to the theory of the German savants is that the number of fillets implies an equable, not a Julian year It is probably for this reason that it is rejected by Sir George Cornewall Lewis. The antiquity of the octæteris in Greece must therefore rest for the present with Eudoxus of Cnidus Greswell, K H , I, 40, contends that the octæteris was employed in Greece before the time of Solon and in another work, F C , I, 67, he traces it in Egypt back to B C. 1261; but these dates and the arguments by which they are supported, are of very doubtful validity. See 1980 lunations further on

198 lunations.—The hekkaidekæteris, or double octæteris cycle It was used to adjust the solar and lunar calendars of Greece It loses about $3\frac{1}{2}$ days on the moon: Geminus, "Uranologium," about B C 80 Greswell, F C , I, 105, is of opinion that it was nearly as ancient as the octæteris, but was little employed, because it had no practical advantages over the the other See 1980 lunations.

223 lunations.—The great Ecliptical Cycle, already introduced under the heading of 6585⅔ days. As there stated, this significant cycle is not a diurnal, but a lunar one. To couch it in days or years is apt to be misleading. It has sometimes been called the Nodical cycle. According to Lockyer this also is wrong: the Nodical cycle consisting of 230 lunations, or 6793½ days, q. v. The Ecliptical cycle begins with a conjunction of the sun and moon (new moon) and continues until the sun and moon (some say also the node) return to the same positions as at the outset. This occurs in 223 lunations, or 18 years and ten (or 11) days and seven, (or eight), hours. Brennand says "and *eighteen* hours." During this period there will usually occur 41 solar and 29 lunar eclipses. At the end of the period the same routine of eclipses will begin to recur, and they will happen on or about the same days of the equable solar year. A cycle composed of three Ecliptical cycles, or 669 lunations, will bring the eclipses to the day and almost to the hour required by the rule. See 6585⅔ days and 658 years.

230 lunations.—Revolution of the moon's node. Lockyer. See 6793½ days.

235 lunations.—Metonic Cycle, so named after Meton of Athens, its Greek discoverer, B. C. 432. During the course of this cycle and upon a given system of intercalation the new and full moons return to the same days of the (30-day) month. Consequently the cycle was not employed until after the year was divided into 12 months, which, as before stated, took place in various states some time between the eighth and sixth centuries B. C. The priests of Meton's time were so delighted with a discovery that enabled them to identify and retain their lunar festivals in a solar calendar, that they loaded the astronomer with honors, called his Cycle the Golden and set it up in the Athenian pynx in letters of gold; at all events, they said in after times that they had done so, which, as things go, is much the same thing. Bentley and Greswell, who argued that the Metonic cycle was necessarily connected with the Julian year, which it is not, traced this cycle back to India B. C., 946; Japan, 660; China, 657; Siam, 545; and Egypt (Ptolemaic,) 360. All these dates, except perhaps the first one, are possible. Greswell, F. C., I, 109, 579-83. The Metonic cycle is purely lunar; and the practice of stating it in days (6939d. 14h. 27m.) or in years (about 19) is misleading. Its epoch in Athens was Hecatombian 1st (July 15th) B. C. 432. Diodorus, II, iii, says that in the Island of the Hyperboreans they observe a cycle of 19 years, during which "the stars perform their courses and return to the same point;

and therefore the Greeks call this revolution of 19 years the Great Year " Dr Whewell says that the Metonic cycle is still used to calculate the new moon for the time of Easter   Cf Sir Geo. Cornewall Lewis

309 lunations.—Apis cycle During this period and upon a given system of intercalation, (the equable year, with five epagomenæ,) the lunar and solar dates in the equable year are restored   A very high antiquity has been claimed for this cycle; but for such antiquity there appears to be no sufficient warrant. The Apis cycle was celebrated by the Egyptian priests with great rejoicings and was made the occasion when a calf, called the Apis, was exhibited in the temple at Memphis, which it was claimed had been foaled upon a cow by lightning from heaven. This fable led to the worship of the calf as a heaven-born creature For slaying the Apis of his time the Egyptian priests blackened the character of Cambyses to all eternity   Herodotus, II, 153; III, 27 Dupuis, following Plutarch and Jablowski, appears to regard the Apis cycle of the Egyptians as a solar period of exactly 25 years, when the sun and moon came into conjunction.   Plutarch, de Isis; Jablowski, IV, 2, Dupuis, II, i, 125   This is not accurate 309 lunations equal 9124d 22h 50m 37 56s , while 25 equable years equal 9125 days; and 25 Julian years equal 9131¼ days See 550 years

360 lunations.—The Moslem cycle, sometimes called the cycle of the Hegira; though it is believed to be much older than the Hegira. According to Suidas, the Egyptians of the Ptolemaic period had a 30-year cycle, called the Mneius, which, although it has been argued was a solar cycle, yet it appears more likely to have been a lunar one of 360 lunations. This cycle has also been traced to Medina and Mecca, A D 383. In A D 630 the Moslem calendar was reformed by Mahomet and its epoch changed to Moharram 1st (July 16th) A D. 622. In Hegira 211, or A D. 826, it was again reformed   Greswell. About the beginning of the tenth century of our æra the Moslem calendar was again reformed by the Caliph Mutadid Albiruni. The Moslem year consists of 12 lunar months of alternately 30 and 29 days, aggregating 354, sometimes 355 days The 360 months' cycle is employed to adjust the civil to the natural months   The calendar is strictly lunar, the 12 months in the aggregate being reckoned at 12 times 29d 12h 44m , which is but 2 84 seconds short of the truth   It takes more than 500 years to restore the commencement of the year to the same solar day of the Julian calendar   meanwhile the dates recede ten to 12 days every year

532 lunations.—The twelfth part (roughly) of the Dionysian, or Paschal, 'cycle of 532 years, q v

669 lunations.—Three Ecliptical cycles of 223 lunations, q v. It was sometimes used in place of the former, as being more exact See 19,756 days

730 lunations.—A luni-solar cycle ascribed by Hellenic tradition to Pythagoras, sometimes to Philolaus of Croton, a disciple of the Pythagorian school It is contended by Greswell that this cycle was employed by Œnopides of Chios, another Pythagorian; and that its epoch was affixed by him to the solar term of the Olympic games, on June 25, B C 544 Cf Ælian in Greswell, K H , I, 440, and F C , I, 557 The number of days reckoned to this cycle was 21,557, or a few hours more than 59 Julian years

940 lunations.—The Calippic cycle, invented by Calippus of Cyzicus, who fixed its epoch in Hecatombeon 1st, then June 28th, B. C. 330, the supposed year of its invention It consists of four Metonic cycles and was employed or offered for the same purpose, for which it was somewhat better suited than the former

1980 lunations.—Twenty octæteric cycles each of 99 lunations, q v. This cycle has been deduced from an inscription (Corp In-scrip Græcorum No. 71) which Boeckh attributes to about B. C. 445 Greswell is of opinion that a cycle of 1979 lunations, equal to 58,441 days, 40 minutes and 12 7659 seconds, was used in Greece, so early as and perhaps before the time of Solon, as the equivalent of 160 Julian years, or 58,440 days, leaving a fraction over of one day and a few minutes and seconds to be intercalated at the termination of the cycle. To bring the 1979 lunations to the result mentioned, he uses a lunation of 29d. 12h 44m. 2 5532s , which, according to Lock-yer, is incorrect. If it be admitted that Greswell's standard of a lunation was actually used in Greece at any time—and this is not im-possible—this fact, coupled with the use of a cycle of 1979 lunations, would carry a knowledge of the Julian year in Greece backward to B C. 592, the year indicated by Greswell, K H , I, 41. But the discovery of a tablet which records a cycle of 1980 lunations does not prove the use of a cycle of 1979 lunations The antiquity of the Julian year in Greece must therefore rest for the present with Œnop-ides, who, however, possessed no means of enacting it into law

3055 lunations.—See 247 years

3760 lunations.—See 304 years

4267 lunations.—By comparing the observations of the Chal-deans with his own, Hipparchus discovered that the shortest period in which the lunar eclipses (this does not include the solar) return in the same order was 126,007 days and one hour. In this period he found 4267 lunations. From this he concluded that the lunar month contained 29d 12h. 44m. 3⅗s. It is not known that the cycle of the lunar eclipses was ever turned to religious or astrological account

6585 months.—The ancient Brahminical and Hindu Divine Year, consisting of 6585 civil months, (each of 36 days,) or 658 solar years, or 36 Ecliptical cycles. Such was the measure of this cycle at the time when the year was divided into ten months. When afterwards the year was divided into 12 months the Divine year continued to consist of 658 solar years, but it was upon the basis shown elsewhere here n. At the beginning of each of these periods of 658 years the Creator was expected to appear on earth incarnated, the miraculous occurrence being called an avatar, or avatara. The dates of these periods are set forth in Chap VI of Avatars. The use of this Indian Divine year by the Assyrians is proved by the intervals between the incarnation of Del-Issus, B. C 2064, Nin-Ies, B C 1406, and Nebo-Nazaru, B. C. 748. Its use by the Greeks is proved by the intervals between the incarnation of Chres, B C. 2064, and Jasius, B C 1406. Its use by the Jews is proved by their Anno Mundi, B C 3670, which is the date of the sixth incarnation of Iesnu, or just one Indian Divine year before the Calijoga. Its use by the Romans, both before and after the Christian æra, is shown by the numerous pretenders to divinity who appeared at or near the beginning of the Indian Divine years, and proclaimed themselves to be the Son of God, predicted in the Sibylline books. Especially is it shown by the public and official recognition and impious worship of Augustus Quirinus Dionysius, as god upon earth, theos, divos, the living god, the sacrosanct, the messiah, the saviour, the promised prince of peace, who it was pretended was born of the Virgin Maia and who at his death ascended bodily to heaven. Finally, its recognition by the Latin Sacred College is evinced by the date assigned by that institution to the Nativity of Jesus, which is just one Indian Divine year from the nativity of the Brahmo-Buddhic incarnation, it is also proved by the papal celebrations of the Ludi sæculares and by numerous other astrological dates and features of the Roman Church

7491 lunations.—Cycle mentioned in Higgins' "Celtic Druids," p. 48, as being equal to 600 Julian years of 365 days, 5 hours, 51 minutes. But as there is no Julian year of this length, which is known to have ever been in use, his computation appears to be artificial and constructed to support theories which had no footing in actual practice.

Moreover, it makes the lunation equal to 29d 6h. 6m. 37.92s , which is not within six hours of the truth He says: "Supposing this cycle were correct to a second, if on the 1st of January at noon, a new moon took place, it would take place again in exactly 600 years, at the same moment of the day and under all the same circumstances." Higgins believed this to be the cycle mentioned by Josephus, Antiq., I, 3; but see remarks herein under 600 years

7520 lunations.—See 608 years.

22,300 lunations.—One hundred Ecliptical cycles each of 223 lunations. Jules Oppert says the Chaldeans and Egyptians used an Ecliptical cycle of 1805 years, or 22,325 lunations, "during which the eclipses return to the same order " This computation exceeds the fact by 25 lunations, the true multiple of the Ecliptical cycle consisting of 22,300 lunations If Oppert is correct, and he is very high authority in such matters, then the Chaldean and Egyptian divine year consisted of 659 instead of 658 years, as with the Hindus, Greeks and Romans Cf Gustave Oppert, op. cit , p. 331

1 year.—Formerly it meant the interval occupied by the sun in performing his apparent course through the ecliptic It now means the time taken by the earth to revolve in its orbit around the sun Bailly very justly remarked that the precise determination of the year was one of the masterpieces of astronomy, and even to-day some thirty-odd different determinations could be adduced, each of which furnished the foundation for theories upon which the learned world has been content at one time or another to rest its astrological and even its astronomical systems. According to Dr Greswell, the word "year" is immediately from the old Saxon *iar* But it is in fact derived more remotely from the Greek *ver*, whence vernal, the spring, or prime-time, printemps, the ver of the annus, or circle (Haliburton, 41) Its still more remote origin is oriental The Syrian month Iyar and the Hebrew month Jar, Iar, or Iyar, both of which anciently commenced either on the vernal equinox, or else, like the Roman Palalia, about the first day of our May, were probably derived from the same word and connected with, the idea that henceforth, from this moment, the reckoning of time commenced Greswell, F C , Introd , 80, fixes, with confidence, the origin of the Hebrew names of the months in B C 524. Nevertheless jar, iar, ear, ver, or year, meaning the prime-time, may have been of far more remoter origin and may even have preceded the computation of time by years, for, as we shall presently see, time was anciently computed by the seasons.

Year of 1, 2, or 3 months.—Diodorus says that at one time the Egyptians had "years' of one month, Censorinus says they had years of two months   Both of these authors may be correct.   They also state that the Egyptians had years of three months, corresponding to the seasons   This may also be correct.   On the other hand, the years of one or two months may be merely deductions made in the attempt to accept, or account, for the immense antiquity in "years" which the Egyptians claimed for their royal dynasties. For example, Diodorus says that if the Egyptian gods reigned from 300 to 1200 years each, this must mean months, for "even at this day, now that there are twelve months to the year, many persons live a hundred years " The years of three months each are undoubtedly matters of fact.   The year, as now understood, is not a very ancient measure of time, simply because it was impossible to compute or mark the year with precision   The earliest form of the calendar was probably lunar, but as the use of a lunar calendar inevitably leads to the ascendancy of hierarchs and the slavery and degradation of the masses, there must have come a period in the history of all peoples when the computation and regulation of time was wrested from the temples and conferred upon the State   That period has never been traced higher than Ies Chrishna, or the first Buddha of India, and it is seriously to be doubted if any valid evidence exists to establish a solar year, whether of 365, 360, or any other number of days, earlier than the date assigned to that mythical, but popularly accepted lawgiver   The earliest form of the solar calendar seems to have been a year of about 90 days   After the mythical period, their years, says Diodorus, writing of the Egyptians, were the same as our seasons, (in Greek, *horas*, of which there were four to the year)   Diogenes says in his Life of Thales, that the astronomer confined his attention largely to the tropics (solstices) and equinoxes, because he was satisfied from the most searching investigations that "nothing else could be determined positively." As Thales was a Phœnician by extraction and a Greek by birth, this must be taken to roughly express the limits of both Eastern and Western experience on the subject at this period, namely, that no better measure of time had yet been discovered than that of reckoning it by seasons   We shall presently see that this practice had led to the civil year of 360 days, divided into eight months each of 45 days; yet the civil year is not an astronomical interval and therefore is not embraced in the remark attributed to Thales.   In addition to the years first above mentioned, Censorinus says that the Arcadians (like the Egyptians) had years of three months; whilst the Carians and Acarnanians had years of six months each   These last probably consisted of two seasons, or horas, the first commencing in our May, the other in our November, but the practice of thus dividing time is comparatively modern and belongs to the second Buddhic period.   Censorinus also asserts that under King Ison (whoever he was) the Egyptians had years of four months each, but if so, then it was when the year was divided into eight months each of 45 days   Cf Dio Sic., I, 26, Censorinus, XIX; Varro, in Lactantius, II, 12; Pliny, VII, 49; Manetho, apud Eusebius, "Chron.;" Philostratus, Diogenes, Plutarch, in "Numa," Solinus; Macrobius, Augustin of Hippo; etc.

Year of 8 months.—The season of 90 days must have proved inconveniently brief for long reckonings and inconveniently long for short reckonings   Still, anxious to avoid the trap of a lunar year, into which it must be inferred they had more than once fallen, the nations of antiquity, instinctively groping their way toward emancipation from Brahminical tyranny, next adopted a solar year of 360 days, divided into eight half-seasons each of 45 days. The evidences which establish this form of calendar are: 1, the number of the gods or kabirim who presided over the months, of which gods there were remotely but eight, (Euterpe, 46); 2, the ancient eight-sign zodiacs, of which one is now in the British Museum; 3, and the days of the solar festivals, which now fall on such odd days of the month as could only have been occasioned by an alteration of the calendar from a year of eight months to one of ten months and, still later, to one of 12 months

Year of 10 months.—The principal evidences which support an ancient year of ten months are as follows: 1, the alteration of the zodiac, which previous to the second Buddhic period, contained but ten signs, 2, the dislocation of the zodiac and the constellations, which formerly agreed, but do so no longer; 3, the numerical names of the Roman months, wh~h plainly indicate that formerly the whole number was ten, 4, the repetition or duplication of two names in each and all the foreign calendars, which indicates that formerly there were but ten months, 5, the present appearance of many ancient stone calendars and planispheres which shows that they have been altered from a decimal to a duodecimal division; 6, the Roman method of dividing the month, which was originally by ides, (eighteen days), and nones (nine days), but was afterwards altered to ides, nones and calends, of unequal lengths and awkward arrangement, 7, the number of the gods, patriarchs, dactyles, laws, prytanes,

dicasts, judices, etc., which anciently was ten and was afterwards
altered to 12, 8, the epochs of the solar festivals, which now fall on
days that from their oddity, for example, Lady Day, St. John's Day
and Christmas, on the 25th and Michelmas on the 29th of a month,
imply an alteration of the calendar from a decimal to a duodecimal
division; 9, the cross-quarter days, which unmistakeably indicate the
alteration; 10, the explicit testimony of several ancient authors; besides many other evidences.

It may here be remarked that the peculiar subdivision of the Roman month seems to have had its precedent in India, some remains
of which subdivision were observed by Sonnerat. The Hindu days
of the moon were called Tides, which suggests Ides. The first of these
was called Predame, the analogue of Pridus. The ninth was called
Naomi, or Navami, the analogue of nones. "Voyage aux Indes,"
I, 240-49   The Indian months began sometimes on the 7th and at
others on the 13th of the Roman months. This resembled the Roman ides, which fell variously on the 15th or else the 13th of the 30-
day month.

Year of 11 months.—See Chap II, herein

Year of 12 lunar months.—Livy ascribes the 12 months' lunar
year of Rome to Numa, while Julianus Græchianus credits it to Tarquin   Cf. Censorinus.

Year of 12 civil months.—The earliest form of this year was
the equable, consisting of 365 days, of which 360 were apportioned
to 12 civil months and five were intercalated annually, or at some less
frequent period   In the latter case the epagomenæ were usually
formed into a supernumerary month every four, five, or six years
The later form of the 12 months' year was the Julian, which consisted and still consists of 365¼ days. It has been argued that before the calendar reform of Cæsar, the odd 5¼ days were intercalated,
both in Greece and Rome, in the same manner as had been the odd
five days of the equable year; but whether this was the fact or not,
Cæsar distributed five of these days among the various months, leaving only one-quarter of a day to be intercalated. This was and is still
done by making every fourth year one day longer than the others

The exact length of the natural tropical year, as determined by
Pope Gregory in 1582, is 365d. 5h 48m 49 7s , or 11m 10.3s shorter
than the Julian year, which therefore in the course of the sixteen
centuries since its establishment in Rome, had advanced the calendar
more than ten days   This difference formed the basis (though not
the pretext) of the calend: "reform" of Gregory, one feature of

which consisted of dropping ten days from the calendar, or counting October 5, 1582, as October 15, 1582. Upon Gregory's basis the difference between the Gregorian and the Julian calendars now (A D. 1900) amounts to 12 days. This is shown in the difference between the Christian date of Western Europe and the Christian date of Greece and Russia, both of which states still employ the calendar of Cæsar. Assuming the Gregorian day to be correct, the real difference exceeds 15 days. But modern astronomical investigation proves that Pope Gregory was wrong and that the true length of the tropical year is 365d. 5h. 48m. 46s. (Newcomb) The difference is too small to require any further adjustment of the calendar

Year of 30 months.—Greswell, F. C , II, 139.

2 years.—The dieteris, a solar cycle for intercalating an extra lunar month It was made the occasion of a festival to Dionysius. Censorinus, XVIII

3 years.—The trieteris, a cycle of three years. Censorinus.

4=year Olympiads. A cycle of four solar years, at the end of which, it is assumed by the Augustan historians, that the epagomenæ were intercalated, and the added interval devoted to rejoicings These took the form of athletic contests, known as the Olympian games. According to their account, Corœbus was successful at the first games of the four-year Olympiads: therefore this series was called by his name, to distinguish it from the earlier series of five-year Olympiads, next to be mentioned. The epoch was Hecatombian 1st, which corresponded with the summer solstice, an agreement that was afterwards destroyed by the degenerate employment of lunar, or lunisolar, calendars The Romans, who would have nothing to do with lunar calendars, reckoned the four-year Olympiads (in their twelve-months year) from July 1st.

5=year Vedic cycle, or cycle employed in the Indian Vedas, or sacred scriptures, which Max Muller regards as the most ancient works extant "The month is lunar, but at the end and in the middle of the quinquennial period an intercalation is admitted by doubling one month. Accordingly, the cycle comprises three common lunar years, besides two others, each of which contains thirteen lunations, altogether five years. The year is divided into six seasons and each month into two half-months. A complete lunation is measured by 30 lunar days, some of which, of course, must in alternate months be sunk, to make the dates agree with the Nychthemera, for which purpose the 62nd day appears to be deducted. Thus the cycle of five years consists of 1860 lunar days or 1830 Nychthemera, subject

to further correction.   The zodiac is divided (in the Vedas) into 27
asterisms or signs, the first of which, both in the Jyotish and the
Vedas, is Crittica, or the Pleiades "   .   .   .   The measure
of a day by 30 hours and that of an hour by 60 minutes are explained in Colebrooke's Essays, I, 106   The cycle of five years
was expanded to one of 60 years.   Brennand, "Hindu Astron.," 60
This was probably after the determination of the period of Jupiter.

   5=year Olympiads   At the remotest period to which Greek history can be traced the epagomenæ were intercalated every five years
and the supernumerary month (of 25 days) was devoted to a festival,
with rejoicings and games, which became the origin of the Ischenia,
Cronia, or Saturnalia.   The establishment of the five-year Olympiads
was attributed by the Greeks to Jasius and the Ten Dactyles, B C.
1406: but, in fact, they cannot be traced back earlier than the Vene-
tian Ischenus, after whom they were originally named and whose æra
was B C. 1219   Furgault, 199, attributes the Greek pentæteris to
Bacchus.   In B. C. 884, according to Eratosthenes, or B C 828,
according to Callimachus, this festival, which had fallen into neglect,
was revived by King Iphitus, in honor of Jupiter, that newly-dis-
covered god, for whom the Greeks had forsaken their faithful, but
now unfashionable, Ischenus, whose later name of Issus, Nissus, or
Dionysius is, however, still firmly attached to the rivers and towns
of Greece and of the Greek colonies in Asia Minor.   The festival
was held at Pisa, on the banks of the Alpheus, near the great temple
of Ischenus, afterwards dedicated to Jupiter at Olympia, and was
observed down to the period of Augustus.   The Scythians, or Goths,
more faithful to their ancient worship than the Greeks, observed the
quinquennial Olympiads down to the last days of Augustus.   "In
Scythia nobis quinquennis Olympias acta est"   Ovid's Pontine Epistles, IV, 6.   In Rome the quinquennial Olympian festivals were practically abolished by Augustus, who deprived them of their sacred
character and gave them a new name.   They lingered until abolished by Theodosius, A D 394   In modern times the Olympian
games, consisting of mere athletic contests, having no connection
with the calendar, nor with astrology, nor religion, were revived by
Mr. Zappas, A D 1858, and again by the efforts of some other
wealthy Greek, in A D 1896, on which last occasion they were celebrated in the restored stadium of Athens.

   5=year lustrum   A cycle of five solar years, the end of which
was celebrated by the Romans with expiatory sacrifices   There can
be little   t the lustrum w s similar to and had its origin in

the five-year Olympiads. It is said to have been instituted in Rome B. C. 472. Censorinus XVIII ascribes its origin to Servius Tullius (B. C. 578). The lustra were last celebrated A. D. 74.

8 years.—The octæteris of 99 lunations, or, approximately, eight Julian years. The discovery of this cycle is attributed by Censorinus, XVIII, either to Cleostratus of Tenidos (B. C. 536), or else to Eudoxus of Cnidus (fourth Century B. C.) See 99 lunations. The Dalmatæ of the Adriatic, probably connected with the Veneti, redivided their lands every eighth year. Strabo, VII, v, 5.

11 years, plus. Cycle of the Sun Spots as determined by Schwabe, of Dessau, from observations made during the period A. D. 1826-72, "rather more than 11 years." Am. Cyc. Brit., art. "Astronomy."

12 years.—The Cycle of Jupiter, or Jove, and the orbital period of that planet. This cycle was probably known in India so early as the 12th Century B. C. and in Chaldea not long afterwards. (See Chapter V, herein). From Chaldea the discovery made its way to Egypt and Greece, in both of which countries it exercised an important influence upon astrological and religious belief. The Jovian cult was probably introduced into Greece before the time of Iphitus, because, as shown above, he adapted the five-year Ischenia (Olympiads) to its ceremonial; yet the Jovian cult, under another name, *e. g.*, the Isthenian, Pelopian, or Cronian, may have preceded a knowledge of the Jovian cycle. Censorinus calls it "the Chaldean or Great year"; Pausanias, "the Great Year." The more exact period of Jupiter's orbit is 12 years and five days. Scaliger shows that "from the earliest times" the 12-year cycle was common to the Taters (Mongols, Mantchus and Igurians), the Tibetans, Chinese, Siamese and Japanese. Plutarch says of the 60-year cycle, "It is the original cycle known to all astronomers," meaning very ancient.

15 years.—Cycle of the Indiction. A cycle of 15 solar years, equal to three lustra, employed by the Romans for levying taxes and counting the population. According to Gregory VII., (A.D. 1073-80) and as set forth in L'art de Verifier les Dates and in the various chronological works and Dictionaries of Dates based upon it, the Indictions commenced with the æra of Constantine the Great, January 1, A. D. 313; but they really had a much more ancient origin. They are mentioned by Malala and the Paschal Chronicon as of B. C. 45 and by Pliny the Younger in the reign of Trajan: Nec novis indictionibus pressi ad tributa deficiant. Both Scaliger and the Abbé Lenglet d Fresnoy, unwilling to mention the true date of the Roman

Indictions, have attributed them to a slightly older date than they merit, namely, the Cæsarian æra of Antioch, B. C 48   Picot, I, 151 The history of this cycle is preserved in the New Testament and the Monumentum Ancyranum.   It was originally established B C. 45, or 30 and permanently confirmed by Augustus after the pacification of Syria and before the death of Herod   This was Anno Augusto 1, or B C 15   Its epoch for the Oriental provinces was September 1st; for the Occident, September 24th   The Hebrew lunar calendar has a cycle of 15 years, during which the days of the septuary week return to the same days of the same month

16 years.—Geminus mentions an intercalary cycle of 16 and and another one of 160 years, to correct the departure from the moon in the octæteric period.   Dodwell, de Cyc , p 173, cited by Lewis, p. 119.

18 years.   (Approx)—The Ecliptical cycle of 223 lunations

19 years.   (Approx)—Metonic cycle of 235 lunations.

20 years.—Cycle of the Chibchas   See A D 1 in Ch VII

24 years.—Cycle mentioned in Livy, I, 19   Macrobius, Sat I, 13, explains it by supposing that Numa was aware of the Julian year and used a triple octæteris, i e , a cycle of 297 months, or, approximately, 24 Julian years, to adjust his calendar   All this is possible, but it ill agrees with the preposterous 304-day year which the chronologists have attributed to the Roman lawgiver.

25 years.—Eikosipentæteris, or Apis cycle, strictly 24 years and 359 days, or 309 lunations, q. v.   Sapi is the Hindu word for a cow, from which Haliburton infers that Apis and Serapis are drawn "Festival of the Dead," p. 83   Herodotus, in Clio 7, evidently used this period for a generation   For " 505 " of his corrupt text, read 550, which, being divided by 22, gives 25 years

28 years.—Dominical cycle   If it were not for leap-years, every seventh year would bring the New Year day to the same day of the septuary week   In consequence of leap year, it requires 28 years to effect this return   Hales, I, 59   It cannot be older than tempo Nebo-Nazaru, when the septuary week was established in the Occident, and it may not be older than than the Augustan period, when names were first given to such days by the Romans.

30 years.—Druidical cycle (Pliny, N H , XVI, 95); probably derived from the Jovian, the sexagesimal, etc   The same period was reckoned as a generation, an average reign, and "an Age," both by the Greeks and the Northern nations. Dio. Sic , book I, p. 65 ; Greswell, F C., Intro., 21; Pliny, II, 6, and Vettius Valens, lib III, p

90; the last named writers also call it the period of Saturn, which, however, is in fact, less than 29½ years. A 30-year cycle is mentioned in the Rosetta stone A 30-year cycle also belongs to the religion of Ies Chrishna See "Story of the Gods," IV, 4 Also to that of Mahomet. See A. D 622

33 years.—Lesser Manvantara cycle The usual lifetime or reign of astrological incarnations, or demi-gods, founded on the astronomical fact that it requires 33 years to carry the beginning of the lunar year through all the seasons to the same solar point and conjunction again See Tatius under B C 769, Pisistratus, B C 527; Alexander the Great, B C 332; and Theodoric, A D 493

52 years.—Intercalary cycle of the Aztecs, who, every 52 years, added sometimes 12, sometimes 13, days to the equable year, to bring it to the Julian See A D 1090

54 years.—Three Ecliptical cycles, aggregating 669 lunations, equal to, approximately, 54 years and one month This cycle was used by the Chaldeans.

59 years.—The cycle of 730 lunations, q v If 29½ days are reckoned to a lunation, 730 lunations would make 21,535 days, which is exactly equal to 59 equable years. These rude equivalents were employed by Philolaus the Pythagorian, who intercalated 21 months into this cycle, to adjust the equable and lunar years Censorinus, XVIII. Greswell ascribes this cycle to Œnopides See K.H , IV, 639 *n*, and F. C , I, 577, 608 Lewis says it is defective and probably corrupt

60 years.—Sexagesimal solar or sidereal cycle, a multiple of the Jovian. The Jovian cycle appears to have been used in the Orient as early at least as the 12th century B. C , but in Greece not earlier than the tenth century B C See Chapter V on the Jovian cycle

72 years.—A "taurus " The period of 72 years measured the manvatara of Manu It is the interval during which the year of the Pleiades gains one day on the tropical year. Haliburton, " Festival of the Dead," p 99 On p 59 of the same work he makes the Pleiades gain one day in 71 years and elsewhere one day in 71 3-7 years. This uncertainty hardly justifies him in applying the "taurus," as he does, to "the 72 sons of Noah "

82 years.—Cycle of Democritus of Abdera, into which he intercalated 28 months Censorinus, XVIII. The æra of Democritus was B. C. 460-355, for he lived to the extreme age of 105 years The cycle of Democritus seems to have been a lunar cycle of 1050 lunations, having for its equivalent a Julian solar cycle of about 82 years

As shown by Sir George Cornewall Lewis, the cycle is faulty; nevertheless it corroborates a knowledge of the Julian year at this early period

84 years.—The Jewish paschal cycle of 1039 lunations, was the equivalent of (approximately) 84 Julian years It consisted of four Metonic and one octæteric cycle Greswell, F C , Intro , 191 , I, 68. This cycle was invented by the Jews. Brady I, 294 It was invented by the Jews before the Christian æra, in order to determine the civil solar date of the Passover festival in a lunar calendar Lyons, op. cit , p 16 It was invented by the Jews during the Roman imperial age. Appleton's Cyc , art. ''Chronology ''

90 years.—Graharparivritti cycles of sourthern India, the first one of which was fixed in the 3078th year of the Calijoga, or B. C. 24 The Pandits' ''Chronology.'' This appears to be a variation of the Jovian and sexagesimal cycles The Pandits do not state whether the Graharparivritti cycles were sidereal or solar.

95 years.—Augustan paschal cycle, consisting of five Metonic cycles, or 1175 lunations, the original epoch of which was the Ascension Day of Divus Augustus Quirinus Dionysius, August 29th. This cycle has been employed to mark the return and week-day of Easter, by means of the Dominical letter in the series A to G. It is supposed to be mentioned in the Chronicle of Bede as the ''laterculus septizonii,'' or septizodii The date of Bede's Chronicle is commonly fixed in A D. 731, but, as shown by Wright and others, no certain reliance can be placed upon this date as a guide to the age of the matters mentioned in the Chronicle Rev Dr Greswell has proved that there is no historical warrant for attributing this cycle to Cyril, the '' Christian patriarch of Alexandria,'' in the fifth century, nor for attributing it to the particular period A. D. 437-52, as is done by Rev. Dr Hales. Greswell has also proved that the original epoch of this cycle was August 29th It is evidently an Augustan paschal cycle, vamped by the Latin church at some period later than the eighth century, by removing its epoch to Easter and attributing its invention to an imaginary official

108 years.—A generation, according to some ancient authors Nisard's Censorinus, *note* to chap XVII See 540 years, herein

110 years.—The Sæcular cycle, celebrated in Rome by the Ludi sæculares, or Sæcular games, every 110 years They are alluded to by Horace, Virgil, Suetonius, Pliny and numerous other Roman authors. Herodian, lib , II, p. 405, says that they were mentioned in the Sibylls Dupuis, II, ii, 47, thinks they were of Bacchanalian (really Buddhic) origin. These games celebrated one-sixth of the Divine year (658 common years) of the Romans and Etruscans. Analogy suggests—though we have no record of the fact—that the $2\frac{2}{3}$ months in excess of one-sixth of the Divine year, measured by this cycle, were anciently sunk from the calendar every 110 years: a suggestion that may throw some light on the 80 days deficiency which Cæsar found in the calendar of Sylla and the two years of difference between Piso's æra of Romulus and the Italiote æra of Procas For a similar practice see cycle of 116 years The proper periods of the Sæcular games were A U 110, 220, 330, 440, 550, 660, 770, etc , and until the time of Augustus they were usually celebrated in those years. But that personage, in order to prove that he was the Messiah and Prince of Peace fortold in the Sibylls in connection with the sixth Ludi sæculares, sank 78 years from the Roman calendar and recelebrated the sixth as the seventh Ludi in A U 738, when he was apotheosised and proclaimed in Rome as the Son of God, or Mediator, inter dies et homines The sunken period of 78 years was, many centuries later, reduced by the Christian church to 63 years, possibly by introducing the following superfluous years in the calendar, as indicated by the chronology of Nicephorus in the reign of Tiberius, 1; Nero, 1, Pertinax, 1; Diocletian, 2; Constantine II., 1; Valens, 2; Theodosius, 1, Arcadius, 1; Leo, 1; Justin, II, 4; total 15. The new dates were then probably introduced into all the ancient works that fell into the hands of the Sacred College.

116 years.—Intercalary cycle of the Southern Indian Kollam æra, upon whose return 30 days are intercalated into a Julian Calendar. See A D, 825, Southern India.

120 years.—If instead of intercalating, as we now do, one day every fourth year, to bring the equable to the Julian year, we reserved these odd days until the 120th year and then added a civil month of 30 days to the Calendar, the final result would be the same. This sort of intercalation, marked by a great festival, is asserted by Prof Flinders Petrie to have been practised in Egypt at a remote period The festival is quite possible, but in assuming that it marked the antiquity of such an intercalation, that eminent Egyptologist is evidently mistaken. He quotes with approval Prof Mahler of Vienna, who believed that he found the evidences of such an intercalation in an inscription of "Thotmes III ," whom he dates in "1503 to 1449 B C." It is plain that no festival which celebrated an equation of equable and Julian years could have been celebrated before the Julian year was known. It was certainly unknown to Herodotus, who studied in Egypt; and there is as yet no evidence which establishes a knowledge of it anywhere previous to the period of the Second Buddha Albiruni, p. 12, says that the Persians of his time, about A D 1000, intercalated a month every 120 years Hyde ascribes this cycle to Giemshid, but a Julian year of such antiquity is doubtful. As a Persian discovery it may have been ancient enough to have been carried into Egypt when that country was conquered by Cambyses But this is mere conjecture. It is the same with the thirty-day civil month, which the use of the 120-year cycle and the observance of the festival, implies There is no evidence of its use before the period of the Second Buddha On the contrary, the archaeological and literary evidences, prove the common use of a year of ten months each of 36 days before that period. and Egypt was no exception to this rule As to the credibility of Egyptian dates, the Rev Dr Greswell, who examined them with great care, long since pronounced a verdict which every fresh archaeological discovery has only tended to confirm they are utterly false and unreliable In the effort to exaggerate their own antiquity and to conceal their racial origin, the Egyptians invented hundreds of imaginary gods and kings, whose fabulous exploits they commemorated in epigraphs of a long subsequent age. They were the worthy forerunners of the classical mythologists and the medieval monks. Prof. Petrie's remarks appeared in the London Times of October 10, 1897. Prof Lauth says that the Egyptian cycle of 120 years was called Hanti, a word that suggests duality He is therefore of opinion that this cycle was merely a double period of 60 years. Jules Oppert evidently regards it as aggregating 24 lustra See 432,000 years, in which this combination appears The reason for doubling the sossos or Jovian cycle of 60 years is suggested under B C. 703, Persia, in Chap VII hereof It was to harmonise the ten and 12 months' years It had previously been employed for this purpose in China Prof Lauth's statement is from Gustav Oppert, op cit. p 333

160 years.—It is suggested by Geminus, Dodwell, Lewis, and the Encyc Brit Art " Calendar" that a cycle of this length was proposed by the Greek astronomers of the fifth or sixth century B C , for the purpose of synchronizing the Solonic lunar year of $6 \times 30 + 6 \times 29 = 354$ days with the Julian year of $365\frac{1}{4}$ days The octaeteris actually employed consisted of $354 \times 8 + 3 \times 30 = 2922$ days, which is 1 528 days, or about 36 hours short of 99 lunations In 160 years, an interval twenty times the length of the octaeteris, this would amount to about 30 days, or one month, which it is further suggested was proposed to be omitted from the calendar   The presumption that the exact Julian year was known at this early period is explicitly contradicted by the testimony of Censorinus and it cannot be admitted without positive proof   The nearest approach to it was the year of Œnopides. See 365¼ days, 1980 lunations and 16 years.

200 years.—Ducenarium, or "luni-solar medieval cycle" of Armenia.   Greswell, F C , I, 561

247 years. (Approx)—Thirteen Metonic cycles   See 3055 lunations

304 years. (Approx)—Sixteen Metonic cycles.   See 3760 lunations   Censorinus, XVIII, attributes this cycle to Hipparchus, who intercalated in it 112 months and called it the Great Year.   See 608-year cycle.   Dr. Greswell believes that this cycle (which implies a division of the year into 12 civil months averaging 30 days each, with five intercalaries) can be traced to India B C 946, but this is very doubtful.   F C , I, 68 *n*   Its attribution by Censorinus to Hipparchus is far more likely to be correct

312 years.—Aztec cycle, composed of six luni-solar cycles of 52 years.   It is also connected with the luni-solar cycle of 200 years. Greswell, F C , I, 561

360 years.—The Surya Siddhanta, I, 14, says that six times 60 sidereal years make a "divine" year.   This interval was evidently used as a means of harmonising the mean sidereal day of 23h 56m (approx.) and the mean solar day of 24h , the difference being 4m (approx)   In six years (not 60 years, as stated by Greswell,) the difference would be 24m and in 360 years, 24 hours, or one day   It does not appear to have been connected (as Greswell supposes) with the cycle of the eclipses.

418 years.—Cycle used by Ptolemy   It consisted of five and a-half Calippic cycles, each of (approx) 76 years   Albiruni

500 years.—Chinese "phen," corrupted by the Greeks to "phenix," or the so-called Phœnix cycle and supposed by Greswell to have consisted of exactly 500 years; but this period is as fanciful as the tale of the oft reincarnated phœnix bird, which is attached to the cycle itself   The various MSS. of Pliny relating to this cycle (N H.X, 2,) read 540, 511 and 560 years.   Syncellus and Suidas say 654 years. Tacitus gives one of the phœnix periods at 1461 years, which really is the Sothic cycle, q v   Solinus says the phœnix cycle is not 540 but 12,954 years, which is Cicero's Great Year and is really one-half of the Precessional Year   The phen, or phenix period was probably the Oriental manvantara, or one-tenth of the Earth's life, which the Egyptians, when their year was altered from ten to 12 months, reduced to one-twelfth, thus 6586—12=550 years, (approx.) the probable Egyptian phenix cycle   See cycle of 550 years, below.   In any case, it is astrological and not astronomical

504 years.—Cycle of Hipparchus   Dupuis, III, 11, 339

509 years.—Divine year of Manilius cited in Pliny, N H , X, 11, 1. This is one-twelfth of 6108 years, q v

511 years.—See 500 years   See also the pretended Hyksos period in chap X.

532 years.—The Dionysian cycle, or Divine year of the Dionysians, at the end of which Dionysius would return to earth and inaugurate a new æra of peace and happiness to mankind   As this cycle was afterwards adopted by the church of Rome, called the Paschal cycle and employed to calculate the return of the moon, from which Easter is dated, its history may repay some research

I   The Dionysian cycle consists of 532 equable years and 140 days over, or of 532 Julian years and seven days over; or of 194,320 days; or of 28 Metonic cycles; or of 6580 lunar revolutions; or of 28 by 19, the multiplication of a solar and lunar cycle of years.

II   It is a compound of the Metonic and solar cycles, so that it not only gives the moon on the day of the 30-day month; it also gives the day of the septuary week of such moon.

III. It was not used by the Greeks in their achme   They had no septuary week   It was not used by the Romans of the republic, nor by the Romans of the empire, until after the revival of the Dionysian cult

IV   It is pretended by the church of Rome and repeated by Blair and other chronologists that this cycle was employed by Victorius, a Christian monk, in A D. 463.   It is not disputed that Victorius employed it; but no valid evidence has been offered to prove that he was a Christian and not a Dionysian monk.

V. It is pretended by the church of Rome that this cycle was employed by Dionysius Exiguus, a Scythian Christian monk, in A. D 524, to calculate the nativity of Christ   To this pretension it is to be objected that Dionysius Exiguus, as a Christian monk, in or about A D. 524, is unknown to history; and that the chronological canon which goes by his name really measures a Dionysian Divine year from the Egyptian Apotheosis of Augustus B. C 8,—who was worshipped as the incarnation of Dionysius—to the year imputed to Dionysius Exiguus, namely, A. D. 524; a circumstance that throws suspicion on its Roman and rather betrays its Alexandrian origin.   Indeed some chronologists call it the Alexandrian cycle   An engraving of Augustus as Dionysius, taken from an antique statue, will be found in Duruy's History of Rome   Besides this one, there are innumerable ancient monuments in bronze and marble which attest the long and widespread existence of the Augustan cult.

VI   The Dionysian cycle, or divine year, is mentioned by Albiruni, a Moslem writer, A D 973-1048, who says that "the Jews had a cycle of 532 years, called the Major Cycle, consisting of 6580 months " (Albiruni, 4to ed , 1879, p 63)   This is unquestionably the same cycle.   It is the degenerate descendant of the Buddhic divine year of 552 years.   This Buddhic interval was a solar divine year; whilst its progeny was lunar

VII   The fact that the Dionysian divine year contains almost the same number of lunar months, (6580), as the Hindu divine year contains of astrological months, (6585⅔), may be merely a coincidence, yet such coincidence could hardly have been without its influence in persuading the Dionysians to accept this cycle as their divine year in place of the Oriental one

VIII.   The first valid mention of the Dionysian divine year as a Christian paschal cycle occurs in Argyrus, who wrote A D 1372, but there is reason to believe that its adoption as such is really due to Pope Gregory VII , A. D 1080, in whose pontificate had occurred the reform of the Persian calendar by Omar Kayyam, A. D 1079   It is also to be noticed that within a year or two of this date, the Armenians changed their divine year from 552 to 532 years, that is to say, from the ancient or Buddhic-Dionysian to the Augusto-Dionysian standard   This last mentioned change may be attributed to the influence of Rome

IX.   Dr Greswell reluctantly admits that the canon imputed to Theophilus of Alexandria was "set back purposely " from A. D 385 to A D 380, and that the canon of Dionysius Exiguus "was set back a paschal period of 532 years, from A D 524 to B C. 9 " (Read B. C 8.)   If it was really "set back " it must have been set back from the end of, at least, the second Augusto-Dionysian divine year, A D 1056; because, merely to set it back from the end of the first one, A. D 524, was in fact not to set it back at all.   Dr. Greswell might have admitted much more and still have kept safely within the lines of historical candor and ecclesiastical prudence

540 years.—See 500 years and 2700 years; also 108 years

550 years.—Twenty-two Apis cycles each of 25 years. See Herod.,

Clio, 7, and read 550 for 505; the former being evidently what was meant by the historian

552 years.—Buddhic divine year   In Armenia, the first of these cycles began B C 552, the second A D 0, or A. D 1 (Greswell says A D 2) and the third one A. D 552, while the fourth one should have begun A D 1104   But it appears that two or three years after the reform of the Persian calendar by Omar Kayyam, A D. 1079, the Armenians prefered to compute time by Divine years of 532, instead of 552 years, thus following the example set them by the Jews, namely, of obliterating, by means of a lunar reckoning, the venerable but now despised memorials of Buddha   Cf Greswell, F C , Intro , 17

555 years.—One-tenth of the cycle of Aretes   See 5552 years
560 years.—See 550 years

600 years.—There is no known cycle of 600 years, either astronomical or astrological; yet this measure of time was often used by ancient writers, for example, Herodotus, Josephus, Censorinus, and others   Bunsen offers an explanation of this period as used by Josephus, but the explanation is far from satisfactory. See "Egypt's place in History," III, 387, 406   It appears rather to be a round statement of the Divine year, whether the latter consisted of 666, 658, 656, 608, 552, 550, or 532 years, which it did at various times and places   The dominant measures of the Divine year were the Brahminical of 658 common years, the Buddhic of 552 years and the later Buddhic, or Dionysian, of 532 years; the others were only of local or transient acceptance   The custom of employing the phrase "600 years" for the Divine year may have arisen from the Chaldean metrological system, which was based on the fifth multiple of the period of Jupiter, thus, $12 \times 5 = 60 \times 10 = 600$ These numbers appear upon our clepsydras, sun-dials and clocks, the origin of all of which was Chaldean   Haliburton, "Festival of the Dead," p 99, says that "the cycle of 600 years was the great lunar cycle or cycle of the Bull"; and he instances its employment in the 600 years of Noah, when the flood of waters was on the earth   There is hardly sufficient warrant either for the assertion or the theory. Consult note to Bohn's Pliny II, 9 (12), and see 7491 lunations herein

608 years. (Approx)—Thirty-two Metonic cycles, the double of the 304-year cycle   The cycle of 608 years (really 7520 lunations) was misleadingly called by Hipparchus the Great Year, and mistaken by Geodfrey Higgins for the Divine Year. The undue sanctity which the Greek astronomer attributed to this cycle was derived from the

same source as the sanctity of the Metonic or Golden Cycle: both
of these cycles served the objects, by conserving and arranging the
lunar festivals, of the temples. But in fact the 608-year cycle had
nothing whatever to do with the Divine year, or with the Messiah;
the years of whose reincarnation, sojourn upon earth, etc , though
deduced from the lunar Cycle of the Eclipses, were invariably solar,
and not lunar, nor luni-solar years   The priests of antiquity used
to amuse themselves and mystify the vulgar by employing the numerical elements of this cycle (the Greeks expressed their numbers
in letters) with which to spell significant names   As no limits were
set to the subdivision of the whole sum, it resulted that in fact almost
any names could be spelled from it   Numerous examples occur in
Higgins' "Anacalypsis" and Eadie's " Biblical Encyclopedia " For a
similar practice in more modern times see the 666-year cycle herein

630 years.—Divine year of the Etruscans, as shown by the interval of 105 years between the first four Ludi Sæculares known to Roman history. See chapter III herein

640 years.—Phenix period, or Divine year, supposed by Greswell
to have been established B C. 798. Greswell K H , VI, 644

649 years.—Divine year of the Second Adventists   If the Cycle
of the Eclipses be multiplied by 36, the quotient is 649 solar years
and a fraction, thus $6585\frac{1}{3} \times 36 = 237{,}072$ days $\div 365$, (or $365\frac{1}{4}$
days) $= 649$ years and a fraction   This is the Divine year of the
modern Christian sect called Second Adventists. It is as fanciful as
any of the rest. It ignores the astrological construction of the ancient Divine year and substitutes for it a basis which is partly astronomical; when, in fact, astronomy knows nothing of Divine years.
It arbitrarily multiplies the Eclipse cycle by 36; whereas it might with
as good reason be multiplied by 72, or any other number   By these
means the Second Adventists predicted with confidence the end of
the " Gentile times" which was to usher the Second coming of Christ
on Easter Day, April 10th, 1898   .

654 years.—The Phenix cycle of Syncellus and Suidas   See 500
years.

656 years.—Panionic cycle, or Divine year of the Ionians. These
years fell in B. C. 1248, and 592 and in A. D 36   Greswell, K. H
III, 373.

658 years.—Divine year of India, Persia, Chaldea, Egypt, Greece
and Rome. This year is based on the Cycle of the Eclipses, which consists of 223 lunations, or $6585\frac{2}{3}$ days. Upon this astronomical fact
was built the astrological fancy that the period of Days must be com-

plemented by one of Months and by another one of Years.   Hence
a system of 6585⅔ days called "The Period"; of 6585⅔ months,
(ten to the year, or 658 solar years), called the manvantara, or else
the Divine, or Messianic year; and of 6585⅔ years, which was regarded as the total Lifetime of the Earth, or of Mankind, when the
World was to come to an End   Although the mischievous zeal of the
Hindu priests has furnished us with a series of avatars and manvan-
taras running back to the 68th Century B. C , there is no reliable
proof that the Divine year, or any Divine year, was used before the
fifteenth century B C in India, (æra of Chrishna,) or before the 12th
century B C in the Greek states   All incarnations, or Divine years,
relating to those countries before these dates, and many perhaps of
later dates, are apparently of long subsequent invention

662 years.—A Divine year which is gained by omitting the last
figure from 12 Armenian cycles of 552 years   It was used for a time
in Etruria.   See Chapter III

665 years.—A Divine year; origin, medieval.   See 9977 years

666 years.—The Apocalyptic cycle, so called from its mention
in the 13th chapter of Revelations   This is apparently an Egypto-
Buddhic, or Osirian, form of the Divine year, employed in Egypt
and in the Egyptian dependency of Syria   It was also used for a
brief period in Etruria   See chapter III   This cycle results from
dividing the Earth's Life of 240 million years by the ancient Hindu
cycle of the Solar Precession, which was 36,000 years   The puerile
practice of spelling names from any Greek letters which, when added
together, are sufficient to compose the whole number 666, is alluded
to in Eadie's "Biblical Encyclopedia," art "Numbers" It appears
that the names of Nero, Mahomet, Martin Luther, Napoleon Buonaparte, and other "enemies" of the Church, have thus been spelled
out

1000 years.—The Hindus of Southern India divide the Kollam
age (Parasurama) into cycles of 1000 years, or millenials   As the
Kollam reckoning began in Calijoga 1927, equal to B. C 1176, the
present, or current, period falls into the fourth millenial cycle   Thus:
the First extends from B. C. 1176 to B C. 176; the Second, B. C 176
to A. D 825; the Third, A D. 825 to A D. 1825, the Fourth, A. D.
1825 to A. D 2825   For a different reckoning of these millenials see
B. C. 4825   For Abyssinian millenium, or Year of Grace, see A. D.
1348 and Greswell, F. C., Intro. 16.

1440 years.—Persian cycle, probably sidereal   Dupuis, III,
ii, 339.

1460 years.—The Sothic, or Canicular, cycle of Egypt. It was a sidereal cycle, which was reckoned from the rising of the dog-star at Heliopolis and was based upon the difference between the sidereal and tropical years, which in the interval of this cycle amounts to exactly one year· in other words, 1460 sidereal years equal 1461 tropical. The same difference exists between the Julian and equable years; hence 1460 Julian equal 1461 equable. An intercalation of one year at the end of the Sothic cycle restored the tropical to the sidereal and the equable to the Julian reckoning The period when this cycle was first employed could hardly have been earlier than the employment of a Julian calendar in Egypt; and this, as shown under "365 ¼ days," was about B C 547, the period of the second Hermes (Buddha). According to Censorinus, this cycle of 1460 years was mentioned by Aristotle. It is also mentioned by Horapollo, (Ptolemaic period), Dion Cassius, Tacitus and Theon of Alexandria. The last-mentioned authority states that the Sothiacal cycle of Egypt began in the reign of Menephres, 1605 years before the termination of the Æra Augusti Upon the assumption that at the conclusion of the Æra Augusti the latter was immediately followed by the Æra Diocletiano, A. D. 284, then the Æra Augusti ended with A D. 283, and 1605 years before this was B. C. 1322, which therefore was the epoch of the Sothiacal cycle and the regnal year of Menephres But the calculation is open to a question of several years concerning the beginning and ending (if indeed there was properly any ending,) of the Æra Augusti· the MSS of Theon are somewhat corrupt; the period of the author is not certain; and an Egyptian king called Menephres is unknown either to history or archæology. The Sothiacal period of Theon begins with the æra of Ies Chrishna (see B. C. 1315); and as both the epoch of the cycle, Thoth 1st, the Seven Stars of the Pleiades and the ceremonies observed at the rising of Sothis, were connected with the worship of Iesiris, the period of Theon is probably nothing more than an astrological deduction connected with the pretended æra of the first Buddha, Osiris, or Hermes. However, the cycle itself is astronomical. Though it may be older in Egypt than the worship of Isis and Osiris, we have no proof of the fact Haliburton connects the sidereal year with the worship of Osiris and makes the dates of the festivals such that they tally with our Cross Quarter days. The heliacal rising of the Pleiades in Egypt took place about 30 or 40 days after the summer solstice, which would tally with Lammas; the Festival of the Dead occurred at Martinmas, and the feast of Lanthorns at Candlemas

1800 years.—See 21,600 years

2300 years.—Du Chesaux, a French biblical chronologist and Second Adventist of the last century, constructed a cycle of 2300 solar years from the "2300 days" of Daniel, VIII, 14 Du Chesaux's cycle of years is composed of 122 Metonic, (lunar,) cycles and its equivalent in years is therefore inexact, because no whole number of lunar cycles will make any whole number of solar years, and if the 2300 years be not exactly 2300 years, then there is no warrant for translating Daniel's "days" into "years" The author of this piece of patchwork invented two other "cycles" of similar construction and thus complacently alluded to his own handiwork: "Who can have taught their author (here he means Daniel) the marvellous relation 'between the periods he employed and the movements of the heavenly bodies? . . . Is it possible, considering all these points, to fail to recognise in the Author of these ancient books, the Creator of the heavens and the earth and of the sea and of the things which to them belong?" Chambers, "Astron," 1890, II, 463

2484 years.—Lifetime of the World Aristarchus, in Censorinus, XVIII

2520 years.—An astrological result attained by multiplying the number of eclipses in an Ecliptical cycle by the number of days in an ancient month, thus $70 \times 36 = 2520$ It is not known to what use, if any, this "cycle" was put

2700 years.—Hindu Cycle of the Lokkal, mentioned in the Puranas and by Vridda Garga, an astronomer, whose æra is placed at the period of the Mahabharata wars The Lokkal is sometimes called the Line of the Rishis Rishi means an inspired writer (of the Vedas) The term Seven Rishis was also applied to the seven stars of Ursa Major, of which Marisha (Arcturus) is the leader The Lokkal is a period of 2700 years, during which Ursa Major is supposed in the Puranas to make the revolution of the ecliptic, which the Hindus divide into 27 lunar mansions, or asterisms, thus giving 100 degrees of movement to each mansion This cycle of 2700 years is mentioned in the Brahma Siddhanta of Sacalya, but not in the Surya Siddhanta. The supposed rate of motion was rejected by Nrisinha, doubted by Bhascara and avoided by Muniswara in his Siddhanta Sarvabauma Camalacara, while admitting that the Puranas affirmed the cycle and the rate of motion, seems piously doubtful about endorsing it On the other hand, Lalla and Varaha Mihira affirm its correctness Brennand, "Hindu Astron.," thinks that the 100 years solstice to an asterism is a mistake, for 1000 years, made in copying the ancient scriptures; the actual movement as determined by later investigation, being .960 years to the asterism, or 25,920 years to the Precession of the Equinoxes. He thinks that the Line of the Rishis, at the rate of 27,000 years to the Precession, was fixed so early as 1590 B C and that the correct period of the Precession (25,920 years) was known so early as the tenth century B C He goes on to say that "Although the epoch 3102 B C. was probably arrived at by calculation backward, yet the epoch 1590 B C (the Line of the Rishis, commencing with the first of Magha) was one fixed by observation of the then astronomers and always referred to subsequently as the 'Line of the Rishis' then established " Op cit , 82 According to Gen. Cunningham, the epochs of the Lokkals are fixed in B C 6777, 4077, 1377, A D. 1323, etc , while Varaha Mihira and the later astronomers fix them in B C. 6077, ?377, 677, A D 2023, etc Consult 21,600 years, farther on.

3000 years.—Imaginary cycle of the metempsychosis, as mentioned by the Egyptian priests to Herodotus See Euterpe, 123 This cycle is also mentioned by Servius, a Latin grammarian of the fourth century of our æra

3600 years.—An astrological cycle mentioned by Dupuis and Greswell, the last of whom blunders in connecting it with the ecliptical cycle It is evidently the tenth power of the 360-year cycle mentioned in the Surya Siddhanta

5552 years.—An astrological cycle mentioned by Aretes of Dyrrachium, cited in Censorinus, XVIII.

6000 years.—Lifetime of the world, according to the ancient Hindu astrologers This period has been variously fixed at 6000, 6080, 6108 (Manilius), 6130, 6500, 6585⅔, 6586, 6600 and 6666 years, in each case the determination being based on the cycle of the moon's node as computed at various times. The notion was that the earth bore to the sun the same relation that the moon bore to the earth; and as the moon completed its nodical cycle in so many days, so the earth ran its course in the same number of years During this lifetime the earth would be regenerated ten times by the incarnations of the Creator, as Vishnu or Ies Chrishna.

6585 2-3 years.—An astrological cycle consisting of ten Divine years, which, according to an almost universal belief among ancient nations, marked the Lifetime of the World. when it would come to an end and mankind would be summoned to Judgment before the Creator See 6585 days, 6585 months, etc. The non-fulfillment of this prediction may have given rise to the expression in the liturgy of "world without end " The ten incarnations of Vishnu, the ten ages of Etruria, etc , were connected with this astrological conceit Webster's Dictionary, article "Cycles," mistakenly alludes to it as "a period of about 6586 years, the time of the revolution of the moon's node, called saros " This cycle was evidently known to the Hindus at the period of the Indian expedition of Seleucus, because their Anno Munci, as reported by Megasthenes, was based upon it Indeed it may safely be carried backward to the period of the first Buddha, because the doctrine of the ten avatars, or avataras, was derived from it, or else from its teleological basis, which was the Cycle of the Eclipses It lost credit with the learned after the discovery of the Precession of the Equinoxes.

7777 years.—Cycle mentioned by Plutarch Dupuis, III, ii, 339.

7980 years.—So-called " Julian " cycle, invented by Joseph Scaliger, A D. 1583, to avoid the uncertainty and complexity of astrological and religious æras. It was constructed by multiplying a solar cycle, 28 years, an indiction 15 years, and the approximate period of a Metonic cycle 19 years, thus $28 \times 15 \times 19 = 7980$ The first year of this cycle was Year 1 of the Sun, Year 1 of a series of Indictions carried backward and Year 1 of the Moon; a triple conjunction that only happens once in 7980 years In other words, during this interval "there are not two years which have the same Golden number, accompanied with the same Solar cycle and the same Roman Indiction " The first year of this period is 4713 B C , which was adopted because each of the three other cycles had the value of "one" in that year.   This period will continue until the year A D 3267 Lockyer. The Julian cycle has been used by some astronomers and chronologists, but owing to its employment of the Metonic cycle, as though it were a solar one, which it is not, its further use is of doubtful wisdom Its only practical recommendation is that of avoiding the inconvenient and confusing " A D " and " B C " periods, whose influence in muddling chronology and hiding the alterations of the Calendar is referred to elsewhere.

9977 years.—An astrological cycle of 15 Divine years, each of 665 common years Dupuis, III, ii, 339, ascribes this cycle to Sextus Empiricus, who flourished in the third century of our æra

10,800 years.—One-half of the period accorded to the precession of the equinoxes, by Heraclitus of Ephesus, B. C. 513. See 21,600 years Dupuis, III, ii, 339, ascribes this cycle to both Heraclitus and Linus.

10,884 years.—One-half of the equinoxial precession, according to Dion, in Censorinus, XVIII

12,000 years.—"The modern Parsee books" say that "12,000 years is to be the term of the human race" Bunsen's "Egypt," ed 1859, III, 519 According to the Aitareya Brahmana, VII, 15, the terms Kali, Dvapara, Treta and Krta are derived from the ace, deuce, tré, and quart of the dice. From these elements the priests manufactured the 1200, 2400, 3600 and 4800 years, which make up the 12,000 years of these four ages Gustav Oppert, "Bharatavarsa, or India," 1893, p 328 All this is post-Buddhic

12,854 years.—One-half of the equinoxial precession, according to one MS. of Cicero, in Hortensium. See 12,954 years and cf Greswell, F. C., III, 211, *n*.

12,954 years.—One-half of the equinoxial precession, according to another MS. of Cicero, in Hortensium. Servius ad Æneid, III, 284, says 12,954, while ad Æneid, I, 269, he has 12,554 years.

15,000 years.—One-half of the equinoxial precession, according to Macrobius Dupuis, III, II, 339.

18,000 years.—Brahminical cycle of the equinoxial precession. This appears to be merely an inference drawn from the allowance of 1800 years to the zodion, as explained under 21,600 years, q v. If so, it belongs to the period of the Brahminical restoration, which succeeded the introduction of Buddhism Dupuis, III, II, 339, who ascribes this cycle to Heraclitus (fl 513 B C) cites Plutarch, de placit philos, I, II, c 32, and Stobæus, phys., I, I, c. 11.

19,440 years.—Hindu equinoxial precession of 54 years to the degree Asiat Res, vol II, 238

21,000 years.—Cycle of the Apsides "The line joining the aphelion and perihelion points (of the earth's orbit), termed the line of apsides, changes its direction at such a rate that in 21,000 years it makes a complete revolution . . . In A. D. 6485 the perihelion point will correspond to the vernal equinox." Lockyer, 216 In B C. 4004 it had to start at the aphelion . This was the year when, according to Greswell, the Universe was created; hence from B C. 4004 to A D 6485 is 10,490 years, which is one-half of the cycle of the apsides. The full cycle, according to Greswell, is therefore 20,980 years, or 20 years less than Lockyer's cycle, which, if Greswell is right, began 20 years before the Creation of the universe! According to Andrew Laing, "Human Origins," (pp 301-310,) 21,000 years represents the precession of the equinoxes. In this statement he is opposed to all modern observation.

21,600 years.—The most ancient Greek measurement of the precession of the equinoxes, that made by Heraclitus of Ephesus, who flourished B. C. 513 It gave 2160 years to the zodion, equal to 21,600 years to the zodiac of ten zodions When the zodiac was divided into twelve zodions the precessional movement became 1800 years to the sign. Higgins, in his Anacalypsis, II, 397, has evidently confused these details. It also consists of eight Indian lokkals each of 2700 years, and may be of Oriental origin See 129,600 years.

24,000 years.—Indian cycle of the precession; according to Bailley, Drummond, Le Gentil and Dupuis III, 11, 289, most of whom regarded it to be as ancient as the æra of the first Buddha See Buddha, p 6, in " Story of the Gods " The 24,000-year cycle was ¹₍ₙₑd by Aryabhala and other Indian astronomers, A. D. 499, all of whom appeared to have been either ignorant or disdainful of the very different determinations of the Greeks. (Cf Duff Rickmers, 37)

24,800 years.—Cycle of the precession according to Cassini· eighteenth century.

24,925 years.—The sum total of the reign of gods, heroes and kings in Egypt, according to Manetho. evidently an astrological farrago based on the cycle of the equinoxial precession

25,200 years.—Cycle of the precession as determined by Ulugh Beg, A. D 1447, viz , one degree in 70 years

25,748 years.—According to Rev Dr Hales, Chron , p 78, the cycle of the precession was computed by Hipparchus at 50⅓ s per year, or a revolution in 25,748 years Contrariwise, Sir Geo Cornewall Lewis says that Hipparchus computed the precession at not less than 36 nor more than 59 seconds to the year This would make the cycle vary from 36,000 to 22,000 years, and render the computation of little value. See 25,920 years

25,812 years.—Cycle of the precession. Dupuis, I, 119. Apparently modern.

25,816 years.—Cycle of the precession Tycho Brahe sixteenth century

25,820 years.—Cycle of the precession. Riccioli: 17th century The Hindus are also said to have had the same determination date not given Drummond ascribes it to the "ancient Persians."

25,868 years.—Cycle of the precession Sir John Herschel.

25,908 years.—Cycle of the precession Tacitus, de Orat , XVI.

25,920 years.—Cycle of the precession, as computed by Hipparchus, according to Higgins, Anacal., I, 194, and Hislop, "666," p. 192 But Greswell, F. C , III, 460, and K H , II, 48, says that Hipparchus reckoned 100 years to to the *degree*. hence 100 × 360 = 36.000 years to the cycle, while Lewis says his computation varied from 22,000 to 36 000 years.

25,972 years,—Cycle of the precession, according to Rambosson, one of the most recent writers on the subject

27,000 years.—Hindu cycle of the precession, computed, according to Brennand, in 1590 B C and corrected to 25,920 years so early as the tenth century B C. See 2,700 years.

36,000 years.—Hindu cycle of the precession. Dupuis, III, ii, 157 For its attribution to Hipparchus, see 25,748 and 25,920 years.

36,525 years.—Astrological Annus Magnus of the Ptolemaic Egyptians, produced by multiplying the Sothiacal cycle of 1461 equable years by 25 years, the measure of the Apis cycle Syncellus, in Greswell, F. C., III, 39; Bunsen, III, 67 It embraces "30 dynasties in 113 descents." Gustav Oppert, "Bharatavarsa," p. 331. "Among the Egyptians there is a certain tablet called the Old Chronicle, containing 30 dynasties in 113 descents, during the long period of 36,525 years " F Hall's edition of the Vishnu Purana, I, 49; Cory's "Fragments," p 89 This is mere astrological nonsense, which could hardly have been invented earlier than the Ptolemaic period.

39,180 years.—The Babylonians fixed the deluge of Adrahasis 39,180 years before their "historical" period, B C. 2517 Jules Oppert believes the first figure to have been made of 12 Sothiacal cycles, each of 1460 years, plus 12 "lunar cycles," each of 1805 years; or of 653 sossos, each of 60 years. The last is possible, the first is inadmissable until a lunar cycle of 1805 years is established See 22,300 lunations. Gustav Oppert's "Bharatavarsa," p 331.

100,020 years.—Cycle of Orpheus, in Censorinus, XVIII

129,000 years.—Cycle of Plato Dupuis, III, ii, 339

129,600 years.—Chinese cosmic cycle, probably modern and evidently composed of six Hindu precessions, each of 21,600 years. Messrs. Croll and Laing have improved on this.

210,000 years.—Cycle of the eccentricity of the equinoxial precession, consisting of ten precessions, each of 21,000 years, a recent discovery of Croll, cited by Laing, "Human Origins," 311.

300,000 years.—Astrological Great Year of Firmicus, who is said to have flourished A D 334-55. Greswell, F C , III, 38

350,635 years.—Cycle of the "restitution of Saturn," according to Achilles Tatius, an Alexandrian ecclesiastic of the sixth century Dupuis, III, ii, 339.

400,000 years.—Astrological Great Year of the Hindus, which began with Calijoga B C 3102, and is called the Age of Degeneracy Halhed's Hindu Code of Manu, p. xxxviii

432,000 years.—Chaldean astrological cycle mentioned by Berosus in Syncellus. This is probably 12 precessions of 36,000 years, or else one-tenth of the Hindu cycle of 4,320,000 years. Jules Oppert, who is high authority in oriental religions and astrology, says it is probably gained by multiplying two sossos by twenty-four lustra, thus 60 × 60 × 24 × 5=432,000. "La poême Chaldeen du déluge," Paris, 1885, cited approvingly by Gustav Oppert, librarian of Calcutta If this is correct it proves the use of the lustrum, pentæteris, or five-year period, by the Babylonians and by the Hindus, from whom the Babylonians got the 432,000-year cycle

1,600,000 years.—Hindu astrological Dvapar Joga, ending with the commencement of the Calijoga. Halhed, op cit

1,753,200 years.—"Great Year "of Nicetas Acominatus, a Byzantine historian who died A D 1216 Dupuis, III, 11, 339.

2,400,000 years.—Hindu astrological Tirtah Joga, (Age of Sin,) the institution of which ended with the commencement of the Dvapar Joga. This cycle implied acceptance of the doctrine of Original Sin Halhed, op cit.

3,200,000 years.—Hindu astrological Age of Purity, which ended with the Downfall of Man and the commencement of the Treta Joga. Halhed, op cit.

3,600,000 years.—Astrological cycle of Cassander, in Censorinus, XVIII.

4,320,000 years.—Hindu astrological cycle, representing the Lifetime of the World Dupuis, I, 164, believed that this was gained by adding together the first, second, third and fourth powers of 432,000 years

6,570,000 years.—Cycle of Diogenes. Dupuis, III, 11, 339 It appears to be a multiple of the Divine year.

240,000,000 years.—Astrological Lifetime of the World, consisting of 6666 precessions of 36,000 years each; a Hindu concert, probably ancient.

CHAPTER IX.

CHRONOLOGICAL PROBLEMS AND SOLUTIONS.

THE chief sources of error in chronology and of confusion in ancient history are, First, the employment of lunar calendars; Second, the alterations in the year of Rome and the Olympiads which were made by Augustus as afterwards modified by the Latin Sacred College: and Third, the employment of "A D." and "B. C" dates. The confusion produced by lunar, or luni-solar, calendars has been of so varied a character that it is difficult to convey an adequate appreciation of it to persons not especially skilled in chronology. Suffice it to say that such calendars have been used as artifices to shuffle out of view the most significant customs and important events: with the object to substitute in their places the myths and fables of superstition The ancient priests made such liberal use of these artifices that it may be asserted with little fear of contradiction that history only begins with the establishment of solar calendars; and that previous to this first charter of human progress, for such it is, there is nothing recorded which possesses any historical value The confusion occasioned by alterations of the calendar will be illustrated by some examples further on. The inconvenience of "A. D" and "B. C " dates was realised three centuries ago by Scaliger, who sought to remedy it by offering to the world the so-called Julian Æra Although but little use has hitherto been made of his suggestion, it can easily be shown that this is a reform which, shirk it as we may, must nevertheless precede any attempt to establish upon a sure foundation such literary fragments and archæological monuments of the past as time and proscription have spared to the modern world.

Take, for example, the text of the present work, Chapter VIII, year 1503 There it says that "to made the true date, *deduct* the 78 years *sunk* by Augustus " It seems strange that to make a true date we should have to *deduct* a number of years which have in fact already been *sunk* from the tables of chronology; yet this is quite right. In correcting dates thus vitiated, the same number must be *deducted* from "A D." dates which have to be *added* to "B. C." dates. The proof of this is readily seen by referring to the intervals between the divine years in Tables A and D   Moreover, the reader will discover that the æras of Ies Chrishna, Buddha, Augustus and Jesus are all one and the same, and that they have only been made to *seem* different through the misleading media of altered calendars and æras.

In the foregoing Chronology numerous examples have been given of calendrical alterations, it is now proposed to add some others from extraneous sources

Tacitus, in his Annals, XV, 41, says that the interval of time between the Foundation of Rome and the Burning by the Gauls was precisely the same as that between the Burning by the Gauls and the conflagration in the reign of Nero. According to our present chronology the Foundation was in B. C. 753 and the burning by the Gauls in B C 384. This is an interval of 369 years. From the burning by the Gauls to the conflagration in the reign of Nero, July, A D. 64, is 447 full years and a fraction   Deduct 369 from 447 and the quotient is 78 years, which is the measure of the excess of the later period over the earlier one. Tacitus says that in fact the two periods were exactly equal   our chronology makes one of them longer than the other by 78 years   It is impossible that 78 years of chronology and history could have been fabricated and stuffed into the most recent and best known annals of Rome. The calendar of the later Republican and early Imperial periods of Rome may have been altered to the extemt of ten or 15 years without attracting attention; but not to the extent of 78 years. The alteration, whenever it was made, must therefore have been attached to a period long past, that is to say, to the earlier period, before B. C. 384   The nature of the alteration was therefore to sink 78 years from the calendar. Who made this alteration, when was it made; what was its object? Remember that Tacitus was a priest and a member of the Sacred College of Rome, and therefore one whose statement on this subject possesses the full force of official authority   The subject has thus far been blinked by historians and churchmen, but it should be blinked no longer. Where are those 78 years of Roman experience and of Roman history? Is mankind to be perpetually robbed of that valuable, that inestimable portion of its inheritance which is to be found in the history of the greatest state of antiquity?

Tacitus Annals, VI, 28, says that from the third Ptolemy to Tiberius "the interval is not quite two hundred and fifty years." According to our chronology the interval between the first regnal years of these monarchs, B C 247 to A D. 14, is 261 years   Here is a discrepancy of eleven or more years, probably of 15 years, the number of years inserted into the calendar by the Latin Sacred College

In the first example, the recensors employed by the Latin Sacred College evidently made no alteration of the dates in the text; probably for the reason that not being specific, their significance was not perceived In the second one, the dates were practically specific, and the recensors, in order to make them conform to their general system of chronology, were obliged to alter them That they did their work badly was no fault of the men, but of the system

The Ludi Sæculares were required to be celebrated once in 110 years. Augustus celebrated them in B C 15. They were next due in A D 94, or 95 But "Claudius," (says Suetonius,) "assuming that Augustus had wrongfully anticipated the Ludi Sæculares, and that he had celebrated them out of their true season, caused them to be re-celebrated," after an interval of 78 years [1] Suetonius says that several persons took part in both of these Ludi, which could hardly have been the case had they been 78 years apart. Pliny even names one of these persons. The interval between the Ludi Sæeculares of Augustus and Claudius, which was really 78 years, is stated in modern editions of Pliny, N H , VII, 49, at only 63 years This must be the work of the Latin Sacred College, which gave us our present mutilated MSS of the Roman encyclopedist The reduction of the 78 years of calendrical alteration effected by Augustus, to the 63 years of dislocation shown in Pliny, could not have been effected in the days of Pliny, but is evidently the work of long subsequent ages. Tacitus says that "the chronology of Augustus differed from that of Claudius," which is precisely what we are endeavouring to prove But in the face of the worship of himself as the Son of God, which Augustus had established, the true chronology of Claudius had no chance to succeed, and it fell before the false chronology of Augustus, so that the next Ludi were celebrated by Domitian in A D 94, or 95. The 63 years of dislocation in the calendar of Rome, which was mainly created by Augustus (i e , 78 years, less 15 years, since restored) and which Claudius tried in vain to rectify, still remain We are in fact 63 years farther from the reputed Foundation of Rome and the events connected with that period than what our chronology permits us to believe. As Augustus sunk his 78 years from a remote period of Rome's history, his alteration of the calendar may be regarded as having no longer any practical importance. But this would

---

[1] It is not known how far this attempt of Claudius to restore the chronology of Rome was carried It evidently failed with his death, when the Augustan chronology was everywhere revived.

be a mistake; because such alteration vitiates all foreign dates which have to be converted into Roman   The 15 years restored to the calendar by the Latin authorities stand in a worse category   The canon of Nicephorus perhaps indicates in what manner these 15 years were restored to the calendar, but no matter how or when it was done, it has robbed us of the knowledge of that due succession of historical events which would enable us to utilise the experience of the past Until our chronology is rectified, Roman history will have to be written over and over again, without its being able to impart to mankind any convincing lessons in either religion or politics   "The laws relating to religious matters were kept secret by the Pontiffs that they might hold the minds of the multitude in bondage," said Livy (VI,1). "The chronology of Augustus differed from that of Claudius," said Tacitus.   "Roman history has been falsified and its monuments destroyed," said Plutarch (on the Future of the Romans)   From these deliberate verdicts of antiquity there can be no appeal, except to archæology and a scientific arrangement of dates

---

Pausanias, I, 379, says that the Third Age of Greece began in Olym. xxiii, 4, that is, B C 685   But the Third Age was the æra of Nebo Nazaru and Phoroneus, B C 748, (see chapter VI;) a difference of just 63 years from the date in Pausanias, the text of which has evidently been altered since the time when the 63 years difference was fixed   As previously shown, this was done probably during the pontificate of Gregory VII

Dunlop calls attention to several anachronisms and chronological puzzles some of which appear to have arisen from the repeated alteration of the Roman calendar.   For example, Attius the comic poet, was born B C. 170; yet this same Attius refused to rise from his seat in the College of Poets upon the entrance of Julius Cæsar, who was not born until B C 100 and would hardly have entered the College until B. C. 70, when Attius was long since dead and buried. Cicero, who was born B. C. 106 and wrote his "Brutus" in B. C. 45, says that he consulted this same Attius concerning the merits of that work. According to the received chronology the dead poet was still living

---

Catullus, the poet, died, says Eusebius, in A U. 696, others say A U 705; yet Cicero records that Catullus' satire upon Cæsar and Mamurra was newly written in A U. 708, when Cæsar rewarded the deceased poet for it with a supper'   Other instances of this sort are mentioned in Dunlop's "Roman Literature," vol II, pp 195, 204, 220, 223, 231, 232, 239 and 275 and in the last chapter of Michelet's "Roman Republic "

The chronology of Albiruni gives the following dates: From the "first year" of Cyrus to the "reign" of Alexander, 222 years; to the 11th-century-Jewish-and-Christian date of the nativity of "Messiah," 304; to the "first year" of Iesdegird, 638⅔ years; total, from Cyrus to Iesdigerd, 1164⅔, or, from Alexander to Iesdigerd, 942⅔ years The discrepancy between this and the chronology which is accepted at the present time is about 15 years.

It was the custom of the Romans, upon a general and permanent peace, to close the temple of Janus Quirinus, the Prince of Peace, probably as a sign that no further supplications or sacrifices of lambs were to be exacted or required Ovid, Fasti, I, 283, gives the poetical reason that Peace was locked within, that it might not escape; but at present the origin of the custom is of no consequence The temple is said to have been first closed at the termination of the first Punic war, when Titus Manlius was consul. Livy, I, 19; Vell., II, 38; Serv Virg , I, 294; VII, 607 Livy fixes this date in A U 519; Lenglet, A. U 513; and Adams, A U 529 Odd as it may seem, all these dates appear to be correct; Livy's date being the basis of the others Adams' date is due to the ten years' difference between the Greek and Roman Anno Mundi; while Lenglet's date shows the 15 years' alteration of the Augustan dates effected by the Latin Sacred College.   It may be added that the Temple of Janus was closed a second time before Augustus closed it thrice at short intervals Suet., August., 21. But even about the second closing, (to say nothing more of the first), there is a contention, which is due entirely to the mischievous and perplexing shifting of the calendar, already so often mentioned in this work.

Mionnet's voluminous work on Ancient Coins, Paris ed. 1806-37, describes a number of Roman imperial coins, commencing with Nerva and ending with Alexander Severus, the dates upon which are evidently in the regnal year of Augustus, B. C 28 These dates should therefore be 28 years older than the Christian regnal years of the sovereigns whose effigies and names are associated with them. But in fact they are all, without exception, just 43 years older; proving that 15 years have since been sunk from the Christian æra, A. D , by adding that number of years to the Augustan æra, B C. For example, the coins of Geta are dated "255" According to the received chronology this sovereign began to reign and died A D 211-12 The difference between 212 and 255 is 43 years, making it appear that his coins were dated in an æra which began B C. 43, whereas no such æra is known and it is evident from other circumstances that the æra intended was that of Augustus and the Foundation of the Empire.

Diadumenianus is another sovereign who reigned but a single year, which, according to the received chronology was A D 217-18 Yet his coins, also evidently dated from the regnal year of Augustus, bear the figure "261" Deduct 218 from 261 and the remainder is 43; whereas, if the Christian chronology were correct, there should only be a difference of 28 years, that being the number of years B C when by such chronology, the Empire was founded by Augustus

From the first year of the last Vicramaditya, the son of Bahram-Gur, A D 441 or 442, (a date reckoned from the Calijoga,) to the Hegira, A D. 622, (a date reckoned from the Christian æra,) the Hindus compute 196 years, yet, according to our chronology, the difference is only 181 years: a discrepancy of 15 years Col. Wilford, Asiat. Res., IX, 202.

The Hindu date when the Vernal equinox corresponded with the first point of Cartica is B C. 1426, while according to "modern computation" it was B. C 1350 Brennand's "Hindu Astronomy," p. 54 Here is a discrepancy of 76 years, the same as is shown in our chapter on the Ludi Sæculares This interval leads to the suspicion that the "modern computation" cited by Brennand is based on an Augustan, not a Christian year

These evidences concerning the dislocation of Roman chronology could be continued almost indefinitely. Enough has been shown to prove to the most unwilling reader that the calendar has been altered and that, in this respect and the important consequences that flow from it, the Christian world has been grossly deceived.

CHAPTER X

MANETHO'S FALSE CHRONOLOGY

MANETHO, an Egyptian priest, in the service of Ptolemy, surnamed the "Saviour," one of the minor "incarnations," to whom fell a portion of the vast empire established by that greater incarnation, Alexander of Macedon, has left us, in fragments preserved and perhaps altered by Berosus, Josephus and Syncellus, a list of Egyptian dynasties and kings, which, if correct and successive, and if to each were allowed twice or thrice the ordinary regnal period of earthly potentates, would carry the government of Egypt back to a remote antiquity. Manetho's list gives us 30 dynasties, which for convenience have been divided by modern commentators into the Old, the Middle and the New empires. The Egyptologists accept all this as authentic and fancy they see a confirmation of it in the monuments

If there is any truth at all in Manetho, such truth is limited to the regnal names of the New Empire; for his kings of the Old Empire, as such, never existed at all; and those of the Middle Empire are largely apochryphal   Such in effect was the opinion of Petavius, who so long ago as 1627 came to the conclusion that "the Egyptian dynasties are fabulous" Wilkinson, Hincks, Greswell and other more modern critics have come to the same conclusion   the chronology is false and worthless   Even Bunsen, who attempted to restore the chronology, which he "analysed in connection with the Scriptural data" (Egypt, I, 253) completely failed Syncellus said that Manetho was "led astray," while Bunsen condemned both Syncellus and Manetho, charging the latter with nothing less than patchwork, fraud and imposture   (I, 228)

Josephus, who was anxious to prove the great antiquity of the Jews, and to corroborate their story of the exile in Egypt, very cleverly made use of Manetho's account of the conquest of that country by the Hyksos, in assuming that the latter were Jews, but, like most casuists, he proved to much. Here is his statement "I will set down Manetho's very words, as if I were to bring the man himself into court as a witness. 'There was a king of ours (says Manetho) whose name was Timaus.   Under him it came to pass, I know not now, that God was averse to us, and there came, after a surprising manner, men of ignoble birth, out of the eastern parts, and had boldness enough to make an expedition into our country and with ease subdued it by force, yet without our hazarding a battle ' " Manetho then gives the names and regnal periods of the first six stranger kings, viz , Salatis, 13; Beon, 44; Apachnas, 13½; Apophis, 61; Janus, 50; Assis, 49, altogether, 230½ years "These people," continues Josephus, still quoting Manetho, "and their descendants kept possession of Egypt 511 years   Then the Egyptians under King Alisphragmuthosis rose against them and in the reign of his son, Thummosis, they induced them to depart to Judea, where they built Jerusalem." Such is Josephus' case. As to his own account of the period of this pretended invasion of Egypt by the Jews, namely, "393 years before Danaus came to Argos " and of their removal to Judea, namely, "almost a thousand years before the siege of Troy," it adds nothing whatever to his case; because we know that the events themselves never took place; that Danaus was merely the Hindu sign of the zodiacal Archer and that the siege of Troy was a mythos   Egypt was not conquered by the Jews, but by the Hyksos   Nor is the date true even when applied to the Hyksos, for " Danaus in Argos " relates to the feigned incarnation of Ies Chres, the Son of God, from whom and his Eight curctes in the island of Crete, Danaus brought the Word which made him (a fabulous) king of Argos   The date of this incarnation was approximately B B 2064   That of the next one, Jasius, with his Ten dactyles, also of Crete, was approximately B. C 1406 This was, approximately, the date of the actual invasion of Egypt by the Hyksos By confusing the two incarnations, the shrewd Josephus added 658 years to his proofs of Jewish antiquity But the whole thing is fabulous; the Exile, the Eis-o-dus, or Exodus, the incarnations of Chres and Jasius, and the six kings who reigned 230½ years, these are all plainly astrological.   Even Timaus, who, according to Manetho, lost Egypt to the Hyksos, was obviously meant for Tammuz, Son of God, the Mighty in battle, the Nissus of the XXIVth Psalm, the Jasius of the Cretans, the Dio-Nissos of the Athenians, the god who was worshipped by Manetho's royal master   in other words, an astrological myth, in whose heavenly character it is evident that Manetho, a priest of the old school, did not entirely believe   This is the witness whom Josephus, an ancient Roman casuist and the Egyptologists who are modern casuists, call to support their several contentions a Greek fabulist, steeped in astrology and cunning, ready, even out of the word

"Hyksos" to coin the lies of "Shepherd kings" and "Captive-kings," whereas, as shown by Pococke, it was merely the proper name of the Scythian tribe, the Hucsos, who issued from the Euxine and overran Egypt. To crown all, Josephus himself, in another place, calls this same Manetho, his own witness, an ariant liar (Contra Apion I, 27.)

All the ancient peoples believed themselves to be autochthonous and each affected to trace their origin from the gods. The Chinese, the Indians, the Assyrians, the Chaldeans, the Jews, the Egyptians, the Greeks, and even the Romans, all followed the same practice. Consequently they carried their chronologies back to the remotest periods, when, according to their several beliefs, man first lived in civilised communities. The Chinese annals begin with Fo-hi—a Buddho-Solar divinity—and their cycles of time, with the accession of Yao, an impersonation of the planet Jove, whom they called a Son of God, and whose æra, according to Father Du Halde (I, 282), was B C 2337, or according to Bunsen (III, 388) B C 2163. The Calijoga of the Brahmins began B. C. 3102, the Buddho-Brahmins carried their series of incarnations far beyond this period, and their successors the Brahmo-Buddhists (the existing Hindus) carried theirs still further. Neither of them altered the Calijoga; they merely belittled its antiquity by creating still more ancient æras.

The "History of Assyria," which was written by Herodotus and to which he refers in his Clio, 184, has not been permitted to reach us. It is abundantly evident that his surviving work was tampered with, both before and after the æra of Christianity. Yet it still retains traces of the incarnations of Bel, or Bel-Issus, or the Lord Ies, born of the Virgin Semiramis, or Semia-rama, the Divine Token, which Philo Byblius, following Sanchoniathon, fixed about the end of the 15th or the beginning of the 14th century B. C. and the ecclesiastical writers Eusebius, Syncellus, Helvicus and Petavius, carried backward a Divine Year earlier, to about B C 2064. The earliest Assyrian date which is clearly mentioned by Herodotus, does not carry us beyond the epoch of that incarnation of the deity who was known in Assyria as Tiglath Pil-Esar II, and in Babylon as Nebo-Nazaru, or Nabon-Issa, B.C. 747. The astronomical observations, which, during the Alexandrian æra, were carried by Berosus from Babylon to Cos, only extend backward to the same period. This was also the limit of Ptolemy's astronomical records. Yet Aristotle is made to say that the Chaldean observations extended backward twenty centuries and Rawlinson assures us that their exact date is inscribed upon the baked-clay tablets found in the ruins. He says they commenced B C. 2234. Unless the clay tablets were fabricated after the period of Tiglath-pil-Esar II., in order to carry the Assyrian line of incarnations one Divine Year further back than the Belus of B C 1406 and they fell under the observation only of highly privileged persons, like Aristotle, it is inexplicable that they were but imperfectly known to Berosus, who had been a priest of Belus at Babylon and was an astronomer and the author of a history of Chaldea; and it is astonishing that they should have been ignored by Ptolemy, who was also an astronomer It was Freret's suspicion that these tablets were anachronical forgeries; a suspicion that is reduced almost to a certainty by their duodecimal division of the year; for, at the period to which they refer, the Assyrian and Babylonian years were in point of fact divided into ten months and not into 12, as the Egyptologists imagine, the division into 12 months being always Buddhic or Bacchic, and that too of the second Buddhic period

When we come to Græco-Egyptian chronology it is evident that the subject is obscured by fables and impostures of the grossest description. The 341 historical kings and the period of 11,340 years, from Menes to Sethon, (Euterpe, 142,) is obviously an astrological mythos This period, if we allow 26 years for the reign of either Menes or Sethon, amounts to an average of exactly $33\frac{1}{3}$ years, to each reign, thus $341 \times 33\frac{1}{3} = 11,366$ Now deduct this number from 12,000, which according to Le Gentil, was half of the Precessional Year of the Hindus, (and therefore also of the Egyptians), and the remainder is what? Precisely 660 years, a Great Year, the period of an incarnation, the annualised cycle of the Moon's node, the sixth power of the ludi sæculares In other words, when the astrological dynasties of Egypt ended in Sethon, who was a priest of Vulcan, and when, in consequence of that misfortune, the empire split up into a dodekarky, the rival priests of Apis hailed as their incarnation, the Over-lord of the Twelve, who, when he had overthrown the rest, reigned as Psammetichus To complete the mythos and the Great Year the priests were obliged to predict another incarnation who was to come one divine year later.[1] Herodotus is careful to tell us that these dates are from the Egyptian priests. Manetho, who abused him for his caution, (Josephus on Apion, I, 14,) fills up the idle tale with the names of kings who never existed and of whom no genuine re-

---

[1] One divine year after the Psammetichus brings the computation to the incarnation of Augustus, thus 673 less 658 equals 15, the year B. C of Augustus, or 666 (Bunsen) less 658 equals 8, the year B C of Augustus in Egypt The whole thing is astrological

mains have ever been found. Mr Laing, in " Human Origins," after dividing this nonsense by two, accepts a moiety. But why divide it by two, why not accept the lot, aye, even the "fifteen thousand years since Bacchus " of the Egyptian priests (Euterpe, 145;) or the "seventeen thousand years before the reign of Amasis," when, according to the same mendacious authority, the Egyptians changed their gods from Eight to Twelve (Euterpe, 43 and 156;) or the 24,000 years of gods, heroes and kings, which make up Manetho's full precessional list? Bunsen, 1, 69, says 24,935; but in being thus precise this Egyptologist has overshot his mark [2]

It is only too evident that, except perhaps a name here and there and except the dynasties of the New Empire, Manetho's lists are worthless. The supposed corroborations upon the monuments found in recent years, amount to nothing, for many of these were altered in ancient times by the erasure of certain names and the substitution of others.[3] The only Egytian date which has survived the wreck of time is the so-called æra of Menephres, B C 1322, preserved by Theon. This may have once been regarded as the æra of the so-called New Empire which began immediately after the expulsion of the Hyksos. But we now know that the pretended æra of Menephres is merely astrological Bunsen computes that during the (supposed) 511 years of the Hyksos in Egypt they had 65 kings, an average of about eight years to each reign. Add these 511 years to Theon s 1322 and we have B C 1833 as the earliest date which the ancients

---

[2] Josephus says the Hyksos reigned 511 years, Brugsch says five dynasties aggregating 500 years, Laing says one dynasty of 259 years, contemporaneous with the Theban dynasty, which reigned over Upper Egypt during 260 years Brugsch shows that during the strictly historical period, that is to say, from the beginning of the XXVIth dynasty B C 666, to Alexander the Great, B C 332, (an interval of 334 years,) there reigned in Egypt 24 kings, an average of about 14½ years to each reign Previous to this period he has, besides the Hyksos, 106 kings reigning between B C. 4400 (Menes) and B C 666. Deduct the Hyksos interval of 500 years, leaves 3234 years with 106 kings, an average of 30½ years each; which is double the ordinary measure As the periods of the 106 kings are computed by assuming their reigns in *most* cases to have lasted 33 years, or an average of 30½ years each for all of them, and as the actual reign during the historical period was only 14½ years, it cannot be regarded as unfair if Brugsch's 30½ are reduced to 14½ years. In such case 106x14½ =1537 years, will cover all the dynasties except the Hyksos, from Psammetichus B. C. 666 (or B. C 673) back to Menes Add Mr. Laing's 260 years for the Hyksos and we have the following result 666 plus 1537 plus 260=2463 B C for the æra of Menes, if indeed Menes ever existed at all, which is much to be doubted ; for the æra to which this computation assigns him is itself astrological It is that of Ies Chres, the Cretan son of God.

[3] This is abundantly shown by Perrot and Chipiez, " Egyptian Art ," 1, 233, 244 It

preserved of any supposed historical event relating to Egypt, beyond the fact that some kind of people must have dwelt there whom the Hyksos conquered, and that some of these may have left monuments But all these dates are unsafe; for the æra of Menephres proves to be merely a Sothic astrological period and the 511 years sojourn of the Hyksos, a fragment of the Buddhic astrological circle of 550 years.[4] Indeed, the invasion, (not the sojourn) of the Hyksos is about the earliest well authenticated event that we know of concerning ancient Egypt; and it is doubtful if more than a few of the existing monuments are earlier than that period   Manetho, indeed, says that the Hyksos destroyed everything; but as Josephus himself remarked, Manetho is not to be trusted, and as the antiquarians Perrot and Chipiez distinctly assert, this is false; for the Hyksos left the earlier monuments unmutilated, and so they stand to-day.

The oldest æra of the Greeks, B C 2064, was that of the mythical Chres and his Eight curetes or apostles, who were called the Danoi This was a legend of the sun-worship, the date of its invention being unknown.   The next oldest was the Brahminical myth of Jasius and the Ten dactyles of Mount Ida, whose æra was one Brahminical cycle (658 years) later than Chres, or B C. 1406.   Then we have the æra of Ischenou, B C. 1219.   Finally, in B C 748 (another 658-year cycle) we have Iacchus, Inachus, or Bacchus, and the Twelve apostles: only, be it observed, that these dates have often been confused.   Chres has been put for Jasius and Jasius for Chres   For example, Herodotus (Euterpe, 145) shifts Bacchus into the period of Chres, or Cres, by alleging that he was born at Nyssa in Ethiopia (evidently to account

has also been shown by Maspero, Naville, Edwards and others.   "The names and titles of Rameses II. were reengraved over the erased names of Usertesen III and other earlier kings." . .   "The royal ovals on the front of the throne (of the colossal Hyksos statue found at Bubastis and now in the British Museum) had been erased and reengraved by Rameses II , the vacant spaces at each side being filled in with six columns of inscription in honour of Osorkon II.   Here, then, was a twofold usurpation (and forgery) and no trace left of the original legend" (inscription,)   "The name of Apepi (a Hyksos king) has been hammered out, but is still traceable on the right shoulder (of another statue) the place being reengraved with the cartouches of Meneptah " . . .   "Maspero has discovered that the cartouches of Piseb-khanu are also carved over an erasure "   "'The work of Ramesis II at Bubastis (Tel Basta) was chiefly a work of usurpation,'" (wrote M Naville, who in 1889 discovered these remains)   "'I never saw so many erased inscriptions.   I have very carefully examined all the large architraves, upon which the hieroglyphics measure two feet in height, and there is *not one* which is not engraved upon an erased surface.'"   Amelia B. Edwards, in the Century Magazine, January, 1890

[4] See Chap. VII, under ' 500 years," for a " phen " of 511 years mentioned by Pliny.

for his woolly head) "about 1600 years before my time"; whereas it is quite evident from what he says in Euterpe, 43 and 145, and from what Sanchoniathon says of the Cabirim, that the system of Eight gods preceded that of Twelve, and that Bacchus was connected with the latter and not with the former.[5] It is also evident from Euterpe, 51, that Herodotus himseif was a worshipper of Bacchus and an initiate of the Eleusinian mysteries.

The Hebrew æras and chronology were based upon the pedigrees and lives of their kings, heroes and patriarchs, until they ended (or began) with Adam, whose æra they calculated backward to the year B. C. 3760. The rabbis even gave us the day and hour of his birth. This was exactly one divine year before the Calijoga, and beyond any doubt whatever, it was based upon that æra.

The Roman æra, B. C. 753, is evidently another perversion of one of the Bacchic incarnations: for it roughly agrees with the period when Numa is said to have changed the year of the Romans from 10 to twelve months and added two more gods, Janus and Februus, to their theogony. (Livy, I, 19; Plutarch in Numa, I, 83). The Roman chronology of the Augustan æra did not ascend beyond the Bacchic period. For example, Julius Cæsar, who was annointed in the Serapion as the Son of God, December 25, B. C. 48, claimed his descent through Venus, the Mother of God, who was a divinity of the Bacchic cult.

We have now before us all the more important æras and chronologies known to the ancients. Their earliest plausible dates in the Orient were China, 2163, and Brahminical India, 3102, B. C. In the Occident the earliest plausible dates were, Assyria, 2064; Egypt, 2064; Greece and Rome, 2064, and Judea, 3760, B. C. To begin with, all these dates are those of avatars or incarnations. They are not historical, but astrological; and, as matters of fact, are not worth a moment's consideration. As matters of ancient opinion, however, they furnish us with useful guides to chronology and an important historical inference. The inference is that when they were offered for popular belief their authors knew of no older dates; and this inference, if well founded, completely destroys both Manetho's chronology and the deductions which have been drawn from it.

For example, if the Greeks before the Alexandrian æra had any reason to suppose, either from the written histories or monuments of Egypt—both of which were familiar to them, for the men who left us

---

[5] The text of Herodotus omits to mention the intermediate system of Ten gods: an almost certain indication that it has been "revised."

the Rosetta Stone could certainly read the hieroglyphics better than
we can—that there was any Egyptian history earlier than their own
Cres (or Iacchus), they would most likely have ascended to a higher
date, in order to prove, as Herodotus says the Phrygians did, (Euterpe, 2,)that their own incarnation was the more ancient and venerable. If the Jews, whose sacred books are credited to an earlier period
than the Alexandrian æra, and whom it must be supposed were also
acquainted with Egyptian literature and archæology, had any reason
to believe that the Egyptian annals ascended higher than their own
date of B C 3760, they would scarcely have been content to place
the birth of Adam in that year. It is the same with all the others
Each nation of antiquity went back far enough in its chronology to
prove itself to be heaven-descended   It results that none of them
suspected that the civilization of Egypt or Chaldea was believed by
anybody to be more ancient than the date affixed to their own civilisation, and as they lived from two to three thousand years nearer to
the beginning of Egypt and Chaldea than the modern Egyptologist,
we are compelled to prefer their testimony to his   That testimony is
to the effect that Manetho's dynasties are false; and that few or none
of the Egyptian or Chaldean epigraphic monuments are older than
about B. C. 1500 to 2000   The further inference to be drawn from
this comparison of æras is, that if we consider the Orient and Occident
separately, the longest or most ancient chronologies are those which
were probably fabricated latest, and the longest tale of all was that
of Manetho.

CHAPTER XI.

FORGERIES IN STONE.

JUST as there is scarcely a writing of the past that has not been corrupted, so there is scarcely a piece of ancient sculpture in our museums that has not been mutilated. The eminent antiquarian Feuardent accused Gen. Cesnola, or the professors and artists who worked under his directions, or upon his advice, of "building up" his collection of Cypriote antiquities, or at least a part of it, with fragments belonging to originally unconnected figures. The curators of the Roman museums did all this and much more. They altered the attributes of the marble deities and effaced the names of the artists who sculptured them; they forged names and dates; they mutilated zodiacs and planispheres; they obliterated some inscriptions, interpolated others, and deliberately destroyed those which they did not choose to alter or efface. Dr. Clarke alleges that such has been the fate of all the antiquities of the Crimea. In 1893 I had occasion to examine some ancient coins in the Paris Collection and while doing so I alluded, in hearing of the Assistant Curator, M. Cazenove, to the ancient year of ten months. To this M. Cazenove, albeit in many respects an accomplished numismatist, replied that there was no ancient year of ten months. It was in vain that I cited Livy, Ovid, Virgil, Censorinus, the numerical names of our months, and other evidences. He would not have it. Even when one of the other Curators came to my support, M. Cazenove continued to deny the ancient division of the year into ten months, On this subject there exists such an ample accumulation of evidences that only he who does not wish to believe, can fail to be convinced on the subject. To this evidence I propose to add, by way of example, the testimony of two stone monuments now in the Louvre. One of these is a Roman sundial and calendar, which has been altered from ten to twelve months, the other is an Egypto-Grecian planisphere similarly altered, but containing more convincing evidences of the forgery.

Roman Sun Dial and Calendar, Louvre, Mu., No. 2. This is a work of Pentilicon marble, discovered in the spring of 1792, at Gabies, by

Gavin Hamilton, a Scotch painter.[1] It has probably been altered or restored by Franzoni and was formerly in the Villa Borghese, Salle de Gabies, No. 16.

The modern parts are the heads of Mercury, Vulcan, Neptune, Juno, Apollo, Minerva and Jupiter; the lance and a piece of the table; the ends of the noses of Venus, Cupid, Mars, Diana and Ceres; Vesta's chin; nearly all of the lamp belonging to Vesta; the screech owls; the ram; the dove; finally the left arm of the Virgin.

This unique monument has severely tried the sagacity of the learned, who do not yet agree upon its signification. It is apparently composed of two different parts, independent of each other. In the middle of a circular table, is a sort of flat hollow, forming a patella, or disc, on which is (now) sculptured the heads of twelve Olympian divinities. All these heads appear full-faced with the exception of Ceres. From left to right they appear in the following order:

Neptune; on his left, a trident.

Juno crowned; to the left, a sceptre.

Apollo; his hair wreathed with a strophe; on his left, a sceptre.

Minerva, helmeted; on her right, a lance. The crown of the helmet is decorated with a seated sphinx. Two screech owls are perched upon the volutes of the visor.

Jupiter; on his left, a thunderbolt.

Venus crowned; on her left, a sceptre. Between Venus and Mars is placed a nude Cupid with its arms around the necks of the couple.

Mars, beardless; his helmet ornamented with griffins.

Diana; with bow and quiver over the left shoulder.

Ceres; (Visconti says Vesta;) the head bound with a strophe, turned towards Diana.

Vesta, (Visconti says Ceres).

Mercury, beardless; a winged wand on his left.

Vulcan, a round bonnet on his head, a sceptre on his left.

Upon the edge, or periphery of the table, are the twelve signs of the zodiac, accompanied by the emblem of the tutelar divinity who presides over each month of the year. These signs and emblems do not correspond with the heads carved upon the flat of the disc; and most of the conjectures that have been brought forward to establish their connection, have only served to complicate the subject. The

---

[1] Gabies, or Gabii, about 16 miles E. S. E. from Rome, possessed a temple of Juno, in which that goddess was worshipped with peculiar ceremonies, the priests wearing their dress in a characteristic manner. Virgil's Æneid, vii, 612 and 682.

eminent antiquarian Visconti is of opinion that we have here a veritable Roman calendar.

The heads of the five divinities, Jupiter, Juno, Minerva, Ceres and Diana, seem to correspond with the months indicated by the zodiac upon the edge; but not so the other seven gods.

Ceres has preserved the place she occupies in the zodiacal system; Mars and Mercury have changed theirs; the union of Mars with Venus and of Mercury with Vesta (or Ceres) is apparently maintained with design; Diana and Apollo are opposite each other. Most of this is the result of modern alterations.

All that can be positively affirmed is that this monument belongs to the Roman religion, the god Mars being there represented by a she-wolf; that it was probably made by a Roman artist, the diameter of the patella measuring exactly one Roman cubit, or about $17\frac{1}{2}$ inches; that the zodions of the 12-sign zodiac are not complementary with the heads of the gods; that the sculptor apparently wished to create an astronomical instrument, the moveable surface of which could be turned according to the march of time, or the wants of the operator; that the hollow in the middle of the disc, now composed of a vast number of small pieces not all of them antique, served as a sun-dial, because traces of the needles that pointed out the divisions of time and the thin plates of metal that upheld the hemisphere, can still be seen.

There can be no question that this monument was originallp sculptured with ten gods, which were afterwards altered to twelve; hence the incongruity between the figures on the disc and those on the periphery: the latter being probably of later date than the former. To these incongruities the modern " restorer " has added his own.

The Egypto-Grecian Planisphere, Louvre Mu., No. 4. This relic of antiquity consists at present of two fragments of white marble, which were excavated from a trench upon Mount Aventine in Rome during the year 1705. It was formerly in the Vatican Museum. It is a fragment of a Greco-Egyptian planisphere, reconstructed in 1705 by Francesco Bianchini, a Catholic antiquarian and astrologer of Verona.

The engraving is traced with a point (a graving tool) upon a slab of square marble, each side of which measures $28\frac{1}{8}$ inches, that is to say, exactly two Roman feet.

The radius taken between the exterior border of the medallion and the inner border of the great circle measures 7¼ inches, or exactly ten Roman digits The diameter of the large circle is 27 digits

Three-fourths of this interesting monument are lost or mutilated; the remaining portion only enables us to conjecture the principal design, not to reconstruct the whole

B de Montfaucon, in his "Antiquity Explained" (t I, pl 234, and suppl , t I, 17 b, p 43) published a fragment of a similar planisphere, a plan for the restoration of which he found among the manuscripts of Peiresc, 1580-1637, at the Saint Victor library.

The middle medallion represents a large bearded serpent, or dragon, turned to the left, the head turned downwards In the folds of the serpent, which take the form of an S, are seen two she-bears with open mouths, a little one running to the right and a larger, and higher, one running to the left It is easy to recognise in these the two familiar constellations of the Northern heavens. the Little and Great Bear.

This medallion is surrounded by four concentric circles, divided into 12 parts (dodecatemoria) by means of 12 straight lines, which start from the centre These lines may be wholly or partly modern

The middle zone encloses a zodiac of ten signs

Humboldt discovered in these signs certain analogies with the ancient Hindu zodiac The Horse, which corresponds with our sign of the Lion, occupies the same place in the Tartar, Hindu and Tibetan zodiacs. The Eagle, (?) Dog. and Serpent are met with not only among the Oriental zodiacs, but also among those of aboriginal Mexico; while the Goat occupies one of the lunar mansions of Hindostan

The two other circles enclose the signs of two Egypto-Greek zodiacs, one of 12 and one of ten signs There is no difference, either in the figures or the costumes The marble here is much mutilated The omitted signs are the Archer and Fishes An attempt, however, has been made to insert the Archer, so that there are permissably 11 signs The Ram and the Bull are decorated with dorsal bandelets, such as were put upon the victims on the day of sacrifice The Twins are represented by a nude youth carrying a club, and a nude girl with dishevelled hair, who, with one hand holds a lyre, resting upon a cippus, while her right arm is locked about her brother's neck.[2]

Cancer has the usual form of a crab The Balance is held in the

[2] The Count de Clarac's engraving of this monument is not exact. See Hugin, Astronomicon, ii, 22, p 472

lowered right hand of a young man, clothed with a chlamys. The Archer is represented by a Centaur letting fly an arrow. The double line which separates these two zodiacs may signify the Equator.

We arrive at a narrow border encumbered with Greek numerical signs, most of them in relief, a few of them engraved with the trait. As there are five such signs to each of the twelve constellations of the inner zodiac, Bianchini held that these numbers represented the epagomenæ, which the Greeks placed under the special guardianship of the five planets: Saturn, Jupiter, Mars, Venus, and Mercury. M. Lebroune treats them as mere gnostic absurdities.

With one exception, the signs of the 12-sign zodiacal planisphere agree with the lists of Ptolemy (Tetrabillon, I, 21) and of Julius Fir. micus Maternus, (Astronomicon, ii, 6.)

The letters employed differ from the ordinary alphabet, *e. g.*, in the form of the *sigma*, which is replaced by a Roman S. As to those which are engraved with the trait, (namely, the first sigma of the Ram, omega of the Bull and omega of the Balance) their object is not discernible.

In the original design the 36 days of the month are followed by secondary divinities who presided over the ten months of the year. Of these divinities only eight are left, differing from one another in form, costume and attributes. These are in a procession towards the right.

Chontare has the upper part of the body naked and he carries a two-edged sacrificial axe upon the left shoulder, as if he were going to sacrifice the ram of the zodiac. Chontachre, with a hawk's head, holds a ring in the lowered right hand. Some years ago this ring held a cross, but this has recently been chiseled away. Seket, clothed with a mantle, holds two rings, which also held crosses, which have recently been chiseled off. Choon, with a jackal's head, is also clothed with a mantle. Ero, nearly all destroyed, carries a sceptre. The fragment of the lower part commences with the 18th, or middle day, of the month, or Aphoso, the upper part of whose body is naked. He carries a ring (which some years ago held a cross) in his right hand and a stick in his left. Souchoé and Ptèchouli, both draped in the same manner, have their right hands advanced, and in the left, each holds a ring, from which the pendent cross has been destroyed. Chontare, again, with the bull's head, the upper part of the body naked, carries a sceptre.

It is unnecessary to remark that these figures are not strictly Egyptian. In passing into the domain of Greek astrology they underwent modifications which altered their previous character   Among the later modifications is the mutilation and chiseling of the crosses.

The proper names given above are Grecianized after Hephistion's list [8] Upon the periphery of the central design are placed the busts of the seven planetary gods, at the rate of three gods to each constellation   These gods can be easily recognised by their attributes. (See Lersch, Bonner Jahrbucher, vol IV, p 163)

Cronos, or Saturn, is clothed with a mantle, the head is veiled; he holds a harp   Zeus, or Jupiter, carries a sceptre; Ares, or Mars, is helmeted; he has a large belt over the left shoulder and is armed with a lance   Helios, or the Sun, wears a chlamys over the shoulder; his head is encircled with seven rays   Aphroditus, or Venus, is nude; she is decorated with a necklace and holds in her left hand a mirror. Hermes, or Mercury, has a winged head and a wand in his hand. Selene, or the Moon, has a crescent above the forehead.   The heads of these divinities are each backed by a disk, halo, or nimbus, similar to those of the later Byzantine saints

If the restoration of the destroyed parts is correctly surmised, it will be seen that, after the system of Ptolemy, the seven gods are repeated five times   Mars, by opening and ending the procession, makes the 36th god, answering to the 36 days of the month in the year of ten months

Formerly the four corners of the marble were occupied with the effigies of the four principal winds   Only one is left, perhaps the easterly wind, Subsolanus, who blows to the right.   His hair is dishevelled and upon the forehead is an ornament which one might take for a pen   An analogous bust is seen among the fragments of Peiresc, previously mentioned   All the parts engraved with traits were originally painted red   As to the age of the monument it can scarcely be much earlier than the Ptolemaic period.

When the planisphere was reconstructed, the following inscription was put upon it: "Fragmentum planisphærii, ursarum et draconis imaginibus inscripti iuxta Phenicios et Græcos, necnon XII asterismis borealibus Chaldæ orum et signis zodiaci, decanis ac terminus Ægyptiis vii planetarum. Effossum in monte Aventino, anno MDCCV "

The following table shows the two Ten-sign zodiacs of this calendar and the one mentioned by Baron von Humboldt:

---

[3] Biot, " Memoires de l'Academie des Inscriptions," 1846, vol XVI, ii, p 88· Abbildungen, " Symbolik," pl 19   The hieroglyphic groups are reunited after R. Lepsius, "Chron Egyp ," I, 66-77, 551

Egyptian, ten signs, Exterior zone.	Chaldean, ten signs, Middle zone.	Hindu, ten signs. Humboldt.	The Ten Syrian Months. Nicholas. (4).
Twins	Serpent	Fishes	Sabat
Crab	Crab	Bull	Adar
Lion	Horse	Horse	Nissan
Virgin	Lion? [5]	Virgin	Iyar
Balance	Goat	Balance	Sivan
Scorpion	Cow	Warrior?	Thamuz
Goat	Eagle	Dwarf	Ab
Aquarius	Bear	Man-lion	Eloul
Ram	Quadruped [6]	Bear	Tesri
Bull	Dog	Tortoise	Kanun

Such is a faithful description of these marbles at the present time. The nature of the alterations makes it evident that a portion of them were effected in ancient times in order to conceal the Ten months year, while another portion were made in modern times in order to efface those sacred symbols which we have borrowed from obsolete religions and falsely claim to be peculiar to our own. Perrot and Chipiez, "Egyptian Art," I, 233, 241, inform us that King Psousennes carved upon the sphinxes of a Hyksos monarch, his own false and anacronical cartouch. Are we, who deface and pervert the religious monuments of the past, any better than the royal Egyptian forger?

[4] To these ten months were afterwards added Tisri II and Kanun II, making twelve. These duplicate months were inserted (at least they so appear now) immediately after those of the same names. The Jews had the same months, except that they added Heshvan and Tebet, after Tisri and Kanun and changed the latter to Kislev. In their lunar calendar they also had a 13th month, which was added in embolismic years. This was called Adar Sheni. The solar year commenced on or about the vernal equinox and with the suggestive month of N'Issan.

[5] Mutilated; hind-part only remains of what seems to be a lion.

[6] Mutilated; possibly a deer.

CHAPTER XII.

THE MESSIAH.

HISTORIANS of the Roman republic have too commonly betrayed a tendency to find the cause of its decline in the working of some one or other defective institute of that great state, some institute that was especially inimical to the writer, as the establishment of colonies, the unequal distribution of opportunity, wealth, lands, or political power, or the growth of slavery, or the evils of the monetary system. But a broader survey of the subject rather leads to the conclusion that no single cause is sufficient to account for the devolution of events which followed the Punic wars. The downfall of the republic and the erection of the empire appear to have been due in part to all of these circumstances and perhaps also to others, among not the least of which were religion and the various branches of knowledge and belief upon which religion was founded. After striving in vain to uphold the tottering republic, Cicero lived long enough to perceive that the catastrophe was inevitable and that neither could he retard it, nor Cæsar accelerate it.[1] Rome was no longer a small commonwealth of free citizens, rendered more or less equal in rank by a substantial equality of fortune, attainments and political power. It had become a populous and unwieldy empire, composed of many conquered nations and tribes, differing in race, religion, language, history and degrees of social development. The republican constitution, which had sufficiently well fitted the infancy of this state, and which, had the state grown less rapidly, might have been gradually altered to suit its greatly altered manhood, was, under the circumstances, antequated and useless, as a means of repressing disorder, or preserving the peace. This constitution had been overthrown by Marius and Sylla. The Civil Wars had supplemented the existing orders of priests, patricians, plebians and slaves, with what was substantially a new social caste, the equites, or knights—the future farmers of the revenues and the lords of feudal manors. When

---

[1] "Cæsar is no less under the control of circumstances than we are under the control of Cæsar." Letter of Cicero to Papirius Pætus, dated A. U. 707?

to the already vast territorial possessions of the Commonwealth were afterwards added nearly the whole of Transalpine Europe, and of Asia Minor and Egypt, the republican constitution utterly broke down. The year that saw Pompey invested with the supreme power of the Roman State, added further dignities and privileges to the new order of aristocrats. [2] These developments of caste were sure presages of the Empire. [3]

In both of the last dictatorships all the civil powers of the State had been entrusted to one man, in the hope of securing order and tranquility; in both cases the trust had failed to secure its object. To keep together so vast an empire, to assimilate under one government such heterogeneous populations as had recently been brought under its sway; to command the respect of distant kings; to curb the ambition and repress the avarice of proconsuls who had become mightier than kings; and to conserve the private fortunes that had been carved out of the dying republic; some greater elements of power and authority and some more efficacious means of subordination were required to be wielded at Rome than those which had failed in the hands of Sylla and Pompey. Take, for example, the case of Parthia. This state had formerly been subject successively to the divine monarchs of Media, Persia and Syro-Macedonia: it had emancipated itself from their controul; it had deified its own sovereigns and these had become subject to a Roman proconsul. The involution of heavenly rank therefore stood as follows: the sovereign of Media was a god; the sovereign of Persia was a higher god, because he had overthrown the former one and substituted himself in his place as an object of worship. For a similar reason the Seleucidæ and Arsacidæ were gods, of still higher rank, until we come to Pompey, who was by parity of reasoning the highest of gods, that is to say, the god of gods, because he overthrew the entire succession of these divinities; he was mightier than them all.

The additional powers and discipline which for these reasons were needed to maintain the ascendancy of Rome were found in the pecu-

[2] Dio., xxxvi, 25; Juv., iii, 159; xiv, 324; Adams, 21.

[3] So far was Cicero from sharing this opinion that he actually regarded the new order of nobles, when they should unite with the ancient noblesse of the Senate, as an additional guarantee for the permanency and security of the Republic. Cicero, however, as his letters abundantly prove, was a poor politician. Indeed this Upas tree of caste grew so rapidly that, in his second philipic, he was obliged to confess that during his own lifetime he had witnessed the Dictatorship of Sylla, the Lordship of Cinna, and the Monarchy of Cæsar. But even here his vision was very limited; it was not a Monarchy, but an Hierarchy, that had grown up under his eyes. Orat., ii. 105.

liar organization and privileges of the Sacred college and in the mysteries of religion. These the ambitious and unscrupulous Cæsar hastened to seize with the office of high-priest and the assumption of sacerdotal powers, which, in proportion as they exceeded the attributes of earthly kings, rivalled those of gods To this discipline and subordination was added that moral influence which the church alone could wield, the influence of blind faith, of religious myths and superstition, the respect for ecclesiastical displeasure, the fear of committing sacrilege, and the dread of excommunication and anathema. [4] These are elements of power and government which no statesman, in any age, can afford to despise, and which we may feel assured were not permitted to lie unused by so profound a politician as Julius Cæsar The example of other states may also have contributed to bring about the Roman hierarchy Hindostan, China, Japan, Persia, Chaldea, Egypt, Greece, Etruria and numerous other states of antiquity had been hierarchies Archaic Rome itself had been an hierarchy Gaul was an hierarchy Many of these hierarchies survived to Cæsar's time, and some of them, although all were decaying, were among the richest and most populous states then in existence.

Cæsar has left us in no doubt with regard to his design The conquest of India by Alexander had brought anew to the western world the entire flood of Brahminical myths [5] The eleventh, a supplementary incarnation of Vishnu (zodion of Pisces) was at hand, and Cæsar, (who, among his many gifts, was an accomplished master of astrology,) had evidently determined to become its hero, for he publicly and ostentatiously proclaimed his descent from the goddess Maria or Venus, and attested his official acts with a seal which bore her effigy. Marcus Cœlius, writing to Cicero in A U 704, alluded to Cæsar as " our heavenly-descended chief," a proof that such was the character of his pretensions [6] But there are many more proofs to come Cæsar's further plans were cut short by the dagger of his friend Brutus, but they are clearly discernible in the constitution which was developed by his adopted son, Augustus, and which, beyond some impairment of the first article, continued to remain essentially the fundamental law of the whole empire, until the Moslem revolt in the seventh century withdrew the eastern provinces from Rome, the revolt of the bishops of Rome in the eighth century withdrew the western

[4] Cicero, de l egibus, ii, 7

[5] It is to these myths, many of which reached the Romans through Assyria, that Tacitus seems to allude by the term "judicial astrology " Annals, ii, 27, passim.

[6] Suet Jul vi, Dio , xi iv, Melmoth's Letters of Cicero, vii, 7.

provinces, and the Latin conquest of Constantinople in the 13th century destroyed all that was left of the ancient imperial authority.

The first and most important article in the constitution of this empire was the extraordinary one of the Emperor's deification. Both in Spain and Gaul Cæsar must have heard of Hesus, the Messiah, whose effigy stood at every cross-road, whose crosses were worn upon the breast of every warrior, and whose second coming, which had been long predicted by the Druid astrologers, coincided very closely with the period of his own invasion of those countries. Indeed, it is not at all improbable that, like Musa, Pizarro and Cortes, of later ages, he made use of this superstition to represent himself or permit himself to be regarded as the Expected One, in order to render his march of conquest the more easy and rapid. However this may be, it was probably less the imaginary incarnation of Hesus than the actual example of Alexander which afforded to Julius Cæsar the precedent which he followed in his own deification. "When he was in Spain he bestowed his leisure hours in reading the history of Alexander, and was so much affected by it that he sat pensive a long time, and being asked the reason, he said, 'Is it not sufficient cause for concern to reflect that Alexander at my age reigned over numerous conquered countries, whilst I, as yet, have not one glorious achievement to boast?'"[7] Not only the example of Alexander, but the similarity of circumstances, helped to make a divinity of Cæsar. After the battle of Pharsalia the world was at his feet; and among the numerous potentates who were swayed by his nod were many who were themselves gods, and, as such, were worshipped by their degraded subjects.[8]

From Pharsalia Cæsar went to Egypt. He arrived in Alexandria October 6th, B. C. 48, and remained there until the month of March.[9] It was during this interval that, following in the footsteps of the Macedonian conqueror, he permitted himself, on Brumalia, or the winter solstice, A. U. 706, to be deified in the temple of Jupiter Ammon and hailed by its subservient priests as the Son of God,[10] and it

---

[7] Plutarch, in Julius Cæsar. The official seal of Augustus was an effigy of Alexander the Great. Suetonius, in Aug., 49.

[8] In after times similar empires, whose Asiatic origin is plainly stamped upon their religious remains, were discovered and destroyed by the astonished Spaniards in distant Mexico and Peru. Mr. Bryce (Holy Roman Empire, 251,) notices the resemblance between the sacred empires of the Cæsars and the Caliphs, but omits to mention the most important respect in which they differed, namely, in the deification and adoration of the sovereign.   [9] Simcox.

[10] It was customary with the pagan Romans to bestow a new name upon those who were honoured with the rites of deification, as afterwards it was with the Christians to

was in this same temple, after his death and pretended ascension to heaven, (of which more anon,) that Octavius, the Augustus, his adopted son and successor, paid him the reverence due to God the Father. Cæsar returned to Rome through Syria, and on the way he stopped at Piscenus, or Pesinus, in Galatia, the seat of the religion of Maia, Mother of the Gods. Here, if we can place any faith in the accusation which both Cicero aad Brutus assisted to repel, his assassination was planned (though the plan miscarried) by Deiotaurus, the sacred king of the Galatians [11]. However, it was not in Galatia that a tragic and untimely death was destined to overtake him, but in Rome.

The assumption of an heavenly origin entirely changed the character and demeanour of Julius. Upon his return to the capitol he became difficult of access and was rarely seen in public, except when affairs of state rendered it necessary for him to consult with the patricians of the Senate. He placed his own statue on a sculptured horse which had once supported the figure of Alexander the Great. This was in front of the temple of Venus Genetrix [12]. Other statues of himself were placed among those of the gods in the various temples and carried in the processions of the circus. Even these tokens scarced sufficed to absorb that religious fervour and popular reverence for his person and name, which was soon to become the scandal of the provinces and the watchword for assassination in the capital. He was presented with sacred vestments, with a sacred image of himself to be borne in his chariot, with a sacred throne and a sacred bed [13]. To mark the sacred character of his residence it was surmounted by a steeple. This architectural device was an Egyptian symbol of ecclesiastical and sacerdotal authority, the Roman name for which was fastigium. "Divus Julius habuit pulvinar, simulacrum, fastigium,

---

those who were canonized as saints. On this occasion Caius received the sacerdotal name of Julus, or Julius, really copied from the Indian Houli, but feigned to be taken from Julius, the son of Æneas, from whom his family subsequently affected to trace their descent. In all the earlier works referring to him he is called Caius Cæsar, and sometimes simply Caius. Mr. Higgins has collected many curious observations relating to the name of Julius, which he connects with the festival of Yule and the custom of the Yule-log. Brumalia is from Brouma, or Brumess, one of the names or titles of Bacchus. This deity, whom the medieval monks consigned to revelry and intoxication, was anciently worshipped as the pure, the chaste, the joyous Messiah. He was the Son of God, immaculately conceived by the virgin Maia, or Ceres, sometimes called Semele.   [11] Cicero, Letters, III, 25, Orat. pro Deiotaurus

[12] Lanciani, "Pagan and Christian Rome," p 54

[13] Suet, in Jul, 76 App., Bell Civ., III, p. 494

flaminem, etc." The god Julius had shrines, an image, a steeple, priests, and so on.[14] The steeple of the Regia probably also contained a chime of bells like the temple of Jupiter.[15] Speaking of the omens that, it was believed, preceded the assassination of Julius, Plutarch, in his life of that divinity, says, "Calphurnia dreamed that the steeple fell down, which, according to Livy, the Senate ordered to be erected upon Cæsar's residence, by way of distinction."[16] The temples of Julius Cæsar bore the appellation of Heroum Juleum, or Julian chapels, and contained his effigy and that of Venus, Mother of God.[17] "On certain occasions, in the exercise of his high pontifical office, he appeared in all the pomp of the Babylonian costume, in robes of scarlet, with the Crosier in his hand, wearing the Mitre and bearing the Keys."[18]

Of the numerous statues made of him at, or shortly after, this period, but few have survived the devastation of the iconoclasts, or the corroding hand of time. Among them is the magnificent bust, which still adorns the Pontifical palace at Rome. Upon the head of the deity is seen the sacred mantle, or peplum, which marks his heavenly character.

When the tremendous commotion caused by the death of Julius Cæsar had spent itself in civil wars, and in the firm establishment of the Messianic religion and ritual, Augustus ascended the sacred throne of his martyred sire and was in turn addressed as the Son of God, whilst Julius was worshipped as the Father.[19] The flamens of the Sacred college erected and consecrated to the worship of Julius Cæsar a magnificent temple in Rome, and for its services, as well as for those of the provincial temples which might be consecrated to the same god, they organized a body of priests called the Julii, or Juliani.[20] These priests were selected from the most ancient order, the Luperci, of whom Ovid says that they were instituted by Evander,[21] and to which order none could belong but the members of noble families. This priesthood was not abolished until the time of Anastasius Silentiarius in the sixth century;[22] so that as Juliani they

---

[14] Cic., II Philipic, (Orat., II, 106.) [15] Suet., Aug., 91.

[16] Plut., in vita; Pliny, XXXV, 12, s. 45; XXXVI, 5; Paus., 54; and Cic. Flor., IV, 2.

[17] Rev. A. Herbert, "Nimrod," I, 455. [18] Rev. A. Hislop, "Two Babylons," p. 241.

[19] Manilius, "Astronomica," quoted farther on; Ovid, Fasti, III, 155-9.

[20] Dio., XLVII, 18; Dio. Cas., 45; Plut., in Rom.; Virgil, Aen., VIII, 663.

[21] Fasti, II, 279; see also Livy, I, 5.

[22] So says Onuphrius Panvinius, a learned Augustine monk of Verona, 1529-68, the author of the "Lives of the Popes" and other works.

held together from first to last for nearly six hundred years. The first bishop or chief priest of the Julian cult was Marc Antony.[23] No person who fled to a temple of Julius for sanctuary could be taken from it for punishment, a privilege which had never been granted before, not even to the temples and sanctuaries of Jupiter. Except when Augustus caused the son of Marc Antony to be dragged from one and slain,[24] the shrines of Julius were always regarded as inviolable.[25] Under the Triumvirate and during the early portion of the reign of Augustus, the worship of Julius Cæsar and the erection of temples, sanctuaries, shrines and altars consecrated to this worship was carried to all parts of the empire and enforced by precept, example and military power. Upon these altars costly offerings and bloody sacrifices were made. One of the latter consisted of 300 senators and equites, who were coldly slaughtered by order of Augustus upon the ides of March, A. U. 713, on a Julian altar at Perugia, to propitiate the god Divus Julius.[26] Official oaths were formulated in the name of Julius Cæsar, and to violate them was deemed a more heinous crime and punished with greater severity than any other perjury.[27]

The naming of one of the months of the year after the god Julius, which was done during the consulship of Marc Antony, is, by itself, no evidence of his deification; but the practice of other nations, the precedent afforded by the Athenian god Demetrius, the subsequent naming of a month after the deified Augustus, and the fact that the Romans never adopted any names in place of the ancient numerical names of the months, except the names of gods, lends it great significance. Many attempts were made to name the months after various emperors who followed Augustus, but they all failed. April was for a brief time called Neronius, May, Claudius, and June, Germanicus.[28] Tiberius, who refused to be deified, or worshipped as a

---

[23] "As Jove, as Mars, as Quirinus have their priests, so is Marc Antony priest of the god Julius." "Est ergo flamen, ut Jovi, ut Marti, ut Quirino, sic Divo Julio, Marcus Antonius." Cicero, II Philipic

[24] Suet., Aug., 17.   [25] Adams, 264.

[26] Suet., Aug., 15, Dio., XLVIII, 14, Seneca de Clem., I, 11, App. de Bell. Civ., lib. v. This horrible rite celebrated the conclusion of the Civil War, the Ascension of Julius to Heaven and the Advent of Augustus as the Prince of Peace. In the time of Julius Cæsar human sacrifices were only made to Mars; in that of Augustus they were made to Julius the Father

[27] Dio., XIV, 6 and 50, Tac., Ann., I, 73; Codex, IV, 1, 2, Codex, II, 4, 41, Digest, XII, 2, 13, Tertull Apol., 18, Cicero de Legibus, II, 7.

[28] Tacitus, Ann., XV, 12 and 74.

god, also refused to permit his name to be substituted for November. [29]

In remote times the Roman year was divided into ten months, named Primus, Secundus, Tertius, Quartus, Quintilis, Sextilis, Septembris, Octobris, Novembris and Decembris, the year beginning with the vernal equinox, which was made to fall on the first day of March and the months containing 36 days each. After the adoption of the gods Mars, Aphrodite, Maia and Juno into the Roman pantheon their names were conferred upon the first four months of the year, instead of Primus, Secundus, Tertius and Quartus. This calendar was reformed by the Decemvirs, in the sacred name of "Numa." They divided the year into 12 months with intercalary days and conferred upon the supplementary months the names of the gods Janus and Februus. [30] When Julius Cæsar was deified his name was given to what was originally the fifth month of the year, or Quintilis. When Octavius Augustus Cæsar was deified his sacerdotal name was given to the original sixth month, or Sextilis. [31] The remaining months still bear their ancient ordinal names.

If all other evidences had perished, the names of the months alone would have been sufficient to afford a clue to the worship of Julius Cæsar. The inveteracy of custom, the respect for tradition, the practical inconvenience that arises from changes of any kind, all combine to resist innovation, so that when innovation does occur, as in the case of changed names of the months, it may be tolerably certain that powerful motives or irresistible influences lurk beneath. If such be the case, even at the present time, when intelligence is universally diffused and public opinion is guided by an unfettered press, it may be imagined how much more emphatically it was the case when mankind was steeped in superstition, when every life was in danger, and when innovation had to resist not only the inveteracy of custom, but the mandates of revengeful and absolute power. [32]

[29] In 796, after Pope Leo III. had sent the keys and standard of Rome and other tokens of his submission to Charlemagne, the latter gave twelve German names to the months of the year, but they all fell flat; the people would not accept them.

[30] Brumalia, or the winter solstice, was anciently the first day of the year. Beginning the year a week after the winter solstice was an innovation.

[31] Macrobius, Sat., I, 12, says the change was made in the Senate on motion of the tribune Pacuvius and leaves us the inference that it was done during the lifetime of Augustus. The inference is corroborated by John of Nikios.

[32] Other attempts have been made both in ancient and modern times to change the Roman names of the months, but they all proved abortive.

If the reader is surprised and shocked at the impiety of a religion such as we have described, let it be remembered that the minds of the Romans were prepared for it by the familiar worship of the Lares or the manes of their ancestors; [33] by the depravity which they themselves had ascribed to many of their Homeric gods, by the Messianic incarnations which had gone before, among them that of their own Janus Quirinus; [34] and especially by the nearer incarnations and worship of Alexander the Great, Demetrius Poliorcetes and Titus Flamininus, by the anarchy, bloodshed and brutalizing triumphs [35] and spectacles which civil wars and foreign conquests had recently brought beneath their eyes, [36] by the transcendent services, both military and civil, which Julius had rendered to the State; and by his illustrious descent, his alleged miraculous birth, [37] his brilliant and varied attainments, [38] his extraordinary courage and sagacity, his personal magnetism, his profuse liberality, the magnificence and glamour of his surroundings and the legitimate authority he wielded both as sovereign and high-priest. [39] Even Pompey's triumph had helped to pave the way for the deification of his rival and successor. Among the kings who had paid homage to Pompey was that scion of the Arsa-

[33] Virgil, Aeneid, IX, 255, Tooke's Pantheon, 279

[34] Julius Proculus swore that Romulus appeared to him and ordered him to inform the Senate that he had been called to the assembly of the gods, and that sacrifices should be made to him under the name of Quirinus. Plutarch, in Rom , Livy, I, 16 and Dio Halicar The figures of Romulus appear clad in the trabea, a robe of state, which implies an ecclesiastical as well as secular dignity. The lituus, or staff of augury, in his hand, survives in the crosier Bell's Pantheon

[35] The elation produced by a military triumph was such as to render it necessary to place behind the victor's back, a slave, whose office it was to remind him that he was but a mortal' Pliny, XXIII, 1, p 4 Was it the victor's elation, or a popular dread of the example set by Scipio, Sylla, and Pompey?

[36] The people of Paris, scarcely over a century ago, worshipped a Goddess of Reason, personified by a beautiful young woman.

[37] Julius Cæsar was born exactly 658 years, less ten years, after the incarnation of Nabon-Issus This interval was the celebrated astrological cycle or one-tenth of the annualized cycle of the moon's node, which was the proper time for the recurrence of an incarnation. The æra of Mahomet is exactly 658 years, plus ten years after the deification of Cæsar. These differences of ten years may be due to the subsequent alteration of the Alexandrian æra, alluded to elsewhere in this work The accepted year of Cæsar's birth and that of Mahomet's Flight, were probably both "adjusted" by the astrologers

[38] "Cæsar had capacity, sense, memory, learning, foresight, reflection and spirit." Cic , II Phil., 45.

[39] "The deified Julius, a most perfect specimen, as well of the divinity of heaven, as of the human intellect." Valerius Maximus, VIII, 2.

cides, whose arrogant line had exacted a worship due alone to the Creator. Pompey, as though persuaded that no one less than a god could receive homage from a god, caused an image of himself, in gold and pearls, to be carried in the most brilliant procession that the world ever saw; leaving his son Sextus to complete the impious pretension which the father had perhaps merely suggested. [40]

The Roman dominion was no longer Italy, no longer Europe, but the earth. At the feet of Pompey 12 tributary kings had laid their crowns; at the tread of the Julian legions the earth seemed to tremble and empires fell to pieces. Love, admiration, respect, veneration, are feelings which failed to express the idolatry of a sensuous and embruted population, toward a being so exalted, so gifted, so brilliant, so god-like, above all, so powerful, as Julius Cæsar, whose slightest word sufficed to condemn a kingdom to destruction, whose merest glance of favour meant fortune, preferment, power, opportunity, livings, endowments, license, satiety, all that men, that hierophants, that nations, coveted. Adoration was alone sufficient to express the feelings of the Roman populace toward him who reigned over the vast empire which they had acquired and the innumerable kingdoms they had enslaved. But a few years later Tiberius was actually upbraided because he refused to be deified and because he persisted in reminding the Romans that he was but a mortal. [41] We may be certain that Julius had little need to command deification; his crime was that he permitted and accepted it.

If, after all these evidences and considerations, the prevalence of this form of anthropomorphism should still excite his incredulity, let the reader turn to a passage in Ezekiel, and read of that prince of Tyre who was rebuked and devoted to destruction, because in his pride he claimed to be a god. Next let him open the Antiquities of Josephus, XIX, viii, 2, and he will learn that Agrippa, the tributary king of Judea, etc., under Claudius Cæsar, appeared at a public festival in Cæsarea in a "garment made wholly of silver and of a texture truly wonderful, and coming into the theatre early in the day, when the silver of his garment, illuminated by the sun's rays, was so resplendent as to send a horror over those who looked intently upon him, his sycophants cried out, some from one place and some from

---

[40] Among the kings devoted to Pompey, but who survived him, was Deiotaurus of Galatia, whose name also implies the assumption of a divine character. The abbé Lenglet de Fresnoy dates the deification of Sextus Pompey as the "Son of Neptune" in B. C. 37. Chronol., I, 474. Neptune was the god who presided over the zodiacal Fishes.   [41] Tac. Ann., IV, 38.

another, that he was a god, and they added, ' Be thou merciful to us, for though we have hitherto reverenced thee only as a man, yet shall we henceforth own thee as superior to mortal nature.' " Unfortunately for this would-be deity, he was shortly afterwards taken with a colic and died in great pain, perhaps poisoned by some obscure Brutus of Judea. [42]

It is not necessary to account for such a worship by recalling the depravity of the age A country could be named where similar depravity exists to-day, yet where there is no worship of the reigning sovereign. It was due to faith, habit, custom, example, in short, to the fact that the Romans lived nearly two thousand years nearer to the Brahminical myth of the Incarnation than we do Our task is to relate the historical fact, we leave to others the less invidious burden of its explanation, only let them take heed, in such explanation, of other phases of religion; of the Hanging Fakirs, the Stylites, the Chainwearers and Grasseaters of the imperial æra, of the Agapemonæ of England, the Shakers and Mormons of America, and the other strange rites or beliefs that mankind have practised or endured [43]

[42] This story of Agrippa, or Herod, is briefly told in Acts XII, 22, where the scene, however, is changed to Tyre The following example of human-worship belongs to the present time

Calcutta, June 20, 1894 —Yesterday the Queen's statue at Madras was smeared (annointed) with Hindu religious marks on the forehead, neck and breast The police inquiry has resulted in the opinion being expressed that it was the work of a Hindu who desired to worship the statue This is not the first time that such a smearing (annointing) has taken place. Some time ago a carpenter was caught in the act of decorating the statue with garlands, and marks similar to those now found were detected on that occasion He said that he was worshipping the Great Maharanee, who, he hoped, would protect him and give him plenty of work The Inspector of Police, in whose division the statue is situated, says that he himself has noticed people burning incense, breaking cocoanuts, and prostrating themselves in worship before it Correspondence London Times

[43] See my Essay on "The Druses of Galilee" Materials for a history of the Druses will be found in Ezekiel, Josephus, Pausanias, De Sacy, Didron, Churchill and other works The Jezites, an ancient "Christian sect" in Persia, are described by Noel, article "Jezd" The Stylites, Grasseaters, and other "Christian" sects of a later period are mentioned in most of the early ecclesiastical "histories " The Galilean Chainwearers are described by the Emperor Julian, in the fragment preserved by Cyril of Alexandria A modern incarnation of the deity in the kingdom of Ava is mentioned by Upham A re-incarnation of Salivahana was to "come off" in 1895. So late as 1781, Sir William Hamilton, the English ambassador to the Court of Naples, found that phallic symbols were publicly worshipped in the Christian churches of Isnernia and Daniano Meredith's pages are crowded with evidences on this subject. The images of the Sibyls were retained in the Christian church of Sienna Bell s Pantheon, II, 237 The Agapemonæ was an English Christian sect of the present century, whose abominable rites are alluded to by the Rev Mr. Baring-Gould. For the blasphemous monkish tale of the marriage of St. Dunstan's mother to the Almighty, see Brady's Clavis Calendaria, I, 388.

As in the case of other successful deifications or apotheoses, that of Julius Cæsar was made the beginning of a new æra. This one began with the date of his deification in the temple of Jupiter Ammon, on the winter solstice of the year B. C. 48. As it coincided closely with the date of the battle of Pharsalia, Tacitus and other pagan dissenters from Julianism, who could not change the æra, called it, or have been made by their redactors to call it, the æra of that battle; and as it also coincided within a year or two of the alleged freedom of Antioch, the Christian monks, who could not change it, called it by the name of that event. As such it was employed by the putative Evagrius, in the sixth century, and explained away by Pope Gregory XIII. in the 16th century. [44]

Even after the deification of Julius was ratified by the senate of Rome, two years later, the Julian æra was reckoned from the original deification, and, as such, it was introduced into all parts of the empire, with, possibly, the exception of Antioch, for this exception is by no means certain. This subject, as well as the absence of all mention of the Christian æra by the Christian writers down to the pontificate of Gregory II., has received attention in another place.

The worship of Divus Julius was encouraged and supported both by the Triumvirate, who assumed the government of the Roman world after his death, and by Octavius, the Augustus, who succeeded the Triumvirate. Nay more, Augustus had the address to cause his own worship to be added to that of Julius. The latter was now impiously addressed as the Supreme Being, the former became the Son of God, and as such he is announced upon his coins and other monuments. But this did not last long. Even the Son of God did not appear to be a title sufficiently exalted to suit the devotees of the Augustus; and in numerous contemporary inscriptions, both in Rome, Greece and Asia, he is termed Deos, or Theos, which means not the Son of God, nor one of the gods, but the living god, the Creator, Optimo Maximo. However, Divus Filius, Æsar and Quirinus seem to have been the titles by which Octavius himself preferred to be called.

---

[44] Says Gregory: "Antioch, in honour of the emperor, fixed its æra in Caius Julius Cæsar and made this year of grace, the first." "Works," London, ed. 1665, p. 156, cited in Evagrius, note to 11, 12. The Holy father then admits some instances of its use (as though such instances were rare) and ascribes its adoption to the free prerogatives of the city, secured to it by Julius Cæsar. If the granting of such freedom to cities was sufficient to cause a change of the æra it may be asked why is it that Antioch stands almost alone in this respect, and why is it that nearly all other æras are those of pretended incarnations or deifications, and not of freedom conferred upon cities?

The worship of Augustus was not, as the ecclesiastical schools have insinuated, a mere lip-service, a meaningless mode of saluting the sovereign-pontiff, an effusive form of adulation or flattery to the emperor of Rome; it was the worship of a personage who was believed to be supernatural, omniscient, all-powerful and beneficent, the re-incarnation of Quirinus, the Son of the god Apollo and of the wife-virgin Maia, [45] the god whose coming was foretold by the Cumæan Sibyl, whose sway was to extend over the whole earth; whose Conception and Birth were both miraculous, and whose Advent was to usher in the Golden Age of Peace and Plenty and to banish Sin forever. Such was his character in Rome. In Greece he was worshipped as Dionysos; in Egypt as Thurinus; in Iberia and Gaul as Æsar, or Hesus; and in Germany as Baldir; for all of these titles and many others will be found on his monuments, or have been preserved by his biographers.

The most effective reply that can be made to those historians who have ignored the worship of Augustus—and who, when they have not concealed its evidences, have passed them over, or sought to belittle them—is to read a letter from one of the worshippers of this god, written from Tomis, a Roman outpost, near the mouths of the Danube [46] addressed to Græcinus, in Rome, and dated, according to our chronology, A D 15, or shortly after the death and Ascension of Augustus. The writer of this letter was no less a person than the poet Ovid, or Publius Ovidius Naso, a nobleman of the equestrian order, then 58 years of age and, as his other writings testify, in the full possession of his faculties.

"Nor is my piety unknown. this distant land sees a shrine of our Lord Augustus erected in my house. Together with him stand his son and wife (his priestess), deities scarcely less than our Lord himself .   . As oft as the day arises, so often do I address my prayers to them, together with offerings of frankincense. Shouldst thou enquire, the whole of Pontus will confirm my words, and attest my sincerity; nor is my religion less known to strangers   .
Though fortune is not equal to my inclination in such duties, I willingly devote to this worship such means as I command   .
Cæsar! Thou, who art summoned to the gods above, thou too, from whom nothing can be concealed, thou knowest this to be true!

[45] For Maia, Atia, etc , see the author's monograph on "The Mother of the Gods."
[46] The Danube was originally called the Issus, afterward, the Matous. Malte-Brun's Geog

In thy place among the stars, fixed in the arch of the skies, thou hearest my prayers, which I utter with anxious lips!"

This evidence does not stand alone. Throughout all of Ovid's Letters, of which 36 remain to us, throughout all of his Elegies, of which 50 remain, throughout all his Fasti, of which six entire books remain, he repeatedly addresses the then living Augustus as God, or the Son of God, the Great Deity, the Heaven-born, the Divine, the Omniscient, the Beneficent, the Just, the Long-suffering, the Merciful God. It may serve the purposes of perversion to explain this away, it may afford a refuge for obstinacy or delusion to dismiss it with affectations of incredulity or contempt; but this is no answer to the fact; for fact it unquestionably is, not alone upon the testimony of Ovid, but upon that also of numerous other intelligent, respectable and even illustrious witnesses, that is to say, the testimony of Virgil, Horace, Manilius, Pliny, Suetonius and others. What is insisted upon is that, Augustus Cæsar, by his contemporaries, was believed to be, and was actually worshipped as a god; with bell, book, candle, steeple, frankincense, rosary, cross, mitre, temples, priesthood, benefices and ritual; in short, with all the outward marks of superstition, credulity, piety and devotion. There is nothing impossible about this; and the evidence of this worship is so valid, circumstantial and overwhelming, that to refuse assent to it, is to put reason out of court altogether. The witnesses are not phantoms, the wild creations of credulous minds; their writings are not anonymous patchworks, undated, unlocated and unsigned; they do not stand unsupported by archæology, inscriptions, coins, calendars, or popular customs; on the contrary, they are corroborated and buttressed by all these classes of evidence. The witnesses are men of reputation, their writings are among the masterpieces of the world, which it would be impossible to imitate and difficult to alter without detection, whilst the monuments which support them are numbered by myriads and found in every conceivable locality, from the Roman slabs in the mosque of Ancyra, to the coins rescued from buried Pompeii; both of which, as well as a vast number of other inscriptions and coins, proclaim the divinity and universal worship of Augustus throughout the Roman world.

And mark this: that in actual history great events do not occur alone. They appear neither unheralded nor unsung. Minor events start forth to presage them; others proclaim their occurrence; still others attest and exalt their significance; whilst a numerous progeny of facts remain behind to corroborate their appearance upon the

world's stage and to definitely mark their æra. The presages of the
Augustan incarnation were the previous assumptions of divinity by
Alexander the Great, the Ptolemies, the Selucidæ, Demetrius Poliorcetes, the Arsacidæ, Titus Quinctius Flamininus, the abortive attempts of Scipio, Sylla, Sertorius and Pompey, and the successful
one of Julius Cæsar   It was the bestowal of Cæsar's empire, Spiritual
and Temporal, upon his adopted son Augustus, that directly led to
the worship of the latter.   The assumption of divinity by the various
sovereigns and heroes mentioned, are historical facts which no amount
of sophistry can belittle or set aside; they are the historical circumstances that presaged and led up the worship of Augustus   In false
history and false philosophy there is no such evolution.   Take for
example the incarnations of Nebo-Nazaru, Hesus and Salivahana
What preceded these fictions? Nothing.   What accompanied them?
Nothing   What followed them? Nothing, but other fictions   What
evidences of their occurrence exists within two hundred years of the
time assigned to them? None whatever.   What valid evidence, at
any ime? None at all   They were myths of the cloisters, unconnected with any real event, fabricated centuries after the date assigned to them, and supported only by forgery, imposture and alterations of the calendar

When the tremendous commotion caused by the assassination of
Julius Cæsar had spent itself in civil wars and in the firm establishment of the Messianic religion and ritual, when Actium was won, and
Egypt and Asia were reconquered, Augustus ascended the throne of
his martyred Sire and was in turn annointed, addressed and worshipped as the Son of God, whilst Julius was tacitly worshipped as the
Father   Most of the ancient books were now destroyed; the writers
of the old school were executed or banished, the republican calendar
was altered, and a conclave of historians and mythological poets was
encouraged and rewarded, who re-wrote the history of Rome and
erected for posterity a body of elegant fiction and imposture, which
nineteen centuries of time have not yet sufficed to wholly overthrow
or eradicate

These statements are not mere opinions, they are based upon evidences so valid, so numerous and so convincing that they would tri-
umphantly withstand the severest scrutiny of a court of law.

According to the received chronology, Cæpius, or, he who was afterwards called Caius Julius Cæsar Octavianus, and still later the
Augustus, was born September 23, A. U. 692, began to reign February 26 U 711 and died August 29, A U 768, aged 76 years

lacking one month. [47]   He was the son of Maia, as she was called by
Horace and the inscription at Lyons, while Suetonius says her name
was Atia, a niece of Julius Cæsar.   His putative father was Caius
Octavianus; a citizen of Rome and the son of a baker.   At the age
of four years Augustus lost his father.   He was then adopted by
Phillipus and afterwards at the age of puberty by Julius Cæsar, as his

[47] The chronology is based on the dates which appear in the Testament of Augustus,
engraved on the walls of his temple at Ancyra. According to Mr. John M. Kinneir's
"Journey through Asia Minor," ed. 1818, p. 70, this monument has been tampered
with, therefore until the dates are corroborated by some valid monument, as yet not
exposed to the work of forgers, they must not be regarded as conclusive, especially
as Josephus says that Augustus died at the age of seventy-six, while Eutropius, vii, 8,
says that he died at the age of eighty-six. The monument says "I am now in my
seventy-sixth year," which, if Josepus is right, was the year of his death. Of course
this is possible; but in view of the testimony of Eutropius and Kinneir, it looks suspicious. The Ancyran monument says that Augustus was nineteen years of age when
Hirtius and Pansa were consuls and when—after their mysterious death during the
same year—he got his first consulship. This was the year following the assassination
of Julius Cæsar, or (by our chronology) A. U. 711. As it is from this year that the
reign—not the Advent, nor the Apotheosis, nor the Ascension, but the reign—of Augustus is commonly reckoned and, as according to Josephus, he died at the age of
seventy-six years, therefore he died in 768 and was born in 692. If the student will take
the trouble to compare these dates with those in any modern date-book, he will observe
several discrepancies and he will have to choose between the monument and the chronologists. Suetonius says that Augustus was born the day when the conspiracy of
Catiline was debated in the Senate, but this does not help us, for the year of Rome
is wanting, as indeed it is in most of the ancient works which have been submitted to
the scrutiny of the Sacred College. Josephus evidently counts Augustus' reign from
February 26 of the year, when, according to Tacitus, Hirtius and Pansa were consuls. As it does not appear that Augustus succeeded Hirtius and Pansa on February
26, Josephus probably derived this particular day from that of the Apotheosis of A. U.
738. This last was the New-Year day of the Augustan Aera, which was observed
during the lifetime of Augustus, but was afterwards superceded by an æra, the year,
(not the day,) of which, was counted from the Ascension. It will be observed that
Eutropius, Josephus and the Treatise on Oratory which is commonly ascribed to Tacitus, all count the reign of Augustus from his first consulate, or, which is practically
the same thing, from the deaths of Hirtius and Pansa. Although Augustus does not
claim so much in his Testament, he begins its chronicles at the same time. Strictly
speaking, he was at that time a consul of the republic, and that, too, with Pedius for
his colleague. The Triumvirate had yet to be formed and dissolved; Greece, Africa
and Asia had to be conquered; and the empire organised. Until these objects were
achieved Augustus did not reign; and when he did reign he was careful rather to claim
less than more authority than he had really acquired. With regard to his Aera, there
is no evidence that it was employed earlier than his return from Syria and the celebration of the Ludi Sæculares and Ludi Augustales. The date, February 26, is from the
"six months and two days" of Josephus, reckoned backward from the day of Augustus' death.

own son   When Cæsar was assasinated, Augustus was still in his teens.   When, in accordance with the Treaty of Brundusium, Augustus divided the world with Marc Antony, giving to the latter the Eastern, and retaining for himself Rome and the Western Empire, he had but barely attained the age of manhood   After the departure of Marc Antony, one of the first acts of Augustus was the destruction of Perugia, a city which refused to acknowledge his authority   The fall of this place was followed by the sacrificial Placation of Julius the Father   In this atrocious rite, some authors allege that the consul, Lucius Antony, (brother of Marc) besides Cannutius C. Flavius, Clodius Bithynicus, and the principal magistrates and council of Perugia, together with 300 senators and knights, were immolated as human sacrifices, upon an altar of Julius, erected for the occasion [48] The greater part of the abominable auto da fé was executed in the presence of Augustus himself, whose only reply to those who implored and shrieked for mercy, was. "You must die."

Let those who contend that the worship of Julius and Augustus was merely a form, ponder over this horrible event   So soon as the gruesome business was over, Augustus prepared for his own elevation to the godship   Such of the ancient literature as was not destroyed, was perverted, the Sibylline books [49] being among those preserved, because they were found to contain the prophecy of his Advent, which, according to the subservient interpretation of Virgil, was to occur this same year, that is to say, in the consulate of Pollio, A U 713, when the world would be at peace, the temple of Janus closed, and the Golden Age would begin   Unfortunately for this pretty scheme, Marc Antony, grown jealous of Augustus, made war upon him; and the temple of Janus had to be re-opened; so that the god of the Western world was fain to postpone his intended elevation until the god of the East was subdued   The memorable victory of Actium was won in A U. 723   It was in this year that Herod is said to have paid a relief of 800 talents to Augustus, who confirmed him, for the second time, in his vassal kingdom of Judea, an act, which the Ro-

[48] Suet in Aug.

[49] There were ten Sibyls and ten books and ten decemviri to take charge of them In Roman legend the books are mentioned in connection with Tarquin the Proud, in Roman history they first explicitly appear in the consulate of Lucretius, A. U 292, although they are alluded to as nothing new   Livy, I, 7, III, 10, V, 13, etc   In the Augustan age it was pretended that they had been destroyed during the Marsic war A.U. 670, whereupon new copies were collected from the Sibylline oracles throughout the empire and deposited by Augustus under the statue of Apollo on the Palatine Hill. Suet , Aug , 31; Dio., 17.

mans called "the Grace of God," but which the Jews attributed to
bribery at court. In the following year Augustus entered Asia and
Egypt at the head of an immense army; when Antony and Cleopatra,
in despair, committed suicide. In this year the conqueror pretended
to have opened the Suez Canal and thus placed Rome in direct communication with India; whereas, it was in fact done several years
previously by Julius Cæsar; although in the meanwhile the canal may
have filled up with sand and have required dredging. The monument
of Ancyra asserts that in his seventh consulate Octavius was recognised as the Augustus, or Holy one; a statement that agrees with
Censorinus, who says that he received the title of Augustus in A. U.
726. This was probably true as to the Orient, but it does not appear
that the title was assumed in Rome until the year known to us as
A. U. 738. [50]

In A. U. 730 Herod is said to have rebuilt the temple of Jerusalem
and dedicated it to Jehovah. In the upper city he erected another
edifice of greater magnitude, which he called the Cæsarium, and
dedicated it to Augustus. He also built a temple to Augustus in
Strato's Tower, "which," says Josephus, "was excellent, both for
beauty and size; and therein was a colossal image of Augustus, not
less than that of Jupiter Olympus, which it was made to resemble."
Herod rebuilt Samaria, renamed it Sebastos, the Greek form of Augustus, and erected therein a temple to the worship of that god. Indeed he repaired many places and erected temples and statues of
Augustus in them, and called them Cæsarea, Augusta and the like.
In the 192nd four-year Olympiad, answering to A. U. 745, Herod
even went so far in his homage of Augustus, as to revive the panageia of Jasius, or the fifty-months each of 36 days, or five-year

[50] According to the monument at Ancyra, which was erected after Octavius had
been consul 14 times, imperator 20 times and tribune 38 times, therefore according to
our chronology, after A. U. 762, Octavius had been named Sebastos (at least in the
Orient) in his sixth consulate. According to the chronology which has been supplied
to us, this was in A. U. 724; yet Eutropius, VII, 8, says that Augustus returned to
Rome in the 12th year from his first consulate, which agrees with A. U. 723. Censorinus says the title of "Augustus, D. F.," was conferred by the Senate, January 16,
in the year of his seventh consulate, when his colleague was M. Vipsanius Agrippa,
Cos., III. This answers to our A. U. 725, or 726; so that, like Julius Cæsar, Octavius appears to have been deified in Egypt first, and in Rome two years later. Some
authors make a difference of three years between these dates. The Roman deification
seems to have been immediately followed by the Triumph and the Sæcular games of
A. U. 738 (Censorinus), yet there are 14 or 15 years between the two dates, during
which the history of Octavius is barren of events.

Olympian games and to call them "Cæsar's games " For the expenses of their observance he devoted certain revenues in perpetuity. (Josephus, Wars, xxi) His coins were stamped with the Buddhic or Osirian sacred monogram ☧ which was afterwards appropriated by the medieval historians of Christianity

After the subjection of Egypt, Augustus, at the head of vast forces, visited Tyre, Sidon, Samos, Ancyra, Cyzicus and other places in Asia ; in all of which he received a homage due alone to gods To crown these supernal triumphs, he recovered from the Parthian king, Phraates, the Roman standards, captured years before from Crassus and thus relieved the arms of Rome from the only stain that rested upon them According to the Ancyran inscription, Augustus returned from Syria to Rome during the consulship of Q Lucretius Vispillo The day was afterwards celebrated as Augustalia, October 12 The chronologists place this consulship in A. U 737, whereas Eutropius says that Augustus returned 12 years after his first consulship: a discrepancy of 14 or 15 years The conqueror brought with him the acknowledged empire of the world He was therefore fully prepared to assume that divine elevation for which every preparation had been made during his absence from the capital

According to the chronology arranged for the occasion, it was just seven cycles, each of 110 years, from the apotheosis of Romulus, by whose sacred name of Janus Quirinus, Augustus desired himself to be called The pretension was that Augustus was the reincarnation of Janus Quirinus, or Romulus; therefore, the temples erected to his worship in the west were commonly dedicated to Augustus and Roma; the images of the latter being merely those of a beautiful matron. With the street effigies of Augustus, of which Ovid informs us there were a thousand in Rome alone, the members of Augustus' family, the Holy Family, as Ovid calls it, namely, his wife, Livia, and one of his adopted sons, Drusus—both of whom were canonized—were sometimes associated Many of these effigies continued in use for centuries, and some of them are possibly doing service yet From the year of the apotheosis, that is to say, A. U. 738, began a new æra It was in this year, says Lenormant, that Augustus assumed those rights of coinage which ever afterwards remained the prerogative of the sovereign-pontiff [51] The new year day of this æra was originally February 26 This was eventually altered to December 25.

---

[51] It was in A. U. 738 that Augustus assumed those rights of coinage which ever afterwards remained the prerogative of the sovereign-pontiff Lenormant, ii, 214.

Except in the Iberian peninsular, where the custom of employing the Julian æra prevailed down to a recent period, the Augustan æra, since masked under other names, served for the dates of the Roman world, until some time after the reign of Justinian II., when, without any unnecessary disturbance of recorded dates, the years, which were formerly reckoned from A. U. 738, were reckoned from A. U. 753. [52] When the chronology of the Augustan period is closely examined it will be found to have been altered by the Latin Sacred College to the extent of 15 years. Proofs of this alteration of the calendar appear upon examining the Timæan and Ciceronian æra of Romulus; the dates of the Ludi Sæculares given by Censorinus; the erroneous æras ascribed by modern chronologists to Augustus' principal Triumph; the conflicting dates ascribed to the consulates of Augustus by Suetonius and Eutropius, or inscribed on the monuments at Ancyra and elsewhere; the dated coins of Rome and its provinces; besides other circumstances, which it would be tedious to rehearse in this place.

To prepare for the Apotheosis of A. U. 738, the Augustan historians and poets—bearing in mind the slaughter of Perugia; the ungrateful murders of Cicero and Lucius Antony; the tragic death of Marc Antony and Cleopatra; the mysterious banishment of Ovid; the condemnation of Afidius Memla, and many other similar circumstances—now tuned and struck anew their mendacious lyres. Let us listen to some of their strains, first disposing of the too premature pæans of Virgil, which he sang in his Fourth Eclogue:

"The last Great Æra foretold by the Cumæan Sibyl is now arrived; the Cycles begin anew. Now returns the Golden Age of Saturn, now appears the Immaculate Virgin. (This was Maia, the virgin mother of Augustus). Now descends from Heaven a divine Nativity. O! chaste Lucina, (this was the goddess of maternity), speed the Mother's pains, haste the glorious Birth, and usher in the reign of thy Apollo. In thy consulship, O! Pollio, shall happen this glorious Advent, and the great months shall then begin to roll. Thenceforth whatever vestige of Original Sin remains, shall be swept away from earth forever, and the Son of God shall be the Prince of Peace!"

As before intimated, this strain was sung too prematurely, and the battle of Actium had yet to be fought and won before the Messianic and Apotheosis project could be realised. Meanwhile no glorious Advent is recorded, no great months began to roll, no Great Æra was commenced, no Cycles were renewed, the peace was postponed,

[52] See "Middle Ages Revisited," Appendix on "Chronology of Augustus."

the temple of Janus was reopened, and Original Sin has retained its
place in the liturgy of the Roman church to the present day

The Pollio alluded to in this Eclogue was Caius Asinius Pollio,
born A. U 678, died A U. 757, an orator, poet, historian, politician,
warrior, governor of Gaul, courtier and time-server.   He was with
Julius Cæsar when he passed the Rubicon and again at Pharsalia
Pollio was named as consul with Cn Domitius Calvinus, for the year
713, but, although the year goes by their names, such was the confusion of the times that neither of them actually filled the consular
chair   After the death of Cæsar, Pollio took sides with Marc Antony,
but, either from the desperate circumstances of the latter or because
he was bribed with the consulship, Pollio, before the slaughter of
Perugia, went over to Augustus   It was he, who, introducing Virgil
to Mæcenas, procured for the poet the restitution and enlargement
of his landed estates and earned for himself the immortality conferred
by the mention of his name in the Eclogues.   His own works, of
which there were several, have all disappeared.   The capitulation of
Perugia, the holocaust of human victims sacrificed upon the altar of
Julius the Father, the Treaty of Brundusium, and the departure of
Antony for the east, all occurred during the nominal consulship of
Pollio, and they marked both the advent of Augustus Cæsar and the
assumed restoration of peace to the Roman world [53]

We now begin with the literature of the triumph, deification and
Apotheosis, which followed Augustus' return from Asia.   In pursuance of the astrology which Rome had gathered from Etruria, Greece,
Pontus, Galilee, Syria, Egypt, Spain and Gaul, indeed from every
source whence came the heterogeneous materials which now composed her military forces and her millions of slaves, it was necessary
to show that the Incarnation was connected with previous incarnations, that it occurred at the beginning of a new divine cycle, that
it was the issue of a divine father and mortal mother, that the mother
was a wife-virgin; that the birth happened at the end of ten solar
months; that it occurred in an obscure place; that it was foretold by
prophecy or sacred oracle; that it was presaged or accompanied by
prodigies of Nature, that the divinity of the child was recognized by
sages; that the Holy One exhibited extraordinary signs of precocity
and wisdom, that his destruction was sought by the ruling powers,
whose precautions were of course defeated; that he worked miracles,
that he exhibited a profound humility; that his apotheosis would

[53] Appian, de Bell Civ , Dio Cass.; Livy, Ep , 126, Suet , in Aug.

bring peace on earth, and that he would finally ascend to heaven, there to join the Father. Accordingly, the Augustan writers furnished all these materials.

The first day of the Apotheosis, February 26, was that of the Nebo-Nazarene nativity; whilst the year was that of the Ludi Sæculares, dating from the Apotheosis of Romulus. Suetonius tells us concerning the Nativity that Atia or Maia having, in the absence of her husband, gone to the temple of Apollo at midnight, there fell asleep; and in that condition was approached by a serpent. Upon awakening, she seemed, for reasons stated by the chronicler, to be aware of what had happened. In the tenth month she was delivered of Augustus, who became known as the Son of the god Apollo. The birth occurred in Velitre, a village some twenty miles from Rome, and in a small and humble cottage, which ever afterwards was held Sacred. Even the owner of the house, having incautiously approached it, was blasted by lightning from heaven. The birth of Augustus was foretold not only by the Cumæan Sibyl, it was predicted by a divine oracle delivered in Velitre and by a prodigy that had happened publicly in Rome five or six months before the Nativity and was the occasion of the intended Slaughter of Innocents presently to be mentioned. Before the Nativity, Maia dreamt that her body was scattered to the stars and encompassed the universe. After the Nativity, Octavianus, her earthly husband, dreamt he saw the bright beams of the Sun emanate from her person; and when he sacrificed, where Alexander the Great had formerly sacrificed and had seen a miracle, namely, at a temple of Dionysius or Bacchus in Thrace, Octavianus saw a similar miracle: a sheet of flame ascended from the altar, enveloped the steeple and mounted high to heaven. On the following night Octavianus dreamt he saw the Infant Augustus grasping the Thunderbolt and wearing the Sceptre and Robe of Jupiter, his head surrounded by a radiance of glory, and his chariot decked with laurel, while yoked to it were six steeds of purest white. When, before the Nativity, the divine oracle at Velitre predicted that "Nature was about to bring forth a Prince over the Roman people," the Senate passed an Act, A. U. 692, ordering that "No male child born that year should be reared or brought up." Thus, every boy born within the Roman pale was devoted to destruction, and a frightful Slaughter of Innocents would have ensued, had not those who expected children, removed the tablets of the law from the walls of the ærarium; and thus defeated the atrocious edict. When the sage and astrologer, P. Nigidius, learnt that Atia had been delivered of Augustus, he

openly proclaimed that the Lord of the Universe was born.   While
Augustus was yet an infant, he arose from his cradle at night and
next morning he was found upon the roof of the house, facing Apollo,
or the rising Sun.   On the city side of the house a multitude of frogs
maintained a deafening clamour   So soon as Augustus was old
enough to speak, he commanded these animals to keep silence, and
from that moment they were completely hushed

When, at a later period, Augustus went with M Vipsanius Agrippa
to the study of Theogenes, the astrologer, at Apollonia, and there
divulged the hour of his nativity, Theogenes fell down and worshipped him as God, (adoravitque eum) [54]   At a later period he was
worshipped by Lepidus, the Pontifex Maximus of Rome [55]   Among
the miracles that Augustus wrought, his merest touch was sufficient
to cure deformity or disease; and so universally was his divine origin
and attributes acknowledged that many people, in dying, left their
entire fortunes to the Sacred fisc, in gratitude, as they themselves
expressed it, for having been permitted to live during the incarnation
and earthly sojourn of this Son of God   Suetonius (Aug 100) informs us that in the course of twenty years private individuals bequeathed to Augustus no less than 35 million aurei, equal to about 40
million sovereigns or half-eagles of the present weight and standard
In addition to these legacies, numerous vassal princes left their entire patrimonies to this Messiah.

To evince his humility, once a year, Augustus, veiled in the sacred
peplum, stood at the porch of the Regia and received alms from the
pious   His Apotheosis not only brought profound peace to the Roman world, so that the temple of Janus was permanently closed, it
marked a new Æra   At his death, concludes Suetonius, "there was
not wanting a person of prætorian rank who saw his spirit ascend to
Heaven."   The name of this privileged witness was the senator
Numericus Atticus   The Ascension of Augustus is engraved upon
the great cameo, from the spoils of Constantinople, presented by
Baldwin II , to Louis IX , and now in the Cabinet of France. A fac-
simile of it is published in Duruy's "History of Rome "

Having thus briefly sketched the history of the Augustan worship,
it is next in order to call those contemporary witnesses who attested
this worship, or who sang its praises.   We have already heard Ovid,
Virgil and Suetonius   We will now turn to a later work of Virgil;
and also to Horace, Manilius, Tacitus and others

[54] Suet., in Aug.   The Roman term for astrologer was "mathematician."
[55] Manning's Xiphilinus, I, 114

Says Virgil (Æneid VI, 789-93):

This is Cæsar and the Holy Family
Spanning the spacious axle of heaven,
This is He, whom thou hast oft heard promised thee,
Augustus Cæsar, Son of God, who
Shall restore the Golden Age to Latium.

Says Horace (Book I):

"Come we entreat thee, Divine Apollo, thy brilliant shoulders robed in clouds . . . Kind Maia's wingéd Child, if with change of shape thou dost take on earth the form of a Youth, deigning to be styled the Avenger of Cæsar, late mayest thou return to Heaven."

Again:

"Father and Guardian of the human race, mayest thou (great Jove) reign with Augustus, thy second in power . . . Inferior only to thee, He shall rule with equity the wide world."

And as if not satisfied with these expressions, Horace elsewhere adds that of "Præsens divus habebitur Augustus": We have with us, the living god Augustus.

Listen to Manilius, (Astronomica, I, 7-10:)

"It is thee, Augustus, thyself a god, and the Prince and Father of his Country, who by divine law reigneth over the universe, and who awaiteth his place in heaven with the Father, who inspires me to sing these sublime themes."

Again, (I, 773-5:)

"The Julian family sprung from Venus and descended from the skies, returns again to heaven, where reigns Augustus with Jupiter the Father."[56]

Were it necessary, these testimonies could be greatly multipled; but they would fatigue the reader. The temples at Ancyra and Ephesus, besides myriads of coins and inscriptions, still extant, hail Augustus as Divus Filius, or the Son of God; the medal published by Father Hardouin in his work on Ancient Coins, pourtrays the pontifical hat of Augustus surmounted by a Latin cross; whilst Horace and some of the inscriptions allude to the god as the Son of Maia, who, as we know, was universally recognized as the Mother of God. [57]

Coveting deification, Augustus neither commanded himself to be deified, nor to be worshipped; but with the prudence and deviousness that characterized all his measures, he munificently rewarded those

[56] It did not appear to present any difficulties to the Roman mind that the Augustus should have been successively regarded as the Son of Julius the Father, Apollo the Father and the coadjutor of Jupiter the Father. Historical incarnations are far more intractable than mythical ones, and demand a much larger degree of credulity on the part of the worshipper.

[57] At Lyons a temple was erected to Mercurio Augusto et Maiæ Augustæ. Duruy's Hist. Rome.

who set the example of addressing and worshipping him as the Supreme Being, whilst he heavily and cruelly punished those who neglected this impious homage. Arminius complained to his soldiers
that the Romans had made Augustus a god. This was not strictly correct: Augustus had made himself a god, as Scipio and Sylla had attempted to do, and as Titus Flamininus, Sertorius and Julius Cæsar
had actually done, before him.

By securing and uniting in his own person the tribunitian, consular,
censorial and sacerdotal functions; by suppressing the quæstors, and
by taking the appointment of the prætors into his own hands, Augustus stealthily and noiselessly secured all those powers of the state
which Julius had grasped with ruder hands, but had suddenly lost at
the foot of Pompey's statue These usurpations having been confirmed
by a trembling senate, Augustus was raised almost in fact, as well as
in name, to that deified rank which Julius had established, but so
briefly enjoyed.

With the consular power Augustus acquired lawful command over
the army, navy and militia, lawful control over the provinces and the
right to deal with tributary or vassal kingdoms; with the censorial power and the suppression of the quæstors he obtained control
of the tithes and other revenues, the administration of the treasury,
the construction and repair of public works and the right to enquire
into the private affairs of citizens, both by confession and otherwise;
the last a most potent instrument of tyranny With the acquisition
of the tribunitian power his person became Sacred and his decrees
Inviolable and Infallible. Tremendous as were these powers, they
were increased by the law of sacred treason, or Læsa Majestas, which
made it a capital crime even to speak of him irreverently. He also
acquired the lawful right to arbitrarily convene or dismiss the senate
Through the appointment of prætors he exercised a powerful influence upon the magistracy and the administration of justice Finally,
with the office of supreme-pontiff he acquired lawful authority over
the priesthood, the flamens, augurs, bishops, curates, vestal virgins,
temples, sanctuaries, shrines and monasteries, over the calendar, over
the coinage, over the fisc and over all sacerdotal institutes, prerogatives, rites, ceremonies, festivals, holidays, dedications and canoni-
zations; as well as over marriages, divorces, adoptions, testaments,
and benefices, or church livings; in short, he became the Supreme
Lord over all that immense class of subjects embraced by the Roman
imperial, censorial, fiscal and ecclesiastical systems

After he had acquired these powers he appointed a new set of officers, of his own creation and dependent upon himself, to whom he assigned their execution or enjoyment. In carrying out these measures, Augustus was evidently guided by legal advice. Force was seldom manifested; injustice was not openly displayed; and the rights of property, office, title, privilege, or custom, were rarely violated without a plausible pretext. The forms of law, which had grown up under the republican constitution, were employed to destroy the last vestiges of liberty; and the empire was enchained, subdued and crushed as completely as though its master was indeed endowed with the supernatural powers attributed to him by his sycophants and devotees.

The college of Augusine priests was elevated to the same rank as the four other great religious colleges; the function of the first-named one being to establish rites, offer prayers, chaunt hymns and accept sacrifices, in the temples sacred to Augustus. The worship of Augustus, Son of God, was officially incorporated into the religion of the empire; every city of the empire had an augustal flamen, every house an augustal shrine; succeeding emperors themselves sacrificed to Augustus, and irreverence to this deity was visited with the severest penalties. Afidius Memla, for refusing to take his oath of office in the name of the divine Augustus, was ejected from the senate, and the ancient city of Czyicus, for neglecting the worship of Augustus, the Son of God, was deprived of its privileges. During the reign of Tiberius the head was removed from an image of Augustus and placed upon another image, possibly of the same god. This offense was regarded with such profound horror that it was brought to the attention of the senate, who ordered several persons, suspected of knowing its author, to be put to the torture until they confessed his name. When this was discovered the offender was summarily executed. For changing one's clothes in the presence of an image of Augustus the penalty was death. For whipping a slave near the shrine of Augustus the punishment was death. For defacing a coin which bore the effigy of Augustus the penalty was death, not because it was a coin, but because it bore the image of the god. This is proved by the next instance. For defacing the effigy of Augustus on a ring the penalty was death. For accepting honours in a colony on the same day that somewhat similar honours had been decreed to Augustus the penalty was death. It has been insinuated that the worship of Augustus was an idle form, an empty, meaningless ceremony, a mode of flattery, like that alleged to be still rendered to some eastern potentates. To complete this assurance it will be necessary to prove that the thumbscrew, the rack,

the headsman's block, the axe, and the bloody remains of Roman
citizens stuck upon lances at the city gates, the remains of men who
had been executed for sacrilege to the god Augustus, were also illu-
sions; that Suetonius, Tacitus, Josephus, Pliny and the other post-
Augustan writers on this subject have transmitted to us a mass of
falsehoods without the extenuating motive of either religion, interest,
or ambition, that the myriads of Roman coins, found in the most
distant places, stamped with the rayed image of Augustus and proclaiming him in explicit words the Theos, or living god, the Sebastos,
or Holy One, or else the Son of God, are forgeries, and that the temples erected in his honour and in which worship and sacrifices to him
were conducted by a hired priesthood and enforced upon the people,
were so many figments of the imagination ⁵⁸

Costly temples, altars and images were erected to Augustus in
Rome, Nola, Pompeii, Athens, Piscennus, Proconnesus, Tomis, Byzantium, Cyzicus, Antioch, Ancyra, Samaria, Jerusalem, Alexandria,
Lyons and Vienne, (in Gaul,) Leon and Terracona, (in Spain,) and
numerous other cities, the remains, in some cases almost complete
remains, of which are still extant; the worship of Augustus was regu-
larly conducted in all these places, and all classes of men were compelled to bow to his images and to worship them, upon the penalty of
death ⁵⁹ In Italy no such compulsion was necessary   Indeed, this
worship stood in such high estimation that petty images of Augustus
were used as charms, which were suspended or worn upon the person;
and the larger images of his incarnation, which were erected in highways and public places, were, in the absence of a temple, resorted to
for sanctuary and respected as such

On the numerous votive tablets and other monuments erected to
the worship of Augustus he is variously addressed as Liber Pater Augustus, with the thyrsus of Bacchus (3046), Jupiter Optimus Maximus Augustus (6423), Apollo Augustus (534), Serapis Augustus (4044),
Saturnus Augustus (1796), Savus Augustus (3896), Savus Adsalluta
(5134), Sedatus Augustus (3922), Salus Augustus (4162), Mercurius
Augustus (1434), Æsus, Baldir, etc , the numbers being those of the

⁵⁸ The coins with the rayed images and sacred titles of Augustus are depicted and
described in Cohen's " Monnaies Imperiales," 1, 107, etc   They are also mentioned
in Lenormant, II, 170, and in many other numismatic works

⁵⁹ Soranus, a Latin poet, in the reign of Julius Cæsar, was put to death upon the
charge of betraying a secret   He acknowled no god but the Soul of the Universe
Lempriere, in " Valerius " It is therefore likely that his real offence was the refusal
to worship the sovereign-pontiff.

inscriptions in Mommsen's "Corpus Inscriptionum Latinorum."

Lanciani informs us that of the vast number of structures on the Palatine Hill which comprised the palaces of he Cæsars " but one section alone remained unaltered throughout all the ages." [60] This was the section built by Augustus; the one in which he dwelt. It was destroyed in 1549. To this may be added the fact that of all the memorials of the distant past which the Vatican preserves with the most jealous care is the marble image of Divus Augustus. Like reverence, however, has not been extended by the Italian government to his sepulchre, which, it is stated, has recently been subjected to indignity. [61]

The church of Augustus tolerated no rivalry and permitted no heresies. Agrippa, whose great services to the state might have evoked a popularity inconvenient to the Augustus, died suddenly at the age of 51 years. After the death of Augustus, and by order of Livia, the innocent sons of Agrippa were put to death. [62] In the reign of Tiberius, Caius Silanus, proconsul of Asia, being accused of irreverence to the god Augustus, was excommunicated and banished to Cythera. [63] The Egyptians and Jews in the city of Rome were ordered to renounce their impious worship or leave Italy at short notice. Four thousand of them were transported. [64] Junius, who pretended to be able to raise the dead, was forbidden to practice his art. The Chaldean astrologers, and afterwards all astrologers, magi, and worshippers of strange gods, were banished out of Italy. [65]

After the death of the Augustus, which occurred, according to the received chronology, in A. D. 14, the army of office-holders, priests, sycophants and panders, who filled the capital, hastened to transfer their scandalous homage to Tiberius, his successor. For this they were at once rebuked by Tiberius, who reminded them that he was no god, but like themselves a mere human being; and he forbade them to address him by any sacred title, or even to swear by his name. Yet such an impetus had this worship received that his edict was evaded, and the courtiers swore by the emperor's Genius. It was perhaps to avoid a homage which he was powerless to prevent that Tiberius removed to Capri, where he resided until he died. In Rome he sternly en-

[60] Lanciani's "Ancient Rome," p. 109.

[61] London Weekly Graphic, Nov. 14, 1874.

[62] In like manner Tiberius permitted his favorite, Sejanus, to erect images of himself in Rome: then he destroyed him.

[63] Tacitus, Ann., III, 68.   [64] Tacitus Ann., II, 86.

[65] Tacitus, Ann., II, 28-32.

forced the worship of Augustus, although in the provicces he added
or permitted that of himself   He must have reduced the number, or
else the emoluments, which Augustus had awarded to the Roman
ecclesiastics, [66] for, without any other assignable cause of offense, the
works written after his death, most of which were the product of
their busy pens, sought to blacken his memory with hints of crimes
which it was impossible for a man of his venerable age to commit

After the death of Tiberius the superstition of Rome attached
itself to Caligula, and made him a god   Philo of Alexandria affords
us a glimpse of this impious worship in his account of an embassy
which he headed on behalf of the Jews   The Alexandrians sent a
counter embassy to thwart him, and they met in the imperial presence under the following circumstances:

"Caius (Caligula) was engaged at this time in transforming the
garden of the Lamias into a royal residence, and the rival embassies
were summoned thither   They found him hurrying from room to
room, surrounded by architects and workmen, to whom he was giving
directions; and they were compelled to follow in his train   Stopping
to address the Jews he asked· 'Are you the god-haters who deny my
divinity, which all the rest of the world acknowledges?'   The Alexandrian envoys hastened to put in their word. 'Lord, these Jews
alone have refused to sacrifice to your welfare'   Said the Jews
'Nay, oh Lord, this is a slander.   We sacrificed for you not once,
but thrice; first, when you assumed the empire, then, when you recovered from your illness; and again, for your success against the
Germans'   'Yes,' observed Caligula, 'You sacrificed *for* me; but
not *to* me,' and thereupon he hurried to another room, the Jews
trembling and their rivals jeering, as in a play"   A similar avoidance
of this worship at Jerusalem is mentioned by Josephus; and when
the procurator of Judea attempted to set up a statue of Caligula in
the Temple, the dagger of some Judean Brutus alone prevented the
profanation

After Caligula came Claudius.   He also demanded to be worshipped as a god.   Josephus has preserved the text of an edict in which
Claudius admits that the Jews had been unjustly treated by Caligula,
because they had refused to worship him as god, contrary to the
charters of privileges which they claimed to have obtained from Julius and Augustus, and Claudius orders these charters to be respected [67]   This edict was no doubt procured through bribery of the
court officials, for Claudius soon forgot all about it and demanded

[66] Suet , Aug , 30   [67] Josephus, Ant., XIX, v, 2

from the Jews similar worship to himself. Rather than submit to it, the Jewish people came before Petronius en masse and told him he might slay them all, for they would never yield to such a demand; whereupon he wrote to Claudius that if he insisted upon being worshipped in Judea, he would soon reign over a desert. Before Petronius received the reply of Claudius, the dagger had also dispatched the latter; but not before his insistence upon being worshipped in Britain had sacrificed the heroic Boadicea and the entire nation of the Iesini; who were as resolute as the Jews on this subject. The levity of Nero and the short reigns of Galba, Otho and Vitellius, diverted the worship of the reigning sovereigns to the dead and canonized Augustus, Son of God. But it appeared again in the reigns of Vespasian and Titus, who were also worshipped as incarnations of the deity. In the reigns of Domitian and Nerva, both of whom assumed to be the Creator and demanded and received divine homage, this blasphemous and happily always declining worship received a further check; so that when Trajan ascended the throne, Tacitus was enabled to write the passage already quoted concerning the reign of Augustus: "The reverence due to the gods was no longer exclusive. Augustus claimed equal worship. Temples were built and statues were erected to him; a mortal man was adored; and priests and pontiffs were appointed to pay him impious homage."

Following Trajan were Hadrian, Antoninus, Marcus Aurelius, Commodus, Pertinax and Aurelian, all of whom demanded and accepted divine homage. But this was almost the last of it. The repugnance and resistance, which had begun in the provinces, afterwards manifested itself in the intellectual centres of the empire; and though it was attempted again and again to return to the worship of Augustus, the attempt failed; so that in the place of an odious and degrading religion, Elagabalus deemed it feasible to revive the ancient worship of the Sun. The theogonies of Hesiod and Homer, [68] of Virgil and Ovid, were obsolete; the Julian and Augustan worship had become obsolete; and the worship of living emperors was repugnant to the spirit of the West. Although this was the period of those numerous Mithraic monuments which now appear in the archæological museums of Rome, Paris, London, York and Newcastle, the religion of the Sun made but little headway. The legions accepted it, but that was all. Mithraism, too, was obsolete. Its vital force was long since spent. Elagabalus was supported by some of the best families of Rome, but the weakness of his cause and the

[68] Cicero de Div., 17, 38, 67, 126, 248, 262, especially 126.

opposition and hatred of the Augustan priesthood, whose livings it endangered, thwarted his object; and have since loaded his name with obloquy. His plan of directing into a purer channel the superstition and religious fervour of his countrymen, though delayed for three-fourths of a century by the Roman ecclesiastics, was nevertheless carried out more successfully by Diocletian, who revived the Sun-worship which Elagabalus had established But the revival was only accomplished at the cost of dividing the empire into four satrapies; and with this division, what remained of the worship of Augustus fell, to rise no more. In its place and in the place of the ephemeral Mithraism and of the Dionysian worship, which, according to the coins of the period, succeeded it for a brief interval, arose that later religion of the West, which conserved the fruits of military conquests, that, without it, might have been made in vain and that absorbed all the other religions which these conquests had brought together.

Emperor-worship is not so much the product of the Orient as it is of those vast hierarchies which could only arise in the Orient, so long as the Occident remained comparatively destitute of population The agglomeration of an extensive empire, embracing numerous races and tribes of men, differing from each other in origin, aptitudes, mythology and religion—especially when such an agglomeration is followed by the practice of transplantation and fusion, the whole empire being governed by a single hierarch—has always been followed by emperor-worship

The empires of India, Persia, Assyria, Egypt, Macedon and Rome, were all of this character, they all practiced the transplantation and fusion of the people whom they conquered; they were all governed by hierarchs; and these hierarchs were always worshipped by their subjects Some traces of the Oriental tendency to worship human gods is observable even in modern times. To-day, in Madras, the the statue of the British queen-empress is annointed with consecrated oil, strewn with flowers, propitiated with offerings of frankincense, and worshipped on bended knees by the natives, who call it the great Maharanee, or Queen of Queens, the Holy One, the Supreme God That these are acts of piety and not of flattery, is evident from the fact that they are done furtively and in defiance of the police; who are instructed to prevent them

If on the one hand, extensive empire and hierarchical government furnished the ground of emperor-worship, on the other hand, the mythology of the Orient supplied the seed The incarnations of Bel-Issus, Nin-Ies, Tiglath-pil-Esar, Cyrus, Darius, Rhamses, Alexander the Great, the Ptolemies, the Selucidæ, and the other personages alluded to herein, formed a series of Asiatic gods as well marked as any generation of monsters traced by the philosophic eye of Darwin. Even this line of gods, which, with perhaps one or two doubtful exceptions, consisted of actual historical personages, was complemented by another series of wholly mythological beings. Such were the incarnations of Vishnu, Ies Chrishna, and the Brahminical Buddha of the Hindus; Assui, of Assyria, Nebo-Nazaiu, of Babylon, Osiris and Horus, of Egypt; Ormudz, of Persia; and Ischenou, Chres, Jasius and Bacchus, of Greece.

Water will not rise above its own level. Man will not worship a god who is either above or below the poise of his own comprehension. The gods have therefore this useful function: they furnish an infallible barometer of the human intellect. Measured by this scale, the worship of Augustus was not at the period of his advent below the comprehension of the West, for, with the exception of the stubborn Northmen, we hear of no dissatisfaction with it. Rural Italy, Gaul, Spain, Pannonia and Southern Germany, all accepted or endured it; Britain, Saxony and Scandinavia alone rejected it Nor was it below the comprehension of Egypt and Asia Minor, for only in Judea do any serious revolts against it appear in the chronicles of the times. But if, with the heroic exceptions mentioned, the rural populations endured it without repugnance, the great cities of the empire, such as Antioch, Alexandria, Athens and Rome, found it too degrading for continued acceptance. It was these centres of intellectual activity that gave effect to the revolts which emperor-worship had provoked in Britain, Frisia, Saxony and Judea; and it was out of this combination of popular resistance and intellectual disgust that arose a long and deadly struggle against the worship of Augustus and the wide-spread and firmly-rooted superstitions upon which it was founded; a struggle which finally ended in the adoption of Christianity. [69]

[69] The coins of Augustus commonly have the rayed image of that personage, with the legend DIVVS AVGVSTVS, or AVGVSTVS DIVVS FILIVS. This style was afterwards followed on the coins stamped with the effigy of Christ, the first one of which was issued by Justinian II, Rhinotmetus, about the year A. D. 705, with the legend d N IhS. CPS REX REGNANTIVM. There were several issues of these coins and some slight variations in the spelling. The small "h" is really a Greek "e," while the capital "P" is really a Greek "R" Sabatier's Byzantine Coins, Justinian II., No. 2. For Divos and Divus on Coins of Julius and Augustus, see Humphreys' "Coin Collector's Manual," plate 8.

FINIS.

INDEX.

CORRIGENDA.

PAGE.	LINE.	
12	39	For *remins* read *reminds*
26	4	After *appears* insert *as B C 816*.
38	11	After *return* insert *of*
42	14	After *annualized* insert *nodical*
44	1	After *at* insert *the.*
47	31	For *Psammeticus* read *Psammetichus*
51	19	After *Rama* insert *or.*
58	12	*Divitiacus B C 57* should precede *Deiotaurus B C.53.*
98	20	For *548* read *584.*
135	30	For *548* read *584*
148	11	For *at* read *about*
158	24	For *af* read *of*
162	1	For *Achæn* read *Achæan*
162	3	For *Maccabean* read *Maccabæan.*
181	38	For *Oxyges* read *Ogyges.*
186	22	For *aided* read *sided.*
249	30	For *calendar year* read *year calendar.*
255	39	For *remoter* read *remote*
261	6	For *Tenidos* read *Tenedos*

THE CAMBRIDGE ENCYCLOPEDIA CO , *publishers of historical and reference works, 62 Reade Street, New York, beg to announce the following partial list of their publications for the Autumn and Winter of 1899–1900 :*

The Worship of Augustus Caesar ; derived from a study of coins, monuments, calendars, æras and astrological cycles, the whole establishing a New Chronology of History and Religion, by Alex. Del Mar, formerly Director of the U. S Bureau of Statistics, 8vo, pp 400; cloth, $3

The Middle Ages Revisited ; or the Roman Government and Religion from Augustus to the Fall of Constantinople, by Alex Del Mar, 8vo, pp 600, $4

Ancient Britain ; in the light of modern archæological discoveries, by Alex Del Mar; 8vo, pp 250; cloth, $2

History of Money in America ; from the Discovery, to the Foundation of the American Constitution, by Alex. Del Mar, 8vo, pp. 200; cloth, $1 50

The Science of Money ; or The Principles deducible from its History, ancient and modern, by Alex Del Mar; 8vo, pp 226; cloth, $1

Barbara Villiers ; a History of Monetary Crimes, by Alex. Del Mar, 8vo, pp. 110; cloth, 75 cents

The Beneficent Effects of Silver Money during the 17th Century, by Alex Del Mar; 8vo, pamphlet, seventh edition; 10 cents

The Venus di Milo and its relation to the Greek worship, by William Maude; 12mo, pp. 24 *Edition de luxe*, illustrated, 50 cents.

Life of the Emperor Hadrian, by Ælius Spartianus; trans into English by William Maude; 8vo, pp 100; cloth, $1

The Fluctuations of Gold, by Baron Alex von Humboldt; trans. into English by William Maude, 8vo, pp 100, cloth, $1

The Law of Money, by Francois Grimaudet, Solicitor to the French Mint under Henry III ; trans. by William Maude; 8vo, pp. 128; cloth, $1

THE CAMBRIDGE ENCYCLOPEDIA CO , *publishers of historical and reference works, 62 Reade Street, New York, beg to announce the following* ADDITIONAL LIST OF THEIR PUBLICATIONS:

Etching; its technical process and its history, by S R Koehler; new edition, illustrated by numerous plates and reproductions, folio, pp 260 *Edition de luxe,* cloth and gold; only 100 copies printed, $10

Pharisees and Alligators, by Max O'Rell; 8vo, pp. 240; cloth, $1

Sketches by Max O'Rell I, Jacques Bonhomme; II, The Auvergnats; III, John Bull on the Continent; IV, From my Letter Box; 8vo, pp 168; paper, 50 cents.

A Mother's Song, in Five Cantos, by Mary D. Brine; illustrated by Miss C. A Northam; 4to, pp. 60; cloth and gold. *Edition de luxe,* $1

Sweet Twilight Dreams; being Poems and Pictures of Life and Nature, selected from English and American poets, and profusely illustrated by twenty eminent artists, 4to, pp. 80; cloth and gold, $1

Sunlight and Shade; a Holiday gift book of Poems, profusely illustrated by twenty-five eminent artists; 4to, pp. 192; $1

History of Yachting; 1850 to 1900, by Capt Coffin and others, with 125 splendid illustrations, by Fred Cozzens and other artists; 4to, pp 225 *Edition de luxe,* cloth, $5

Movement, or Action in Art, as illustrated from the designs of the most eminent artists, ancient and modern, by W. H. Beard, with 225 original drawings by the author; large 12mo, pp 360, $1.

Economic Philosophy, by Van Buren Denslow, LL. D., formerly of the New York *Tribune*; 8vo, pp 800, $2

History of Money in Ancient States, by Alex Del Mar; 8vo, pp 400, $3

Life of Hon. Alex. Del Mar, by J K. H Willcox, 8vo, pamphlet; third edition, 25 cents

CPSIA information can be obtained
at www.ICGtesting.com
Printed in the USA
LVHW080552190122
708822LV00009BA/464